SOCIALIST REGISTER 2015

SOCIALIST REGISTER 2 0 1 5

TRANSFORMING CLASSES

Edited by LEO PANITCH and GREG ALBO

THE MERLIN PRESS
MONTHLY REVIEW PRESS
FERNWOOD PUBLISHING

First published in 2014
by The Merlin Press Ltd.
99B Wallis Road
London
E9 5LN

www.merlinpress.co.uk

British Library Cataloguing in Publication Data is available from the British
Library

ISSN. 0081-0606

Published in the UK by The Merlin Press
ISBN. 978-0-85036-621-1 Paperback
ISBN. 978-0-85036-620-4 Hardback

Published in the USA by Monthly Review Press
ISBN. 978-1-58367-481-9 Paperback

Published in Canada by Fernwood Publishing
ISBN. 978-1-55266-689-0 Paperback

Printed in the EU on behalf of LPPS Ltd, Wellingborough, Northants

CONTENTS

CONTRIBUTORS

Ricardo Antunes is a professor of sociology at the State University of Campinas, Brazil.

Sam Ashman is associate professor in the Department of Economics and Econometrics at the University of Johannesburg.

Rishi Awatramani is organizing director at Virginia New Majority Student Power Network.

Joel Beinin is professor of Middle East history at Stanford University.

Andreas Bieler is professor of political economy and fellow of the Centre for the Study of Social and Global Justice at Nottingham University, UK.

Timothy David Clark is a research associate at Willow Springs Strategic Solutions in Calgary, Alberta.

Marie Duboc is professor of political science at the Eberhard Karls University in Tübingen, Germany.

Mark Dudzic is a labour activist and served as National Organizer and Chairman of the United States Labor Party.

Fuat Ercan is a professor in the Department of Economics at Marmara University, Istanbul.

Roland Erne teaches international and comparative employment relations at University College Dublin, Ireland.

Susan Ferguson is an associate professor in digital media and journalism at Wilfrid Laurier University, Waterloo, Ontario.

Lin Chun is an associate professor in comparative politics in the Department of Government at the London School of Economics and Political Science.

Randy Martin is professor of art and public policy at the Tisch School of the Arts, New York University.

Jane McAlevey is a union organizer, doctoral candidate at CUNY Graduate Center and author of *Raising Expectations*.

John McCullough is associate professor in the Department of Film at York University, Toronto.

David McNally is a professor of political science at York University in Toronto.

Kim Moody is a senior research fellow at the University of Hertfordshire, UK.

Şebnem Oğuz is associate professor of political science and international relations at Baskent University in Ankara.

Nicolas Pons-Vignon is a senior researcher in the School of Economic and Business Sciences, University of Witwatersrand, Johannesburg.

Charles Post is a professor of sociology at the Borough of Manhattan Community College-CUNY.

Hugo Radice is life fellow at the School of Politics and International Studies, University of Leeds.

Adolph Reed Jr is a professor of political science at the University of Pennsylvania.

Supriya RoyChowdhury is a professor of political science at the Institute for Social and Economic Change, Bangalore.

Achin Vanaik is professor emeritus of international relations and global politics at the University of Delhi.

Steve Williams is a San Francisco-based organizer and co-founder of POWER.

George Wright is professor emeritus in political science at the California State University, Chico.

PREFACE

By devoting the 2015 *Socialist Register* to investigating class formation and class strategies on a global scale, as we also did the 2014 volume marking the *Register*'s fiftieth anniversary, we were going against fashion in quite deliberately emphasizing the fundamental importance of class analysis, class discourse and class politics for the twenty-first century. It has unfortunately been the case that even in left circles over the past several decades any talk of class, let alone class struggle, became decidedly unfashionable. Of course, this was in many ways a very old story. When the *Register* was founded in 1964, the irrelevance of class had already been proclaimed in mainstream intellectual circles, and this was increasingly echoed by the leaders of social democratic parties. Twenty years later, as the political compass of even the more radical left began to swing to a proliferation of 'other' identities, Ralph Miliband faced this head-on in the 1983 *Register*: 'Socialist work means intervention in all the many different areas of life in which class struggle occurs: for class struggle must be taken to mean not only the permanent struggle between capital and labour, crucial though that remains, but the struggle against racial and sex discrimination, the struggle against arbitrary state and police power, the struggle against the ideological hegemony of the conservative forces, and the struggle for new and radically different defence and foreign policies'. Yet, amidst an endless stream of images across the new communication technologies, the left's attention became more and more focused on those very spaces of 'civil society' and the 'global economy' in which class relations and class struggles seemed all too little visible.

This remained largely the case in the first years of the new millennium, even as the representatives of the global ruling classes, in response to the challenges issued by 'anti-globalization' protests, already started wringing their hands once a year about the world's poor at gatherings like the World Economic Forum in Davos. The first great capitalist crisis of the twenty-first century that erupted in 2008 only seemed to confirm that the fundamental chasm before contemporary capitalism lay somewhere in the symbolic and fictitious world of credit-money and not in the class relations of contemporary finance and production − at least until Occupy issued a new class discourse, in the stark form of a struggle between the one per cent and 'we', the 99 per cent. Now, over the year between the publication of the 50th annual volume of the *Register* and this, the 51st, what has been appropriately coined 'the Piketty bubble' – i.e., the extraordinary amount of mainstream attention devoted to the publication of Thomas Piketty's *Capital in the Twenty-First Century* – seems to have justified, however unintentionally, our decision to produce two successive volumes devoted to sustaining, sharpening and spreading class analysis.

Piketty's analysis of the inherent, persistent, law-like structure of inequality between capital and labour is explicitly cast in terms of comparing centiles rather than classes. As he puts it in a section of his book headed 'Class Struggle or Centile Struggle?': 'The concepts of deciles and centiles are rather abstract and undoubtedly lack a certain poetry. It is easier for most people to identify with groups with which they are familiar: peasants or nobles, proletarians or bourgeois, office workers or top managers, waiters or traders. But the beauty of deciles is precisely that they enable us to compare inequalities that would otherwise be incomparable, using a common language that should in principle be acceptable to everyone'. Yes, it is in fact easier to get mainstream attention, and even approval, this way. But it is more instructive, and more dangerous to the power structures that sustain capitalist inequality, to think of class not 'as a structure, nor even as a "category", but as something which in fact happens ... in human relationships'. These famous words are from the 1963 preface to *The Making of English Working Class* by Edward Thompson, who was very much present at the conception of the *Socialist Register* the same year. 'The finest-meshed sociological net cannot give us a pure specimen of class, any more than it can give us one of deference or of love. The relationship must always be embodied in real people and a real context'.

It is in this sense that last year's volume, *Registering Class*, took a quite different tack from Piketty's by locating growing social inequalities not in an empiricist account of trends in the accumulation of assets relative to rates to growth, but in the political conditions and social struggles allowing the spread and deepening of capitalist social relations. In this vein, 'capital' cannot be examined only in its manifestations as wealth, as important as that is for understanding the parameters of power in capitalist societies. The essays in last year's *Register* on the changing configuration of the capitalist classes sought to provide a careful accounting of the concrete, material ways capital is organized and exercises its power and hegemony so as to extract and accumulate its wealth in the twenty-first century. However useful his data set and all the attention he draws to persistent and growing inequality,

Piketty tells us next to nothing of these issues. If he provides a certain break with neoclassical economics, Piketty nevertheless returns us to a sociology of classes as statistical artifacts of income and asset brackets, rather than that of classes as a specific ensemble of social relations, experienced and organized in particular ways, to explain the historical form, trends and contradictions of wealth and income inequalities. In this paradoxical world, it is income and assets which explain classes, rather than historical class relations that explain the accumulation and social forms of wealth. This is far removed from an understanding of class as a social process, made and remade in class struggle through which working-class people collectively organize to overcome, or all too often to reinforce, divisions amongst themselves, in the context of the socioeconomic and political inequalities of capitalist class relations.

The current volume, *Transforming Classes*, takes as its departure point class relations in this latter sense – the way working classes are being made and remade in the struggles against neoliberalism, austerity and authoritarian governments. Indeed, the purpose here is to take an account of the balance of class forces, the old and emerging forms of workplace and political organization, and the strategies being debated and adapted in different zones of the world. The volume begins with an essay that cuts new ground in theorizing the working-class experience from the prism of social reproduction, wherein race, gender, ethnicity and migration are all constitutive of class and necessarily define key features of the terrain of class struggle. As much in the advanced capitalist countries as in the most imperialized zones of the Global South – in fact, through their mutual imbrication in global labour markets – workers' livelihoods, particularly those of migrants, are directly connected to household formation across borders. Taking up this concern to develop a truly global awareness of the transformations of social classes and class politics, the essays that follow – as authoritative in their appraisals as in their range – focus not only on such key developing capitalist countries as India, South Africa, Turkey, Egypt, Brazil and Chile, but also on the momentous political and discursive dimensions of the capitalist transformation of class relations in China under the auspices of the ruling Communist Party. And no less indispensable to the overall assessment of global capitalism are the essays here that attend to the advanced capitalist world. In both trying to understand the transformations which the so-called new middle classes have been going through as well as the state of trade unionism in Europe and North America, these essays focus on the need to develop an adequate class theory and class politics for today. In this respect, the four essays that compose the symposium on 'Labour and the Left in the USA', with which this volume concludes, provide not only sober readings but also shed light on promising campaigns for new working-class organizations in and beyond the workplace even in the imperial centre of world capitalism.

Both volumes on class began from a workshop held in Toronto in February 2013. Over the last year, we solicited a number of additional essays as the volume's themes cohered and new class struggles burst forward requiring analysis and debate. We want to thank all our contributors for their essays, as well as Ana and Robert McLuhan for their excellent translation of Ricardo Antunes's essay from Portuguese. We are especially grateful to Colin Leys, Alan Zuege and Adam Hilton, who provided not only invaluable editorial assistance but also considerable help in conceiving the volume. Adrian Howe and Tony Zurbrugg at Merlin Press are also once again due our gratitude for being such sympathetic and supportive publishers, as is Louis Mackay for yet another imaginative cover.

The *Socialist Register* begins its second half-century with some reorganization and renewal of its editorial collective. With this volume, Vivek Chibber joins Colin Leys and Alfredo Saad-Filho as an associate editor, and while Hidayat (Gerard) Greenfield is departing due to his heavy international trade union responsibilities, we are pleased to announce that Lin Chun, Hannes Lacher, Şebnem Oğuz and Stephanie Ross are coming on board as new contributing editors. As with Madeleine Davis and Ray Kiely who joined us last year, we very much look forward to their active collaboration on the *Register*.

It would be remiss of us not to mention the deaths of Stuart Hall, Norman Geras and Tony Benn over the last year. The importance of Stuart Hall's attempt to rethink class in the formation of the British New Left was highlighted in Madeleine Davis's essay on the lineages of the *Socialist Register* in last year's volume, as was his contribution to 'the battle for socialist ideas' (the title of his 1982 *Register* essay) in the face of the bankruptcy of Labourism and the rise of Thatcherism. Although Norman Geras resigned as a contributing editor in 2003, we will always value his contribution of five outstanding essays over the previous decade on socialist morals, ethics, hope and vision. Tony Benn himself contributed to the 1989 volume with an essay on 'Obstacles to Reform in Britain', and to the 2003 volume with an interview on 'Bush and Blair: Iraq and the UK's American Viceroy'. His appreciation of the *Register* long graced our volumes' back covers. We can do no better to express our own appreciation of Tony Benn than to say that his definition of his original purpose in seeking nomination as a candidate to become a Member of Parliament in 1950 as to 'make, teach and keep socialists' well expresses the *Register*'s continuing purpose.

LP

GA

July 2014

PRECARIOUS MIGRANTS:
GENDER, RACE AND THE SOCIAL
REPRODUCTION OF A GLOBAL WORKING CLASS

SUSAN FERGUSON AND DAVID MCNALLY

'This guestworker program's the closest thing I've ever seen to slavery'.[1]

'No one pays attention to these killings, but the secret of the world is hidden in them'.[2]

Each of the quotes above speaks to a distinct aspect of contemporary capitalism in North America: the first refers to America's migrant labour system; the second references Mexico's *maquiladora* factory zone and the epidemic of murders of women working there. In truth, these apparently distinct systems form a unity. North America's 'guestworker' programmes and Mexico's deregulated labour regimes are interlocking spaces in the social geography and political economy of neoliberal capitalism. These zones of precarity comprise reconfigured spaces of capital, work, gender, race and social reproduction in late capitalism. Linked in obvious ways by flows of capital they are equally connected by movements of people, particularly the migrant workers who represent the ideal precarious labourer of the neoliberal era. Yet another spatial flow defines this economic geography: the cross-border movement of wages that connects otherwise separated sites of labour and domestic social reproduction. Wages rarely sustain just the immediate producer; they also reproduce her family members. And in the case of migrant workers, such reproduction frequently involves remittance across borders – and transnational survival networks. At least half a billion people on the planet receive wage remittances. The sending of the latter also follows a powerfully gendered pattern, as female migrants send higher shares of their earnings to family members in their countries of origin.

Small academic industries have emerged in the study of both migrant labour and *maquila* factory systems. And recently, economists have paid increased attention to the financial flows attendant on wage remittances.[3]

Studies that map out the complex interrelations between cross-border movements of capital, labour and wages in the social reproduction of class relations in all their multi-dimensionality are much less developed. This essay proposes some conceptual guidelines for theorizing those relations. While its frame of reference is global, its focus is on North American movements of capital, people and wages – and the associated regimes governing (gendered and racialized) migrant labour, border security, and financial remittances – as these are paradigmatic of genuinely worldwide social processes. In suggesting pathways toward theorizing the inner connections among these seemingly disparate phenomena, we explore patterns of primitive accumulation, dispossession, capital flows, migration, racialization, work and gender relations in an effort to illuminate crucial dimensions of the social reproduction of capital and labour today.

Our work in this area is inspired by a Marxist-feminist approach that understands social reproduction in terms of the inner connections of household, neighbourhood and community activities with the monetized social activities (predominantly wage-labour) necessary to market-dependent reproduction, wherein food, housing, transportation, clothing and so on must be purchased as commodities. The term 'monetized activities' points to the fact that, while wage-labour is the principal means of subsistence for the dispossessed, activities such as street-vending, selling sex and independent domestic production are also part of the social picture. As much as monetized practices are decisive in a capitalist market society, they are crucially interconnected with domestic and neighbourhood activities ranging from cooking and cleaning to childcare and recreation. An adequate theorization of the *total* social reproduction of the capital-labour relation thus requires a multi-dimensional analysis which, while acknowledging the decisive role of waged-work and other monetized practices, situates these within a nexus of practices through which working-class life is produced and reproduced.

In exploring the interconnections between workplaces and households, social reproduction theory as it developed within Marxist-feminism has enabled deeper understanding of the interrelations of gender and class in modern capitalism. While underlining this accomplishment, we are nonetheless dissatisfied that a considerable amount of work in this tradition has operated within a national framework by taking the nation-state as *the* macro-level site for the social reproduction of labouring people. The result has been a neglect of more global social processes (by all means bound up with relations among states) and patterns of transnational social reproduction. Fortunately, some important critical work has opened more promising directions in recent years by conceptualizing social reproduction in its interrelations with the global political economy.[4]

The shortcomings of the 'methodological nationalism' within one influential strain of social reproduction analysis are threefold. First, in not situating the national within the global, this approach fails to grasp nation-states as determinate locations within a system of global economics and geopolitics.[5] The result is an underestimation of the global dynamics that significantly drive 'national' policies regulating labour markets, immigration, education and so on. Secondly, it loses sight of international processes of dispossession and primitive accumulation which, among other things, generate *global reserves of labour-power* whose cross-border movements are at the heart of the worldwide production and reproduction of capital and labour.[6] Finally, inadequate theorization of the global space of capitalist production and reproduction tends to obscure the *central* roles of racism and imperialism in the constitution of the actual relations of capital and of the complexly differentiated global working class.

This means situating the social reproduction of working classes in relation to the hierarchically structured *global market in human labour-power*. The distinct national spaces within the world market in labour are linked together as elements of a complex social whole constituted by racialized forms of citizenship and non-membership, and differentiated domains of 'security' and precarity, all governed by an overriding logic of control and exploitation of labour. Seen in these terms, the social reproduction of the global working class crucially entails processes of migration and racialization that are *inseparable* from its class and gender dimensions.[7] The deepening of a social reproduction analysis centred on the (hierarchically and racially) differentiated global labour market is thus vital to a robust analysis of working-class formation today.

PRIMITIVE ACCUMULATION, DISPOSSESSION AND THE GLOBAL LABOUR MARKET

'Capital needs the means of production and labour-power of the whole globe'
– Rosa Luxemburg[8]

Marx was well aware that capital has to ensure the reproduction of a working class sufficient to meet the demands of accumulation, thereby circumventing sustained labour shortages. He understood that capital does not directly produce labour power and therefore requires some specific social process to ensure adequate supplies of that crucial commodity. Yet his account of this process – what he described as 'the capitalist law of population' – is significantly flawed. In Chapter 25 of *Capital*, he argues that a section of the working class is regularly made redundant due to ongoing mechanization of production. Since mechanization is labour-displacing, the capitalist mode of production will systematically generate a reserve army of labour – a mass of unemployed workers – whose growth in numbers is tendentially inexhaustible. The dynamic of labour-displacing accumulation constitutes, he claims, 'a law of population peculiar to the capitalist mode of production'. And because this surplus population is always available for exploitation, it 'forms a disposable industrial reserve army, which belongs to capital just as absolutely as if the latter had bred it at its own cost'.[9]

All of this pivots, however, on a tacit assumption: that the rate of biological reproduction typical of early English capitalism will remain largely unchanged. Yet Marx does not provide any *social* account as to why this should be so, defaulting instead to a naturalistic assumption: when it comes to 'the maintenance and reproduction of the working class', he writes, capital 'may safely leave this to the worker's drives for self-preservation and propagation'.[10] This, however, treats workers' generational reproduction as a *strictly* naturo-biological process, rather than as a biologically-grounded domain of human material life that is socially mediated and hence historically variable. Equally damaging, his naturalistic premise has been empirically refuted. Throughout nineteenth-century industrialization, working-class women in Europe and North America increasingly asserted control over biological reproduction, precipitating a sharp and continuous decline in pregnancies, childbirth and household size. This dramatic development, which halved the average number of children borne by married women in Europe, (once dubbed by Seccombe 'The Great Proletarian Fertility Decline') demonstrates that the generational renewal of the working class is a socio-historical process, powerfully influenced by women's reproductive choices.[11] Instead of leaving this process 'to the worker's drives for self-preservation and propagation', as Marx suggested, capital increasingly turned to the state, promoting laws that strictly regulated birth control and abortion, while also advancing immigration policies that reflected capital's need for a substantial reserve army of labour.

To be sure, Marx's 'law' looked more compelling during his own lifetime, as European capitalism experienced such growing labour surpluses that widespread emigration was the norm. Over the course of the century before the First World War, for instance, 50 million people left Europe.[12] While specific nation-states had especially high rates of emigration – Italy and Ireland, for instance – the trend also held for industrialized Britain and Germany. Much of this had to do with ongoing processes of internal primitive accumulation that displaced rural producers from the land and drove them into markets in wage-labour – something that does not figure formally in the workings of Marx's 'law', and a point to which we shall return. Even when significant internal reserves were available, emigration coexisted with immigration, particularly of the casual, seasonal and low-wage variety. By the middle of the nineteenth century, European labour markets had begun to manifest patterns of ethno-national segmentation, with poorly-paid, casual and seasonal manual work often attracting large numbers of migrants from poorer zones of Europe, such as Ireland, Italy, Scandinavia and Russia.

Such patterns became increasingly significant in the twentieth century, particularly during the sustained economic expansion after the Second World War, when major industrial economies became systematic importers of labour-power. As with early modes of appropriating labour in the Americas, these patterns were profoundly racialized, with migration flows frequently tracking (in reverse) the paths of earlier colonization with, for instance, Algerians working in France, Indonesians in the Netherlands, Indians in Britain, Mexicans in the US. The demographic reasons for policies of incorporating migrant labour are clear enough, since, contrary to Marx's expectation, declining domestic birthrates have not been adequate to reproduce national stocks of labour-power in the Global North. The UN Population Fund estimates that without immigration the population of Europe will contract by nearly 125 million by 2050. Japan faces a similar conundrum. As for the United States, in 1970 immigrants made up five per cent of the workforce; forty years later, they made up more than 16 per cent. Equally significant, immigrants accounted for approximately half of the growth of the US labour force between 1995 and 2010. In other words, without large-scale imports of foreign-born labour, American capitalism would have experienced acute shortages.[13]

It must be insisted, however, that there is more than demographics at work here, especially in the neoliberal period. Much migrant labour, particularly when it comes under programmes that stipulate 'temporary servitude', or arrives in the form of undocumented workers lacking civil and labour rights, constitutes a vulnerable and hyper-precarious section of the working class whose insecurity contributes to the lowering of general levels of real wages and job and social protections. Only anti-racist forms of labour organizing show any real capacity for countering such tendencies – a point to which we shall return.

It seems abundantly clear that heightened precarity of migrant workers is deliberate social policy. Consider, first, the case of the United States. Since the signing of the North American Free Trade Agreement (NAFTA) between Mexico, Canada and the US, capital has moved more freely throughout the area while labour, particularly racialized Mexican labour, has moved more unfreely. Each year, the H-2 programme provides over 100,000 migrant labourers for US business, more than half of them in agriculture – and under conditions of enormous civil and social restriction which are tantamount to bonded labour. In sheer numerical terms, of course, this 'official' inflow has been overshadowed by the tripling of undocumented ('illegal') workers in the US since the inauguration of NAFTA – from four to 12 million, the vast majority of them from Latin America. And the *proportion* of Mexicans entering the US without authorization has soared from one-quarter during the 1980s to fully 84 per cent by the 2000s.[14] Huge numbers are moving as a result of accelerated displacements from the land and destruction of state-industries and services induced by NAFTA. Some of the displaced move to places where US and other foreign capital has set up inside Mexico – overwhelmingly the *maquila* zones adjacent to the American border – while others cross over, with or without authorization, in search of work in the US job market. Whereas the Mexican-born population in the US was 2.2 million in 1980, it was 12 million by 2006, more than half of them undocumented.[15] So significant is this shift that one out of every three Mexicans working for wages is employed in the US, while one-quarter of all industrial workers in Mexico are either in the *maquilas* or other continentally integrated industries.[16] In short, there is a direct link between accelerated primitive accumulation under NAFTA and the construction of a truly continental labour market.

NAFTA and neoliberal policy have thus promoted continental flows of both capital and labour, one liberalized and the other punitively policed. Indeed, the deliberate thrust of US immigration policy in the NAFTA era has been to simultaneously criminalize border crossings by Mexican workers while methodically increasing the employment of unauthorized Mexican labour – and thereby to construct what has rightly been called a *crimmigration* system.[17] In 2012 alone, the Obama administration pumped almost $12 billion into Customs and Border Protection, increasing surveillance systems and doubling the number of Border Patrol agents.[18] Notwithstanding the growing number of deportations, the purpose of inhumane and punitive border enforcement is not principally to deport undocumented workers, but to deepen their condition of *deportability*. Rather than an end in itself, deportation is a means to intensify the profound vulnerability of workers who live with the knowledge that they are inherently deportable.[19] Deportability reinforces those deeply racialized forms of precarity under which migrant labourers comprise a 'permanent labor force of the temporarily employed'.[20]

While the Canadian programme for promoting precarious migrant labour is configured differently – in good measure because Canada does not share a border with Mexico – the effects follow the same neoliberal model in shifting from an emphasis on permanent settlement to modes of 'transient servitude'. The latter is regulated through the Temporary Foreign Worker Program (TFWP), which ties work permits directly to employment status, restricts mobility rights, prohibits most temporary workers from applying for work permits or changes in immigration status while inside the country, and limits most workers to a maximum of four years in Canada. Hyperprecarious migrant labour under the TFWP has soared since 2000. In the early 1980s there were fewer than 40,000 workers in Canada under the predecessor programme of the TFWP; by 2012 there were nearly half a million, as the annual number of temporary migrant workers admitted tripled to 300,000 in the first decade of the 2000s. Moreover, temporary migrants were increasingly to be found in notoriously labour-intensive, low-wage and non-union sectors, such as retail, accommodation and food services, among others.[21]

While deportability is an ever-present threat, legally enforced *transient migrancy* plays the crucial role in the Canadian programme. The four-year restriction means that, 'while the TFWP is becoming more permanent and persistent, the individual TFWs remain steadfastly temporary. Each year tens of thousands of TFWs leave the country as their work permits expire, only to be replaced by tens of thousands of new TFWs'.[22] Temporary migrant workers in Canada are thus meant to be fully disposable. Not only can they be ejected from employment; they can also be geographically expelled from the nation-state. As a result, they occupy the extreme end of the precarity scale. Large numbers are paid less than the legal minimum wage, are frequently unpaid for overtime hours and sometimes have costs for employer-provided housing deducted directly from their paychecks.[23] In every meaningful sense of the word, Canada's temporary migrant workers are bonded labourers, tied to employers, deprived of basic civil rights and subject to systematic economic and social abuse.

The neoliberal phase of 'free trade' agreements, such as NAFTA, has thus involved a significant reorientation in global labour migration. Not only are the dominant capitalist nations systematic importers of surplus labour generated elsewhere (particularly the Global South); they have also constructed an array of coercive immigration regimes designed to cheapen migrant labour by restricting its social and political rights. Immigrant labour has always arrived with a variety of (frequently limited) legal statuses – from those who have been given a relatively straightforward track to permanent residence and citizenship (often for ethno-racial reasons) to those who come as temporary foreign workers and experience forms of legal bondage in the 'host' country, to those who enter without documentation of any sort, making them hyper-precarious. As the US and Canadian cases demonstrate, the latter forms of temporary and undocumented immigration figure decisively under neoliberalism and its recent 'age of austerity'.

It follows that global processes of dispossession and migration should be considered central to the capitalist law of population. In fact, Marx may have sensed this when he rounded out his discussion of the ostensible 'law' with considerations on Ireland and its migrant workers. Here, he touched on colonialism, centralization of land ownership in Ireland, massive emigration and the vital role of wage remittances from Irish-Americans.[24] In the course of raising questions of colonialism, dispossession, displacement from the land and migration, Marx gestured toward a considerably more productive line of theoretical investigation, one that analyzes the social reproduction of labour power in relation to global processes of primitive accumulation and the movements of labouring people they induce.[25]

Marx's tantalizing – but theoretically underdeveloped – comments in this area remind us that the coerced mass movement of peoples is nothing new to the neoliberal era of capitalism. In fact, in many non-capitalist modes of production slavery has been a key social mechanism for appropriating labour-powers developed outside a given society. Historically, the enslavement of women, for their reproductive capacities as well as their direct labour, has loomed particularly large in this regard.[26] And throughout the bourgeois epoch, the dispossession of workers on the peripheries of the capitalist economy has consistently served as a means of producing additional (and massive) supplies of labour-power, particularly for the colonial extensions in the Americas. During the rise of capitalism, notes one historian, 'The creation and survival of economic enterprises across imperial borders in mining, agriculture, distributive trades and services, depended on the availability of coerced unfree labour'.[27] Today, this predominantly takes the form of precarious (and intricately bonded) migrant labour.

Speaking schematically, we can identify three main forms of appropriating massive supplies of dispossessed people from the peripheries of the system: 1) slavery and indentured servitude in the seventeenth and eighteenth centuries, which saw probably hundreds of thousands of Irish children, women and men sold as slaves, only to be dramatically exceeded by the sale of about 12 million enslaved Africans; 2) the so-called 'coolie labour' system, under which at least 12 million workers from India and another five to six million from other parts of Asia were sold into contracted servitude; and 3) the modern system of hyper-precarious migrant labour.[28] Each of these modes of appropriating labour-power has pivoted on global regimes of racialization and colonial and postcolonial subordination.

What is unique about the neoliberal period, therefore, is not that racialized labour-power is appropriated from the peripheries of the global system. That has been a constant of the capitalist mode of production. Instead, the key development has been the massive expansion of the global labour reserve as a result of the most accelerated and extensive processes of primitive accumulation in world history. This has facilitated the construction of neoliberal forms of migrant precarity, which contribute centrally to the reorganization of the global labour market in ways that facilitate the reproduction of capital at the expense of the reproduction of working-class households.

GLOBAL DISPOSSESSION IN THE NEOLIBERAL ERA

A central feature of the neoliberal era has been the *globalization of primitive accumulation.* Unrelenting, large-scale processes of dispossession have dramatically swelled the size of the global labour reserve, while also rendering it more international than ever before. Capital has increasingly moved to where such reserves are to be found – China and East Asia generally, Mexico, Eastern Europe and many other regions – at the same time as it has repressively incorporated tens of millions of migrant workers into the spaces of the Global North. Precise measures of either the global working class and/or that component of it that comprises the world reserve army of labour are of course impossible. To begin, social classes are dynamic formations in time, their boundaries shifting with reconfigurations of life and labour. Nevertheless, the basic trends can be grasped statistically. The global working class has grown by at least two-thirds (and has perhaps doubled) across the neoliberal period, from something between 1.5 to 2 billion people reliant on selling their labour-power in 1980 to over 3 billion today – with half or more of this number making up the global reserve army.[29] This is a stunning increase in dispossession and proletarianization – and one that has been utterly crucial to the neoliberal reorganization of the capitalist world economy.[30]

Of course, capital does not set out to dispossess people as an end in itself. Dispossession is a means to an end: the transformation of economic 'assets', particularly land, from common or public ownership or non-capitalist usage (e.g. by peasants) into elements of capital, i.e. means of production mobilized for the production of surplus value. Neoliberalism has dramatically deepened myriad social processes that dispossess small producers for just such reasons, in the process driving forward worldwide proletarianization. As it is impossible to provide here a comprehensive overview of these processes, we shall merely itemize some of them:

- Land grabs, including giant land leases, for purposes of export-oriented agribusiness, large-scale mining and oil exploration, and conversion to bio-fuels[31]
- Giant dam projects and land enclosures for industrial development that displace communities of rural producers[32]
- Migration due to climate change that renders whole regions less capable of sustaining agriculture and pasturage[33]
- Appropriation of land in order to monopolize (and privatize) sources of fresh water, or to develop lucrative eco-tourism[34]
- Privatization of communal lands and neoliberal reforms (including government exploitation of 'natural disasters') that dispossess agrarian producers[35]
- Use of civil wars and armed conflicts as means of displacement[36]

Huge numbers of people dispossessed by such means relocate as *internal* migrants within the nation-states to which they legally belong. China has at least 150 million rural-to-urban migrants, who suffer from systemic discrimination in housing, access to social services and legal rights while living outside the towns or villages from which they have moved. Similar patterns prevail in Mexico, where internal migrants suffer related forms of oppression. Not all displaced migrants head to the Global North, of course. The states of the Persian Gulf are massively reliant on migrants, particularly from South Asia, importing 8.5 million by the early 2000s.[37] One observes similar patterns in other parts of the 'newly industrializing' world. In Brazil, the number of migrant labourers increased 50 per cent in just two years (2010 to 2012), while in Chile the number of migrants tripled in a decade.[38]

As for Mexico, during the 1990s alone at least one million small farmers were displaced, as trade liberalization and imports from agribusiness undercut local producers. Such processes continue, as increasingly marketized and liberalized economics drive ongoing dispossession and profound polarizations of wealth and poverty. Large numbers of dispossessed agrarian producers have migrated to the *maquila* zones in search of wage-labour, with women forming an increasingly significant proportion of this internal migration. This has given Mexico an internal low-wage export manufacturing zone, often described as having four essential characteristics: 1) feminization of the workforce; 2) extreme workforce segmentation with less 'skilled' and feminized workers earning much less; 3) reduced real wages across the board; 4) extreme anti-union policies.[39] Displacement has also driven mass processes of cross-border migration. And, contrary to official rhetoric about border protection, the impetus of US capital has been to draw ever-larger reserves of cheap labour into the US itself, including six million Latina/ Latino immigrants during 2000–08.[40]

As is always the case in the capitalist mode of production, the relation between capital and labour is two-sided. While labour constitutes a source of surplus value and profit for capital, it is also true that, for labour, capital comprises a source of wages with which working-class households can be reproduced. Each in short is a means to the reproduction of the other, albeit in a massively unbalanced and exploitative relation. In the case of migrant labourers, much social reproduction occurs at sites significantly separated from the spaces of capitalist production – and frequently by way of geographic separations that involve cross-border movements. The result, as we discuss in the next section, is a spatial rescaling of households in which cross-border wage remittances figure centrally in reproducing labour-power at sites where the costs of doing so are sharply lower than they would be near the sites of waged employment. In the decade prior to 2012, wage remittances tripled worldwide, topping $530 billion for officially recorded flows – more than three times global aid budgets. For countries such as El Salvador, Jamaica, Nicaragua, Jordan, Yemen and Eritrea, wage remittances boosted gross national product by more than 10 per cent.[41] Moreover, relative shares of remittances vary according to gender and status: women typically send a larger share of their wages to their home country than do men, and temporary migrants send a larger share than do permanent ones.[42]

In the Mexican case, the sums involved are striking. According to the World Bank, wage remittances from Mexican workers in the US nearly quadrupled in the first eight years of this century, from $7.5 billion to $28 billion per annum – an amount equivalent to nearly three per cent of Mexican GDP.[43] These cross-border movements of workers and the counter-flows of their wages via remittances doubly benefit capital: first, by bringing precarious and relatively cheap migrant labour to sites of work in the United States and Canada; and second, by enabling the reproduction of the next generation of labourers in Mexico, where the costs of life are lower and for whose public services capital in the US and Canada pay nothing. But in addition to benefiting capital, these reverse flows of labour and wages rescale relations of gender, childhood, kinship and social reproduction.

TRANSNATIONAL HOUSEHOLDS:
NEW CONFIGURATIONS OF GENDER AND CLASS

Thus far, we have only addressed what might be termed 'first-order' social reproduction: the biological and daily regeneration of migrant workers themselves, and their households. In this section, we focus on migrant paid domestic and agricultural labour in the US and Canada, two sectors that have figured prominently in the social organization of North America's precarious workforce. Research into these workers' survival strategies reveals the otherwise hidden practical activities and relations undergirding global labour reserves. It reminds us that the tripartite dynamic of the flow of capital, labour and wages across borders involves very real social relations sustained by people who strive to meet their needs by acting (through their paid and unpaid labour) within a world in which capital's drive to accumulate is a persistent limit.

Many studies explore how the constrained forms of migrant workers' self- and household reproduction rely on and reproduce systems of racism and sexism. Our aim here is to shift the lens slightly, in order to show how their (complexly racialized and gendered) survival strategies figure in the global social reproduction of *class*. Theorizing first-order social reproduction of migrant workers, in particular the establishment of transnational households, as integral moments in the renewal of waged labour highlights the variegated forms in which capitalist social relations radically separate sites of production from sites of social reproduction. And precisely because this spatial rescaling occurs in and through a world that is segmented into hierarchically ordered nation-states policed by immigration and border regimes, we must conceive of the contemporary working class as formed in and through gendered *and* racialized relations. Such an approach can also clarify the ways in which racism and sexism are reproduced through global dynamics of dispossession and accumulation. In other words, a global social reproduction perspective facilitates an understanding of class in which dynamics of gender and race are internally related parts of a complex social whole.

Migrant workers' transnational households and networks, and the state policies supporting these, institutionalize dramatically lower costs of social reproduction. Capital and the state in North America regularly draw from a pool of effectively 'cost free' labour power on whose past social reproduction they have not spent a dime. And because they deny or restrict migrant access to state resources and services, receiving nations also invest comparatively little in the current migrant workforce's *ongoing* regeneration. Undocumented workers, having the least access to resources, and being most vulnerable to criminalization and employer abuse, are generally the most cost-free workers. Yet legal migrants too, particularly those governed by seasonal and temporary worker programmes, have limited and uneven claims on social services. Working disproportionately in industries, such as agriculture, that typically fall outside regular labour protection laws, they are vulnerable to significant medical costs while largely deprived of basic employment standards around overtime, unionization and vacation pay. Domestic workers have had greater success in their quest for improved employment standards in recent years. Yet because they perform affective care work in private households, and are subject to hyper-personalized supervision, violations of those standards are not uncommon.[44] Moreover, with transiency, secondary citizenship status and labour immobility built into their contracts, all migrants have little leverage when it comes to challenging these conditions of social reproduction.

Such restrictions perpetuate migrants' socio-spatial segregation from the citizen population, and impose a lower overall standard of first-order social reproduction. Crowded housing (the median space per person in US-residing Latino households is 350 square feet, 80 square feet less than that of the average family living below the poverty line), inadequate schooling and healthcare, lack of health and safety protection in workplaces all contribute to defining a new, cheaper, norm.[45] Not only do these conditions devalue migrant workers' status and worth in the popular imaginary, the new norm places competitive pressure on what the citizen workforce can demand in wages and benefits. Substandard conditions of migrant workers' social reproduction thus simultaneously rationalize and institutionalize a racialized regime of cheap labour.

This is not to deny that the low-end, 'first-world' wages migrants receive improve their monetary standard of living as well as that of their households back home. For the most part, they do.[46] But geographically dispersed households suffer greatly from emotional and social costs of separation. Migrants have responded to policies disallowing or making it difficult to immigrate if pregnant or accompanied by dependents with complex transnational survival strategies.[47] On the one hand, transnational households and community networks represent creative cross-border survival strategies designed to meet the socio-material and affective needs of the workers and their families. Important as they are to resisting or managing capitalist imperatives as well as gendered and racialized relations, transnational families and other cross-border practices and institutions nevertheless constitute a central mechanism in perpetuating the cheap social reproduction of the current and future working class.[48] Sustained by wages paid to migrant workers which are divided between their self-reproduction and that of families back home or elsewhere, transnational households are imbricated in the workings of global capitalism, all the more so as the flow of remittances from the more to less capitalistically advanced societies has become deeply embedded in the social and economic fabric of the sending country. Remittances to Mexico in 2005, for instance, represented 160.7 per cent of net foreign direct investment, and have continued at such levels.[49] Because they are primarily spent on private consumption, they raise local living standards and shore up local economies. More than this, the Mexican government encourages migrants (with promises to match contributions) to funnel a proportion of remittances into what would otherwise be state social reproductive services such as community infrastructure projects, thus boosting public investment as well.

As a way to encourage the export of labour power, many states in the Global South have assumed an ever-growing proportion of skills training and worker recruitment costs. For example, in 2006 the Philippines implemented the Household Service Workers policy (HSWP) intended to 'professionalize migrant domestic work and minimize vulnerabilities'.[50] The policy regulates worker recruitment and deployment processes, while also establishing state assessment, training and upgrading programmes (including both domestic skills accreditation and cultural and language training) for potential migrants. Similar state support for foreign recruitment and deployment of local labour power is intensifying in the Caribbean. Such policies simultaneously relieve receiving nations of key social reproductive costs associated with training and culturally preparing workers to enter their labour markets *and* deepen the sending country's investment in and commitment to migrant labour as a 'development' strategy.

Yet the limits to such a strategy are clear. To begin, in exporting their nation's labour power, sending countries effectively lose a potential productive resource, one in which they have made at least some degree of social investment. Moreover, sending countries, which are usually heavily dependent upon commodity export markets, march to the beat of an international drummer – in this case, the more capitalistically developed states which orchestrate the terms of free trade agreements, IMF loans and structural adjustment policies, and which impose restrictive immigration and border control regimes. The latter insure that the flow of foreign capital into labour-exporting countries does not disrupt the continual reproduction of precarious labour, but instead consolidates migrant precarity. For instance, rather than diversified socio-economic development, foreign capital in Mexico fosters differentiated forms of precarious labour, suspending social and legal rights in *Maquila* zones, to such an extent that the hardships of international migration and/or lack of status in another country is often viewed as preferable to working legally within one's own borders. But as sending countries pursue development strategies linked to exporting cheap labour, they are likely to continue and possibly step up efforts to facilitate the migration of their native population, and reproduce and intensify their subordinate position in the world capitalist economy. As a result, unlike the children of citizen households in receiving countries, children of migrants' transnational families are largely destined to join the global reserve army of labour. Rescaled survival strategies (e.g., transnational families and other networks) are thus a crucial mechanism for the relatively cheap social reproduction of not only current precarious labour power, but also that of the future.

To grasp the significance of this shift toward institutionalizing degraded conditions and cheaper social reproduction, it is helpful to compare the contemporary immigration regime of transient servitude to earlier periods in which immigration frequently led to full citizenship and assimilation. During the 1910s and 1920s, for instance, US state and community resources were leveraged to educate immigrant women in the art of promoting supposedly American values and morals in their child-rearing and other domestic work.[51] The goal was to develop an immigrant workforce that approached American citizen norms (which while deeply racialized, gendered and class-differentiated nonetheless did not legally differentiate immigrants from citizens in terms of access to state and employment-based social reproduction support).[52] Today, however, the neoliberal capitalist goal is to create and sustain a temporary migrant workforce that is differentiated from the citizen workforce, whose everyday life and longer-term expectations are so degraded that they can often be viewed and treated as *disposable*.[53] The disposability of such workers rationalizes and promotes the neoliberal era shift in the institutions and practices of social reproduction. As we have outlined, this shift involves policies designed both to offload social responsibility, and where migrants are concerned, to outlaw, discourage and/or offshore biological reproduction. Instead of instruction in parenting, many women migrants today are either denied reproduction rights by the terms of their migration or, as in many *maquilas*, plied with birth control pills by their bosses.

The concept of disposability involves the devaluation of household labour of social reproduction as much as degradation of waged labour in the workplace, highlighting the multiple sites of capitalism's essential impulse to treat labour power as merely a commodity. The fact that '[f]oreign labor is desired but the person in whom it is embodied is not desired' is a fundamental contradiction that the current regime of transient servitude is designed to manage.[54] In so doing it draws on and reinforces deeply racialized and gendered institutions, practices and ideologies. Capital does not simply need labour power to function, it needs exploitable labour power. And the more desperate, anxious and insecure a life is – the closer it resembles 'bare life' – the more susceptible it is to exploitation. In other words, 'social processes of abjection … [produce] subjects that can be exploited not only because they are able to sell their capacities as labor power … but also because they bear *second skins* that command a low price'.[55] Indeed, a feminine 'second skin' is crucial to the *maquilas'* reliance on disposability as a central strategy. High female turnover in the factories is attributed to women's lack of interest and loyalty to their jobs, which in turn justifies withholding skills training from them. Yet managers will routinely engage in sexual harassment of pregnant women and surveillance of reproductive cycles to justify firings. The Mexican woman worker in the *maquilas* is a 'subject formed in the flux between waste and value,' suggests Melissa Wright. 'She can be nothing other than a temporary worker, one whose intrinsic value does not mature, grow, and increase over time … [one who represents] the permanent labor force of the temporarily employed'.[56]

Such cultural devaluation has put women at risk of even more violent forms of oppression. Since 1993, at least 1,400 girls and women have been murdered (and frequently raped and mutilated) in the Chihuahua free trade zone of Ciudad Juarez – many of them during late night commutes to and from the factories.[57] Juarez also has the highest rate of domestic violence in Mexico. Prior to the *maquila* development of the early 1990s, however, murders of women were extremely rare in the city. But as the state withdrew services in line with NAFTA policies, drug cartels competed with state military might to patrol the region. At the same time, gender relations were being rescaled as many young, mostly single women experienced the partial financial and sexual empowerment and independence that comes with their status as wage earners. Such a disruption of gender norms has, in many cases, heightened male insecurity, contributing to a hyper-masculinized culture in which the sex trade flourishes alongside the drug trade, and in which women workers tread a jagged path between economic value (as breadwinners) and social devaluation (as disposable workers).[58]

While clearly not all migrant workers negotiate femicidal circumstances, the spatial rescaling and debased conditions of their social reproduction ensures that they all do bear second skins, based upon gender and racial oppression. Their abject status, reproduced through longstanding forms of domination, works to perpetuate the same: insofar as migrants' below-standard wages, work and life conditions are culturally devalued yet economically critical to capitalist expansion, they are set up to be both loathed and feared, a threat to 'citizen' morals and jobs.

A social reproduction feminist approach is attentive to such dehumanization because it extends and historicizes Marx's theorization of the two-sidedness of labour power. While capitalism requires labour power *qua* commodity, it has no (internal) mechanism to create and sustain it. Rather, the commodity labour power can only be reproduced *socially*, by (geo-politically, bio-physically differentiated) people with needs and emotions that exceed their mere reproduction. The state can and does aid and abet capital in meeting its need for labour power of course, but the drive to accumulate puts continual pressure to deny the (costly) humanity of real people, to deny the 'excess' needs thrown up by socially embodied human life and to impose 'bare life' instead. Capitalism's drive to proletarianize labour is thus bound up with a reliance on gendered and racialized relations that mark the processes of replenishing this and succeeding generations of workers.

MIGRANT JUSTICE AND WORKING-CLASS POLITICS

If working classes are to be understood as formations, rather than structures, this is in part because of the *making* of class relations and experience by workers themselves.[59] And, as we have argued, these relations and experiences are multi-dimensional, while also governed in this society by an overriding social logic based on market dependence and capital accumulation. By tracing the patterns of gender and racialization that are constitutive of working-class formation *from the start*, we can illuminate the ways in which movements for gender and racial justice are central features of class struggle. It follows that most significant social struggles are not uni-dimensional: however much they may exhibit class features, such struggles also frequently express challenges to gender, racial and sexual orders.[60]

It is in this spirit that we have insisted on delineating the complex patterns by which labour migration has become central to the reproduction of hundreds of millions of working-class households, whose wellbeing relies on wage remittances. But labour and the wage system always involve conflict. And since in the case of migrant workers these conflicts almost always raise issues of racism, sexism and political inequality, this underscores the strategic importance of migrant justice for any meaningful working-class politics today. This is especially so because anti-migrant politics function as a cutting edge of right-wing mobilizations internationally, be it those of Golden Dawn in Greece, the Front National in France, the Tea Party in the US or conservative forces in Canada. It would be naive to deny that considerable numbers of 'native-born' working-class voters have been attracted to such politics. Part of the responsibility for this lies with trade union leaderships that too often revert to a nativist protectionism – particularly in North America – rather than championing the full political and social rights of all migrant labourers. Notions of 'us' and 'them', of 'citizens' and 'foreigners', are deeply inscribed within the ideological relations of nation-states. Genuinely working-class politics requires an opposition to these categories of bourgeois common sense. Not only do racial and gender justice dictate defence of migrant rights; so does solidarity of workers. When national media in Canada created a furor over temporary migrants 'taking jobs' from Canadian-born workers, one astute analyst observed that the challenge of solidarity involves putting forth demands that turn 'the logic of neoliberalism on its head' and undercut the racialized segmentation of rights and status – by demanding permanent residency for all workers who enter the country.[61] The demand to 'normalize' or 'regularize' the status of all migrants explicitly challenges racialized discourses of 'us' and 'them' by arguing for the equality of *all* workers.

As important as is the struggle for migrant justice in public arenas, no less important are the on-the-ground struggles of migrant workers, who are increasingly fighting back. If the May Day 2006 strike by millions of migrant workers in the US was the most visible manifestation of such struggles, it was far from the only one. Campaigns and strikes in Los Angeles by drywallers, carpenters and janitors have been hugely significant, as was the sit-down strike in Mississippi by migrant workers from India at Signal International, along with the farmworker organizing campaign in the same state.[62] It is also difficult to overstate the importance in the US of the campaigns by the National Domestic Workers Alliance, which have led to the adoption of domestic workers' bills of rights in New York, California and Hawaii. Consistent with the transnational movement of domestic workers, the International Domestic Workers Network has built significant national organizations in Argentina, Brazil, Jamaica, Uruguay and Colombia.[63] Movements of migrant workers have also demonstrated that it is possible to make substantial gains even during the period of global slump that commenced with the financial crisis of 2008-09. A ten-month 'strike' and occupation by 6,000 *sans-papiers* in Paris in 2009 won guarantees of full legal status after five years of residence. And in March 2013, a strike by thousands of mostly immigrant warehouse workers in Italy won regular work permits for many workers using 'illegal' papers.[64]

Writing in 1866, Marx argued that unions,

must now learn to act deliberately as organising centres of the working class in the broad interest of its complete emancipation ... Considering themselves and acting as the champions and representatives of the whole working class, they cannot fail to enlist the non-society [people] into their ranks. They must look carefully after the interests of the worst paid trades ... They must convince the world at large that their efforts, far from being narrow and selfish, aim at the emancipation of the downtrodden millions.[65]

As working-class social reproduction becomes increasingly entangled with new patterns of gendered labour, repressive border regimes and racialized 'crimmigration' policies, genuinely radical working-class politics must challenge assaults on the rights of any and all groups of workers. This can only mean developing a working-class movement that champions every struggle for enhanced social reproduction. It requires seeing working-class struggles based in communities and neighbourhoods – around housing, police harassment, childcare and schooling – as having equal strategic importance to those centred on workplace issues. And it means supporting the struggles of unorganized workers and the unemployed as much as the battles of the organized.

NOTES

1   Former US House and Ways Committee Chairman, Charles Rangel, on CNN's *Lou Dobbs Tonight*, 23 January 2007, as cited by Southern Poverty Law Center, *Close to Slavery: Guestworker Programs in the United States*, Montgomery: Southern Poverty Law Center, 2013, p. 2.

2   Roberto Bolano, *2666*, New York: Picador, 2008, p. 348.

3   See for instance the World Bank's *Migration and Remittances Factbook 2011*, available at http://data.worldbank.org.

4   We refer here not simply to pioneering work in 'transnational feminism', but also to work that conceptualizes social reproduction itself in transnational terms. For a few recent examples, see Sedef Arat-Koc, 'Whose Social Reproduction? Transnational Motherhood and Challenges to Feminist Political Economy', in Kate Bezanson and Meg Luxton, eds., *Social Reproduction: Feminist Political Economy Challenges Neo-Liberalism*, Montreal and Kingston: McGill-Queen's University Press, 2006, pp. 75-92; Isabella Bakker and Rachel Silvey, eds., *Beyond States and Markets: The Challenges of Social Reproduction*, New York: Routledge, 2008, especially ch. 1, 5, 6, 7; Sara Farris, 'Interregional Migration: The Challenge for Gender and Development', *Development*, 53(1), 2010, pp. 98-104; and Ursula Huws, 'The Underpinnings of Class in the Digital Age', *Socialist Register 2014*, Pontypool: Merlin Press, 2013, pp. 80-107.

5   In methodological terms, this requires recognizing the priority of the whole over the parts. In dialectical theory, while the whole has a determinate relation to the parts (which has nothing to do with a mono-causal determinism), the totality is also constituted in and through the systematic relations among the parts, which thus determine the whole that reciprocally determines them. See David McNally, 'The Dialectics of Unity and Difference in the Constitution of Wage-Labour: On Internal Relations and Working Class Formation', *Capital & Class*, forthcoming 2014.

6   We use here the term 'global reserves of labour-power', rather than 'global reserve army of labour', to indicate that not all of these workers are to be located in the *reserve* army. While many seasonal and temporary migrants are to be located in the latter, significant groups of largely female migrant labour, such as nurses and live-in caregivers, experience relatively stable, long-term employment. This point is made nicely by Sara Farris, 'Neoliberalism, Migrant Women, and the Commodification of Care', *S&F Online*, published by Barnard Center for Research on Women, 11-12 (Fall 2012/Spring2013), available at http://sfonline.barnard.edu.

7   See Himani Bannerji, *Thinking Through: Essay on Marxism, Feminism and Anti-Racism*, Toronto: Women's Press, 1995; and Susan Ferguson, 'Canadian Contributions to Social Reproduction Feminism: Race and Embodied Labor', *Race, Gender & Class*, 15(1-2), 2008.

8   Rosa Luxemburg, *The Accumulation of Capital*, New York: Monthly Review Press, 1968, p. 365.

9   Karl Marx, *Capital, Volume I*, Harmondsworth: Penguin, 1976, pp. 783-4.

10   Marx, *Capital*, p. 718.

11   Wally Seccombe, *Weathering the Storm: Working-Class Families from the Industrial Revolution to the Fertility Decline*, London: Verso, 1993, ch. 5.

12   Saskia Sassen, *Guests and Aliens*, New York: New Press, 1999, pp. 42-3.

13   Audrey Singer, 'Immigrant Workers in the United States Labor Force', Brookings Research Paper, 15 March 2012, available at http://www.brookings.edu.

14   Richard Vogel, 'Transient Servitude: The U.S. Guest Worker Program for Exploiting Mexican and Central American Workers', *Monthly Review*, 58(8), 2007.

15   Rahel Kunz, 'The Crisis of Social Reproduction in Rural Mexico: Challenging the "Reprivatization of Social Reproduction" Thesis', *International Review of Political Economy*, 17(5), 2010, p. 920.

16   Richard Roman and Edur Velasco Arregui, *Continental Crucible: Big Business, Workers and Unions in the Transformation of North America*, Halifax and Winnipeg: Fernwood Publishing, 2013, p. 74.

17   Nicole Trujillo-Pagan, 'Emphasizing the "Complex" in the "Immigration Industrial Complex"', *Critical Sociology*, 40(1), 2014, p. 30.

18   Clare Long, 'Obama's red line on "good deportations" is inhumane – and he has crossed it', *The Guardian*, 24 April 2014.

19   N. De Genova, 'The legal production of Mexican/migrant "illegality"', *Latino Studies*, 2(2), pp. 160-85; Trujillo-Pagan, 'Emphasizing the "Complex"', pp. 35-7.

20   Melissa W. Wright, *Disposable Women and Other Myths of Global Capitalism*, New York: Routledge, 2006, p. 88.

21   Salima Valiani, 'The Rise of Temporary Migration and Employer-Driven Immigration in Canada', in L. Goldring and P. Landolt, eds., *Producing and Negotiating Non-Citizenship: Precarious Legal Status in Canada*, Toronto: University of Toronto Press, 2013, ch. 3; Jason Foster, 'Making Temporary Permanent: The Silent Transformation of the Temporary Foreign Worker Program, *Just Labour*, 19(Autumn), 2012, pp. 22-46.

22   Foster, 'Making Temporary Permanent', p. 40.

23   Karl Flecker, 'The Truth about Canada's Temporary Foreign Worker Program', *Our Times*, January 2013, available at http://ourtimes.ca.

24   Marx, *Capital*, pp. 854-62.

25   A good case could be made that this theoretical direction is quite close to the spirit of crucial sections of Marx's famous discussion in Part 8 of *Capital* (v. 1), particularly to the fascinating analysis in Chapter 31 of enslavement of indigenous and African peoples by capital alongside war and colonialism as 'chief moments' of primitive accumulation.

26   Joseph C. Miller, 'Domiciled and Dominated: Slaving as a History of Women', in Gwyn Campbell, Suzanne Miers and Joseph C. Miller, eds., *Women and Slavery*, v. 2, Athens: Ohio University Press, 2008, pp. 284-312.

27   Hilary Beckles, 'The Colours of Property: Brown, White and Black Chattels and their Responses on the Caribbean Frontier', *Slavery & Abolition*, 15(2), 1994, p. 36.

28   We are somewhat modifying here the schema developed by Lydia Potts in *The World Labour Market: A History of Migration*, London: Zed Books, 1990.

29   See Ajit K. Gose, Nomaan Maji and Christopher Ernst, *The Global Employment Challenge*, Geneva: International Labour Organization, 2008, pp. 9-10. See also Raul Delgado Wise, 'The Migration and Labor Question Today: Imperialism, Unequal Development, and Forced Migration', *Monthly Review*, 64(9), 2013; and J. Foster, R. McChesney and R. Jamil Jonna, 'The Global Reserve Army of Labor and the New Imperialism', *Monthly Review*, 63(6), 2011.

30   We consider the proletariat to consist of all those dispossessed of means of producing for themselves and thus reliant for their subsistence and reproduction on the market. To be a proletarian is thus not identical with being a wage-labourer. See Bryan Palmer, 'Reconsiderations of Class: Precariousness as Proletarianization', *Socialist Register 2014*, pp. 40-62.

31   See Stefano Liberti, *Land Grabbing: Journeys in the New Imperialism,* London: Verso, 2013; and Todd Gordon, *Imperialist Canada*, Winnipeg: Arbeiter Ring Publishing, 2010.

32   See Judith Whitehead, *Development and Dispossession in the Narmada Valley*, Delhi: Pearson, 2010; and David McNally, *Global Slump: The Economics and Politics of Crisis and Resistance*, Oakland: PM Press, 2011, pp. 133-7.

33   Raveena Aulakh, 'On the Border', *Toronto Star*, 30 March 2013.

34   See Jennifer Franco and Sylvia Kay, 'The Global Water Grab: A Primer',13 March 2012, available at http://www.tni.org; and Colette Murray, 'Upon Whose Terms? The Displacement of Afro-Descendent Communities in the

Creation of Cost Rica's National Parks', in Peter Vandergeest, Pablo Idahosa and Pablo S. Bose, eds., *Development's Displacements: Ecologies, Economies, and Cultures at Risk*, Vancouver: UBC Press, 2007.

35   Perhaps the most infamous case here is the role of trade liberalization, and NAFTA especially, in undermining indigenous communal land systems in Mexico. But see also Birgit Englert and Elizabeth Daley, *Women's Land Rights and Privatization in East Africa*, Woodbridge and Rochester: James Currey, 2008.

36   On Colombia, see Sheila Gruner, 'Contested Territories: Development, Displacement, and Social Movements in Colombia' in *Development's Displacements*, pp. 155-86. For a number of African cases, see Madelaine Drohan, *Making a Killing*, Toronto: Random House, 2003.

37   Adam Hanieh, *Lineages of Revolt: Issues of Contemporary Capitalism in the Middle East*, Chicago: Haymarket Books, 2013, p. 129. See also Richard Morin, 'Indentured Servitude in the Persian Gulf', *New York Times*, 14 April 2013.

38   Stephanie Nolen, 'With economic migration come challenges', *Globe and Mail*, 21 December 2013.

39   J. Carillo, 'Maquilizacionde la industria automotriz en México', in J. Carillo, ed., *La Nueva Era de la Industria Automotriz en México*, Tijuana: El Colegio de la Fontera Norte, 1990, as cited in Kathryn Korpniak, *Desert Capitalism*, Montreal: Black Rose Books, 1997, p. 13.

40   Roman and Arregui, *Continental Crucible*, p. 71.

41   Claire Provost, 'Migrants' Billions Put Aid in the Shade', *The Guardian*, 30 January 2013; United Nations Population Fund, *State of World Population 2006, A Passage to Hope: Women and International Migration*, New York: UNFPA, 2006, p. 12.

42   United Nations Population Fund, *State of World Population*, p. 12.

43   World Bank, *Migration and Remittances Factbook 2008*, available at http://econ.worldbank.org.

44   Mark Thomas, 'Labour Migration and Temporary Work: Canada's Foreign-Worker Programs in the "New Economy"', in Norene J. Pupo and Mark Thomas, eds., *Interrogating the New Economy: Restructuring Work in the 21ˢᵗ Century*, Toronto: University of Toronto Press, 2009, pp. 149-72.

45   On housing see Roman and Arregui, *Continental Crucible*, p. 77.

46   Nicola Phillips, 'Migration as Development Strategy? The New Political Economy of Dispossession and Inequality in the Americas', *Review of International Political Economy*, 16(2), 2009, pp. 231-59.

47   Those policies vary by class of foreign worker. See Judy Fudge and Fiona MacPhail, 'The Temporary Foreign Worker Program in Canada: Low-Skilled Workers as an Extreme Form of Flexible Labour', *Comparative Labor Law and Policy Journal*, 31, 2009, pp. 22-23.

48   See for example Kerry Preibisch and Evelyn Encalada Grez, 'Between Hearts and Pockets: Locating the Outcomes of Transnational Homemaking Practices among Mexican Women in Canada's Temporary Migration Programmes', *Citizenship Studies*, 17(6-7), 2013, pp. 785-802.

49   Phillips, 'Migration as Development Strategy?', p. 244.

50 Center for Migrant Advocacy, Survey Research on the Effectiveness of Household Service Workers (HSW) Policy Reform Package, *Migrant Rights Policy Monitor*, July 2011, p. 8, available at http://centerformigrantadvocacy. files.wordpress.com.

51 Grace Chang, *Disposable Domestics: Immigrant Women Workers in the Global Economy*, Cambridge, MA: South End Press, 2000, pp. 99-100.

52 Jim Crow laws, on the other hand, did institute a spatial-legal differentiation, albeit among citizens.

53 Live-in caregivers are arguably less disposable than other migrants, a fact that can be linked to their role in directly reproducing the citizen workforce, as Sara Farris argues in her forthcoming book on femo-nationalism.

54 Michael Kearny, cited in Roman and Arregui, *Continental Crucible*, p. 85.

55 Rosemary Hennessey, *Fires on the Border: The Passionate Politics of Labor Organizing on the Mexican Frontera*, Minneapolis: University of Minnesota, 2013, p. 129, emphasis added.

56 Wright, *Disposable Women*, p. 88.

57 Wright, *Disposable Women*, p. 77.

58 See Hennessey, *Fires on the Border*, pp. 103, 18-32; see Jessica Livingston, 'Murder in Juarez: Gender, Sexual Violence and the Global Assembly Line', *Frontiers: A Journal of Women Studies*, 25(1), 2004, pp. 59-76.

59 See David McNally, '"Unity of the Diverse": Working-Class Formations and Popular Uprisings From Cochabamba to Cairo', in Colin Barker et. al., eds., *Marxism and Social Movements*, Leiden: Brill, 2013, especially pp. 410-2.

60 Our disagreement with intersectional approaches, notwithstanding their many insights, has to do with the idea of pre-constituted relations of class, gender, race and sexuality which then encounter one another (i.e., intersect). Following the internal relations approach, we understand these social relations as mutually co-constitutive at their most foundational levels. We also recognize the need for further work that theorizes additional relations – such as those of ability and sexuality – in the sort of framework we seek to develop.

61 Michal Rozworski, 'The Temporary Foreign Worker Program and Labour Solidarity', 17 April 2014, available at http://politicalehconomy.wordpress. com. See also 'Solidarity with Temporary Foreign Workers', Statement by No One Is Illegal-Vancouver supported by Justicia for Migrant Workers BC, available at http://noii-van.resist.ca.

62 On these struggles see David Bacon, *Illegal People*, Boston: Beacon Press, 2008, pp. 133-42, 167-83; and Immanuel Ness, *Guest Workers and Resistance to Corporate Despotism*, Urbana: University of Illinois Press, 2011, pp. 102-10, 172-4.

63 Michelle Chen, 'Domestic Workers Sow a New Global Movement', *In These Times*, 15 April 2013.

64 See Struggles in Italy, 'Logistics workers national strike', 22 March 2013, available at http://strugglesinitaly.wordpress.com.

65 Karl Marx, 'Instructions for the Delegates of the Provisional General Council, General Questions', 1866, available at http://www.marxists.org.

THE LANGUAGE OF CLASS IN CHINA

LIN CHUN

The post-Mao regime's mantra of *Jiegui* ('getting on the global track'), or willing participation in the latest round of capitalist globalization, has redirected China's development path. The country has now become the world's largest recipient of foreign direct investment, largest trade-dependent exporter, largest energy consumer and largest producer of carbon emissions, mostly at the low end of the global productive chain. As its economy – including its finance and other strategic sectors – becomes ever more open, a deeply problematic national growth pattern based on officially endorsed 'cheap labour' becomes entrenched in the international division of labour, vastly favouring global capital. This pattern also entails a reshaped social structure and reshaped relations of production, above all a renewed validation of the exploitative and repressive power of capital – private and bureaucratic, domestic and transnational – over labour. Fuelling the enormous market expansion of a late capitalism hungry for space, China is also now one of the most environmentally polluted and socially unequal nations on earth. In other words, over half a century after the 1949 revolution, China is again being radically transformed, this time from a variant of state socialism to a variant of state capitalism. The country's double path dependency – on the one hand, from pre-reform Chinese socialism, and on the other, from its newly endorsed globalization – distorts or limits its transition to capitalism, a transition project that is no longer tentative or politically hidden. Yet this project still cannot be openly embraced in official statements due to the enshrined commitment of the People's Republic to socialism and the enduring attachment of the Chinese people to revolutionary and socialist traditions. This peculiar disjunction causes some extraordinary difficulties, not just in the articulation of class politics, but also in the way class politics operate in practice.

The weakness, if not the complete absence, of an independent working-class movement in China cannot be explained by repression alone. Multiple impediments to class consciousness and stronger labour mobilization arise from contradictory social changes and their confusing messages. For example, a singular Chinese phenomenon is a discrepancy between displacement and dispossession, thanks to the fact that the majority of migrant workers from the countryside retain their rural land rights. It is true that the younger generation is increasingly 'landless', in the sense that the initial redistribution of land in the early 1980s, organized on the basis of a newly introduced 'family responsibility' system, has not kept up with demographic changes in many places. However, insofar as the rural households remain protected by certain rights to land, the commodification and proletarianization of labour is fundamentally incomplete. In people's subjective perceptions, when the ambiguity involved in a 'socialist' state taking a capitalist path is set aside, the contrast between visible gains in material prosperity and past scarcity hampers even the most ardent critics of the market transition. Such contradictions function dialectically to stabilize an otherwise crisis-ridden process, in the context of a formerly (and officially still) communist party undergoing a profound self-transformation. Meanwhile, unprecedentedly rapid economic trends also affect culture and social organization in ways ranging from fervent consumerism and the popularity of new communication technologies, to an extensive financialization that destabilizes everything from macroeconomic policy and institutions to household budgets. As labour processes diversify and the young, the better trained, the self-employed and cosmopolitan careerists pursue more autonomy in work and life, exploitation and control must take fresh forms, and so do class identities and struggle.

The refusal of the language of class, to be discussed below, is a titanic act of symbolic violence on the part of the Chinese state, committed as part of a political strategy to make way for 'reform and opening'. The tactic is also evident in official phrases such as 'socialist market economy', 'primary socialist stage', or 'socialism with Chinese characteristics' – all of them largely devoid of socialist content. By the same token, China's working men and women need an alternative vocabulary as a politico-ideological weapon for articulating their situations and demands. At issue is thus not only the way the concept of class is diluted or muted in China's de-revolutionized polity; it is also about the way in which the lack of a language of class-based counter-hegemony helps to explain the lack of counter-hegemonic organizational capacity.[1]

To say this is not to endorse the views of those who imagine that class conflicts can somehow be overcome outside the realm of political economy. The damage caused by the kind of identity politics which involves discursive political attacks on 'class essentialism' are manifest. The alarming retreat from both gender equality and ethnic peace in China, following the imposed denial of class, makes this powerfully clear.[2] In that light class continues to be what the renewal of a multi-dimensioned, universal struggle for liberation ultimately depends on. As Marx famously put it, the working class as the bearer of human emancipation is a class 'which has a universal character because its sufferings are universal, and which does not claim a *particular redress* because the wrong which is done to it is not a *particular wrong* but *wrong in general*'.[3] Such a class thus cannot transform its own conditions without transforming society as a whole. A dialectical rather than a mechanical linkage between 'class' and its 'language', then, has to be constantly made in the very practice of expressing, interrogating and acting on class interests.

The purpose of this essay is to outline the making, unmaking and remaking of the major classes in China since the communist revolution. The communist party and its state and 'ideological state apparatus' have played a pivotal role in that trajectory, mediated by an institutionalized system of language and rhetoric. As official discourse was able to penetrate the infra-politics of everyday speech, the way power is exercised is traceable in its evolving political glossary. In the following sections I aim to clarify the class nature of the party's project in the way it seeks to position China in the global context. I will also trace the changes of class structure in China's market reforms; changes that are closely linked to the expanding global market and affect not only the relations between capital and labour, but also those between the state and labour, and state and capital. My main focus is the peasants-turned-workers and their plight, and hence the question of the class consciousness of a massively enlarged Chinese working class. The realignment of classes, and the corresponding new class lexicon, that will be needed for the impending development of a new transformative project to recapture state power will be noted for future consideration.

'TAKING CLASS STRUGGLE AS THE KEY LINK': REVOLUTION AND THE IDEOLOGY OF SOCIALIST TRANSITION

The party saw revolution as necessitated by the basic contradictions that had to be overcome: contradictions between imperialism and the Chinese nation, and between 'feudalism' (referring to landlordism and premodern social forms in general) and the popular masses. The revolution was thus intrinsically and simultaneously national and social in nature. More creative still was its strategy of seizing power by encircling the cities from their rural peripheries through a 'people's war'. In the Chinese Marxist conception, this revolution, led by a communist party, is defined as '*new* democratic' because its maximum programme contained a socialist ambition. It is thus categorically distinguished from the classical bourgeois revolutions which, while having a democratic aspect, only paved the way for capitalist development.[4] The 'new democratic' revolution relied on a worker-peasant alliance as well as a 'united front' that also included the national bourgeoisie, the progressives and patriots from intermediate social groups, and even an 'enlightened' gentry. The united front was seen as one of the 'three magic weapons' of revolutionary success, along with party construction and armed struggle.[5]

A 'land revolution' in a 'semi-colonial, semi-feudal' society appears problematic to anyone who believes that a large proletariat is needed for any socialist transition.[6] But they are mistaken, both empirically and conceptually, in relation to the Chinese case. In the first half of the twentieth century, China's relatively small working class was significantly larger in size and stronger in political capacity than the weak national bourgeoisie. This asymmetry is explained by the substantial foreign presence in the Chinese economy: workers in foreign-controlled factories were a growing class, while domestic industrialists and merchants were a shrinking one, squeezed by foreign capital. The industrial working class became an independent and vital revolutionary force, taking such tremendously daring actions as the Hunan miners' movements (1922-25), the Guangzhou-Hong Kong general strikes (1925-26) and the three Shanghai workers' uprisings (1926-27). Even after the counterrevolutionary slaughter of 1927, despite their devastating losses, workers became the core of the red army and urban underground party work. In addition, as exemplified by the founders of Marxism themselves, the communist intellectuals were an organic component of the proletariat. 'Petty bourgeois' intellectuals drawn to the Chinese revolution had to temper themselves through guerrilla warfare and grassroots work. These locally specific class factors, the party, workers and sympathetic intellectuals, were what in turn made it possible to educate and organize the poor and middle peasants, who were crucial in enabling the revolution to recruit soldiers and constantly defend and expand its rural bases.

The class basis of any political party and the nature of any national revolution are also determined by the way the country in question is globally located. The effectively proletarian character of China's peasant revolution was also due to the position of the Chinese nation in an epoch of global capitalism and uneven and compressed development.[7] Under siege by competing imperialist forces, the exploited and oppressed 'class' status of China itself gave its resistance a class-like character. It was this condition of a 'nation-class' that allowed the Chinese Communist Party to emerge as an innovative working-class organization, and gave the country's democratic revolution a socialist outlook and aim.[8] These developments, as recognized at the time, were on par with struggles and events elsewhere in the international communist movement. 'Class', either in its conventional or in its extended usage, cannot be a positivist category superficially described by occupations, hierarchies or locations. Its connotation must rather be constructed through the application of a locally and globally appropriate political economy.

This clarification is necessary because dogmatic misconceptions about the Chinese revolution, though not new, still lead to some implausible and politically detrimental conclusions about the present day. It is a gross factual oversimplification to maintain, without distinguishing between Mao's continued revolution and its post-Mao derailing, that due to its 'petty bourgeois' attributes the CCP leadership has undergone a direct transmutation 'from nationalist revolutionaries into a bureaucratic ruling class'. It is also theoretically erroneous to approvingly classify market reforms as the 'consolidation of the bourgeois revolution', needed before the working class would finally grow to make the next move, in the 'correct' sequence of societal evolution.[9] In these perspectives, Chinese socialism either never seriously existed, or was no more than a doomed and parenthetical episode. However, even fair-minded liberals recognize the depth and significance of the Chinese revolution;[10] and astute Marxist analyses show that a decisive degeneration of the party did not seriously occur until after the reform regime embarked on a 'wrong march'.[11] Dismissal of the authenticity and immensity of the socialist experiment in China, and ignorance of the radical differences between the party lines and state policies of the pre- and post-reform eras, also unintentionally echo much of the familiar Cold War narrative. Evident continuities notwithstanding, the latter era was in fact conditioned by its (partial) repudiation of the former's revolutionary and socialist legacies.

The arrogant view that revolutionary Chinese communists, with their petty bourgeois backgrounds, were unable to prepare for a socialist transformation overlooks the historical evidence. It fails to register how quickly and smoothly the communist modernizers nationalized industries and commerce, and collectivized agriculture, in the 1950s. In most sectors nationalization was preceded by a stage of public-private partnership, and the government introduced a novel scheme to give affected capitalists a fixed percentage of dividends in compensation. Collectivization, too, progressed by and large voluntarily 'with neither the violence nor the massive sabotage characteristic of Soviet collectivization'.[12] Missing from the orthodox critiques of all persuasions is the power of politics to redirect history in defiance of the 'normal' historical sequence of capitalism preceding socialism. Worse still, vulgar economism also offers a 'justification' for capitalist measures, including state-imposed and at times violent privatization programmes of publically owned enterprises and services. Remarkably enough, neoliberals find themselves supported by Marxists in treating global integration as something natural. Their reasoning is perfectly in line with Beijing's deformed Marxism, euphemistically interpreted as validating an ultimately unskippable capitalist phase.

As though to mock the charge that the communist project in a peasant China could only be substandard, the new regime proudly described itself as a 'people's democratic dictatorship' rather than a proletarian one. As in Eastern Europe, the former description simply signified majority rule for the people against their enemies. In communist terminology this rhetorical invention signalled a popular front style of politics inherited from the broadly based Chinese revolution, in contrast to the Russian revolution and the more industrialized Soviet Union. Although the Chinese did not shelve the notion of the 'dictatorship of the proletariat', it did not prevail in the country's political discourse until the idea of 'continuing the revolution' came to dominate official ideology in the run-up to the Cultural Revolution.[13] The vitality of the initial linguistic choice deserves special attention, however. It reflected China's fundamental socio-historical conditions in which the peasantry could not be sacrificed to modernization. The peasant population instead must be turned into an agent of socialist transformation, both for their society as much as for themselves. Thus the successive revolutionary movements from 'new democracy' to socialism had duly transcended the Marxian law of industrial proletarianization. As such, the 'people', in its specific historical and discursive frame, was unmistakably a primary marker of class power. The same can be said of the term 'mass line', found throughout the constellation of Chinese communist conceptual constructions. In the same vein, the terms 'women' in relation to women's liberation, and 'nationality' in relation to ethnic equality and solidarity, also have an intrinsic class signification.

While 'the people' was positively defined to include multiple classes, and negatively defined against class enemies, the classes included in 'the people' ceased to exist as economic realities after the land reform and the 'socialist transition' that had been accomplished by 1956: class labels no longer denoted membership of a space in the existing socioeconomic structure when landlordism and capitalism had already been eliminated. Yet such capsule designations, affixed to persons and households according to their categorized economic situations, usually up to three years before the liberation, continued to count heavily in determining people's social and political statuses, and in the long run exhausted and soured the population.[14]

As class labelling became materially baseless, the language of class functioned as an ideological mechanism of mobilization in the new regime's struggle for survival and national development. But there were also other, real and serious, class divisions, quite independent of any remnants of the old class system, that were in contradiction with the egalitarian socialist project. At least three such divisions stand out: the structural inequality between the urban and rural sectors of society, with the latter being subject to the extraction of resources to finance industrialization through 'internal accumulation'; the privileges accorded to higher-ranked cadres; and discrimination against those with a 'bad' class background.[15]

Social inequalities and bureaucratic degeneration worried Mao so much that he called for the resumption of the mass class struggles that at the 1956 party congress had been judged to be over. The Anti-Rightist campaign of 1957, catalyzed in part by the events in Poland and Hungry, led him to declare that 'the principal contradiction in Chinese society' was that existing between the proletariat and bourgeoisie, and between the socialist and capitalist roads. Guided by the idea of 'taking class struggle as the key link', the Lushan conference of 1959, instead of launching, as originally intended, a correction of the ultra-leftism that had been responsible for the failures of the Great Leap Forward, embarked on a campaign against the 'rightist tendency'. In 1962, Mao again reminded his mass followers to 'never forget class struggle' so as to prevent 'capitalist restoration' in a presumably 'very long period of transition from socialism to communism'.[16] These calls were answered by an intense run of further political campaigns. Aside from intensified criticisms of the 'bourgeois rights' that Marx had referred to in the *Critique of the Gotha Program* and the 'three great distinctions' (of urban-rural, industrial-agricultural and mental-manual labour divide), the 'socialist education movement' of 1964-65 targeted corrupt local officials. Always 'culturally' vigilant, the Maoist revolution was promoted also in education, literature and the (performing) arts, so as to 'let the workers, peasants and soldiers occupy the ideological superstructure' of campuses, newspapers and stages. Doctors and other elite intellectuals were urged to serve in the countryside. Mao's keen sense of cultural hegemony found expression in a *cultural* revolution which also had an impact on '1968' in the capitalist heartlands.[17]

The extraordinary Cultural Revolution, doing battle with the party-state itself, was officially launched in 1966 to encourage 'the dark side of our work to be exposed openly, completely, and from bottom up' for socialist rejuvenation, as Mao put it. A few years earlier, he had warned the party to 'guard against revisionism, particularly the emergence of revisionism at the party center'.[18] The theory of the Cultural Revolution especially singled out 'capitalist roaders' from what it saw as a bureaucratized 'new bourgeoisie' within the communist party. Nothing less than a mass counter-movement of the working class and young rebels could bring them down. The methods adopted, known as forms of a 'grand democracy', were specified as 'speaking out freely, airing views fully, big-character posters, and big debates', along with self-organization on legitimate democratic lines. Seemingly an irrational exercise in populist self-destruction, 'grand democracy' aimed to force the ruling apparatus open to popular scrutiny as the only way of rescuing socialism from erosion. But this unprecedented, singular event is not comprehensible without the international context also being taken into account. External contradictions could heighten domestic ones. Among several formidable geopolitical problems, there was a real risk of war. With Vietnam and the Sino-Soviet split in the foreground, China faced both imperialist and 'social imperialist' superpowers.[19]

The inner-party line about the struggle on which the Cultural Revolution was based, theoretically mirroring class struggle in society, turned out to be obscure. The absence of economically definable, exploitative social classes meant a 'categorical breakdown' – i.e. class categories were incapable of identifying the politically most relevant forces in the movement. If the underlining struggle was in reality one between a monopolistic political class and a mass revolt driven by accumulated discontent, the disjunction between class and politics, and between politics and political language, needed to be repaired.[20] Workers (and soldiers) had to be sent to universities, middle schools and many other organizations to stop the turmoil of anarchism and factionalism, with orders that 'the working class must lead in all spheres'. Those who were sent, however, were themselves engaged in quite a few localized 'civil wars' before a 'great unity' could be achieved with the formation of provincial and municipal 'revolutionary committees' in 1967-68. Since the spontaneous organizations were based less on class than on factions, an obvious tension arose between the ideology of class and factional cleavages within the same classes. Ambitious and ambiguous as it was, a Cultural Revolution in search of a yet-to-be-configured target was doomed if only because it came too early, too fast. Indeed, 'while the Cultural Revolution disclosed the problems of socialism, it could not resolve them: the socialist system, such as it was, could not transform the existing power structure without undermining its own foundation'.[21]

The primacy of the friend-enemy antithesis is a political *sine qua non* for a revolutionary people. Revolutions in China, however, consistently inclined to exaggerate *internal* enemies, resulting in excessive purges. The wrong people were persecuted for the wrong reasons, and the physical and psychological suppression of dissent entailed abuses of civil rights and personal injuries. Consequently, resentment and alienation grew to the point that Deng's subsequent policy reorientation initially had a popular mandate. Even if Chinese socialism was pursued against incredible odds, which posed profound moral dilemmas, there can certainly be no excuse for victimization. The confusion of two kinds of contradiction – those 'between the people and their enemies', and those 'among the people themselves', as delineated in Mao's own *Correctly Handling the Contradictions among the People* (1957) – was unforgiveable. Worse still, the disaster did not stop there. It metamorphosed into a crooked fusion of marketization and bureaucratization as the elites attacked in the Cultural Revolution took a horrendous revenge.

'NO ARGUING': THE POLITICS OF CLASS DENIAL

In striking contrast with Maoist ideology and the politics of class struggle, Deng Xiaoping's motto was 'no arguing'. It in effect forbade debating the direction of reform in terms of socialism versus capitalism. At first a pragmatic expedient to deradicalize society, the rule quickly hardened into a dogma of economic development as 'an absolute priority'. Ironically, this ideology against ideology was the product of an intense political struggle in 1978 for 'liberating the mind', with a view to delegitimating any opposition based on socialist moral concerns – a project that anticipated a second round of the 'end of ideology' drive in the reconfiguration of global economics and politics after the Cold War.[22] Central to the process was a tacit refusal of socialist experiments in general, and a frontal denunciation of class struggle in particular. As a key element in the 'depoliticization of the definition of class', the apolitical Weberian language of 'strata' and 'social stratification' was introduced in public communication.[23] The problem, however, is that even if the narrative of class is subverted, the realities speak for themselves. The manifest return of some pre-revolutionary class divisions during the reforms, along with the important formation of some new classes, cannot in the end be concealed. Officially attempted linguistic remedies, from 'common prosperity' and 'harmonious society' to a shared 'Chinese dream', only serve to uneasily epitomize disparities and disharmony.

Hyper growth in China may have contributed to the impressive reduction of abject poverty and a markedly improved standard of living – a feat largely attributable to the infrastructural groundwork that had been laid before. But that growth is also seriously offset by its grave human, social and environmental costs.[24] As the ideology and practice of egalitarianism were 'rationally' condemned for the sake of efficiency, society became more and more polarized. By 2011, the richest 10 per cent of Chinese families had an annual income that was 21 times that of the lowest 10 per cent; and the top 20 per cent of average urban incomes were 67 times as high as those of the bottom 20 per cent of average rural incomes. Slowly falling inequalities have been claimed in a few areas, but the overall trend persists, and on regional, sectoral, ethnic and gender lines as well.[25] Especially feeling the pain are workers on low wages or suffering from arrears of wages; peasants working in unprofitable farming or suffering from land loss and social insecurity; and migrant workers struggling to cope with residential discrimination and family separation (leaving behind their children and elderly relatives in the dilapidated villages) on top of exploitation or sweatshop conditions at their workplaces. If labour in the new China had once enjoyed access to the means of production and political recognition, its commodification negates those fundamental gains. In today's media, the 'leading class' (according to the Constitution) of industrial workers becomes one of the country's 'vulnerable social groups'.

China has 600 to 700 million loosely identified 'farmers', referring mostly to the smallholding agricultural producers still working (more or less) on the land after decollectivization. They have experienced post-communal differentiation, as well as altered and multifaceted relationships with the state. The umbrella category of 'peasantry' thus requires a class analysis of its changing composition.[26] The coming of age of new middle peasants is an important example; the emergence of a class of parasitic landlords as rentiers living on the proceeds of land compensation, in a breakneck process of urbanization, is another.[27] Class agency is thus a real question for the unfolding rural struggles from below over land, for security, against privatization or against the big agribusiness preferred by government policy, and so on. To the extent that peasants can and do reorganize themselves in production, consumer, marketing and other cooperatives, while adopting machinery and green technologies, pursuing a capitalist transformation of agriculture is neither rational nor practical. Above all, the impossibility of endless rural migrants finding stable employment in the cities, let alone all depending on global markets for their food needs, makes basic national grain self-sufficiency a necessity. Retaining their equal rights to the use of collective land, and their close ties to urban workers, a major section of the peasants could well re-emerge as an anti-capitalist political force. Such a force would have little to do with pre-capitalist conservatism, but much to do with the distinctive Chinese tradition of peasant revolution and socialism.

The peasant, meanwhile, is an ever more plastic identity in a transitional economy. Of the 50 per cent of the population designated as 'urban' in

2014, a large number are unsettled. They keep travelling to attend to their land in busy agricultural seasons. Conversely, many rural residents take non-farming jobs. This 'floating' rural–urban dualism has manifold consequences for class analysis. The continuous loss and shortage of farmland due to urban expansion, together with desertification and soil pollution, threaten livelihoods and national viability. This overriding condition solidifies, and demands a clear conception of, the role of land in China, as a means not just of production but also of subsistence. The fact that migrant workers with urban jobs have largely relied on rural resources for their family's reproduction explains the existence of a very cheap labour reserve in China's globalizing market. With the countryside as a social safety valve, the reform regime has enabled global capital to keep exploiting Chinese labour at an extraordinarily high rate.[28] The enormous yet hidden contribution of China's collective land to global capital's accumulation and expansion still awaits conceptual exposure.

The reshaping of the ruling classes, on the other hand, has transformed the 'communist' state. Precisely where the voice of class is shut out, an unholy alliance of private and bureaucratic capital takes an unprecedented form of class rule, incorporating a wing of media and intellectual clients.[29] In recent decades the private sector has grown spectacularly, taking over more than two-thirds of China's 'mixed economy'. Along the way its entrepreneurs – investors and managers, traders, bankers, real estate gamblers, party cadres and academics sitting on boards of trustees – have been politically empowered. Unlike the archetypal indigenous bourgeoisie who sought to 'save the country through industry', and also unlike the nationalist capitalists typical of the East Asian developmental states, China's new bourgeois class consists essentially of profit-seekers. Some were initially enriched by grabbing state assets at knockdown prices during successive waves of privatization. Among these, a particularly notorious example of greed is afforded by the law-breaking 'coal bosses' of 'black mines' who have dared to turn 'cheap labour' into 'cheap lives', with record levels of industrial deaths. More recently, improvements may have been made here and there in the mining industry, but occupational diseases and other work–related casualties remain shockingly prevalent across industries.[30] It is true that lacking credits from state banks, and facing fierce competition (including competing unfairly with foreign capital, owing to a perverse policy preference for the latter),[31] small enterprises often find it difficult to thrive. However, the generalization that private entrepreneurship in China is subjugated to state capital is grossly and deliberately misleading, put forward to justify wholesale privatization. Giant, patrimonial private firms have in fact benefited hugely from legalized or customized special treatment, while obtaining crucial political influence as well.

Among the new elites, the most powerful are those who combine political advantage and economic fortunes in a peculiar market where money and power trade and fuse. A segment of the 'princelings' has managed to leverage their 'background capital' to amass wealth through exceedingly profitable dealings in such areas as energy, utilities, telecommunications, pharmaceuticals, security, insurance, banking, charity foundations and private equity. They also tend to be compradors or agents of global capital, nurtured by a business environment of 'attracting foreign investment' at all cost. The inroads of a deregulated and financialized capitalism, with its local pillars and multinationals increasingly gaining shares in the strategic sectors, have dangerously eroded China's economic independence and capacity. The 'bureaucratic-comprador bourgeoisie' recreated in the process resembles that of the family monopolies under semi-colonialism and the Guomindang kleptocracy, but is far greater in size and power. Potentially belonging to the same class are managers of state-owned conglomerates who are treated like capitalist CEOs. With combined earnings of salary, dividends, bonuses (often paid regardless of performance) and countless sources of grey income, they are paid hundreds of times more than their workers. As such, how public the state sector still is becomes acutely questionable. Clearly, the bizarre duality of bureaucratization and privatization must end. This call for reform, however, must not be confused with neoliberal assaults on public control over the nation's essential resources and commanding-height industries. Such a sector has to be defended (or achieved), not dismantled. Bureaucratic oligarchy is not to be equated with socialist state capital, in which investment decisions can only be authorized democratically.

Popular antipathy is fuelled also by the political corruption of bribery and patronage networks in appointments and promotions. The communist party's class basis has undergone a major conversion since it formally welcomed private entrepreneurs into its ranks as 'advanced elements in the new social strata' in 2002. The national and local People's Congresses have gradually been filled with wealthy and well-connected notables. Governmental and legislative positions – such as party secretaries, NPC deputies and/or representatives of the People's Political Consultative Conference – have been almost overrun by the super rich, who are not only the beneficiaries of a freewheeling 'civil society' of asymmetrically powered 'interest groups', but are also conspicuously advocates, advisers and indeed decision-makers in the policy process.[32] The extent of the rot is revealed in the scandal in Hunan in 2013 (where 56 delegates from Hengyang region were found to have bought their way in the provincial People's Congress with big money), on which the media coverage has been loud.[33] Indeed, the party and its disciplinary organs have finally taken on corruption. Its anti-graft campaign remains highly selective, however, being used as a tool in political and power struggles.[34] Rather than solving the problem of corruption, the party-state has turned it into a regular organizational mechanism of bureaucratic capitalism.[35]

In hindsight, then, we can say that since the capitalist market, which has catalyzed a 'peaceful evolution' of regime change in China, was absent at the time of the Cultural Revolution, that revolution was misconceived and premature. Yet, as the 'cadre lords' sitting on the common people's backs have indeed grown in the marketplace and have overwhelmed resistance, the cultural revolutionary theory about a new bourgeoisie forming within the party has been vindicated. The hybrid formation of a monstrous bureaucratic capitalist class is genuinely tragic from a socialist point of view, in the sense that just as such a class is in the process of consolidating its power, another cultural revolution – this time with an actually existing target – is simply not in the cards today.

The ideological suppression of class politics by renouncing the language of class is thus a sign of the ruling order's fear and sense of crisis. Class awareness and mobilization must be averted. The party, after all, has an intimate experience of arising from workers' and peasants' movements, not to mention the terrifying memory of Maoist anti-bureaucratic campaigns. The positivist chimera of a 'normally' modernizing social stratification represents the pressing need for a collective amnesia in face of a capitalist integration that is tearing Chinese society apart. Successive governments have thus tried hard to muffle social criticism and maintain stability by promoting economic booms as much as by using force. Looking at the history of Chinese communist rule, then, one of the most visible and greatest ironies is that class politics and discourse were taken to an extreme when the country was relatively egalitarian, and thoroughly stifled at a time of intense class polarization and conflict.[36] The latter episode, however, is inexorably prompting its own demise, as the return of class is no longer avoidable.

Interestingly, the baffling category of 'middle class' is exempted from the politics of class denial. The imaginary of such a class is associated with the official slogans of modernization, development and social stability, goals that are made absolute and employed to silence or disarm the exploited classes. Conceptually, the middle class is elusive as a fuzzy constitution without clear boundaries. Sociologists disagree on its defining factors, including income, education, occupation, lifestyle and aspiration, and hence also on any assessment of its size in any given socioeconomic structure. Theoretical difficulties focus on the 'contradictory class locations' (in which some find themselves at the intersection of different classes) as well as on spatial disjunction between domination and exploitation in contemporary capitalism.[37] The classical riddles also persist about whether the lower levels of the 'salaried bourgeoisie' of lawyers, doctors, managers and the like, or non-manual 'brain workers', such as white-collar employees and high-tech professionals, should actually constitute a part of the working class rather than the middle class. The mostly uncritical image of a desirable 'middle class' – fluid, obscure and a by-product of basic class positioning in capitalist modernity – compromises the politically charged subtext of class itself.

In a China where capitalist and post-socialist conditions mingle to erode public belief in equality, and to allow policies that produce inequalities, optimism about a middle class is especially problematic. First, such a class is 'more a discourse than social structure'.[38] Even if middle income earners are all lumped together, they are still proportionally too small to produce any shift towards an 'olive-shaped' society. With traditionally protected state workers losing out in the labour market, and with the unrelenting displacement of peasants, the prerequisite for the expansion of a middle class – deproletarianization – is not there. Secondly, any alleged middle class will be too dependent on the state and state-led development to be expected to be politically active. Its identity, if any, can hardly be of a steady class nature, if only because most of the elements assigned to such a class are tied to the establishment. Thirdly, the moderately wealthy can be arrogant and indifferent toward labour and, for that matter, towards the aggrieved rural poor or ethnic minorities. Their lack of a sense of solidarity with other classes has been shown by case after case of urban homeowners demanding that polluting factories should be moved elsewhere, or of gated residential communities asking that 'low *suzhi*' (culturally defective) migrants, such as garbage collectors, street vendors and prostitutes, be 'cleaned up'.[39] And, finally, middle-class models of civil society, citizenship and democracy are often not relevant to, or compatible with, the concerns of the lower classes.[40] In this connection, China's liberal and neoliberal intellectuals share many biases and weaknesses with an arguably burgeoning middle class. Any projected 'class power' of intellectual politics would be illusory or self-deceptive if its ultimate class dependency is forgotten.

'IT IS RIGHT TO REBEL': LABOUR'S AWAKENING AND THE QUESTION OF CLASS CONSCIOUSNESS

Marx's two-class theory, previously challenged by a peasant communist revolution, is becoming belatedly resonant in China's export-manufacturing development, powered by partial proletarianization. The partially proletarianized consist of both traditional state sector workers and the two generations of new workers who have migrated from the countryside. The former have lost both their 'iron rice bowl' and their social esteem as hallmarks of Chinese socialism, experiencing in particular privatization-induced unemployment. The latter became the protagonists of assembly factories linked to the global market.[41] In hard times, the 'petty bourgeoisie' of technical personnel, small business people and job-hunting college graduates can also be part of the story. *Dagong*, literally 'selling labour', is the common (self-)depiction of a commodified labour force and its multilayered members. From 1991 to 2013 there was a huge increase of 269 million in the urban workforce, 85 per cent of which was accounted for by rural immigration.[42] Precarity through 'informalization' is preferred in the labour market, and through the 'casualization' of employment in the formal economy as well. This has resulted in a swelling pseudo-class of the proletarian 'precariat'.[43] Consider the case of young unmarried women workers as a transient yet substantial component of migrant labour in both the industrial and service sectors (public and domestic, formal and informal).[44] Exploitation and domination multiply by the intersected class, gender and rural-urban differentiations.

Many other cleavages exist, caused by various differences between public and private firms, contracted and 'dispatched' (i.e. subcontracted) jobs and more or less skilled positions. The institutional barriers of residential bifurcation, or work unit-based pay and fringe-benefit differentials, continue to separate workers. Workers also socialize by regional connections and dialect. The changed social contract between workers and a 'workers' state', however, is a common and superseding experience across the board. Particularly worth noting is how China's educated, healthy and dedicated industrial workforce, nurtured by a high level of human capital investment relevant to a low-level national income before economic reform, has been subjugated. This workforce, rather than anything else, is the country's truly great comparative advantage and key to explaining its economic growth.[45] But the failure to appreciate this central contribution to industrial policy and public culture is manifested in the way labour is brutally cheapened in a 'race to the bottom' to reduce labour costs. Appalling conditions have predictably followed, in terms of long hours, meagre pay, missing or incomplete or fake contracts, unfulfilled legal requirements by employers to contribute to pension and other welfare funds, unpaid regular work and overwork, job insecurity, workplace hazards and, not least importantly, lack of respect for workers' dignity. Things have been improving in a few aspects under the pressure of labour shortage in costal regions, and wages are rising. But violations of labour rights remain rampant.

A ruthless pattern has formed in the private sector of working 11 or 12 hours a day, six or seven days a week, lengthy periods of night shifts, restricted living plus routine bullying from harsh shop-floor managers. The pattern has even entrapped student interns and occasionally child labour. A shocking string of suicides at Foxconn in 2010 exposed the extent of abuses and the crimes of a savage labour regime based on collusion between the state and private and foreign capital. The latest surge of labour protests has implicated many more multinationals in an age of global outsourcing. Apart from the Japanese-owned Uniden, a Walmart supplier in Shenzhen, which earlier saw a sporadic five-month strike in 2004, also involved, among others, are Apple, Dell and IBM suppliers (e.g. the Taiwanese-owned Foxconn and Hong Kongese-owned Biel Crystal), Honda plants, Samsung and Flextronics International contractors and Pepsi factories.[46] The Yue Yuen complex in Dongguan, where 40,000 workers went on the largest strike in recent memory in April 2014, supplies products to such footwear giants as Nike, Reebok and Adidas. Conditions in the hidden corners of mining, retailing, construction and service industries tend to be even worse.[47] Even in the public sector, workers are not free from capitalist exploitation and humiliation when the market operates everywhere by the logic of profit.

Class struggle has come to be waged in reality. A once-popular Maoist slogan in line with the ancient idea of the just rebellion against tyranny, 'to rebel is rightful' has returned to vindicate striking workers, revolting peasants and many other protesters and petitioners. Even censored official news outlets admit rising 'mass incidents'. Workers are also getting better organized and more informed about movements elsewhere, near and far, through cell phones, text messages and microblogs (a version of Twitter). In 2012-13, strikes took place in various production sites of Foxconn and Honda. Most recently, workers in a sister factory in Jiangxi acted in solidarity with fellow shoe-making workers on strike in Yue Yuen. Thousands of bus drivers in Shenzhen walked away from work at the same time, as did workers in the China Operations of International Business Machines.

From jumping to kill oneself to collective action for change, what does this development signify? Is it a likely 'historic turning point' for the Chinese working class after decades of defeat, retreat and silence? Is China on its way to be 'the world's class-struggle capital'?[48] While pondering these questions, one must keep in mind the major fact that although official trade unions and government arbitration commissions sometimes side with workers or adopt conciliatory approaches, local authorities often also deploy police to beat and arrest 'troublemakers', as they consider labour organizing a major menace to be suppressed, even on occasion preemptively. Thugs are also frequently hired to violently dispel gathering workers. A necessary concern is thus the altered nature of the state apparatus. In a now outmoded but all too apt terminology, Mao predicted that the communist decay would lead not to bourgeois democracy, but to a capitalist and fascist dictatorship.[49]

But despite the new dynamics of popular struggle, the labour movement in particular is caught in a remarkable post-socialist dilemma. The influences from the socialist past interfere in the present, blurring or blending support and control, consent and coercion, on both sides of industrial relations. The state and its corporatist arm, the All China Federation of Trade Unions, require by law a union branch in every minimally sizeable workplace. Such unions are supposed to act on their workers' behalf and they indeed do, half-heartedly and intermittently, even winning concessions from management.[50] But under a policy guideline that prioritizes a 'good investment environment' such unions cannot be the workers' own, and not just because they hold few democratic elections and barely advance working-class interests. The ambiguity over independent unionization lies in the understanding that it would let a socialist state forgo its moral and material responsibilities for the wellbeing of its workforce. As already evident on the ground, any fair settlement in labour disputes is unlikely, given the sheer imbalance of power between labour and capital. Workers are learning to fight through legal channels only because they have lost a state committed to their fundamental right to both economic security and political recognition.

Most telling is China's reform of labour legislation in relation to the 'rule of law' (which is indispensable for a market economy). The 1994 Labour Law was revised in the 2008 Labour Contract Law, a landmark text for the government's refusal to side with labour on a moral ground beyond legality. Industrial relations are now straightforwardly a matter of legal and procedural, rather than social, justice. Under the current circumstances, a positive upshot of the law is that it requires the formalization of employment through a labour contract. Such requirement could intensify certain forms of discrimination against those considered less economic to employ (e.g. avoiding the cost of maternity leave by not hiring women), but the majority find the requirement beneficial. However, the law as stipulated on paper is not the same as its enforcement. Without the necessary political will to enforce the 1994 law, two decades on, China's legal eight-hour workday is still scarcely followed in the low-end private sector. A large number of urban workers remain not formally contracted. In 2013, no less than 82 per cent of forty million construction workers, for instance, had not signed any labour contracts. Their legal appeals to the relevant government agencies were denied consideration precisely on the ground that without detailed rights specified in a contract they were not covered by the protection of the law![51] The rights of workers in the large informal economy are similarly excluded from the scope of the law. The legalization process itself has also been accompanied by market greed and corruption, which curb the effect of the resulting law.

The problems with a solely legal approach still go farther. Legality is after all also instrumental of containing contentious politics. Insofar as a strike is not really lawful – the clause on the freedom to strike was removed in the 1983 constitutional amendment – strikers can be coerced and their leaders can be sacked or even criminalized or otherwise punished. More subtly, since the legal framework is based on individualized rights, it functions to trim the formation and expression of collective class interests. The Labour Law incorporates workers as atomized contract-takers and market actors essentially subordinated to capital accumulation. Equally problematic is '*weiquan*', or the protection of the right to civic activism. This has attracted much attention from international circles concerned with labour and human rights, but it remains 'a hegemonic discourse propagated by the political and social elites' of middle-class liberals. The campaign for such rights confines disputes and arbitration to an individualistically and reactively framed legal manner. The result 'constitutes a decisive constraint on unions' claims, options, and strategies in their representation efforts'.[52] Just as depoliticized proceduralism treats as inferior the people who ought to be lawmakers themselves (which is after all a fair definition of democracy), unionism or syndicalism cannot be the consciousness of class liberation. A unionized movement for labour rights through 'collective bargaining' may facilitate minor reforms while defusing conscious class struggle.

As workers' outlooks, abilities and militancy in different situations and places develop unevenly, it is difficult to generalize about class consciousness in China. Traditional workers, having lived through class wars and social revolutions, and benefited from honoured entitlements, oppose privatization and its long and painful aftermath. Their nostalgia for the socialist past may involve some romanticization, but mainly they are aware that, beyond individual companies or capitalists, a presently triumphant capitalism has to be countered.[53] This standpoint was made clear, for example, in the 2009 strike in the state-owned Tonghua Steel in Jilin, a major northeastern base of new China's industrialization. New workers, on the other hand, have yet to grasp their own class position independent of the influence of the liberal intellectual 'protectors' of their civic rights. The personal and job mobility and hence fluid identity of younger workers could also be an obstacle to class consciousness, if the classical pattern of working-class formation remains viable at all: class is not fixed at the point of production or distribution. It is formed and transformed culturally as well, and the organization and structure of workers' feelings are fostered by their concentration in shared working and living communities. Three decades into intense market integration, migrant workers have begun to transcend their spontaneous protests over immediate material concerns. The Shenzhen Hengtong rubber factory strike in 2013 was triggered by the installation of cameras to put machine operators under close surveillance without their prior consent. The two groups of workers, traditional and new, are merging in a common search of class subjectivity. The conjuncture of 'state meets capital' – as a worker's poem accurately captures it – necessitates resistance.[54]

At the theoretical level, the long debate in the Marxist canon over Lukács's *History and Class Consciousness* cannot engage us here. Suffice it to note the ongoing relevance of the language of class, of 'commodity fetishism', 'exploitation', 'alienation' and 'surplus value'. It is a conceptual vehicle that workers could employ in surmounting their atomization, dependency and falsely perceived powerlessness. The existing social order is certainly not 'natural' or impossible to resist. China's positioning in the capitalist world does not have to be what it is. And class struggle is the only decisive way for the working class, in 'conscious actions', to defy 'the fate of history'. Whether class consciousness is 'imputed' from within or injected from outside, it is in the practice of class politics that a working class engages in its own making, that it 'historically happens'.[55] However, if class consciousness is both contingent and dependent on the ideological rhythm of class struggle, questions concerning the party and party-class relations remain pivotal. Any new 'modern prince' must still clarify its relationship with the 'popular state' on one hand and the working class on the other.[56] This is highly relevant because of Chinese particularities – the communist party's world historical defeat in its voluntary or suicidal surrender to global capitalism. Yet in light of the party's ability to contrive a unique and brilliant answer to these questions in the earlier revolutionary practices of party construction and the mass line, it is fair to ask whether it really has terminally exhausted its internal and external resources of renovation.

'POLITICS IN COMMAND': THE STATE, DISCURSIVE POWER AND THE RETURN OF CLASS POLITICS

It would be a serious error to treat the question of class and class consciousness in China as something new, forgetting its invaluable national and local histories. That is, at issue in the current Chinese context is not only a 'retreat from class'; it is also the overturning of class power itself. This power was brought into being, in however limited ways, by the communist revolution. Its dismantling is measured by the destruction of the party-state's popular base. This loss of a socialist state, along with the party and its cultural capital and ideological supremacy, is catastrophic for the labouring classes. For a hitherto oppressed people, losing a hard-won state of its own – real or perceived – is losing the whole lot. Differences among modern states, or between variously socialist or variously capitalist natures of a state, have a huge impact on society and the conditions of existence of social classes. Globalization may have generally impinged on the autonomy and capacity of national states; the domestic labour regime under state purview is still what affects workers most.

The notion of state manipulation or management of class is part of a broader theoretical consensus that modernity in general and capitalism in particular have needed state sponsorship from the outset. The territorial state was the 'ultimate linchpin' of capitalist development, not least because capital expansion required a unified national market as well as political power to survive class antagonism.[57] The structural versus instrumentalist interpretations of the state is the focus of several influential debates among Marxists. Concerning the ruling communists as modernizers more specifically, the competing conceptions of state socialism and state capitalism are both pertinent, and the thesis concerning the social democratic state's 'structural dependence on capital' might be borrowed as well.[58] Whatever the theory, empirical observations strongly support the claim that to a large degree the communist party-state controls class differentiation or reconstruction through directing class designations, regulating class relations, containing class conflicts and indeed suppressing class foes.[59] Also likely is a dialectical interaction between a state 'determining' the compass of class, and a class 'ruling' by its embodiment in state machinery and policymaking. The state is 'coloured' accordingly by the dominant class. The awesome power of the post-revolutionary state is part of the story of 'socialism and backwardness' defying the standard contours of history. That such a state has mutated into a comprador-bureaucratic tyranny in China is an indicator of the impact states can have on class structures. But allowing conceptually for a far-reaching state role in class formation and relationships, and rejecting the notion that the state is a neutral force above classes, should not lead to substituting the state for the relations of production. The autonomy of the state remains relative. What recent Chinese history does underline is the expansive reach of the PRC state, aided by its ideological discourse of either class struggle (in the Mao era) or class evasion (in post-Mao reactions).

To achieve clarity about class politics in today's China means, then, seeing popular struggle to restore socialist fundamentals as requiring a phased and probably lengthy process of recreating the party and recapturing the state. The reality is that vested interests have grown so entwined with a still nominally socialist party-state that the latter becomes their best guarantor, even their hostage. On the one hand, the ideology of the 'free' market masks or 'rationalizes' private looting of public assets. On the other, more than a matter of compatibility, neoliberal policies depend on a dictatorial power to be implemented. China's ever more sweeping economic neoliberalization (as shown in Beijing's latest policy package announced in early 2014) only reconfirms this pattern of 'growth' and the class essence of the regime. If reform was initially validated by the crisis of Chinese socialism, the present crises of Chinese capitalism are forcing a reorientation, discarding the imposed rule of 'no arguing'. Such a reorientation would in turn necessitate a reappropriation of the language of socialism. It would naturally begin with an accurate articulation of class conditions and positions since 'it is the discursive structure of political language which conceives and defines [class] interest'. To the extent that language 'as a process of signification' is itself a form of social being, and that the struggle over the 'ideological state apparatus' is necessarily communicative, class analysis is bound to be discursively contentious.[60] Not surprisingly, 'discursive hegemony' has been a catchphrase in Chinese internet complaints since the turn of the century. The renaissance of a class vocabulary must abandon all accumulated baggage of arbitrariness or 'left infantilism'. But for the education and organization of workers, it has to be reutilized since the 'materiality of language itself' has been so powerfully demonstrated throughout China's modern transformations.[61]

'Politics in command' must also be reappropriated. The Maoist idiom was spelled out by the centrality of class struggle, and premised on a decisive role of the party line and cadres. It was also intimately associated with the 'mass line' as a most creative and successful method of the revolution.[62] The usual perception of the mass line as either a condescending elitist tool or a form of populist voluntarism is misguided. It is instead based on a conviction in the agency of the common people and embedded in the project and language of class liberation. It thus cannot be transferable without these contextual references. Since the communist party no longer has any distinct ideological position, and the traditional party-mass relationship no longer exists, the 'mass line' verbally picked up by Xi Jinping sounds merely hollow. It contradicts the corruption-tainted images of officials head-on, and is entirely alien to an all-pervasive monoculture of money and political cynicism. It is also incompatible with the vulnerability of labour and the glamorized hegemonic notion of an all-virtuous market.

To reaccentuate politics is then to seek a counter-transformation of society as much as of perceptions. Just like the formation of conscious classes, the remaking of the masses as a political subject is a process of political struggle, one which would necessarily involve channelling energy and skills toward rebuilding the party with the goal of giving power to the people. This is feasible as a democratic project since the rank-and-file party members are themselves among the masses who need to rise up, although sympathetic elements at all levels of the party would need to be engaged. This would of course have to entail unpacking the meaning of 'democracy' in the shallow and complacent discourse of the mainstream framing of 'political reform', based as it is on capitalist integration. Democracy in China, perhaps more than in those countries which lack a revolutionary socialist experience, needs to be closely guided by the ideas of equality and social justice. Especially in view of the existing state-capital coalition, which could well survive or even control an electoral political process, formal democracy alone will be useless for the working classes concerned with the means of production and surplus retention. The only meaningful measurement instead is whether and how well collective preferences of the common people are articulated and translated into state power and policies.

If neither capitalism nor socialism is teleological, and if class identities and alignment are also open ended, then winning the battle for ideas is where a transformative politics could attract popular agents. Notwithstanding unsolved conceptual issues of unprecedented class differentiations in the 'knowledge economy', the more complex new division of labour in today's 'cognitive capitalism' may be 'changing the balance of forces back in favour of producers'.[63] As a 'hi-tech proletariat' and a 'biopolitical' and 'cyber-productive' labour force grows, the ever more digital and immaterial nature of production and management erodes capital's ability to exploit this new workforce in the way it does with traditional wage labour. More broadly, the inclusive concept of 'classes of labour' comprises all of those who depend directly or indirectly on selling their labour power for their own daily reproduction. A similar Chinese term is the 'labouring people' (*laodong renmin*), which encompasses the vast majority of the population, including the large sections of the 'semi-proletarianized petty bourgeoisie'.[64] Another comparable but also distinct identity is 'commoners' as producers and consumers as well as democratic agents, which presupposes the construction of the commons.[65] This could be the closest to the Marxian generic identification of 'direct producers' reworked against a backdrop of advanced productive forces and socialization of production. Politically, the vast and plurally constituted mass of 'plebeians' do not necessarily undermine class analysis and strategy, since class provides a 'compass of orientation – towards the classes of the people, the exploited, oppressed and disadvantaged in all their variety'.[66] The theoretical question is whether or where 'class' ends in such articulations. The conceptual fact that in Maoist discourse 'class' is core to the 'masses' should be instructive. If Marx privileges the working class in terms of its acquiring consciousness, it is possible to argue that certain other subject positions, such as women facing patriarchy or minorities confronting majority chauvinism, can be privileged in their own ways. Such social groups acquire the consciousness of their suppression in a similar way to workers. That is, their identities may possess a class feature or multiple class features – women, ethnic minorities or migrants could be proper classes understood in their respective relational positions in the given political economy.[67] The point specific to China is then that capitalism is pushing the exploited and oppressed people together into a gigantic political force for reclaiming socialism.

China's landscape of class has twice been transformed since 1949, through a sequence of socioeconomic and political upheavals that have also been marked by a shifting discourse of class. While in the official rhetoric the term 'socialism' is ever emptier, it makes real sense as a protest language in labour and other resistance movements. However, as certain formal commitments and provisions to the labouring classes under the rubric of socialism have not been totally repudiated, they should be defended in the interest of reinstating or establishing class power. The remaking of the state and party must begin with winning back their original constituencies. The fact that the state, despite being aggressively interventionist, can hardly contain mounting social unrest indicates the inevitable return of class identities and politics. The latter is necessarily transformative for an alternative social order in which political power serves the people, and needs dominate profit. This would be a 'war of position' by the common people around organized labour and in alliance with their counterparts in other countries. The tragic course of capitalism with Chinese characteristics and its vicious human and ecological impacts must and can be reversed.

NOTES

1   Eli Friedman, 'China in Revolt', *Jacobin: A Magazine of Culture and Polemic*, 7-8, 2012.

2   Among many discussions on the retreat of gender equality in China, the works cited below focus on women workers who embody both gender and class identities. For the worsening ethnic relations in recent years, see Lin Chun, 'Modernity and the violence of global accumulation: the ethnic question in China', forthcoming in Breno Bringel and Mauricio Domingues, eds., *Global Modernity and Social Contestation*, London: Sage, 2015.

3   Karl Marx, 'Contribution to the Critique of Hegel's Philosophy of Right', in Karl Marx and Friedrich Engels, *Selected Works in One Volume*, London: Lawrence & Wishart, 1968, p. 219.

4   As Marx observed, bourgeois revolutions always advance backwards, breaking into the future with their eyes turned to the past. With an illusion of liberty, it could only liberate men from feudal relations, and then subject them to a new, bourgeois-capitalist mode of exploitation. See Louis Althusser, *Machiavelli and Us*, London: Verso, 1999, pp. 49-50.

5   See especially Mao Zedong, 'An Analysis of Classes in China' (1926), 'The Strategic Questions of the Chinese Revolutionary War' (1936), 'The Chinese Revolution and the Chinese Communist Party' (1939) and 'On New Democracy' (1940), in *The Selected Works of Mao Zedong, vol. 1 and 2*, Beijing: People's Publishing House, 1991.

6   Most recently, for example, see Neil Davidson, *How Revolutionary were the Bourgeois Revolutions?*, Chicago: Haymarket Books, 2012, p. 252; and Neil Faulkner, *A Marxist History of the World: From Neanderthals to Neoliberals*, London: Pluto, 2013, p. 256. Both fail to recognize what was fundamentally new about an otherwise 'bourgeois' revolution in China.

7   As Trotsky explains, 'the privilege of historic backwardness ... permits, or rather compels the adoption of whatever is ready in advance of any specified date, skipping a whole series of intermediate stages'. Hence, this 'leads necessarily to a peculiar combination of different stages in the historic process'. Leon Trotsky, *History of the Russian Revolution*, Ann Arbor, Michigan: University of Michigan Press, 1961, pp. 4-5.

8   Ernest Gellner, in a different theoretical context, once observed that 'only when a nation became a class ... did it become politically conscious and activist ... [as] a nation-for-itself'. Ernest Gellner, *Nations and Nationalism*, 2nd Edition, Oxford: Blackwell, 2006, pp. 116-7.

9   Faulkner, *A Marxist History of the World*, p. 257; Davidson, *How Revolutionary were the Bourgeois Revolutions?*, pp. 252, 621.

10   See the established scholarship in China studies represented by the leading experts since John King Fairbank.

11   Maurice Meisner, 'The Wrong March: China Chooses Stalin's Way', *The Progressive*, 26 October 1986.

12   Mark Selden, 'Cooperation and Conflict: Cooperative and Collective Formation in China's Countryside', in Mark Selden and Victor Lippit, eds., *The Transition to Socialism in China*, Armonk, NY: ME Sharpe, 1982, p. 85.

13   John Starr, *Continuing the Revolution: The Political Thought of Mao*, Princeton: Princeton University Press, 1979. Mao's concern with the consolidation and development of socialism through a continuing revolution can be seen as another version of seeking 'the Machiavellian moment', as discussed in Althusser, *Machiavelli and Us*.

14   Jonathan Unger, *The Transformation of Rural China*, Armonk, NY: ME Sharp, 2002, pp. 29, 223.

15   See especially Richard Kraus, 'Class Conflict and the Vocabulary of Social Analysis in China', *The China Quarterly*, 69(March), 1977.

16   Mao's thoughts as recounted in this paragraph are systematically annotated and analyzed in Stuart Schram, *The Thought of Mao Tse-Tung*, Cambridge: Cambridge University Press, 1989, part 2.

17   Mao's ideas might have directly influenced the Foucauldian critique of 'knowledge/power', but certainly went deeper for their distinctly class oriented insight.

18   'Speech at the Extended Central Work Conference', 30 Jan 1962, *Selected Writings of Mao, vol. 8*, Beijing: People's Publishing House, 1999.

19   John Gittings, *Survey of the Sino-Soviet Dispute: A Commentary and Extracts from the Recent Polemics, 1963-1967*, Oxford: Oxford University Press, 1968.

20   Alessandro Russo, 'The Probable Defeat: Preliminary Notes on the Chinese Cultural Revolution', *Positions*, 6(1), 1998, pp. 185-6.

21   And, 'in terms of the socialist promise of liberation, a revolution orchestrated by those in positions of absolute authority is a contradiction in terms'. Arif Dirlik, 'Back to the Future: Contemporary China in the Perspective of Its Past, circa 1980', *Boundary 2*, 38(1), 2011, pp. 24-5 (written in 1981).

22   Michael Burawoy, 'Neoclassical Sociology: From the End of Communism to the End of Classes', *American Journal of Sociology*, 106(4), 2001, pp. 1099-1100.

23   Dirlik, 'Back to the Future', p. 16. See also Wang Hui, 'The Crisis of Representativeness and Post-Party Politics', *Modern China*, 40(2), 2014, p. 238; and Ann Anagnost, 'From "Class" to "Social Strata": Grasping the Social Totality in Reform-era China', *Third World Quarterly*, 29(3), 2008, pp. 497-9.

24   Minqi Li and Dale Wen, 'China: Hyper-Development and Environmental Crisis', *Socialist Register 2007*, London: Merlin Press, 2006. Questionable is development itself, an internalized assumption in both capitalism and socialism of overcoming 'the anguish of backwardness'.

25   *China News Net*, 18 January 2013; Wang Xiaolu, 'Measuring the Width of the Wealth Gap' and 'The Wealth Gap: Identifying the Problem, Proposing Reforms', *Caixin*, 23 and 27 September 2013. The Gini coefficient data (approaching 0.5 throughout the years in the new century) published by the National Bureau of Statistics and analyzed in the Chinese Academy of Social Sciences annual blue books 'tend to be underestimated because of uncounted grey income and raging corruption statistics'. Ma Jiantang, Bureau Chief, 'The Real Problem with those Gini Numbers', *Caixin*, 5 February 2013.

26   This formulation disregards any conceptual difference between 'peasants' and 'farmers', and indeed both would need further discussions in class terms. A more relevant point is their attachment to the land due to a hard demographic constraint in China on conventional modernization.

27 The level and sources of income could be most indicative of the structural locations in production and productive relations. See He Xuefeng, 'Who are the Peasants?', *Economic Guide*, March 2014; Henry Bernstein, '"The Peasantry" in Global Capitalism: Who, Where and Why?', *Socialist Register 2001*, London: Merlin Press, 2000.

28 The share of 1.2 million Chinese workers in the 2012 profit report on Apple iPhones was only 1.8 per cent, for example. Joint University Student Investigation Team, 'Foxconn, Have you Righted your Wrongs?', *References*, Beijing Huayan Research 11, 18 March 2014.

29 'As political families move into business, private tycoons are entering the political sphere'. James Areddy and James Grimaldi, 'Defying Mao, Rich Chinese Crash the Communist Party', *The Wall Street Journal*, 26 December 2012. See also Bruce Dickson, 'Integrating Wealth and Power in China: The Communist Party's Embrace of the Private Sector', *China Quarterly*, 192(December), 2007.

30 See for example *China's Work Safety Yearbook 2012*, Beijing: China Coal Industry Press, 2013; and Ann Herbert et al., 'National Profile Report on Occupational Safety and Health in China', Geneva: ILO, 2012.

31 This is seen in 'the tax system, subsidies, trade regulations, and access to finance' to the extent that 'domestic and foreign capital effectively operated within different legal parameters' with 'the more favorable laws applied to foreign, not domestic capital'. Leo Panitch and Sam Gindin, *The Making of Global Capitalism: The Political Economy of American Empire*, London: Verso, 2012, p. 296.

32 Seven of the nation's richest multibillionaires attended the 18th party congress in 2012. In the same year, one-third of China's quasi-capitalists were party members, while many also assumed the position of party secretary in their own companies. See the Chinese Academy of Social Sciences, *Blue Book*, 2013; *The Southern Metropolis Daily*, 20 December 2012; Tyler Cowen, 'China Fact of the Day', *Marginal Revolution*, 27 February 2012; John Garnut, 'The Rot Inside', *The Age*, 14 April 2012; David Barboza, 'Billions in Hidden Riches for Family of Chinese Leaders', *New York Times*, 25 October 2012; Stephen Aldred and Irene Jay Liu, 'The Princeling of Private Equity', *Reuters*, 9 April 2014. In rural China, too, business people took party posts in villages and townships through votes for abilities or bribes. Yan Xiaojun, 'To Get Rich is Not only Glorious: Economic Reform and the New Entrepreneurial Party Secretaries', *China Quarterly*, 100(2), 2012.

33 Zhang Lu, 'Hengyang Bribery Not an Isolated Phenomenon', *Caijing.com.cn*, 25 February 2014.

34 The Bo Xilai case is a good example. See Yuezhi Zhao, 'The struggle for Socialism in China: The Bo Xilai saga and beyond', *Monthly Review*, 64(5), 2012.

35 Maurice Meisner, *The Deng Xiaoping Era: An Inquiry into the Fate of Chinese Socialism, 1978–94*, New York: Hill & Wang, 1996, pp. 300-45. In addition, 'patrimonial capitalism' and 'crony capitalism' focus on personal and family networks of the system. According to reports by the International Consortium of Investigative Journalists, the Chinese political and corporate elites, including

relatives of top leaders, have used offshore companies to secretly store their fortunes. An estimated one to four trillion dollars in untraced assets has been moved out of China since 2000. Oliver Campbell, *World Socialist Web Site*, 30 January 2014.

36   Zhao Yuezhi, 'Communication, the Nexus of Class and Nation, and Global Divides: Reflections on China's Post-Revolutionary Experiences', *Nordicom Review*, 30(Jubilee Issue), 2009, p. 97.

37   Pierre Bourdieu, *Distinction: A Social Critique of the Judgment of Taste*, London: Routledge, 1986, ch. 2; Erik Olin Wright et al., *The Debate on Classes*, London: Verso, 1989, pp. 4-6, 24-8.

38   David Goodman, 'Dreams and Aspirations', *Journal of Chinese Political Science*, 19(1), 2014, p. 49; Yingjie Guo, 'Farewell to Class, except the Middle Class: The Politics of Class Analysis in Contemporary China', *The Asia-Pacific Journal*, 26(2), 2009.

39   On *suzhi* as a discursive operator in the neoliberal governance of labour migration, see Yan Hairong, *New Masters, New Servants: Migration, Development, and Women Workers in China*, Durham, NC: Duke University Press, 2008, ch. 3. Treatises based on a class analysis of prostitution in China for and by migrant workers are still lacking. In a recent popular television show, middle-class professionals openly lectured workers to not complain – 'do not use the word "exploitation" so easily, and learn to be thankful to your bosses who give your jobs'. The audience applauded approvingly, leaving the few workers who managed to tell just a tiny bit of their misery speechless, almost in tears.

40   As Maurice Meisner puts it, 'any serious impetus for democratic change will more likely come from the victims, not the beneficiaries, of state-sponsored capitalism'. 'Capitalism, Communism, and Democracy in China: A Review Essay', *The Progressive*, 71(11), 2007, p. 41.

41   Forty million state workers were laid off during 'urban restructuring' in the 1990s. See Thomas Gold, William Hurst, Jaeyon Won and Li Qiang, eds., *Laid-off Workers in a Workers' State: Unemployment with Chinese Characteristics*, London: Palgrave, 2009. The parallel processes of old and new workers in the declining industrial base and a new manufacturing sector respectively are captured in structural overview and personal details in Chin Kwan Lee, *Against the Law: Labor Protests in China's Rustbelt and Sunbelt*, Berkeley: University of California Press, 2007.

42   State Council news conference reported in the *People's Daily*, 21 February 2014. Manufacturing employment has begun to shrink as shown in the newest trend of migrants landing in service jobs more than in factories.

43   Eli Friedman and Ching Kwan Lee, 'Remaking the World of Chinese Labor: A 30-Year Retrospective', *British Journal of Industrial Relations*, 48(3), 2010. As Bryan Palmer argues, precariousness cannot be taken to found a separate and distinct class formation. 'Reconsiderations of Class: Precariousness as Proletarianization', *Socialist Register 2014*, London: Merlin Press, 2013. For the debate, see a useful discussion of 'job classes' versus 'jobless classes' by Philippe Van Parijs, 'A Revolution in Class Theory', in Wright, *Debate on Classes*, ch. 6.

44   They are 'triply coerced by global capitalism, the "socialist" state, and familial patriarchy'. Pun Ngai, *Made in China: Women Factory Workers in a Global Workplace*, Durham, NC: Duke University Press, 2005, pp. 2, 12-15. See also, Yan, *New Masters, New Servants.*

45   Lin Chun, 'What Is China's "Comparative Advantage"?', in T. Y. Cao, ed., *The Chinese Model of Modern Development*, London: Routledge, 2005.

46   There were 202 industrial relations disputes or conflicts in the first quarter of 2014 alone, a 30 per cent increase from the same period in 2013. See Pun Ngai and Jenny Chan, 'Global Capital, the State, and Chinese Workers: The Foxconn Experience', *Modern China*, 38(4), 2012; Jenny Chan, Pun Ngai and Mark Selden, 'Apple et al Create New Working Class', *Asia Times Online*, 29 August 2013; and regular analyses in the *China Labor Bulletin* and on the *World Socialist Web Site.*

47   Pun Ngai et al., 'The China Dream of a Contract: Investigation in the Situation of Labour Contract for Construction Workers in 2013', *References*, 20 Feb 2014; and 'The Living Conditions of Miners in a State Owned Coal Company', *21ccom.net*, 27 March 2014.

48   Mike Davis, 'Spring Confronts Winter', *New Left Review*, 72(November/ December), 2011, p. 15; Minqi Li, 'The Rise of the Working Class and the Future of the Chinese Revolution', *Monthly Review*, 63(2), 2011.

49   Mao, 'Speech at the Extended Central Work Conference', and 'A Comment on Cadres Participating in Manual Labour in Zhejiang', in *The Writings of Mao Zedong since the Founding of the People's Republic, vol. 10*, Beijing: Central Wenxian Publisher, 1998, pp. 297 and 293.

50   China's Trade Union Law (crafted in 1992 and revised in 2001 and 2009) confirms that the unions represent voluntarily associated workers. Its requirement on elected unions has made Walmart among others comply. Among the most optimistic observations, Wadi'h Halabi sees China as a 'union risen to state power' vis-à-vis world capitalism and Chinese unions as a genuine working-class organization and a 'subcommittee of this union in state power'. 'Question of Unions: Understanding China and its Unions', *Political Affairs*, 27 March 2014.

51   Pun et al., 'The China Dream of a Contract'. According to Philip Huang, full time, formally contracted labour is less than 10 per cent of China's combined workforce, urban and rural; and the country's formal economy accounts for only 16.8 per cent of total employment. 'Misleading Chinese Legal and Statistical Categories: Labour, Individual Entities, and Private Enterprises', *Modern China*, 39(4), 2013.

52   Ching Kwan Lee, 'From the Specter of Mao to the Spirit of the Law: Labor Insurgency in China', *Theory and Society*, 31, 2002, p. 197; Anita Chan and Kaxton Siu, 'Class Consciousness of Chinese Migrant Workers in the Pearl River Delta', *Forum Arbeitswelten*, April 2011; Kevin Gray, 'Labour and the State in China's Passive Revolution', *Capital & Class*, 34(3), pp. 450, 459-60.

53   See a case analysis by Lu Xinyu, 'Ruins of the Future: Class and History in Wang Bing's Tiexi District', *New Left Review*, 31(January/February), 2005.

54   'We miners toil to dig out black coal, in the dark; darkness betrays the sun'.
      'Long live the miners', quoted in Pun Ngai, 'Miners in the Historical Tunnel:
      Back to the State or Forward to the Market?', *References*, 18, 25 April 2014. An
      even more politically explicit poem found in a factory dormitory in 1995 reads:
      We are a mass of *dagongzai* [young men who sell labour]
      Coming from the north, coming from the west
      At first we didn't know what *dagongzai* meant
      Now we know, toiling from the sunrise to the sunset
      Toiling with drops of blood and sweat
      Selling our labour to the boss, selling our bodies to the factory
      Do what they dictate to you, no negotiation, no bargaining, but obey
      Money is the magic, and what the capitalists bestow on you
      A commodity, a commodity (quoted in Pun, *Made in China*, p. 23).

55   Georg Lukács, *History and Class Consciousness*, London: Merlin, 1971, p. 178.
      E.P. Thompson, *The Making of the English Working Class*, Harmondsworth:
      Penguin, 1968, pp. 35-6, 213. A focal point of debates centres on Lukács's
      'idealist' horizon in relation to Lenin's unity of class consciousness and the party.
      For a summary of the critiques, see Terry Eagleton, *Ideology: An Introduction*,
      London: Verso, 2007, pp. 94-104. See also John Rees's introduction to Lukács,
      A Defense of History and Class Consciousness: Tailism and the Dialectic, London:
      Verso, 2000.

56   For Antonio Gramsci, the proletarian political party is 'the first cell containing
      the germs of collective will which are striving to become universal and total'.
      But when such a party is 'no longer recognized as the proper expression of
      their class', a crisis of opposition between 'represented and representatives'
      occurs. The bureaucracy of the party then becomes 'the most dangerously
      habitual and conservative force; … standing by itself and feeling independent
      from the masses, the party ends by becoming anachronistic'. Antonio Gramsci,
      The Modern Prince and Other Writings, New York: International Publishers,
      1959, pp. 137, 174-5. This turns out to be rather accurate about the Chinese
      situation today.

57   Henry Heller, *The Birth of Capitalism: A Twenty-First-Century Perspective*,
      London: Pluto, 2011, p. 4. The early modern state in Europe provided an
      essential container for the emergence of capitalism, as seen in the British state's
      mediation between the landed and manufacturing bourgeoisie against workers
      (ch.1 and pp. 210-13). See, more generally, Perry Anderson, *Lineages of the
      Absolutist State*, London: Verso, 1979. Critical of 'class determinism' at the
      expense of state, Ellen Wood argues that that the state, understood broadly
      as an institution of public power, 'has not emerged from class-divisions but
      has, on the contrary, *produced* class-divisions and hence also produced the state
      in the narrow sense'. Ellen Meiksins Wood, *The Ellen Meiksins Wood Reader*,
      Leiden: Brill, 2012, p. 195.

58   Adam Przeworski and Michael Wallerstein, 'Structural Dependence of the
      State on Capital', *American Political Science Review*, 82(1), 1988.

59   Ivan Szelenyi, 'A Theory of Transition', *Modern China*, 34(1), 2008.

60   Gareth Stedman Jones, *Languages of Class: Studies in English Working Class History, 1832-1982*, Cambridge: Cambridge University Press, 1983, pp. 21-2; Joan W. Scott, 'On Language, Gender, and Working Class History', *International Labor and Working Class History*, 31(Spring), 1987, pp. 4-6. It was Maoist politics that pioneered the revolutionary practice of translating ideology into the local lexicon and everyday communication in mass mobilization for social change.

61   Scott, 'On Language', p. 5.

62   Jack Gray, 'Politics in Command: The Maoist Theory of Social Change and Economic Growth', *Political Quarterly*, 45(1), 1974; Maurice Meisner, 'Leninism and Maoism: Some Populist Perspectives on Marxism-Leninism in China', *China Quarterly*, 45(January/March), 1971.

63   Heller, *The Birth of Capitalism*, p. 209. Hardt notes how 'rent' increasingly replaces conventional 'profit' in the hi-tech sectors, where the producers could subvert capitalism ('Production of the Common', in Costas Douzinas and Slavoj Žižek, eds., *The Idea of Communism*, London: Verso, 2010, p. 137). More generally, any rigid defence of private property is flawed due to the trend of socialization of capital and market. See Jeremy Rifkin, *The Third Industrial Revolution: How Lateral Power is Transforming Energy, the Economy, and the World*, London: Palgrave, 2013, pp. 218-21.

64   Henry Bernstein, *Class Dynamics of Agrarian Change*, Sterling, VA: Kumarian Press, 2010; Philip Huang, 'Re-knowing China's Labouring People: Historical Evolution of Labour Legislation and the Present Informal Economy', *Open Times*, 5, 2013.

65   Michael Hardt and Antonio Negri, *Declaration*, New York: Argo-Navis, 2012, p. 104. Their more influential and controversial concept is the 'multitude': whereas 'the people' is formed as a unity by a hegemonic power, 'the multitude is formed through articulations on the plane of immanence without hegemony'. Michael Hardt and Antonio Negri, *Commonwealth*, Cambridge, MA: Belknap Press, 2011, p. 169.

66   Göran Therborn notes especially the largely extra-capitalist, critical force made up of the hundreds of millions of landless peasants, casual labourers and the slum populations as destabilizing for capitalism in his 'Class in the 21ˢᵗ Century', *New Left Review*, 78(November/December), 2012, pp. 26, 29; and 'New masses?', *New Left Review*, 85(January/February), 2014.

67   As Henri Lefebvre puts it in *The Production of Space*, 'the forms of the class struggle are now more varied than formerly', which 'implies the mobilization of differences in a single moment'. Quoted in Neil Smith, *Uneven Development: Nature, Capital, and the Production of Space*, Athens, GA: University of Georgia Press, 2008, pp. 227-8.

INDIA'S LANDMARK ELECTION

ACHIN VANAIK

There are numerous reasons why the 2014 general elections to India's lower house of parliament, the Lok Sabha, constituted a post-independence landmark event. But the most important is that it signifies for the first time ever the replacement of the Indian National Congress by the Hindutva-motivated Bharatiya Janata Party (BJP) as the *central point of reference* of the Indian polity. Add to this a Prime Minister, Narendra Modi, who as Chief Minister of Gujarat state in February-March 2002 oversaw (and for many was directly implicated in) the eruption and prolongation of one of the worst anti-Muslim pogroms since independence. If India is as secular and democratic as so many liberals make it out to be then that alone should have permanently disqualified him from reaching where he now has.[1] This denouement carries profound implications for the foreseeable future that need to be scanned. But first a look at what the voting patterns that emerged have shown.

Of the 543 elected seats the BJP achieved (to its own surprise) a majority of 282, its highest ever tally, while the Congress (never before getting less than a 100) was reduced to 44. The regional allies of the Congress gave the pre-poll coalition of the United Progressive Alliance (UPA) 15 more seats; while the pre-poll regional allies of the BJP – the Shiromani Akali Dal of Punjab (4), the Telegu Desam in the south (17) and the Shiv Sena in Maharastra (18) – helped raise the National Democratic Alliance (NDA) total to 336. The BJP can rule on its own terms and has handed over only minor ministerial berths to its allies. Its previous best was in 1998 with 182 seats and a 26 per cent vote share. This time it secured 31 per cent overall yet obtained a simple seat majority, although previously whenever a party has got a ruling majority the vote share has varied between a low of near 41 per cent to a high of near 49 per cent. What does this signify about the BJP victory?

Even allowing for the disproportion between seats and votes inherent in a first-past-the-post electoral system, this is an exceptionally large imbalance reflecting the fragmentation of the non-BJP vote. With the Congress getting around 19 per cent, regional parties still garnered half the votes polled. It could therefore be argued that the regionalization of the Indian polity inaugurated in the 1991 elections still holds. This view gains credibility from the fact that the key to the BJP's success came from its unexpectedly good performance in two key north Indian states (not ruled by it): Uttar Pradesh, where it won an extraordinary 71 out of 80 seats on a 42 per cent vote share; and 22 out of 40 seats on a vote of 29 per cent in Bihar. Without these two the BJP would not have crossed the 200 seat mark. In Uttar Pradesh, though the Samajwadi Party (SP) was only 1 per cent short of its score in the 2009 elections (23 per cent), its seat tally fell from 23 to 5, while the party of Dalits, the Bahujan Samaj Party (BSP), lost all its 20 seats despite carrying 20 per cent of the vote. In Bihar, regional forces again got reasonable vote shares but lost out seat-wise.

Yes, the BJP benefited from a fragmented opposition vote but one should not underestimate the extent of its breakthrough, magnified as it is by the precipitous decline of the Congress. The latter has no representation now from 14 out of the 29 states of the Union. The BJP is now the only national party making inroads into newer states and even into the former left bastions of West Bengal and Kerala. In West Bengal, where the Left Front ruled for 34 continuous years (1977-2011) under the leadership of the Communist Party of India-Marxist (CPM), the BJP got 17 per cent of the vote compared to the CPM's 22.5 per cent, picking up 2 seats each as the regional Trinamool Congress Party (a former breakaway from the parent Congress) swept 34 out of the 42 seats available. In Kerala, the BJP almost did the unthinkable in coming close to winning one seat and for the first time crossed the 10 per cent vote mark.

If geographical extension was one big gain another has been its social advance across castes, classes and tribes (Adivasis). In Jharkhand state, where the tribal population at 27 per cent is more than triple the national average, the BJP got 12 out of 14 seats. In Uttar Pradesh, the country's most populous state, the BJP won around three-quarters of all upper caste votes and over half of those of the intermediate castes (whose upper layers are largely landed upper/middle peasantry) or 'Other Backward Classes' (OBCs) other than the Yadav community who remained loyal to the SP; and 40 per cent of the Dalit vote, barring the Jatavs who remained loyal to the BSP. In Bihar a similar story prevailed among upper castes with the BJP also securing over half of the lower OBC vote and one-third among Dalits. Lower castes and lower classes broadly overlap. The one social group that remained relatively immune to the Modi appeal were of course the Muslims (overwhelming poor and educationally backward, they form approximately 15 per cent of the population). In fact for the first time ever a majority ruling party will not have a single Muslim MP. Apart from this group much of what should be the natural class constituency of the left voted for the right.

Any attempt to rectify this drift must understand why this happened. In the absence of class mobilizational politics by the left, Modi's promise of better development and governance proved highly attractive. Over the last two decades there has been some 'transformation' of class politics but it has been by and for the right. Of the various processes whose complex interweaving has most shaped the Indian polity over the last three decades – the forward march of Hindutva and of the intermediate castes, Dalit affirmation, Muslim ferment, regional assertions – the one with the most explicit class referent is the emergence of the misnamed but growing 'middle class'. Currently comprising the top 15 to 20 per cent of the 1.2 billion population, this is not a median category providing a social buffer for the dominant classes as in the West, but an elite category of mass proportions. And it has provided the most important base for the rise of reactionary right-wing politics, whether practised by the Congress or by the BJP.

Is the geographical and social expansion of the BJP vote an exceptional one-time affair due primarily to proximate factors like the remarkable nature of the election campaign waged by the Modi-led 'Sangh Parivar' or the family of Hindu Nationalist organizations and fronts of all kinds headed by the Rashriya Swayamsevak Sangh (RSS) or National Volunteer Corps? Certainly the communal riots in Uttar Pradesh of autumn 2013, in which the hand of the Sangh is widely suspected, helped polarize the elections that followed in that state and elsewhere. Moreover, even apart from Modi's own indefatigable efforts – between September 2013 and mid-May 2014 he traversed some 300,000 km, and in the last two months held a daily average of four to five rallies or meetings – this campaign set new standards of money power, technological gadgetry and cadre mobilization on the ground. The total expenditure by government, parties and candidates, projected at Rs. 30,000 crores (probably less than the actual), compares with the $7 billion or Rs. 42,000 crores spent during the US presidential election of 2012. The BJP easily received the lion's share of monies given by a corporate sector (large and medium) strongly biased towards the Modi candidature as the authority figure who could fast track policy clearances in its favour as he had done during his long reign in Gujarat as Chief Minister.

Add to this money power the massive use of social media messaging, of hologram technology to project 3D images of Modi to some 1,350 locations, as well as the manpower strength of the RSS for face-to-face mobilization on the ground. The Congress's campaigning, led by an uninspiring Rahul Gandhi as heir-apparent, was but a pale shadow of this. The BJP high command divided 428 contested constituencies into 'favourable', 'battleground' and 'difficult', assigning more cadres to the latter two for patrolling several hundred thousand polling stations. Voter addresses and telephone numbers were centralized and distributed accordingly with the aim of ensuring a very high turnout, especially of the young.[2] This calculated strategy paid off. Since 1991, whenever the turnout has been over 60 per cent the BJP has done better. This time the turnout at 66 per cent was the highest ever. Among the close to 100 million first-time (18-22 year old) voters, there was a 68 per cent turnout – of which the BJP got the biggest single chunk.

One could argue that India is following in the steps of advanced industrialized democracies, where even in parliamentary systems the mediatization of electoral politicking has meant greater personalization as well as presidentialization. Discussion of programmes and the choices to be made between them – what elections are classically supposed to be about – take more of a back seat to public relations skills in messaging. This is not to say that differences between what contending parties claim to stand for are unimportant. But in a media-soaked context without class mobilization and the political confrontations flowing from this, how these specificities are articulated or obscured can become decisive. Between 1971 and 1989 India had five general elections, two of which (the ending of Emergency Rule in 1977 and the sympathy wave after Mrs. Gandhi's assassination in 1984) were wave-like shifts, and three were referendum-like (with the slogans of 'removing poverty' in 1971, 'bringing back stability' in 1980, 'removing a corrupt regime' in 1989). The pattern of those years was repeated in 2014 but with one crucial difference. This time the central appeal was not a policy promise but a highly personalized one of giving power to a 'strongman saviour' who would then resolve *all* basic ills.

THE LONGER VIEW

However, there are more fundamental reasons for the BJP's and Modi's ascent. It is the culmination of a process going on since at least the late eighties with a neoliberal turn in the economy being accompanied by the rise of a Hindutva-influenced consolidation of 'common sense' socially and a stronger authoritarian inflection politically. These developments have all been normalized and now set the limits of the 'acceptable' range of mainstream discourse on what policies and practices should be followed at the central and provincial levels. The prime culprit is of course the Congress Party whose long-term historical and historic decline through its acts of omission and commission set the stage for the emergence of these developments. In a comparative sense the Congress's decline broadly mirrors the trajectory taken by its 'nationalist populist' equivalents in Latin America, where after prolonged periods of rule – e.g., Peronism in Argentina, Vargism in Brazil, the PRI in Mexico, APRA in Peru, MNR in Bolivia, Acción Democrática in Venezuela – these formations either went into oblivion or transmogrified into smaller, explicitly right-wing parties. But in a few of these countries this created the space where, unlike in India so far, left-wing formations grew much stronger and successfully contested for state power precisely because they struggled to transform oppressive class relations.

There have been three turning points in the story of the Congress's decline. The Congress's dominance in the states was first broken in 1967, partly through defections from its social base and by some party higher-ups. Non-Congress alternatives rose to power in certain states. At the central level, increasing volatility of electoral preferences created wave and referendum-type elections between 1971 and 1989 in which a non-Congress centrist alternative came to power twice (1977 and 1989) but did not last a full term. The second turn was in 1991 when a minority Congress government initially engineered defections and this was followed by a period of coalition rule in which a third non-Congress centrist alternative failed to last a full term in power. In its wake a BJP-led coalition emerged and ruled for a full term. Two Congress-led coalition governments followed it, but now the BJP has replaced the Congress as the most preferred vehicle for carrying on the right-wing agenda of domestic and foreign capital.

In the developing world, national-populist bourgeois parties, with both left and right factions mediated by a holding centre, were a characteristic of the phase of import substitution industrialization developed amidst the space created globally by Cold War systemic hostility. Once ISI gave way to free market fundamentalism and the Communist bloc was no more, the new consensus, in India certainly, was that neoliberal globalization was not just the only but the best direction to take, with mainstream debate confined to how 'welfarist' a face it should have. On the economic front it was the Congress that even in the eighties embarked on the neoliberal journey (legitimized after 1991), and then also initiated the search for a closer strategic relationship with the US and Israel. The BJP-led National Democratic Alliance (NDA) of 1999-2004 further consolidated this approach, but added the nuclear bomb, something it had wanted from even before the Chinese test in 1964. The irony is that the Congress, throughout its decline until 2014, was always more electorally favoured than the BJP by the poor and deprived, but repeatedly betrayed this support base.

The fact is that by the seventies the Congress had lost the organizational structure that had emerged out of its role in the struggle for independence, whereby intermediary bodies headed by powerful local and regional leaders kept it connected to the grassroots. The degeneration continued thereafter with its elite leadership moving steadily away from even the old Nehruvian rhetoric claiming to promote state-led development.[3] Given the social character of the Indian state as it has developed over time – where now Indian and foreign big capital together outweigh the landed elite – this turn further to the right was not at all surprising. It could only have been countered effectively if there was organized class resistance from below, which of course the Congress would not pursue. The non-Congress regional parties were aligned to their own local rural and urban elites, while the BSP got itself mired in an identity politics abjuring cross-caste, lower-class mobilizations. The Congress had become a vast electoral machine whose activists, lacking any ideological commitment or inspiration, were effectively silent except at various election times (local, regional and national). The glue that held the Congress together was its ability to come to power at various levels and thereby sustain the patronage-clientelist links that substituted for it not having any internally democratic structure or a vibrant culture of political discussion and debate. The 'family dynasty' was crucial because only it could serve as final arbiter in the factional conflicts within. Unlike the ideologically driven cadre-based Sangh and left parties, electoral fortune or misfortune plays a much more decisive role for its very survival and well-being.

Ruling classes in capitalist democracies ideally want two 'safe' contending parties so that one or the other can act as the alternative when public discontent with the politics of class war from above becomes too disturbing. So there can still be corporate and media support for the Congress. But this alone cannot resurrect a decaying entity that has to find its own political resources to generate stronger public support, and of this there are no signs yet. The BJP and the Sangh are in a much better position. Neoliberal globalization does not diminish the importance of states, but actually requires states to play the crucial role of stabilizers and legitimizers for its expansion. There is then a dialectic of the international and the national. Growing transnationalization of market relations can happily go hand in hand with the assertion of nationally particularist right-wing politics and ideologies. This is where the Indian specificity of Hindutva comes in and has disproportionately influenced the dominant form of Indian nationalism. This would not have been possible if the Sangh had not been capable of mass mobilizations and of steady, long-term work in the pores of civil society to win adherents and activists to its cultural-political messages of Hindu unity as the way to 'making India strong'.

The Congress not only did not resist the Sangh's activities in this regard, but abetted this process through its own pragmatism, assuaging communal elements among Hindus, Muslims and Sikhs. The Congress failed to confront the Sangh's mass campaign to demolish the Babri Masjid, the famous sixteenth century mosque in Ayodhya, Uttar Pradesh, a campaign which openly defied the constitutional commitments to secularism and left a trail of riots and communal violence against Muslims. After it was destroyed in 1992 amidst a political rally that developed into a riot involving 150,000 people, there were further riots and deaths in Uttar Pradesh and elsewhere. The Congress could have forcefully prevented this demolition but did not; nor were top Sangh leaders ever punished. Indeed, in 1991, the Congress government had enacted a 'Place of Worship (Special Provisions)' Act to protect shrines of all communities from communal vandalism, but kept the Ayodhya Babri Mosque out of its purview. The official Liberhan Commission set up shortly after to investigate the demolition was supposed to submit its report in three months; it actually finally submitted its Report 17 years later in 2009. The Report indicted all the top Sangh leaders including the 'pseudo-moderate' former Prime Minister Atal Bihari Vajpayee as privy to this criminal conspiracy. Not only were these leaders not punished, Vajpayee is now widely portrayed even by 'secular liberals' as something of a 'statesman'.

The underlying reality is that even allowing for the Congress's ineptitude and culpability, the Sangh's Hindutva project could never have advanced as it has if the social and political soil had not been long fertile for its flourishing. Those liberals who have repeatedly waxed eloquent on the virtues of the National Movement, the secularity of the state and its 'remarkable' Constitution have never been prepared to admit this reality.[4] For millennia 'Hinduism' was little more than a compendium label for multiple sects with differing beliefs and rituals possessing no unifying thematic. The Gandhi-led National Movement introduced the poison of religiously inspired appeals that were necessarily oriented towards mobilizing the majority Hindus. Both before and after Gandhi there has been a steady process of what the eminent historian Romila Thapar has called 'syndicated Hinduism'. This has entailed the more or less systematic consolidation of an ever-widening Hindu self-consciousness across castes.[5]

Where once local Hindu and Muslim communities shared more cultural similarities with each other than with their distant co-religionists, today Muslims all over India share a consciousness of being besieged, while a sense of Hindu belonging cuts across castes, sects and even linguistic barriers, even as those identities remain strong and in many cases primary. At the very least this has meant that where a Hindutva-motivated minority harbours genuine hostility towards Muslims the vast majority of Hindus are simply indifferent to the plight of Muslims. The Sachar Committee Report of 2011 highlighted their socioeconomic plight, but its recommendations for affirmative action for Muslims – as given to Dalits, tribals and OBCs – was ignored by the Congress government. The fact is that the Sangh has changed the terms of public discourse, and secularism is now seen as a code word for justifying the 'appeasement' of Muslims, which is 'unfair' to Hindus and a 'diversion' from the more pressing everyday needs of the broader public.

THE EVOLUTION OF THE SANGH PARIVAR

The Indian state formally and legally is still a secular state and this does count for something. But in substantive terms this secularity, always weak to begin with, has eroded to the point where the country's most important religious minority of Muslims are in effect second-class citizens, having less hope than ever of transcending this status. For all the degree of psychological-emotional uplift that lower OBCs, a growing number of Adivasis and the bulk of Dalits may derive from feeling that they are part of a wider Hindu collective which is 'on the rise', in other material ways they too share the plight of fellow Muslims, if not their distinct sense of insecurity of being potential victims of communal violence. Hindu self-consciousness does not automatically translate into Hindutva ideology and politics. But it is no barrier to the latter's growth and spread. One of the most persistent claims of academic political science on India is that, given such unparalleled segmentation across multiple lines of social, cultural, economic, linguistic, religious, racial differentiation, only a broadly centrist-moderate force on social and cultural fronts can hope to come to power at the centre and be stable thereafter. Up to the early eighties the prevailing wisdom was that the BJP had to choose between remaining a party of the Hindu *rassemblement* or else moderating so as to become a mass party and a challenger for central power. Instead the BJP and Sangh moved rightwards, launched the Babri Mosque campaign and came to power eventually in 1998-99. Now, in another twist, they have achieved majority rule by moving further to the right as the choice of its new leader and the latest party manifesto should make clear. This does not mean there are no pressures to 'moderate', but that these would at best be movements towards a 'centre' that has itself moved considerably to the right.

Historically, the Sangh emerged in the mid-twenties as a Hindu nationalist and revivalist force partly inspired by European fascism, but has lasted as long as it has because of the way it has evolved (though retaining some fascist characteristics). The RSS is the parent organization from which emerged various other limbs after independence: the electoral-political wing (called the BJP since the 1980s), the cultural front of Vishwa Hindu Parishad (World Hindu Council created in 1964) and scores of other bodies catering to all groups from Adivasis to professionals. The Sangh has now jettisoned its economic nationalism and thus made itself more than acceptable to globalizing capital (which includes some big Indian capital). But it remains a creature of the hard right whose ultimate objective is establishing a *Hindu Rashtra* ('Hindu nation'), for which a Hindu state in all but name (and perhaps that as well) is seen as a prerequisite. For decades the principal route to this social transformation was seen to lie in civil society, where day-to-day activities and regular mobilizations were to be carried out by ever expanding numbers of highly disciplined and dedicated members. They would be rigorously trained and indoctrinated and connected horizontally by a network of tens of thousands of *shakas* (branches) throughout the country and vertically by a military-like hierarchy of specially chosen full-timers. The transformation sought would be achieved in the long term and independent of the vagaries of who occupied central state power. This began to change in the seventies partly because the RSS appeal was diminishing at least in relation to its grandiose goal, and partly because the Emergency of 1975 (when its members and leaders were imprisoned by Gandhi to give her regime a progressive face) forced it to recognize the importance of state power. This was reinforced when the electoral wing of the Sangh became a component of the ruling Janata Party that ended Emergency Rule in 1977.

By the start of the nineties the Sangh came to the view that capture of power at the state and central level was to be the main route to achieving its goal. Civil society activism of the traditional type remained important in its own right, but would now serve as a complement to the main effort. This naturally meant that the weight within the Sangh of the BJP would become relatively greater even as the compromises forced on the BJP and their policies vis-à-vis other parties would be a source of unease within the RSS. The first BJP-led coalition government of 1999-2004 both strengthened the Sangh as a whole, including the RSS, and frustrated it because many of its key demands were put on hold. But it was the ten years after this when it was out of power that was so disturbing to the Sangh. This created tensions within the BJP leadership between many top party leaders and the RSS hierarchy, which saw this weakened unity and the greater autonomy of the BJP as factors contributing to this political exile.

THE NEW GOVERNMENT

In this respect 2014 is again a turning point. During his reign in Gujarat, Modi had effectively suborned the state-level RSS to himself as Chief Minister and head of the state BJP. Modi was not then a favourite of the RSS top leaders for the prime ministerial candidacy, but enormous pressure from the ranks of the RSS pushed them to propose him despite unhappiness among more senior BJP leaders. The highly personalized character of the campaign and then his astounding victory has enthused as never before the mass membership of the RSS and the other Sangh organizations. Thus the RSS and BJP are now once again unified, but with a new twist. For the first time it is the BJP head, not that of the RSS, that will call the shots in the Sangh overall. This integration means that the ideologically driven concerns of the Sangh will be pursued, but Modi will determine their timing and manner of pursuit. Cabinet formation and reorganization of the Prime Minister's Office confirms that this will be a highly centralized administration under his strong control over all major policies – the same style of functioning as he has shown in Gujarat.

Politically, priority will be given to winning over states where the BJP does not rule and whose assemblies will come up for re-election in 2014 and 2015. Success here will give the BJP easier legislative passage in the upper house, the Rajya Sabha. This will also keep the cadres of the RSS and other Sangh organizations active and motivated. Economically, the new government will seek more foreign investment, especially in infrastructure and defence production, and liberalize accordingly. Modi has admired the East Asian development model of Japan and China and this may lead him to be more cautious than gung-ho about further liberalization of the capital account, though he will push for more FDI into hitherto restricted infrastructural areas. He will seek support from Indian big capital with easier clearances for industry, mining and land acquisitions regardless of environmental considerations. This will likely mean a more ruthlessly repressive approach towards existing popular movements and of their support structures – hence the campaign launched against the more progressive organizations in the voluntary sector. These movements resisting corporate-led exploitation because of their livelihood concerns are being accused of hampering Indian development and by implication therefore of being anti-national. Yet he will probably not scrap existing targeted welfare schemes, but try to run them more effectively and economically. In a taste of things to come, the BJP-ruled state of Rajasthan is proposing changes to existing labour laws that would make industry's firing of workers and hiring of contract labour easier and union recognition (and therefore formation) more difficult.

On foreign policy, Modi has little choice but to promote better relations with the US, as he also will, more enthusiastically, with Israel and Japan. Relations with Pakistan will be trickier because in keeping with his image he will be tempted to respond 'strongly' to cross-border terrorist attacks, even if these cannot be prevented by Islamabad. Besides seeking a complete ban everywhere on cow slaughter, his administration will seek to change school and college syllabi in ways that promote 'Hindu pride' in India's past with little regard for historical accuracy. It will also attempt to recruit the 'right' kind of people at all levels in research and teaching institutions of all kinds. The government will take tentative steps towards abrogating Article 370 of the Constitution. That a Muslim majority region in India should enjoy special autonomy has always been anathema to the Sangh idea of a Hindu Rashtra.

Similarly, there will at some time come a push for a uniform civil code, which would override the existing Muslim personal law. It is the imposition of uniformity on Indian Muslims that is the Sangh's driving motive, not the desire for maximizing secular and gender just laws for all women. The process of identifying Muslim migrants from Bangladesh in search of livelihoods in India has begun with a view to eventually expelling them. Though their only crime is illegal entry, they are dishonestly designated as 'infiltrators' while Hindu migrants from Bangladesh are considered 'refugees' to be helped. Finally, there will also be a push for building a Ram Temple in Ayodhya at the site of the destroyed mosque. This could be done through contrived negotiations with some puppet Muslim religious group or pursued in some other way. It would be a powerful expression of not just the righteous assertion of the true Hindu-ness of India, but also the declaration of a message to India's Muslims that even their existence as second-class citizens must be on terms set by the Sangh. As in all the above-cited cases, the issue is not if but when and how the goals of the Sangh will be pursued.

THE NEWCOMER

No tears should be shed for the decline of the 'secular' Congress. This has created the space not just for the right, but for centrist forces and for a rejuvenated left to grow. A centrist push has come from the newly formed Aam Aadmi Party (AAP) or Common Man Party. The AAP was basically thrown up by the largely urban-based, middle-class anti-corruption movement that erupted in April 2011 and lasted for more than a year, with especially large mobilizations in Delhi. Its symbolic leader was a culturally conservative Gandhian, Anna Hazare, who runs a 'model village community' in Maharashtra. But the real organizers were the group around Arvind Kejriwal, a former civil servant turned social activist. The campaign ended with a Congress promise to pass an Act setting up a powerful and independent monitoring body and Ombudsman to check corruption. Unlike Hazare, who places himself above party affiliations, Kejriwal and cohorts felt that a new party had to be created to cleanse the body politic and that the time was opportune. In late 2013 the AAP was formed (after much grassroots activity) precisely to fight state assembly elections in Delhi in early 2014, very much with an eye to the forthcoming general elections.

Eschewing the presentation of a full-fledged programme, the AAP concentrated on opposing corruption, including illegal corporate funding of parties or bribes for personal or policy favours. It cleverly produced 70 local manifestos for each of the 70 assembly seats in Delhi, focusing on concerns such as protection against crime and harassment and cheap and adequate provision of water and electricity. It used the internet and social media innovatively to make transparent its own funding through high-volume small donations directly from the public as well as getting across its party messages and for recruiting members for a nominal fee. Large numbers of middle-class youth and professionals of all ages joined it in Delhi while it also had a national impact. To the surprise of all, it won 28 seats to the BJP's 32 and the Congress's eight in the Delhi assembly.

Thereafter its troubles began. Initially insisting it would never take support from either the Congress or the BJP, it assumed the reigns of the Delhi government with the Congress's agreement only to resign shortly afterwards on flimsy grounds, essentially because it wanted to concentrate on mass campaigning in the general elections. Its basic strategy even before it fought the Delhi elections was that its breakthrough there would give it the credentials to fight the general elections. It would make a dramatic showing there by garnering between 20 to 40 Lok Sabha seats through simultaneous recruitment and campaigning on a mass scale. With such a performance the AAP could expect to become a major governmental contender by the 2019 elections. The assumption was that a political breakthrough would not have to come through the slow accumulation of members and credibility through years of activity; rather sheer mass disillusionment with both the BJP and the Congress would immediately produce a wave in favour of the new anti-corruption party.

The gamble failed. The electronic and mass media that first strongly welcomed it turned against it, citing its flip flop in Delhi, which had also dismayed many of its own supporters as well as other onlookers. Even as it declared itself in support of the market system and capitalism generally, the AAP's decision to attack crony capitalism – and therefore some of the biggest business houses in the country – alienated the corporatized media. The fact that the AAP also saw itself as a movement–cum–party that would regularly resort to protest actions like mass sit-ins to press its demands made it suspect to elite standards of 'sobriety'. Moreover, standing candidates in over 400 constituencies meant there was little check on their quality, with only Kejriwal having national brand recognition. Its comparatively minimal resources were also stretched to the limit. It obtained a nationwide vote share of 2.3 per cent and only 4 seats (all from the state of Punjab); not bad perhaps for a first time entrant, but way below its expectations.

The AAP's effort to appeal to the widest cross-section of the public was a severe mistake. In presenting itself as a 'non-ideological', pragmatic, problem-solving entity, its ideological fuzziness ('neither left nor right', said its leaders) was a major deficiency in such polarizing times, when clarity of purpose was demanded. And by going so fast so soon it did not erect an internally coherent structure for debate and democratic decision-making to go along with its otherwise positive efforts at setting up neighbourhood committees for regular consultations with the local public. Aiming to challenge both the Congress and the BJP, the AAP can only do so by outflanking them not from the right but from the left. But how far to the left will it tack? This remains quite unclear. Does it have a classic social democratic vision of capitalist development? Or will it remain within the confines of a neoliberalism with a human face?

There is a lesson here to be learnt from the Latin American experience, where in Brazil, Bolivia and Ecuador new parties have developed out of social movements based on the factory working class and/or the poor peasantry and/or the indigenous population. This gave those parties a solid core base whose concerns were reflected in their programmes and in the social character of their activists. Operating from this position of relative strength they then sought to attract sections of the middle class. The AAP trajectory has been the reverse. First attracting middle-class activism, it has sought to extend its appeal downwards. This has already created debilitating tensions and contradictions within. It wants to grow as a movement-cum-party, but also wants to avoid sharp class and caste conflicts, i.e., be a something-for-everybody centrist force. Whether it will survive and grow as such, whether it can be pulled significantly leftwards or whether there will be a substantial left-directed breakaway grouping that wants to engage in more transformative class actions from below are still imponderables.

BUILDING AN ANTI-NEOLIBERAL PLATFORM

In Modi's first victory speech he called for a public mandate of ten years to complete his promised 'transformation'. The challenge then is to build a broad anti-neoliberal platform to prevent and reverse this Hindutva-ized right-wing class project. Where does the left figure in this effort?[6] The parliamentary left of the CPM and the CPI (Communist Party of India) – separated by bureaucratic rivalries, not irresoluble programmatic differences – suffered their worst ever defeat, securing nine and one seats, respectively. Long-term co-optation into the system reduced this left to trying, when in provincial power (West Bengal and Kerala), to become 'better' managers of capitalist development even after its neoliberal turn; and otherwise to being a 'responsible' opposition nationally. Stalinist-Communist collapse put an end to an already ongoing process of ideological demoralization of its cadres, rendering this left for the most part not capable (as it once was) of leading large scale and sustained mass mobilizations (although it remains involved in a few progressive grassroots struggles here and there). This loss of interest in, and capacities to, pursue such politics of mass protest is its real dilemma. In programmatic and policy terms, the left has become in all but name a social democratic force drifting rightwards domestically. It does not oppose state crackdown on 'Naxalites' or defend the right to full self-determination in Kashmir or the Northeast. But it maintains a stance against Western imperialism (its criticisms of Russia and China remain muted) that keeps it to the left of European social democrats.

Indian Maoism for the most part rejects electoral involvement. The CPI-ML (Maoist) is rooted among the poorest and most deprived Dalits and especially Adivasis of central India. It has waged armed struggle against the state for decades and survived, even grown, with a membership estimated in a few tens of thousands. But it fails to recognize the basic strategic dilemma facing Marxist revolutionaries everywhere – how to bring about a fundamental transformation in class power in liberal democratic capitalist societies, even if the strength of their 'best political shell' (as Lenin called it) varies. To be sure, in India liberal democracy is weak and brutalized. But even so, it is still meaningful and real. Moreover, even in backward capitalisms armed apparatuses of the state are strong and can look for outside support whenever seriously threatened. Ruling classes have learnt that if quick victory is not possible prolonging the war plays into their hands. Internal divisions arise among the insurgents and their mass base gets war-wearied. As it is, there is a disjunction between the Maoist base that looks primarily for concrete, near-term improvements in livelihood and the more uncertain, remote and ideologically driven aim of the leadership to capture state power. Over the last two years there have been many more defections and captures from the middle and higher levels of leadership. It is quite possible that the party has passed its peak of strength and influence and is in decline. Certainly the Modi government promises to ruthlessly crush them.

How then is an anti-neoliberal platform to be generated? Neoliberalism emerged through so great a transformation of class relations in favour of capital and against labour that derailing it would itself require a counter-shift in the relationship of forces so profound as to almost certainly put the issue of moving toward a 'twenty-first century socialism' on the agenda. Striving for a reversion to the postwar social democratic heyday is clearly now a chimera.[7] Raising standard social democratic demands such as universalizing free quality healthcare and education, provision of social security, of cheap and adequate public transport and housing, etc. – precisely because they are not achievable – become crucial spurs for generating an anti-capitalist momentum. This would be reinforced by the call for the spread of more direct forms of public participation and democratic decision-making along with existing representative institutions themselves needing change, as for example in moving towards some kind of proportional representation electoral system in India.

Indian economic development even under the new government will guarantee rising discontent, not least because the Modi promise of jobs for all seekers will fail. Two statistics say it all: 93 per cent of India's workforce is in the informal sector (compared to Brazil's 55 per cent); and the number of jobs generated by each percentage increase in economic growth in India actually fell radically from 2000 to 2010.[8] Capital intensity is rising in all sectors. This means that Modi's goal to raise considerably the proportion of industry's contribution to output (from around a quarter of GDP now) will not produce enough jobs, and even those created will be mostly informal and casualized. Accelerating the large-scale industrialization of agriculture, forced land acquisitions for industry and real estate, and more ruthless exploitation of marine, forest and mineral wealth will worsen the plight of the landless, small and marginal farmers, Adivasis and fisherfolk, as well as cause greater ecological devastation. Although over time the rural population will become a minority, it will remain substantial.

Moreover, there will be no 'disappearance of the peasantry' even as class divisions become sharper. Migration of more family members to expanding urban slums in search of livelihoods in the informal sector creates stronger living links between town and country. Contesting urban class disparities and struggles for the 'right to the city' can connect to more traditional demands for land redistribution and secure rural off-farm jobs and decent wages.⁹ Fleshing out such a broad programme for generating a mass struggle momentum from all oppressed sections is vital. But the main issue is how to generate the forces that can wage a prolonged and collective fight for it.

In India, transforming class relations of power must necessarily also be refracted through struggles around other identities of gender, caste, ethnic demarcations of various kinds. Though the majority of Dalits are agricultural proletarians, the majority of the latter are not Dalits. This means cross-caste class solidarities must be built. But this is not what the BSP, the main party of Dalits being led by middle-class aspirations, has so far sought to do. But progressives must nevertheless try and engage with that base through and besides its leadership. One great nightmare for the forces of Hindutva and the dominant classes they most cater to is the coming together of Muslims, Dalits, Adivasis and the most backward sections of the 'middle castes' who, in class terms, have more in common with each other than with others and easily constitute a numerical majority. The point is not to create a mere electoral bloc through promises of sectoral favours. This has been done in the past by both regional parties and the Congress, but does not endure because even as special group needs are to a limited extent addressed, common class needs are not.

Localized agitations in some socially mixed areas against some common oppression, like unwanted mining operations or large scale land displacement/takeovers, have led to collective organization and struggle. There are many such important struggles going on, but it has not been possible to bring them enduringly together even as this is increasingly seen as necessary by many of the leaders of such struggles and by the radical left. A mere stitching together of an artificial coalition – united only by the periodic meetings of representatives passing public resolutions or solidarity messages or even agreeing to put forward an agreed list of electoral candidates – will not do. The AAP reached out to various social movements up and down the country putting their leaders up as party candidates or supporting them as independents, but to no avail. Real solidarity has to come through collective struggles, not just around one group's problems but through involvement in the struggles of others. The first raises sectoral consciousness; the second a wider consciousness of the need for deeper change, a better appreciation of who one's allies are and a greater sense of self-confidence.

This problem of bringing together the politics of the singular and the universal has always required an organizational framework which, like a spider's web, has activists who are fanned out in different areas of struggle, and yet are integrated enough to be able to share experiences and understandings. This requires developing the capacity to shift personnel and resources in accordance with the differing tempos of struggles and the opportunities for rapid advance that arise on one or another front. There is no single party that can play this role today in India. But there are a whole host of groups and social movements that can help form the components of an anti-neoliberal platform. Nor should the existing left be immediately written off. The very shock administered by the scale of the right-wing Hindutva advance can spark a process of more fundamental rethinking and reorganization. In the best case scenario, the parliamentary left would recognize that it must completely jettison its Stalinist legacy organizationally and programmatically; forsake its governing ambitions and the compromises necessitated thereof; concentrate on re-energizing its existing cadres by making extra-parliamentary activity its primary preoccupation; and play a non-manipulative and dedicated supporting role where progressive struggles are already taking place. Internally, there should be a complete revamp to promote freedom of discussion with institutionalized tendency and faction rights; and there should be proportional representation at all levels of the leadership pyramid for such groupings (if they exist) as well as for women, Adivasis and lower castes in proportion to their membership.

The Maoists would need to realize that its current armed struggle strategy is a dead end, learn from the wider non-Maoist, anti-Stalinist Marxist traditions and come above ground to struggle even as they may wish to retain the defensive capacity to effectively protect their social bases against the eventuality of oppressor violence. The Indian state in the past has called for a dialogue with Maoists raising the possibility of mutual agreement on roughly these terms. This may be a deception, but it should be explored. Should New Delhi come to feel in due course that the military balance is so strongly tilted in its favour as to assure early victory then it will no longer be interested in such accommodation.

A more realistic scenario, perhaps, is that the CPI, CPM and CPI-ML (Maoist) will not carry out such self-transformation. In this case a new left will emerge through a process of splits (this has already happened to the student wing of the CPM), recompositions, realignments and fusions via extended dialogue and collaborations between small far left groupings (of which India has quite a few) that are outside the shadow of, and critical of, the big three. This will involve seriously exploring the possibility of engaging with the Bahujan Samaj Party and its Dalit base and of the possibility of a left breakaway from the AAP. There is the obvious necessity of working with the range of progressive social movements, peace groups, progressive medics, lawyers, teachers, the more radical NGOs, etc., up and down the country. These cover the whole range of concerns from civil liberties to the rights of

Adivasis, Muslims, sexual minorities, oppressed ethno-national communities in Kashmir and the northeast, the political under-representation of women, domestic violence and public harassment and workplace discriminations of all kinds. There are the struggles against ecological degradation of nature negatively affecting livelihoods and posing potential dangers caused by 'big development' from big dams to nuclear power stations to the proposed scheme to interlink major rivers.

Let us also not forget that the information and communications revolution has meant that the visibility and awareness of inequalities of income, wealth and power are greater than ever, arousing much stronger comparative dissatisfactions and anger. Mass struggles in other parts of the world now have rapid knock-on effects – witness the flurry of protests involving occupation of public spaces in country after country, even if the specific demands raised were different. Many of these struggles appear not to belong to the arena of class conflict, yet they do. Indeed, they must be taken up. Capitalist ruling classes nationally (as in India) and internationally are far more homogeneous despite all cultural, social and regional differences that exist between and among them. Their lines of coordination are smoother and shorter, their capacities for uniting when required quicker. In contrast, those they oppress are far more heterogeneous in their concerns, their lines of communication dispersed and weaker, their broad unification much more difficult to achieve. But it is because there is ultimately a class homogeneity lying behind this great heterogeneity that it is possible for them to coalesce. When this happens on a sufficient scale a revolutionary transformation of class and social relations can take place. Indian progressives know that times of great adversity are also times of real opportunities and possibilities.

NOTES

1   Precisely this assumption led many after the BJP's election failure in 2009 to underestimate the depth and spread of communal sentiment in milder and more virulent forms and therefore to dismiss the future prospects of the BJP, and particularly of Modi as a potential PM. Since I did not share this underestimation, I feared a BJP comeback, though not as a single majority party and of Modi's possible candidature. See my 'India's Paradigmatic Communal Violence', *Socialist Register 2009*, Pontypool: Merlin Press, 2008, p. 150.
2   *Times of India*, 22 May 2014.
3   Unlike East Asia, India never established a 'developmentalist state'. See Vivek Chibber, 'Reviving the Developmental State?', *Socialist Register 2005*, Pontypool: Merlin Press, 2004; and also his *Locked in Place: State-Building and Late industrialization in India*, Princeton: Princeton University Press, 2003.

4   The Constitution originally did not contain the term secular because of basic disagreements among the predominantly Hindu upper caste members of the Constituent Assembly as to its proper meaning. An amendment by Mrs. Gandhi in 1976, intended to put a gloss on her Emergency Rule, introduced the terms 'secular' and socialist' into the Preamble. An Indian secularism must address Hinduism's justification of the caste system that permeates all religious communities and mocks the very principle basic to secularism of *a priori* equal status of citizens. Caste discrimination was outlawed, but there is no constitutional call for abolishing caste, thereby implying that the *existence* of caste as distinct from practices of discrimination is acceptable. Affirmative action for lower caste Hindus was sanctioned, and then under pressure extended to Dalits among Jains and Sikhs. But excluded to this day are Dalit Christians and Muslims.

5   Romila Thapar, *The Past as Present*, New Delhi: Aleph Book Company, 2014, chap.9.

6   For a more comprehensive treatment of the Indian left see my 'Subcontinental Strategies', *New Left Review*, 70(July/August), 2011.

7   For all the justified criticisms from the left of his dismissal of Marxist economic thinking, Thomas Piketty does have the inestimable merit of recognizing (from within the mainstream of neoclassical economics itself) that the 'golden age' of social democracy is an unrepeatable exception. See his *Capital in the Twenty-First Century*, Cambridge, MA: Harvard University Press, 2014.

8   The employment elasticity of output between 2000 and 2010, when India had high average growth rates, actually fell from 0.44 to 0.01. See S.Mehrotra, A. Gandhi, P. Sahaand and B.K. Sahoo, *Joblessness and Informalization: Challenges to Inclusive Growth in India*, Institute of Applied Manpower Research, Planning Commission, Government of India Publication, Dec. 2012, p. 10.

9   David Harvey, *Rebel Cities: From the Right to the City to the Urban Revolution*, London: Verso, 2012.

BRINGING CLASS BACK IN: INFORMALITY IN BANGALORE

SUPRIYA ROYCHOWDHURY

While the exclusivist nature of capitalist growth, both in developed and developing countries, continues to be a shared concern, the political subjectivity of the poor in the current phase of capitalist development is a relatively unexplored domain. How does one relate economic hardship and deprivation to political action? This essay pursues this question in the context of urban poverty in developing countries. Informal work in which most urban poor seek their livelihood provides the lens through which the question of the poor's political agency is seen.

This question is important to ask in the present juncture for a number of reasons. The links between informal work and urban poverty have been empirically established as well as theorized. However, for much of academic scholarship as well as policy discourses, informal work is not the central, not even an important factor in the understanding of urban poverty. Issues relating to work, wages and employer-provided social insurance rarely feature in research and policy debates, which remain focused on a discourse of basic services and human resources (housing, health, education and so on). The dominant view appears to be that informal workers must look to governments for state-sponsored social security and welfare. What lends credence to this view is of course that a large number of informal workers are self- employed in petty production and lack a defined employer.[1] Although informal workers also include large numbers of wage earners found in a variety of unregulated frameworks, there is an emerging consensus that wage earners also must look only to the state for welfare related matters, rather than battle with private employers on wage-related issues.

The neoliberal state of course may be only reluctantly, rather than actively, engaged in social welfare, and this is an obvious but unacknowledged shortcoming of these theories. More importantly, it may be necessary to underline that the poverty and deprivation of the urban poor emerges from their insertion in the informal economy. The informal sector defines the structural exclusion of informal workers: petty producers/traders for the most part remain outside of mainstream channels of capitalist growth; subsistence and unregulated wage earners may be incorporated into large or medium capitalist enterprises, whether in manufacturing, construction or services, but at terms and conditions which are highly disadvantageous to them. However, the practice and imagination of lower-class urban activism – whether middle-class-led civil society associations or grassroots level organizations of the poor – rarely engage with the idea that informality is closely linked to economic policies and the broader economic structure. Much of this activism remains confined in a clientelist position vis-a-vis the state.

This feature of urban activism can perhaps be seen as part of the complex relationship between theory and practice. The structural exclusion of self-employed petty producers has been seen within the broader canvas of capitalist growth, as those who cannot be integrated within the technologically advanced, capital-intensive structures of the so-called modern economies. Such theorizations enrich our understanding of the dynamics of modern capitalism in developing countries, but perhaps leave little room for imagining a possible politics of informal workers. By its very nature, the domain of petty production eludes a coherent practical politics, and precludes the possibility of carving out a theory of the political subject in the context of urban poverty, inequality and deprivation. If a coherent theorization must necessarily draw on practical politics, a possible politics of the urban poor needs to bring back the centrality of ever larger numbers of wage earners, in a variety of unregulated frameworks, ranging from manufacturing to services, daily wage earners to contract workers, part-time to full-time work, public and private sectors. Efforts to organize wage earners in the unorganized sector are disparate and fragmented. What is notably absent is a framing of the issues in this sector within the broader context of the capital-labour relationship.

In this essay I draw on recent research on women workers in the new and dynamic Ready Made Garments (RMG) export industry in Bangalore.[2] The insertion of a workforce at low wages and working conditions in this rapidly expanding, global supply chain draws attention to the economic and political structures that anchor and support informal wage employment. It may then be necessary to trace the multiple and diverse ways in which the wage relationship manifests itself outside of the small, formal sector. The structural and everyday conflicts of this workforce with management, private capital and, indirectly, the state could be read through classical

Marxist analysis. But could one, then, make a case for a refurbished theory of class and class action, drawing on the wage relationship in the informal sector? And what would a possible politics of class look like in the present scenario? The ambivalence that marks the fledgling workers' movement in these domains indicates that one must now understand class and conflict within the specificity of the current context, determined by the evolving and complex relationship between global and domestic capital and the state.

WHY BANGALORE?

Bangalore is the icon of India's information technology revolution, a dynamic space for the banking, finance and hospitality sectors, and an attractive destination for an upwardly mobile, professional middle and upper class of citizens with multiple channels of connection to the global economy and culture. On the other side, the decline of the old public sector had an inevitable impact on the city's profile, as large campuses of sprawling state-owned companies sold much of their land and downsized their functions and employees. In turn, this led to the gradual decline of the small-scale sector in industry, the growth of which had been largely dependent on its ancillary status to the large public sector.

Thus a tech-savvy middle class emerged to represent Bangalore's new status as India's silicon valley, even as the urban underclass – represented both by large numbers of landless, unskilled rural migrants and residents of old inner-city slums – no longer had state-owned enterprises or the small-scale industries sector as a possible space of employment. Nor could they get a foothold in the city's new economy, led as it is by knowledge- and capital-intensive domains, predominantly in services, such as IT (information technology) and ITES (information technology-enabled services), finance, banking, insurance, real estate and so on. The gap between the rich and the poor is not a new phenomenon in cities of the developing world. But as cities become sites of spectacular wealth and consumption, the widening chasm between those who can access the benefits of global marketization and those who remain on the margins, or are in structurally disadvantageous positions within it, becomes far more stark. These contradictory tendencies are significantly visible in Bangalore.

URBAN POVERTY, WORK AND INFORMALITY IN INDIA

The overall consensus in the literature appears to be that although there was marked acceleration of economic growth after the economic reforms were introduced in 1991, the low share of manufacturing employment in India contrasts sharply with the rapid rise seen, for example, in South Korea, Thailand and China.[3] The largest job creation has been, as is well known, in the service sector. Several scholars have registered a sense of pessimism, particularly regarding the role of IT and ITES in leading development in India insofar as the largest numbers of the workforce do not have access to the necessary skills to be part of these sectors.[4] Interestingly, a recent World Bank publication has sounded a similar cautionary note: 'It is unclear that India's human capital and infrastructure are adequately developed to allow India to leapfrog the labor intensive manufacturing stage and follow the growth path of an upper middle income or even an OECD-type economy'.[5]

The non-availability of organized manufacturing jobs is obviously related to the poverty of the urban underclass. In 2009-10, a quarter of India's urban population lived in poverty. Of this, close to half were working as casual labour, and close to a quarter were self-employed (Table 1). There has occurred a steep rise in the number of workers in the so-called informal sector, both in self-employment and in casual wage work (Table 2). The period from 1999-2000 to 2004-05 records an increase in self-employment for both males and females. The rise is particularly sharp for urban males. The structure of urban employment also shows that among men there has occurred a decline in regular salaried employment and a rise in casual labour.

While a closer analysis of the structure of workforce participation in different categories would be beyond the scope of this essay, I would highlight here that there is indeed a close relationship between unregulated forms of work and the poverty of urban households. Tables 3 and 4 provide a glimpse into informal work in manufacturing and construction. Thus in 1999-2000, 29.6 per cent of workers in the manufacturing sector were poor. Of these, 45.5 per cent were casual labour and 38.2 per cent were self-employed. Similarly in the construction industry, 43.9 per cent were poor in 1999-2000, and of these 53.1 per cent were casual labour and 24.4 per cent were self-employed.[6] Similar patterns are seen in other service-related sectors such as trade, hotels and transport, with high percentages of self-employed and casual workers and high poverty ratios. Industrial growth, as it has occurred, has moved towards high technology, capital-intensive production processes, providing opportunities to those with higher skills and who lack a place in assembly line production processes where large numbers of semi-skilled or on-the-job skilled men and women typically found work in an earlier era. These processes led to the crowding of the urban underclass in low-income, self-employed and casual wage labour.

Table 1: Poverty Across Different Status of Workers, 2009-10 (%)

	Rural	Urban
Self-employed	28.7	24.1
Regular Salaried	18.6	12.5
Casual Labour	46.4	49.6
Total	38.3	25.2

Source: Compiled from National Sample Surveys, various years.

Table 2: Distribution of Urban Workers by Working Status, 1972-2010 (%)

	Self-employed		Regular Salaried		Casual Labour	
Year	Male	Female	Male	Female	Male	Female
1972-73	39.2	48.4	50.7★	27.9★	10.1	23.7
1977-78	40.4	49.5	46.4	24.9	13.2	25.6
1983	40.9	45.8	43.7	25.8	15.4	28.4
1987-88	41.7	47.1	43.7	27.5	14.6	25.4
1993-94	41.7	45.4	42.1	28.6	16.2	26.2
1999-2000	41.5	45.3	41.7	33.3	16.8	21.4
2004-05	44.8	47.7	40.6	35.6	14.6	16.7
2009-10	41.1	41.1	41.9	39.3	17.0	19.6

Source: Compiled from National Sample Surveys, various years. ★Estimate.

Table 3: Workers (15-64 years) in Poverty by Selected Industries
in Urban Areas, 1983-2000 (%)

	1983	1987-88	1993-94	1999–2000
Agriculture	54.4	58.4	52.6	53.1
Mining	31.0	37.5	27.8	28.2
Manufacturing	42.1	38.5	30.4	29.6
Construction	51.4	50.6	44.4	43.9
Trade and hotels	40.9	37.5	31.5	29.2
Transport	39.6	38.4	32.2	32.8
Government and Education	21.4	17.1	11.6	9.6

Source: India: Urban Poverty Report, 2009.

Table 4: Percentage of Workers (15-64 years) by Activity Status and
Industry in Urban Areas, 1999-2000 (%)

	Self-employed	Salaried	Casual labour	Total
Agriculture	41.1	30.4	72.3	53.1
Mining	26.6	18.1	53.8	28.2
Manufacturing	38.2	17.7	45.5	29.6
Construction	24.4	16.7	53.1	43.9
Trade and hotels	28.5	24.9	46.5	29.2
Transport	40.0	18.9	55.4	32.8
Gov't & Education	12.6	8.9	44.1	9.6

Source: Report on Urban Poverty, 2009.

RE-IMAGINING CLASS

Through the nineteenth and twentieth centuries, the growing political
salience of the industrial working class via trade unions and social democratic
parties provided the ideological/political anchoring for redistributive justice
and welfare in advanced industrial countries. The decline of that class began
in the West towards the last quarter of the twentieth century, and its eclipse
has continued through the early part of the twenty-first. In the current
context, welfare itself has become more broadly defined than workers'
rights. Thus we have the new conceptualizations of welfare as citizens'
rather than workers' rights,[7] or as claims of the disadvantaged (handicapped,
elderly, women, children), broadly defined.[8] These kinds of theorizations,
reflecting the reality of western welfare state dynamics, have moved the issue
of welfare away from the working class and its politics.

Developing countries like India present a somewhat more complex
picture for our understanding. The industrial workforce here has rapidly
changed its profile in the last two decades, one could say, without giving
itself the benefit of the kind of sustained growth and empowerment which
the working classes in the West underwent in the last two centuries. The
industrial proletariat showed early signs of maturity and organized political
involvement from the 1920s onwards in the nationalist movement. In
the period following independence, the organized sector of the industrial
workforce became incorporated into the state system through a large public
sector. Although attuned to collective bargaining and other structured
negotiations, this workforce was nevertheless inward-looking, less interested
in broader debates relating to policy than in economic gains and middle-class

aspirations. The organized workforce in the large private sector could be similarly characterized.

Constituting only a small fraction of the country's workforce, organized industrial workers were weakly positioned to provide the political face to demands for justice and welfare, which, in any case, were subject to multiple interpretations by many competing groups defined by crosscutting social identities. The enlargement of the industrial working class as an expected consequence of economic and industrial development, along the western model, did not take place in India. In fact, as the era of economic reforms and globalization took off, the decline of the organized industrial workforce began before its substantive expansion and empowerment could take place. The decline of organized manufacturing and the decimation of trade unions on the one hand, and the growth of employment practices such as outsourcing, home-work and contractualization on the other, have created a workforce diversely located in varied activities which do not offer a ready or easy framework for collective action. The space for welfare demands is now predominantly occupied by social (rather than economic) identity-based organized groups; even erstwhile class-based radical Marxist parties, such as the Communist Party of India (Marxist-Leninist) now speak almost exclusively as advocates of social groups such as tribes. Trade unions, for the most part, see themselves as negotiators between labour and management in specific situations, rather than as espousers of workers' rights within the definitional framework of capital-labour conflict.

The state's position on welfare increasingly has been to provide minimum economic needs (limited days of work at minimum wages, food security) rather than addressing structural issues such as the decline of employment in manufacturing, the increasing casualization of work and so on. Policy interventions by the state, or service delivery interventions by NGOs, into the condition of urban deprivation have been predominantly defined in terms of single issues, that is, provision of services (school mid-day meals, slum development). Within this framework, the urban poor are defined as receivers of services rather than in terms of their structural position in the political economy.

For its part, the world of work, spread widely across a large number of informal occupations – ranging from push-cart or pavement selling to daily wage work in construction sites – does not facilitate collective activism. There may be localized demands for land, water or sanitation, but the nature of such activism is fragmented, issue-based, limited in time and space, lacking a consistent political face. The profile of the worker does not appear as a significant element in the identity of the urban poor. The urban poor, in fact, emerge largely as a fragmented subject, for the most part as consumer of specific items of consumption.

DEBATING INFORMALITY AND ITS POLITICS

Recent theorizations of informality have taken into account the intransigence as well as the vastness of the informal sector in developing economies. Neoclassical economists underline informality's diversity to stress that informality may be a correlate of poverty, not its cause, and to caution against any blanket regulatory policy response.[9] They recommend sector- and scale-specific corrections and stepping up the coverage of state protection to currently uncovered workers, thereby retaining the flexibility and efficiency aspects of informality. Even left-leaning scholars acknowledge that instead of regulating the private employer-employee relationship, what is needed is 'a new Social Contract in which governments would guarantee minimum living standards and security to people as people and not as workers'. As Manuel Castells goes on to say: 'The challenge, then, is how to develop new organizational forms ... how to redefine the struggle for equality in terms other than wage levels, working hours, and benefits attached to conventional employment'.[10]

The specifics of the new organizational forms have proved challenging to theorists of lower-class movements. Partha Chatterjee's by now much discussed and debated concept of 'political society' is an imaginative intervention into the problematic of informal sector politics. He underlined

> the difficulties of class organization in the so-called informal sector of labour, where the capitalist and petty modes of production are intertwined in mutually reinforcing tangle. Despite sincere efforts of many activists, Leninist strategies of working class organization have floundered here. The political leaders of the left have instead turned their attention to ... political society.[11]

In later work, Chatterjee has suggested that the democratic state in India must extend some benefits to lower classes; political society, presumably, acts as the principal vehicle through which lower-class demands get carried to, and claim the attention of, state agencies.[12]

Echoing this, ethnographic work on informal workers, mostly women, spanning India, Mexico and South Africa highlights the importance of

> non-party-political people-based organizations like SEWA [the Self-Employed Women's Association] ... there is no shortage of government

schemes ... what is needed, however, is intermediaries like SEWA to help access these schemes ... *The central policy question, then, is – why are there not more organizations like SEWA?*[13]

A combination of state-sponsored social security and NGO and grassroots activism thus holds out the promise of the future incorporation of informal sector workers within the larger growth story of capitalism.

Finally, others have gone so far as to say that even when workers organize and act as workers (occupational groups, industrial workers), their demands are made to the state rather than to their private employers. Rina Agarwala, in a comparative study of *bidi* (cigarette) and construction workers across three Indian states, found that contemporary movements reflect a gradual shift of attention from employer to the state, from work and wage-related issues to more general social welfare-related rights. According to her, this represents class politics (workers use their worker identity cards to get state-sponsored social insurance) and an alternative labour movement model. 'Significantly, their emerging identity simultaneously asserts their informality and their position within the working class. Their identity is not expressed as an antithesis to capital'. This leads Agarwala to the conclusion that this alternative model 'incorporates the informal sector as an active participant in capitalist growth'.[14]

There is, then, an emerging convergence of opinion towards a matter-of-fact, or even normative, acceptance of informal work as a part of modern capitalism, and an inclination to conceptualize new models of organization, essentially those which work with the state to bring some welfare to the urban poor. Very broadly speaking, the idea that a democratic developmental state must necessarily respond to the needs of the poor appeals to common sense. But it is in fact quite problematic. The democratic state's commitment to the poor cannot be read off from welfarist enactments, in a context where asset distribution remains deeply skewed, and governance of welfare highly flawed.[15] Similarly, Agarwala's assertion that informal workers are acting as a class by seeking welfare from the state, but refraining from wage related demands from their private employers, is very troubling as it fails to address the central issue of income poverty.

Recently, important new research has identified informality as deeply structured by the capital-labour relationship. Scholars have stressed the process of informalization of the formal sector through contractualization, outsourcing and home-based work, and shown how this is pinned to the changing institutional structure of industrial capitalism in the globalization context, where global as well as domestic capital can take advantage of unregulated employment practices. Kalyan Sanyal, in a now widely cited book, distinguishes between two domains of the informal sector.[16] The first involves informalized employment practices, taking place within the circuit of capital as a result of increased competition amidst globalization. The second (and Sanyal's point of departure from other work on the informal sector) involves the continuing displacement of large numbers of both rural and urban underclasses from their traditional means of livelihood: separated from the means of production and survival, they cannot in fact be incorporated within the capitalist structures of production, whether in agriculture or in industry. Thus it is that huge numbers become *self-employed*; given the nature of their operations – minimum capital investment, use of self and/or family labour, meagre earnings at subsistence levels – their singular characteristic feature is that they are, for the most part, disconnected from the mainstream capitalist economy. Nevertheless, this labour force performs a vital function for capital in providing a peripheral basin which can absorb the ever growing numbers who cannot be absorbed into the mainstream economy. Sanyal's central theme of petty production as permanently outside of capital in principle challenges received notions of transformation, as petty producers can never be even the reserve army of labour. And it is consistent with other narratives, such as Barbara Harriss-White's, which see the informal sector as not only a domain manifesting economic inequality, but as involving multiple domains of social discrimination, such as caste, tribe, religion and gender which, in fact, provide the key to the structuration of informality.[17]

While self-employed petty producers are certainly caught in the contradictions of capitalism, the question of their political agency remains a complex challenge. In the absence of the workplace, and a workforce potentially available for unified action on the classical issues of wages, working hours and conditions, informal sector theories have highlighted that petty producers, home-based workers and street sellers now claim urban land as a means to life and livelihood.[18] Land can thus be seen, on this view, to have replaced wages as the most keenly contested urban resource. To what extent does such theorization provide us with conceptual tools for thinking about organized political action of the urban underclass?

First, the nature, as well as the scope, of activism in the domain of land contestations is highly circumscribed in time, space and range of activities.[19] The urban poor's claim to city land remains tied to isolated efforts at claim-staking, organized by NGOs and civil society associations. Secondly, the dynamics of slum land contestation most typically is framed in the discourse of legality/illegality. Thus, slum dwellers are typically seen as illegal encroachers. The demand for slum land, represented by NGOs and slum associations has, however, rarely challenged the legality/illegality paradigm by posing an alternative and specific vision of land redistribution (such as rural land reform). In other words, an alternative vision of urban planning, based on lower class claims to urban land, has never emerged. Finally, it has to be noted that urban land is a finite resource which cannot be reproduced. There are thus natural/physical limits to the redistribution of a finite resource.

It could, then, be argued that locating the petty producer – and land as his/her major resource – at the centre of the urban question to some extent weakens the possibility of imagining a political subject in the context of urban poverty, inequality and deprivation. While petty production is central to the domain of the urban informal sector, ever larger numbers of the urban poor are wage earners in an increasing variety of employment relations which are informal and unregulated, varying from daily wage, contract work, apprenticeships, casual work, in a variety of industries (construction, apparels exports) and services (maintenance, security, hospitality, entertainment, transportation) across the public and private sectors. The insertion of this workforce, often on highly disadvantageous terms and conditions into the evolving structure of manufacture and services in an increasingly globalized setting, calls attention to the economic structures that anchor these inequities. This is why it is necessary to trace the multiple and diverse ways in which the wage relationship manifests itself outside the formal economy.[20]

BANGALORE'S READY MADE GARMENTS INDUSTRY

Karnataka is one of India's fastest growing states.[21] The sectoral trajectory of growth here more or less replicates the national patterns, that is, agriculture remains the largest employer, even though the share of agriculture in GDP has been declining steadily. Comparatively, industry and services show low growth in employment, although the share of both, particularly of services, in GDP is much higher.[22] As a city, Bangalore's growth pattern has been singular, where urban employment is dominated by the service sector.[23]

Once known to be a haven for state-owned industries, since the mid-1990s, the city has seen the dismantling of this structure through closures, privatization, outsourcing, downsizing and the sale of land.[24] A large number of small-scale industrial units in Bangalore had developed as a satellite structure to the large public sector; the extinction of many small industrial units was one result of the drying up of orders from declining government enterprises.[25] If employment in organized manufacturing industries has stagnated, the situation in the small-scale industries (SSI) sector highlights the impact of this decline on the urban poor.

In terms of industrial employment, two main sectors have expanded significantly during the last two decades, both in the context of globalization of the city. First, the growth of the city's economy in terms of IT, ITES, financial services, hospitality and entertainment, as well as up-scale housing requirements of the city's upwardly mobile sections, led to a sustained boom in the construction industry. Secondly, the relatively new Readymade Garments (RMG) exports industry developed as part of the emerging global supply chain in garments production and retail. Both sectors, it is important to note, have played an important role in expanding the city's economic growth as well as employment opportunities for unskilled labour. However, this workforce is largely migrant, non-unionized, and lacking collective bargaining rights to improve their incomes and living standards over time as well as access to education and skills that could lead to occupational and social mobility inter-generationally.[26]

While the textile industry is one of the oldest in India, production and export of Ready Made Garments from India is a relatively recent pheno-menon, increasing exponentially from the mid-1980s onwards. The genesis of the relocation of RMG production from North America and Western Europe to developing countries, particularly in Asia, has been widely chronicled. The availability of relatively cheap labour in these countries has been the driving force of this relocation. The global RMG industry thus emerged as a huge supply chain wherein large retailers and global brands source their supplies from a range of small, medium and large producers in Asian locales, who use a low paid, predominantly female, unskilled workforce for the production of apparels.[27] About 92 per cent of workers in the RMG sector are unorganized (96 per cent of the women, and 86 per cent of the men).

Karnataka, and Bangalore in particular, has been a central player in the growth of garments exports in India. The exact number of production units and workers is not known; however, it is likely that there are around 1,000 units in Bangalore, and around 400,000 workers. A process is underway whereby larger units are emerging on the basis of acquisitions and mergers; at the same time the industry remains essentially diverse in terms of structure, with a large number of firms employing as few as 50-100 employees. Regulated, in principle, through a Minimum Wage Board and formal wage revisions, the RMG industry demonstrates, nevertheless, classic features of informality, with a workforce that is non-unionized and footloose. The dynamics of this industry highlight the deeply structural conflicts between this workforce, on the one hand, and local producers and global brands and retailers, on the other.

Women workers in the RMG industry in Bangalore are predominantly young migrants who have moved to the city from rural or semi-rural areas over the previous 15 years.[28] The educational profile of women workers in RMG clearly indicates that a significant percentage of the women had been exposed to more than eight or nine years of schooling, but lacked in any kind of vocational skills. From our survey it was indicated that almost 15 per cent were illiterate, 24 per cent had studied up to 9th class and 54 per cent up to 10th and above.

In Bangalore the stipulated minimum wage until recently for unskilled RMG workers was 152 Rupees (approximately $2.50) per day.[29] The minimum wage (for 24 days of work) comes out to Rs 3,648, and assuming a household of four, the per capita monthly income would be around Rs 912 (approximately $150), which is just above the urban poverty line for Karnataka, fixed at Rs 892 (approximately $140) per month per capita. Our survey indicated that in terms of monthly wages 124 out of 200 women were receiving in the range of Rs 3,000-3,500 (between $58-60 per month). A large number of the women were married (130), and for 96 the spouse was the main or principal earner. If we assume that for most of these women their income was supplementary to that of their spouses, the total household income would possibly be in the range of Rs 7,000-8,000 (approximately $135) per month. In a context where most of the women were living in nuclear families, consisting of husband, wife and three or four children (only 64 were unmarried), this placed them well above the poverty line (although the garment worker's wage itself fell just short of the stipulated minimum).

We found that 14 out of the 200 women were receiving a salary of Rs 2,000-3,000 ($35-50) per month, and another 38 were receiving in the range of Rs 2,500-3,000 (between $40-50) per month, which means that no less than 25 per cent of the workers earned daily wages of only Rs 125 or less, far below the stipulated minimum wage. Notably, the single earners (50 women) were not necessarily in the low-income category, but the largest numbers were, with average earnings around Rs 3,000 per month. Thus the monthly per capita income for 25 per cent of the households was only Rs 750, well below the urban poverty line in Karnataka. Only 24 of the total of 200 women were earning in the range of Rs 3,500-4,000 and above (approximately $66-70 per month). Overall, then, a large number of women employed in the RMG industry were receiving less than the stipulated minimum wages. In cases where these women were single earners their per capita household incomes placed them below the poverty line.[30]

Working hours fluctuate in this industry, predominantly determined by the pressure of orders from global buyers. In the study almost all workers said that they worked overtime, between one and three hours per day on average. Although the stipulated remuneration for overtime is double pay, only 112 out of 200 women in our study said that they received this; as many as 20 said that they receive no extra pay for overtime work, and the rest said that they receive between single to half pay. As most workers are employed on a piece rate basis, management frequently presents large work targets which naturally require overtime work. Overtime is, therefore, a frequently used instrument to extract more work without adequate compensation, as long hours of unpaid or underpaid overtime effectively amount to a lower wage than is formally recorded. As a management approach this widely shared practice speaks of the industry's built-in tendency to extract maximum value from each worker without adhering to stipulated hours of work or of remuneration.

The average woman migrant who lacks education and skills that she can sell at a higher wage has no option but to accept this coercive exchange. A large number of women told us that if they refuse to do overtime, they are asked to leave, not admitted the following day or verbally told that *'if you don't want to do, there are others looking for your job outside the gate'*. An almost universally reported feature of RMG work life seems to be extremely harsh production targets, implemented by abusive floor supervisors who monitor every minute of the workers' time at the workplace.

The RMG sector provides a space for factory-based, urban employment to thousands of rural/semi-rural women who do not have access to skills, education, social networks or other resources, such as familiarity with English or computers. In this sense this globalized industry provides much needed paid factory employment to migrant women. Yet low wages, insecurity of work and a coercive work environment are the hallmarks of this sector. Not only are jobs unprotected, but the women themselves move frequently within the industry to look for a better environment or settle for part-time domestic service positions. Occupation-related health hazards and long working hours leading to excessive physical strain are frequently cited reasons, alongside shop floor coercion, for quitting work.

COLLECTIVE ACTION

Three organizations mainly address workers issues in the RMG sector in Bangalore: CIVIDEP (Civil Initiatives for Development), an NGO which combines leaders drawn from middle-class activists with former RMG workers; the registered trade union, GATWU (the Garments and Textile Workers Union); and Munnade (a Kannada word, which means 'leading forward'). From the late 1980s, CIVIDEP, whose primary concern was to organize women workers in their residential neighbourhoods, provided significant leadership. It deliberately kept away from the factories, did not directly address wage-related issues and focused instead on activities pertaining to microcredit, awareness-raising and so on. Subsequently, as there was more and more of a perceived need for imparting a more unionized character to workers issues, Munnade and GATWU were formed in the mid-1990s.

Munnade is a grassroots organization of women workers which looks after issues of sexual or verbal harassment within factories, providing counselling and generally working on raising awareness. Local committees of the Munnade are area-based (rather than factory-based), which address gender- and family-related issues as well as training of women leaders. GATWU has a national level presence through its affiliation to the New Trade Union Initiatives (NTUI), the independent union federation which over the last decade has especially concentrated on organizing informal workers. In Bangalore, GATWU works mainly on wage- and work-related issues. As unionization within factories is illegal, most women workers are reluctant to engage in union-like activities. Collective bargaining is unknown in this sector. Thus GATWU's membership currently stands at around 6,000 only, which is a miniscule proportion of the total number of women employed in Bangalore's RMG industry. GATWU's functioning must be seen within the context of these constraints.

While a framework of government regulations has been put in place, through the Minimum Wage Act and the Minimum Wage Board, the implementation of these is hugely flawed.[31] The efforts of the GATWU have therefore been oriented towards implementing the minimum wage. These efforts, however, are confined to negotiations with the Labour Department, participating in Wage Board deliberations or taking up these issues in court.[32] As trade union recognition is absent, the Union is handicapped by having no recourse to collective bargaining mechanisms within factories.[33]

The constraints on collective bargaining reflect the broader politics of trade unionism as well as in the structure of the industry. The mainstream trade unions, including those on the traditional left like CITU (the Centre of Indian Trade Unions) which is politically attached to the Communist Party of India (Marxist), have not engaged in a sustained manner with grassroots issues in the RMG sector. For GATWU, the principal protagonist for RMG women, local level struggles are centred around specific issues, such as protesting sudden dismissals or termination of individual workers. Local struggles, then, are defined more in terms of advocacy at the level of government departments. In the absence of alliances with other unions and political parties such struggles at local level do not translate into an imagination, let alone a moment, of political resistance, and larger mobilizations, despite the NTUI's articulation of the need for this at the national level.

The challenge for the workers' organizations is that, in terms of structure, the industry demonstrates conflicting tendencies. On the one hand, a certain degree of centralization and concentration is taking place.[34] Along with these features, however, in response to the 'great recession' in the West and reduction of orders, the industry has moved towards 'just in time' production, smaller orders, shorter, more flexible delivery times. As such, the industry increasingly uses home-based, piece-rated workers, adopting flexibility and outsourcing as employment practices. Thus even the largest companies hire up to 10-15 per cent piece rate workers for short durations.[35]

Without taking away from the value of small, albeit valuable steps, taken by the GATWU so far, three important limits to collective action could be highlighted here. First, facing a non-unionized factory-based workforce, and additionally an invisible, home-based workforce, the union appears to be trying to wage a classical workers' struggle, while the essential conditions necessary to construct this struggle are denied. Secondly, the profitability of the industry clearly emerges from low wages, unpaid overtime, shop floor coercion, denial of termination benefits and so on. Ideologically, the NTUI does try to do a serious critique of employment relations as perceived within the broader fundamental conflicts of capital and labour, but this rarely reaches or makes an impression on grassroots union activists, let alone informal workers themselves. GATWU, therefore, appears to be walking a tightrope in Bangalore, where the structural factors available to traditional trade unions are unavailable to it, nor is there much discursive space for the NTUI's broader, political/ideological critique.

Finally, we need to see the industry as occupying a shadowy space in the city. Its physical location is in Peenya, an industrial area in western Bangalore, which has been called the graveyard of the failed engineering sector, and makes for its very marginal representation in Bangalore's public domain. The IT and RMG sectors can be said to have made comparable contributions to the city's economic growth. Yet IT has made Bangalore India's Silicon Valley (or the next Singapore), IT leaders straddle regional and national political spaces and IT workers are seen as the face of India's future. On the other hand, the RMG sector has rarely, if ever, stepped out of the shadows of the failed engineering sector. Industry leaders have no visibility or presence in the public domain. A huge and powerless female workforce provides the silent and invisible backbone of a sector that is closely connected to the globalized apparels industry.

Since the roots of urban deprivation remain, then, embedded in the workplace, can the issue of welfare really be addressed, as it is now being done in the development discourse, as distinct from the domain of work? And indeed, can welfare (seen as social security) be delinked from wages, hours of work, pension, severance payment? These are not just academic questions, but also deeply political ones. To what extent can we talk about capitalism without at the same time acknowledging class, and class conflict, even when it is not expressed through an explicit class politics? Class conflict, now all but gone from academic and political discourses, still provides a vital clue to understanding the nature and dynamics of urban deprivation.

NOTES

I am grateful to Aparna Sundar, Carol Upadhyay and Vinay Gidwani for their comments at a presentation of this paper at the National Institute of Advanced Studies, Bangalore, in August 2013, and to Michael Goldman for his comments on an earlier draft. The paper was also presented at the Annual Conference of the Indian Society for Labour Economics, December 2013.

1   In the usage here, petty production includes work in production, trade and services.

2   The empirical materials used in the case study of the Ready Made Garments industry are drawn from a research study entitled, 'Migration, Informal Work and Welfare: A Policy Perspective on Karnataka's Cities', which was sponsored by the Planning Department of the Government of Karnataka, India.

3   A frequently noted feature of the structure of the Indian economy is that while the share of agriculture in GDP has steadily declined, and is now 12 per cent, employment in agriculture remains high at 53 per cent. The share of the manufacturing sector in GDP as well as in employment is around 15 per cent, much less than in other developing countries. Although the share of services in GDP is high and continues to rise (55 per cent in 2011-12), its share in employment is around 25 per cent. See Economic Survey, Government of India, 2012-13, available at http://indiabudget.nic.in; Ahmad Ahsan and Ashish Narain, 'Labor Markets in India: Developments and Challenges', in Sadiq Ahmed, ed., *Job Creation and Poverty Reduction in India*, New Delhi: World Bank and Sage, 2007; S.R. Hashim, 'Economic Development and Urban Poverty', in Ministry of Housing and Urban Poverty Alleviation, Government of India and UNDP, *India: Urban Poverty Report*, New Delhi: Oxford University Press, 2009. The continuing high employment in agriculture, despite low productivity, points to absence of employment opportunities in the other two sectors.

4   See Francine Frankel, *India's Political Economy: The Gradual Revolution, 1947-2004*, Princeton: Princeton University Press, 2005; Atul Kohli, *Poverty Amidst Plenty in the New India*, New York: Cambridge University Press, 2012; Pranab

Bardhan, 'Notes on the Political Economy of India's Tortuous Transition', *Economic and Political Weekly*, 44(49), 2009.

5   Ahsan and Narain, 'Labor Markets in India'.

6   Jeemol Unni, 'The Unorganized Sector and Urban Poverty: Issues of Livelihood', in *India: Urban Poverty Report*; Hashim, 'Economic Development and Urban Poverty'.

7   Manuel Castells, 'World Underneath: The Origins, Dynamics and Effects of the Informal Economy', in Alejandro Portes, M. Castells and L.A. Benton, eds., *Informal Economy: Studies in Advanced and Less Developed Countries*, London: The John Hopkins University Press, 1987, p. 310.

8   Paul Pierson, *The New Politics of the Welfare State*, Baltimore: Johns Hopkins Press, 1996.

9   Basudeb Guha-Khasnobis, Ravi Kanbur and Elinor Ostrom, 'Beyond Formality and Informality', in B. Guha-Khasnobis et al., eds., *Linking the Formal and Informal Economy: Concepts and Policies*, Oxford: Oxford University Press, 2006; Ravi Kanbur, 'Conceptualizing Informality: Regulation and Enforcement', 2009, available at http://kanbur.dyson.cornell.edu.

10   Castells, 'World Underneath', p. 310.

11   Partha Chatterjee, *The Politics of the Governed*, Delhi: Permanent Black, 2004, p. 68.

12   Partha Chatterjee, 'Democracy and Economic Transformation in India', *Economic and Political Weekly*, 46(16), 2008.

13   Namrata Bali, Martha Chen and Ravi Kanbur, eds., 'Bridging Perspectives: The Cornell-Sewa-Wiego Exposure Dialogue Program in Labor, Informal Employment and Poverty', Sewa Academy, 2012, pp. 621-48.

14   Rina Agarwala, 'From Work to Welfare: A New Class Movement in India', in Rina Agarwala and Ronald J. Herring, eds., *Whatever Happened to Class? Reflections from South Asia*, Lanham: Lexington Books, 2009; see also Rina Agarwala, 'The State and Labor Activism: The Case of India', *The Journal of Industrial Relations*, 54(4), 2012.

15   For critiques of Partha Chatterjee's view of Indian democracy, see especially Mary John and Satish Dehpande, 'Theorising the Present: Problems and Possibilities', and Amita Baviskar and Nandini Sundar, 'Democracy versus Economic Transformation', *Economic and Political Weekly*, 43(46), 2008; as well as Supriya Roy Chowdhury, 'Civil Society and the Urban Poor', in Ajay Gudavarthy, ed., *Reframing Democracy and Agency in India: Interrogating Political Society*, London: Anthem Press, 2012.

16   Kalyan Sanyal, *Rethinking Capitalist Development: Primitive Accumulation, Governmentality and Post-Colonial Capitalism*, New Delhi: Routledge, 2007.

17   Barbara Harriss-White and Nandini Gooptu, 'Mapping India's World of Unorganized Labour', *Socialist Register 2001*, London: Merlin Press, 2000. See also Harriss-White, 'Work and Well Being in Informal Economies: The Regulative Role of Institutions of Identity and the State', *World Development*, 38(2), 2010.

18   Kalyan Sanyal and Rajesh Bhattacharya, 'India's Bypass Approach to

Urbanization', *Economic and Political Weekly*, 46(31), 2011; Chatterjee, *Politics of the Governed*.

19   See Supriya RoyChowdhury, 'Slums and Civil Society: The Limits of Urban Activism', in Darshini   Mahadevia, ed., *Inside the Transforming Urban Asia: Processes, Policies and Public Actions*, New Delhi: Concept, 2008; and RoyChowdhury, 'Civil Society and the Urban Poor'.

20   In later work, Sanyal traced the continuous reproduction of the wage relationship in new urban spaces. See Sanyal and Bhattacharya, 'India's Bypass Approach to Urbanization'.

21   During the second half of the 1990s, Karnataka was the only state in India to have experienced a growth rate of more than eight per cent. The economy grew at 7.1 per cent in 2001-02, 9.2 per cent in 2006-07 and 8.2 per cent in 2010-11.

22   In 2012-13, the share of agriculture in the state's GDP was 15 per cent, while the share in employment was as high as 56 per cent. The share of industry and services in GDP was 25 per cent and 56 per cent respectively, while their employment share was 16 per cent and 26 per cent respectively. These figures indicate, as do the national figures, that despite low productivity, agriculture remains the highest employment provider, reflecting absence of commensurate growth of jobs in industry and services.

23   In 2004-05, the service sector accounted for 66 per cent of the total employment in Bangalore, which was higher than the average for million-plus cities (62 per cent) and the average for urban India (57 per cent). M.R. Narayana, 'Globalization and Urban Economic Growth: Evidence for Bangalore, India', *International Journal for Urban and Regional Research*, 35(6), 2011.

24   The number of state-owned enterprises came down from 105 to 80 during the decade of the 2000s.

25   The closure of many small units in the Peenya Industrial Area has drawn much attention as representing the decline of the city's manufacturing hub.

26   See Supriya RoyChowdhury with K.S. James and B.P. Vani, 'Migration, Informal Work and Welfare: A Policy Perspective on Karnataka's Cities', Bangalore: ISEC, chapter 2.

27   The RMG industry constituted 7.87 per cent and 8.37 per cent share in India's total exports during the year 2004-05 and 2005-06, respectively. There are around 30,000 garment manufacturing companies in India producing just for export. Out of this some 5,000 are in the medium to large range. India's exports of RMG in 2005-06 amounted to $8.5 billion, showing a growth of 29.6 per cent over the previous year and a Compounded Annual Growth rate of 8.8 per cent in the preceding periods since 2000-01 when the total exports of RMG were worth $5.569 billion. The literature on labour in global supply chains is large and varied. For a sampling, see M. Vijay Bhaskar, 'Can Cluster Development Programmes Ensure Decent Work? Evidence from Indian MSE Clusters in Global Value Chains', *The Indian Journal of Labour Economics*, 51(3), 2008; Geert De Neeve, 'Power, Inequality and Corporate Social Responsibility: The Politics of Ethical Compliance in the South Indian Garments Industry', *Economic and Political Weekly*, 44(22), 2009; Judith Heyer,

'Social Policy and Labour Standards: A South Indian Case Study', ESRC, May 2011; and Mayumi Murayama, 'Globalization and Female Employment in India and Bangladesh: RMG Workers in Post MFA Era', in Murayama, ed., *Employment in Ready-Made Garments Industry in Post MFA Era: The Case of India, Bangladesh and Sri Lanka*, JRP Series, No. 140, Chiba: Institute of Developing Economies, 2006.

28   I draw here from a survey of 200 women RMG workers in the Peenya Industrial Area. This study, combining questionnaire-based interviews with qualitative discussions, was conducted during 2011-13.

29   It should be noted here that in 2009 the minimum wage for an unskilled worker had been fixed at Rs 172 per day (inclusive of Dearness Allowance) by the Minimum Wages Advisory Board. This has so far not been implemented with any degree of uniformity across the industry.

30   These findings are confirmed by a recent survey of RMG worker wages conducted by the Garments and Textile Workers Union. See GATWU, 'Wage Survey of Garments Sector in Bangalore', 2012.

31   Although a Minimum Wage Board is responsible for the revision of fixation of wages every three years in this sector, after the Wage Notification of 2001 there were no revisions until a Minimum Wage Notification came in 2009. While this Notification brought some much-awaited revisions, the industry failed to implement these for over a year. In response to legal proceedings initiated by GATWU, the Labour Department issued a new Notification in March 2010 diluting the provisions of the 2009 Notification. The claim put forward by the Labour Department was that there had been a 'clerical error' in the 2009 Notification. GATWU moved the High Court on the 2010 Notification and obtained a judgment quashing the notification. According to GATWU members, by not complying with the 2009 Notification, without even a challenge in court against the notification, the industry clearly violated the Minimum Wages Act.

32   An important achievement for the GATWU in recent years has been the securing of Dearness Allowance for workers who are paid above the minimum wage, who had earlier been deprived of this benefit.

33   Trade unions in this sector increasingly rely on retailers' pressure and global NGO-led movements to ensure compliance. On corporate social responsibility in this sector, see De Neeve, 'Power, Inequality and Corporate Social Responsibility'.

34   Six of the largest companies, Bombay Rayon Fashions, Gokaldas Exports, Gokaldas Images, Export Garments, Shahi Exports and Sonal Garments employ together nearly one third of the total strength of RMG workers in Bangalore.

35   See Mohan Mani, 'Issues of Garment Sector Labour and the Global Supply Chain: Some Lessons from Bangalore', unpublished paper, 2012.

NUMSA, THE WORKING CLASS AND SOCIALIST POLITICS IN SOUTH AFRICA

SAM ASHMAN AND NICOLAS PONS-VIGNON

The South African election on the 7 May 2014 marked 20 years since the end of apartheid and the achievement of democracy. The result was hardly surprising, with the African National Congress (ANC) winning 62 per cent of the vote. But the idea of unchanging ANC hegemony is far from accurate. Only 35 per cent of those eligible to vote backed the ANC, a decline from 54 per cent in the first post-apartheid election in 1994. In Gauteng, the biggest centre of industry and most populous province which contains the cities of Johannesburg and Pretoria, the ANC's share of the vote fell from 64 per cent in 2009 to 55 per cent in 2014. The Democratic Alliance (DA), a pro-business party based on old white-led parties and new sections of the black middle class, increased its vote from 17 per cent in 2009 to 22 per cent. But most startling of all, the Economic Freedom Fighters (EFF) of former ANC Youth League leader Julius Malema, formed only eight months ago, won over a million votes (6.4 per cent), gained 25 MPs and is now the second largest party (after the ANC) in both the North West Province (a mining area which includes the town of Marikana) and Limpopo (Malema's home province.) The EFF's slogan is 'Economic Freedom in Our Lifetime'; its supporters wear red berets and greet each other as 'Fighter'; and its success reflects frustration and anger with the slow pace of change since 1994. What is more, the election came amidst considerable turmoil in the labour movement. Three issues are of note and form the backdrop for this essay.

First, the remarkable all-out strike by over 70,000 workers at the world's three major platinum producers: Anglo American Platinum, Lonmin and Impala. The strike lasted for five months over the first half of 2014 and was the biggest strike in South African mining history. The settlement fell short of the workers' demand for a R12,500 living wage, but workers made significant gains and, critically, their union remains unbroken.[1] (The miners' action was almost immediately followed by an all-out strike over pay by 220,000 workers in the steel and engineering sectors.) South Africa's platinum belt has been at the eye of the storm for some time. President Jacob Zuma was forced to cancel a pre-election visit to Marikana, both the centre of the strike area and the site of the massacre of Lonmin platinum workers when they struck in August 2012, for fear of the reception he might receive. The Marikana massacre was a turning point in South African history that is at the centre of the discussion below. The majority of the platinum strikers are members of the Association of Mineworkers and Construction Union (AMCU) which has grown rapidly as the previously dominant National Union of Mineworkers (NUM) – whose leaders are central to the ANC – has degenerated as an effective union force. Although it may not necessarily be articulated in this way by workers and strike leaders, the AMCU action was an expression of workers' independence from the Alliance of the ANC, the South African Communist Party (SACP) and the Confederation of South African Trade Unions (COSATU), which is the largest union federation (NUM, until Marikana, was its largest affiliate). For such a large and important strike to take place outside the auspices of the Alliance, and in the face of the condemnation of much of the Alliance, is a significant departure from the past.[2]

Second, COSATU remains paralyzed by its own internal crisis, and stood apart from the platinum workers' struggle as a result, as it has from the issues around Marikana and the massacre more generally. It is not difficult to see why: NUM may have haemorrhaged members to AMCU, but it remains a powerful force within COSATU, the SACP and the ANC.[3] COSATU is split over how critical its stance toward the ANC should be. Its General Secretary Zwelinzima Vavi – a powerful and popular critic of ANC policy – returned to COSATU in April 2014 after an eight-month suspension orchestrated by the right wing in the federation. A desperate ANC managed to negotiate a ceasefire in COSATU hostilities until after the election, but demanded that Vavi campaign for it. The union federation remains deeply divided, with the leadership of ten unions grouped around President S'Dumo Dlamini, and nine other unions backing Vavi and taking a more critical stance to both ANC and SACP leaderships. The nine have demanded Vavi's reinstatement and a special COSATU congress to elect a new leadership. However, merely reinstating Vavi will not end the tensions, and seeing it in personal terms about Vavi alone is a mistake both as an analysis of the past, and as a strategy to go forward.

Thirdly, there is NUMSA, the National Union of Metalworkers of South Africa. NUMSA is now COSATU's largest affiliate with 338,000 members and the unofficial leader of the left bloc inside COSATU. The resolutions adopted at NUMSA's Special Congress in December 2013 marked the most important rupture in South African politics since 1994. The union refused to endorse the ANC in the election. It called on COSATU to break away from the Alliance. It resolved to organize a new United Front to coordinate struggles in the workplace and communities (much as the United Democratic Front did in the 1980s) and to explore the establishment of a new Movement for Socialism. It is widely speculated that this new Movement for Socialism will eventually contest elections, possibly even the local elections that will take place in 2016, but final decisions about its shape and activities will not be taken until March 2015 and there are different positions and emphases within the union about precisely what form it should take. NUMSA plans also to launch township-based political discussion fora in order to build the United Front so as to include a broad range of forces; to hold nine provincial consultative conferences to further discuss these developments which will lead to a national conference; and to hold a national summit on service delivery to try to link together struggles over service delivery with workers' organization. The union will also explore various recent international examples of building left parties such as those in Venezuela, Brazil, Greece and Germany in order to try to learn lessons in advance of its decisions next year. These steps clearly mean an end to NUMSA's attempts to push the Alliance to the left from within. The establishment of some form of mass, union-based, socialist organization outside of the Alliance would amount to a historic step in the history of the South African labour movement. In addition, NUMSA has resolved to organize across value chains, including announcing that it will organize mineworkers.

As Leonard Gentle has argued, both the split inside COSATU and the emergence of Julius Malema's Economic Freedom Fighters are a consequence of the unravelling of the alliance of forces which removed Mbeki and put Zuma into office.[4] The SACP, COSATU and the ANC Youth League backed Zuma despite the fact he did not promise significant change in policy. The SACP gained cabinet positions as a result of Zuma's victory, a culture of cronyism developed around Zuma, and Malema was expelled when he overplayed his hand. COSATU is now split between those who wish to remain loyal to the ANC/SACP leadership, strategy and policy and those who can see both the failure of ANC policy and feel the pressure of workers and the poor from below. This is explicitly recognized: 'We in NUMSA understand the crisis in COSATU as simply a reflection of the on-going class struggles in the wider South African society in general and inside the ANC led alliance in particular'.[5]

And so it is tempting to argue that the tectonic plates are shifting. Strikes and service delivery protests reflect deep dissatisfaction on the ground. The possibility of some form of workers' party, a historical break from the ANC much debated in the past, now seems a more likely prospect than at any time since 1994. The SACP is in deep crisis, with members on both sides inside the COSATU divide. The possibility of a major regroupment and a new political formation has already boosted many on the left. However, the obstacles and the challenges facing the 'NUMSA moment' are also great. Not least of these is the ANC which, now that the election is behind it, is likely to do all it can to ensure that NUMSA is isolated from the rest of the Alliance as a maverick 'red' union, one possibly to be expelled from COSATU.

This essay explores this turbulent conjuncture. Firstly, we look at the development of the South African economy and the working class after 20 years of neoliberal ANC policy and the effect this has had on the structure and the organization of the working class. Secondly, we look at the move from the 'Marikana moment' to the 'NUMSA moment', and how NUM's degeneration has highlighted the weakness of unions in defending their members. The future for union organizing in the mines could be one of considerable turmoil, with AMCU (with the likely support of NUMSA) and NUM vying to recruit and maintain membership. Thirdly, we look at some of the challenges facing the NUMSA project. Whilst we reject the argument that organized workers are a form of labour aristocracy, and we defend the potential of unions in the twenty-first century to act as a force capable of organizing workplace struggles and linking to communities, the challenges should not be underestimated. A myriad of divisions exist between workers: between the employed and unemployed, permanent workers and the precariously employed, the community (especially youth) and workers, and between workers and social movements.[6] While much may be resolved in the coming months, the 'NUMSA moment' is both a product of the movement from below, and could prove to be a key turning point within it. If NUMSA continues to be bold, it may well succeed in building a movement to attract to it those who are increasingly disillusioned with the ANC and ready to embrace a credible alternative which aims to unite organized labour, township activists and the left. But simultaneously, NUMSA also carries the burden of left hopes and potential organization. Will it fail by seeking to do too much?

CONTINUITY AND CHANGE IN THE
MINERALS-ENERGY COMPLEX

The South African system of accumulation has long been dominated by what Fine and Rustomjee dubbed the 'Minerals-Energy Complex' (MEC).[7] Capital concentrated and evolved around core sectors around mining and minerals processing, with the state providing support for key sectors, particularly through giant electricity and steel parastatals. This was combined with the extreme exploitation and political oppression of the black majority which predated the introduction of apartheid in 1948, but which was systematized by apartheid. The mining and energy core of the economy was, and remains, capital intensive and there are strong linkages within and between the core sectors but relatively few linkages between the core sectors and the rest of the economy. Industrial development thus has been highly skewed, and a large reserve army of labour has been reproduced systematically. Alongside concentration in particular sectors, the economy has also been marked by extremely concentrated patterns of ownership, with the historic division between English-speaking and Afrikaans-speaking capital being eroded over time, and six diversified conglomerate groupings coming to dominate the entire economy by the 1980s.

Whilst undoubtedly much has changed in South Africa since 1994, the bitterness at the base of society is rooted in what hasn't changed. This is graphically seen in the ongoing high levels of unemployment, which is close to 40 per cent of the population if 'discouraged job seekers' are included, with that figure rising for youth unemployment, and poor basic service delivery for housing, water and electricity. At the same time income inequality has actually increased since 1994 as a consequence of rising inequality within the labour market due both to rising unemployment and rising earnings inequality.[8] There has been extensive corporate restructuring across the South African economy in line with the global restructuring of capitalism in accordance with the imperatives of finance. South African conglomerates have 'unbundled' and 'rebundled', internationalizing and financializing their operations whilst focusing on core concerns within South Africa.[9] At the same time finance has grown to 20 per cent of the economy, and job creation since 1994 has largely been in financial and low-value added services.[10] And some 40 per cent of the population remain excluded from the formal financial sector altogether. The bloated and powerful financial sector remains extraordinarily non-developmental. There is a crisis in levels of long-term productive investment whilst the financial system fuels speculation, hoarding and the long-term export of capital. And high interest rates in line with a neoliberal macroeconomic policy framework attract short term 'hot' money inflows, fuelling debt-driven consumption and increasingly indebtedness, including an enormous rise in unsecured lending at the base of society.[11]

Financial groupings, after unbundling from the major conglomerates and undergoing restructuring themselves, have been well placed to benefit from the financialization of the Minerals-Energy Complex, the major feature of South African 'development' since 1994.[12] Combined with the effects of trade liberalization in manufacturing, there has been a relative deindustrialization of the economy. The minerals-energy core of the economy remains central: minerals and mineral-related products continue to make a significant contribution to output. Some 60 per cent of South Africa's exports in 2012 were from gold, platinum group metals, iron ore, coal, motor vehicles, iron and steel and non-ferrous metals; and platinum, coal and gold are the most important contributors both to revenue from mining and to mining employment.[13] Finance, mining and energy interests are also important sources of power in post-apartheid South Africa, acting to defend capital's position (particularly with regard to rent-seeking in mining) and to block alternative policy measures, such as lowering the price of cheaply produced industrial inputs in steel.[14] This domestic power has combined with, as we saw above, the internationalization and financialization of operations.

The eye of the storm has very much been platinum as the platinum miners have demanded a living wage across the sector of R12,500 a month to address low pay. But there remains also what is sometimes referred to as the colonial or the apartheid-era wage gap: the persistent discrepancy between wages earned by black and white workers, the former having allegedly 'low skills'.[15] This gap has combined in recent decades with more general global wage repression. The platinum workers' demands produced an unsurprisingly hysterical response from the employers and the business press who claimed the industry would no longer be able to continue with such an increased labour share of revenues relative to its executives and shareholders.[16] But the biggest mining houses in the platinum industry had enjoyed the years of the commodity boom which lasted until the great crash, during which time (international) shareholders gained extensively, earning very high rates of return on capital as compared to the Johannesburg Stock Exchange Top 40.[17]

The stormy class conflict in the platinum sector needs to be seen in this context. And it highlights more general trends and the failure, despite a plethora of ANC policy proposals, to actually tackle poverty, unemployment and inequality. This is in large part because, under South African neoliberalism, poverty reduction has been couched in 'residual' terms, and constrained by the needs of budget balancing (in quantity) as well as by the pervasive and inefficient implementation of New Public Management practices throughout the state.[18] But a black capitalist elite has emerged, through corporate restructuring in and around the MEC, through the re-allocation of mining rights and the gaining of tenders secured via access to the state.[19] The latter range from large (e.g. the infamous 'arms deal', where Western arms companies promised billions of investment which never materialized) to tiny tenders, which play a key function of rent allocation (and class formation) at the local level.[20] This new elite is not only as non-developmental as its white counterpart, it is embedded deep within ANC structures with Cyril Ramaphosa, former NUM leader, Lonmin executive, and now ANC Deputy President the most obvious case in point. (Ngoako Ramatlhodi, the minerals resources minister appointed just after the May election, was revealed to have R20 million of shares in a 'Black, Economic Empowerment' 'partner' of Anglo American Platinum, according to the *Mail & Guardian*.[21]) Both the white and black elites have been served by the National Treasury and the South African Reserve Bank, which have promoted and extended neoliberalism in South Africa.

POLITICAL LIBERATION, NEOLIBERALISM AND FRAGMENTATION OF LABOUR

The battle to unseat apartheid took place in both factories and communities, with workers contesting despotic, racist workplaces. The emergence and formalization (through trade unions) of resistance to despotism on the factory shop floor spread throughout the country from the 1970s thanks to the development of black trade unions and extended to communities living in townships. There struggles were fought, including consumer boycotts of goods or services provided by white-owned companies. This combination of productive and reproductive struggles retrospectively could be considered 'social movement unionism' (SMU).[22] SMU coalesced for a few years in the United Democratic Front (UDF), and succeeded in forcing the apartheid regime to negotiate a transition, while facilitating the return of the ANC to the fore of South African politics. But while the leaders of the ANC were negotiating the transition, and attempting to ensure an end to the flaring violence, they embraced, without ever saying so explicitly, the neoliberal orientation which had been adopted by the apartheid regime since the late 1970s at the insistence of the powerful conglomerates which own much of the South African economy.

Neoliberalism globally has entailed a restructuring of workplace relations that has led to greater labour casualization and has resulted in growing precariousness, all carried out in the name of the need for greater 'flexibility', though flexibility was an *a posteriori* reason given for the casualization of labour, since the term only emerged in the 1980s.[23] The outsourcing of an ever-larger number of parts of production to third parties or contractors has been a key part of this neoliberal restructuring. In South Africa, where labour-capital relations were characterized by the racial despotism of apartheid, this restructuring has had specific effects. Racism involved both a high tolerance for labour squalor on the part of the employers, not unlike that described by Eric Hobsbawm in the context of early industrialization in Manchester, and a very hands-on control over workers in the productive *and* reproductive spheres, most visible in mining. The rise of black unions, which first focused on unfair decisions by employers, in particular dismissals, contested the discretionary power of employers over the labour process and led employers to seek to reassert their authority. This authoritarian restoration has taken the form of outsourcing, though in a manner markedly more brutal than in the North, causing workers to experience an extreme precariousness reminiscent of the sweating system of the early industrial revolution.

This can be seen through the form taken by the task-based system of remuneration in the forestry sector. There, integrated forestry and forest product companies called grower-processors (GPs) have retained ownership of plantations while outsourcing all silviculture and harvesting from the mid-1980s. In so doing, they have put enormous pressure on contractors to do more with less, leading to the development of chain subcontracting, with a large section of producers operating informally. Pressure has been passed on to workers through unilateral increases in task levels, leaving many to work themselves to death chasing unrealistic task objectives. Many work on weekends to 'make up' for their inability to realize their individual objectives during the normal week; should they get sick, injured or exhausted – increasingly frequent albeit under-reported occurrences – they can seldom if ever get medical attention, nor dream of getting paid (or indeed keeping their job) if they miss a day's work. The payment system indexed on 'performance' is obscure to most workers (as achievements are recorded unilaterally by employers); its beauty for capital is that the decline in individual productivity, caused by the brain drain of both foresters and experienced workers since the start of outsourcing, does not affect downstream profit levels because a less productive worker can be offset by other workers who only get paid for the accomplished labour.

This is not just the case in forestry, as similar processes have been observed in numerous sectors, from agriculture to mining, and across informalized activities. This explains the failure of attempts to build a 'class compromise' to improve productivity in South African workplaces. Such attempts, inspired by the corporatist intent of the post-apartheid industrial relations framework as well as by the then-popular 'flexible specialization' approach, alienated both unions, who were unwilling to be superseded by apolitical works' councils, as well as capital, which was reluctant to relinquish power over the labour process, resorting instead to increased outsourcing which undermined the very basis of co-management.[24]

This response by capital was made easier by the existence of the enormous reserve army of labour which exists as a consequence of the structure of the economy, dominated by the MEC core of capital-intensive sectors, but then reinforced further by rising unemployment, first as a result of trade liberalization and then second by the effects of the global economic crisis compounded by regional poverty and economic crisis, notably in neighbouring Zimbabwe. The result has been a crisis of labour casualization with a marked shrinking of the 'core' permanent workforce and the spread of subcontracting throughout the economy. This of course had a knock-on effect on labour's ability to organize and respond, for the fragmentation of workers dents trade union power. That trade unions which were formerly militant and resilient failed so badly to respond to this attack, albeit common by international standards, was surprising in South Africa. The undermining of workers' rights through the use of third party employers has recently received much attention. COSATU demanded the banning of labour brokers ahead of the 2009 elections although this was to become one of Jacob Zuma's many forgotten promises.

As elsewhere around the world, the fragmentation of labour is the prime challenge for the building of a credible progressive project driven by trade unions. Can NUMSA succeed in rebuilding working-class unity in a context of growing fragmentation? The accusation of representing a 'labour aristocracy', made up of the shrinking core of protected MEC workers unwilling to risk embracing the cause of casual workers, seems unfair when applied to NUMSA. The union has been proactive in the sectors where it is present to leverage its bargaining power to improve and equalize the conditions of workers of all status – whether directly or indirectly employed. In spite of some victories, the challenge remains paramount, as the struggle is far from won even in the core automotive sector (where a number of employers have recently relocated to neighbouring countries), and cannot be limited to these. It is therefore crucial to look at struggles from below alongside struggles from above (for instance around policy orientation) in order to generate the inclusive working-class strength and legitimacy necessary to fight a dominant and confident capitalist class closely aligned – and intertwined – with the state. There are positive signs in this regard, from the commitment to value chain organizing, which holds the potential to link struggles which have been atomized as a result of productive restructuring (and at times poor union strategy), to the insistence on the building of a broad progressive front from below.

FROM THE MARIKANA MOMENT TO THE NUMSA MOMENT

The context of present developments, then, is one of high unemployment and extensive labour casualization, ongoing township protest over service delivery and waves of workers' struggle, with inequality endemic – a South Africa with 'a "world-class" business centre surrounded by human misery … to a significant extent a product of post-apartheid government'.[25] It is not surprising that it is mining which has provided a series of key flashpoints, given how central it has been to the history of capitalism in South Africa, but also to union organization and to the liberation movement as a whole. As we saw above, mining has highlighted key issues: the financialized nature of accumulation, corporate unbundling and internationalization; rewards to both domestic and international finance as an important source of deepening inequality; and also the rise of labour broking and the fragmentation of labour.[26] Corporate control of mining has gone through extensive restructuring, but while black capital has made inroads, much colonial and apartheid era capital remains in control, with new multinational entrants such as Glencore/Xstrata now important players in coal and also platinum. But it was the Marikana massacre, and the strike wave of which it was part, which shined the spotlight not only on the poor pay and working conditions of miners, but also the failure to provide an adequate alternative to what might be called the 'classic' Migrant Labour System (which dominated labour recruitment from the 1920s to the late 1970s) and how these factors have combined with the general failures in social and economic infrastructure provision around housing and health and education across the mining areas and South Africa more generally.[27]

The Migrant Labour System was established by the mining-finance houses, initially in gold, both to ensure its labour supply and to drive out the private recruitment companies which extracted heavy fees from the mining companies. It entailed both racialized workplace organization and a regional system of labour recruitment that drew in labour from across southern Africa, allowed for infrequent visits home and saw workers housed in compounds which acted as a means of labour control, but also, latterly, provided an important site of union organizing.[28] This classic form began to break down from the 1970s onwards as gold price rises increased demand for labour and as Mozambique (which gained independence in 1974) and Malawi became less willing sources of supply, so forcing mine bosses to increase wages in order to attract South African labour.[29] More fundamental change was resisted up until the 1980s, however, when labour militancy profoundly challenged mine labour regimes. Mine bosses used layoffs and casualization through labour broking to try to discipline labour, outsourcing 'non-core' functions. Mining houses began to mix long and short distant migration, and introduce new company housing schemes.[30] Increasingly, the option to take a 'living out' allowance and leave the compounds was introduced and negotiated by NUM. But in the absence of adequate housing provision by either the public or the private sector, this has seen many mineworkers opting to live in 'the shacklands' surrounding the mines, often supporting two families (one in the mining area and one in rural areas). Given how the structure of the economy is so skewed, and how deep is unemployment, mineworkers' wages play a central role in supporting un/under-employed dependents in areas of rural destitution such the Eastern Cape, with one mineworker in South Africa now supporting ten other people. Many mineworkers are also increasingly indebted thanks to the unsecured lending of the 'Mashonisas' and other sectors of South Africa's liberalized financial system.[31]

Forrest points to how the reconfiguration of the Migrant Labour System then combined with post-apartheid legislation to produce contradictory effects.[32] The Minerals Resources and Petroleum Development Act and the Immigration Act of 2002 both emphasized the need for local recruitment of labour and required mining companies to pay special levies if recruiting from overseas. This has further increased short distance migration, though the distances involved may still be hundreds of kilometres. The Bafokeng also challenged mining rights on its land and won an agreement with Impala Platinum to prioritize local labour. Workers get round the definitions however, with retrenched 'migrants' often gaining work through labour brokers as 'locals'. And while the increasing penetration of labour brokers into mining has undermined pay, conditions and union bargaining, it has also eroded the monopoly position of the historic mining recruitment house, TEBA, which has diversified and now has its own financial services section, UBank, in which NUM is a major shareholder.[33] This fracturing of the old recruitment system has also led to union corruption, with NUM officials being accused of gaining jobs for friends and relatives or taking bribes for jobs. The failure of NUM to contest the shareholder-driven accumulation of the mining houses has led to an explosion of resentment, and the rapid rise of AMCU, including the emergence of rank-and-file strike committees during the strike of 2012.[34] Moreover, the exposure of NUM intensified the divisions in COSATU, producing a sharp contrast in response to the massacre between COSATU affiliates, and in their ability to reflect critically about whether they too could face a meltdown in membership in the face of allegations of cosy relationships with employers, issues which affect both sides of the divide within COSATU.[35]

And so the massacre at Marikana in August 2012 lies at the heart of all the issues under discussion. It revealed the intransigence of capital, the lengths to which the ANC was prepared to go to demonstrate its support for the mining houses, and the desperate struggle of workers against low pay and appalling conditions (in both mining and the rural areas). Subsequently, the ANC has hidden behind the ongoing nature of the Marikana Commission of Inquiry to avoid addressing the subject of the massacre substantively, a Commission which, whatever its final report says, has revealed the extraordinarily close collaboration between Lonmin, the police, the ANC and NUM during the course of the strike of 2012.

The emergence of AMCU is also a key feature of the present moment and one which is redrawing the map, at least in terms of industrial relations. For South African elites, the platinum workers' strike was, amongst other things, an acute crisis of crisis management. The ANC leaders set up an emergency task team to bring about a settlement to the dispute – which failed to do so. The ANC leadership could no longer draw upon layers of loyalty to the ANC given AMCU's painful emergence out of NUM, especially in the wake of the Marikana massacre. This was reflected in the vote for the EFF in the 2014 election; indeed, the ANC was the only political party not invited to attend the rally held in Marikana to mark the one-year anniversary of the massacre (every other political party in South Africa attended and addressed the crowds). AMCU's emergence now opens up the possibility of regroupment within and between South Africa's trade union federations alongside the political regroupment initiated by NUMSA.[36] There is speculation that NUMSA and AMCU may now form some kind of alliance, particularly as NUMSA has stated it will organize mineworkers. There are obstacles to such an alliance, but if NUMSA is expelled from COSATU, as is widely predicted, this increases the likelihood of regroupment at the level of union federations and possibly the formation of a new national federation.

The process is fraught with difficulties, with the possibility of many dirty tricks in recruitment battles and even of more killings than we have seen already in mining. NUM is hoping to rise again in platinum, which may have been a distinct possibility if the AMCU strike had been defeated. A further tumultuous period for union organizing in the mines is likely in any case, particularly given that platinum mining houses are threatening major restructuring in the wake of the strike and as a consequence of new plans for mechanization. AMCU and NUMSA both now represent important groups of workers at the core of the MEC. The Alliance must know that it is facing the prospect of important battalions being outside its influence and control. The employers know this too, and have made it clear that an important reason the platinum producers do not wish to relent on the demand for R12,500 was the fear that it would spread – initially to gold where AMCU also has a presence (though it is a minority union), but then to other sectors of mining and beyond.[37] This is now being referred to in the press as 'the Marikana effect' – new demands for a living wage and for a closing of the historic wage gap coming from rank-and-file workers. Mineworkers' demands for a living wage were reflected in NUMSA's negotiating processes, with union members objecting to the usual percentage wage increases.[38] The extent to which the difficulties involved in building new alliances between metal workers and mineworkers can be overcome will be a critical determinant of what lies ahead.

CHALLENGES FACING THE NUMSA PROJECT

The stakes are high for all concerned. NUMSA faces a number of serious challenges in its attempt to build a new movement for socialism in South Africa. Aside from the international opposition an endeavour like this is bound to attract if it shows sign of success (an issue which we will not focus on in this article), there are difficulties within South Africa. NUMSA's approach to a movement for socialism is explicitly inclusive of all progressive forces. The union's Deputy General Secretary Karl Cloete says, 'We want to attract all those who have a left agenda – period'.[39] This is at odds with the attitude of sections of the Alliance towards the many social movements fighting the commercialization of basic services which have challenged the ANC since the late 1990s, and which have been excluded, dismissed (as 'ultra-left' by former President Mbeki) and often targeted by police violence. However, NUMSA is not a social movement but a trade union with strong roots in industrial workplaces and a tradition of democratic control by workers.[40] It intends to remain focused on industrial struggles, even while it hopes to champion a new movement for socialism. This entails some tensions around its legitimacy, and not least in a context where unemployment, under-employment and casualization have become pervasive.

NUMSA is aiming to build on discussions to 'mobilise and conscientize' the working class as part of building left organization to advance the struggle for socialism. NUMSA is comfortable with a Marxist discourse which situates class struggle at the heart of the analysis of capitalism and the practice of building socialism, whatever questions may arise over how this us understood. Many on the South African left had come to criticize such an approach, partly because of their disillusionment with established left parties, in particular the SACP. However, an important feature of the present is the support NUMSA's call has received from many of those associated with social movements, with criticism more likely to be about the slow pace of progress and implementation of NUMSA's resolutions rather than about the goals themselves. Combined with the democratic approach promoted by NUMSA, drawing on its impressive level of internal democracy, this holds a crucial promise for progressive politics in South Africa and beyond. Of course, NUMSA will still also have to deal creatively and inclusively in its relationship with social movements, which have flourished in South Africa, achieving important, if often temporary, victories. Yet social movements, for all their achievements, have dramatically failed in sustaining and growing movements which could challenge neoliberalism, let alone capitalism.

That said, some have asked whether NUMSA has done 'an assessment of the appropriateness of the trade union form in the context of the changing working-class under neoliberalism'.[41] The big question, however, with regards to a trade union's ability to mobilize for broad social change hinges on how we understand 'the working class'. If the latter is seen as limited to workers employed and unionized, then its shrinking size may justify recent claims that movements which focus on reproductive issues, especially through the contestation of commodified basic services, may offer a broader base for struggle.[42] But it also important to keep in mind the limitations of these movements as agents of transformation. It is further necessary to challenge the notion that the 'working class' can be understood in such narrow terms, or sub-divided between proletariat and precariat.[43] Notions of an increasingly fragmented working class, from which the poor are sometimes excluded (if not outright opposed to workers) have flourished, not least in South Africa, since the 1970s.[44] Today, they reflect a 'counter-movement' away from a focus on unemployment as the key socioeconomic indicator towards a renewed interest in 'poverty', whether multi-dimensional, chronic or otherwise described.[45] In South Africa, as in many parts of the world, many people are employed *and* poor. Indeed, labour squalor (mostly affecting blacks) has always been a constitutive feature of southern African capitalism.[46]

But what matters politically today is that the victory of the Tripartite Alliance against apartheid has been associated with deepening labour casualization. In spite of the presence of COSATU and the SACP in the ruling coalition, workers are losing ground in the class struggle in South Africa. It is indeed in this light that the fragmentation of the working class ought to be understood. Neoliberalism is the result of deliberate strategies by capital to weaken the power of organized labour, and trade unions in South Africa often have failed to respond to the onslaught, and particularly to the rise of 'labour brokers' across the economy. But while this has fostered pessimism regarding trade unions' progressive potential, the response to capitalist divide-and-rule strategies cannot stem from an acceptance of their consequence (a fragmented working class), but from rebuilding an inclusive approach to the working class.[47]

What is striking in South Africa is that, in spite of a limited albeit much-advertised social grant programme, survival still hinges on the wages of those who are separated from the means of production and depend on access to wage labour for their reproduction. This takes two complementary forms: the importance of access to (often casual and poorly paid) wage labour for the survival of the poorest; and the prevalence of wage transfers within kin networks, as we pointed to with mineworkers, which explain why many share the same class identity regardless of their individual occupational status.[48] Class identities in South African townships are shaped by 'dependence on employment and the mixing of worlds of work at the household level and over the lifetime of an individual'.[49] The casualized nature of the labour market in South Africa means that the same individual is likely to experience alternate periods of unemployment and employment, the same affecting other members of one's extended family. Indeed, in spite of the weakening of organized labour, working-class consciousness and activism is incredibly resilient in South Africa. This is not only true in mining but also in agriculture, a sector where formal union organizing is extremely weak.[50] This labour activism, which is of course an essential part of the (hitherto scattered) 'rebellion of the poor', represents a crucial opportunity for NUMSA, and its ability to draw on it and give it organizational support will be critical to its success. NUMSA is indeed intending to build on movements wherever they exist, in workplaces or communities, in a spirit of raising class consciousness.[51]

Whether or not NUMSA, and a workers' party formed in the not too distant future, can successfully challenge South African neoliberalism, will depend on the outcome of a whole series of immediate challenges, which will determine what kind of an organization is born, what forces it will bring under its umbrella and what sort of party it will be. First and foremost is the question of the degree of support for NUMSA and the extent to which the rest of the Alliance can succeed in isolating NUMSA and its allies. NUMSA is likely to attract the vehement opposition of both capital and the ANC-controlled state; the resources available to counter the new movement for socialism are far greater than those available to build it. Furthermore, it is likely that the SACP will attempt to discredit NUMSA by proposing its own blueprint for the elusive 'second stage' of the National Democratic Revolution, as it is now dubbed. The vitriolic debates which have already occurred between NUMSA's Irvin Jim and the SACP's Jeremy Cronin are likely only to increase in number and intensity.

Second, there is the question of the future trajectory of COSATU. The stance to be taken by the left unions and the many socialists within the federation is at this stage unclear. NUMSA's ability to hold firm and carry out its ambitious programme of movement-building will hinge on the success of its grassroots mobilization of workers; but it will also depend on the alliances it will forge with those social movements disillusioned with the ANC and other unions. NUMSA's day of action on 19 March 2014 against the youth wage subsidy was well supported by its own members as well as by some social movement activists. But it was not supported by other left unions within COSATU. If a divide opens up between them and NUMSA, it will weaken the movement and any future party. If NUMSA is expelled from COSATU, the response of the other left unions will be critical, and so will the stance of COSATU general secretary Vavi – which will inevitably also raise the question of whether Vavi will join a new left organization. If he were to do so, he would strengthen its ability to reach out to workers and others disillusioned with ANC policy, but also – very significantly – to rank-and-file supporters of the SACP, of which he is a leading member with a strong base.[52]

Third, there is the question of how what is being done now will impact on what sort of party is to be built. The likelihood of a new party looking more like the (early period) Brazilian PT would be increased if the above scenario with Vavi unfolds. Paradoxically, the more broadly based and successful a new party is, the more parliamentary it is likely to be, with less emphasis on class struggle from below. The union is undertaking 'fact finding' missions, looking at the international left – Venezuela, Brazil, Germany, Greece as well as historical experiences such as that of Solidarity in Poland. There is also much to be learned about why so many traditional social democratic parties have rejected socialism and embraced neoliberalism, as has the ANC in South Africa, while largely retaining union political support.[53] But there are not only many different experiences, there are many different possible narratives of, and conclusions from, these different experiences. A lot is to be learned in a short space of time.

The fact that the current contestation in South Africa, driven by a radical union and involving a growing number of workers, combines a powerful counter-movement to neoliberalism with a socialist political vision is of global significance. The scale of the task is great. The class struggle in South Africa today is turbulent and intensely fought. Should the NUMSA initiative fail, the left in South Africa is likely to be put back decades. But the past achievements of the South African working class, alongside the bold steps taken by NUMSA so far, provide grounds for optimism. What is taking place in South Africa today shows considerable potential for once again inspiring the left around the world.

NOTES

We would like to thank Ben Fine, Salim Vally and Karl von Holdt for their comments on this article in draft.

1   For a detailed analysis of what the settlement means for different grades see Gilad Isaacs, 'Who Won the Platinum Strike? The Figures Speak', available at http://groundup.org.za.
2   For example, Gwede Mantashe, the secretary general of the ANC (and former secretary general of NUM and former chairperson of the SACP), suggested that the platinum strike was 'political' (meaning aimed at the ANC) because AMCU is supported by 'white foreign nationals'.
3   Following the election, Zuma appointed Senzeni Zokwana, NUM president at the time of the Marikana massacre and SACP national chairperson, to his new cabinet as Minister for Agriculture, Forestry and Fisheries. Zokwana was immediately engulfed in scandal when *City Press* revealed that he pays his personal cattle herder just R26 a day (about US $2), that the cattle herder works seven days a week and that he lives in a dilapidated iron shack. The minimum wage for farm workers is R558 a week. *Business Day* claimed last year that Zokwana earned R1.2 million a year as NUM President though others claim that the figure is higher. SACP General Secretary Blade Nzimande defended Zokwana by arguing that 'Comrade Zokwana is a mine worker who is not paid an executive's salary'. Zokwana later agreed to increase the worker's pay.
4   Leonard Gentle, 'Forging a New Movement: NUMSA and the Shift in South Africa's Politics', The South African Civil Society Information Service, 28 January 2014, available at http://sacsis.org.za.
5   NUMSA, 'NUMSA Views on The State of Class Struggles in South Africa and the Crisis in COSATU', available at http://www.numsa.org.za.
6   For a discussion of some of these issues see Dale T. McKinley, 'Labour and Community in Transition: Alliances for Public Services in South Africa', Municipal Services Project, Occasional Paper No. 24, June 2014.
7   Ben Fine and Zavareh Rustomjee, *The Political Economy of South Africa: From Minerals-Energy Complex to Industrialization*, London: Hurst, 1996.
8   Murray Liebbrandt, Ingrid Woolard, Arden Finn and Jonathan Argent, 'Trends in South African Income Distribution and Poverty Since the Fall of Apartheid', OECD Social, Employment and Migration Working Papers, No. 101, OECD Publishing, available at http://www.oecd-ilibrary.org.

9   Sam Ashman, Ben Fine and Susan Newman, 'The Crisis in South Africa: Neoliberalism, Financialization and Uneven and Combined Development', *Socialist Register 2011*, Pontypool: Merlin Press, 2010, pp. 174-95.

10   Fiona Tregenna, 'How Significant is Intersectoral Outsourcing of Employment in South Africa?', *Industrial and Corporate Change*, 19(5), 2010, pp. 1427-57.

11   Milford Bateman, 'From Magic Bullet to the Marikana Massacre: The Rise and Fall of Microcredit in Post-apartheid South Africa', *Le Monde Diplomatique*, November 2012, available at: http://mondediplo.com; Patrick Bond, 'Debt, Uneven Development and Capitalist Crisis in South Africa: From Moody's Macroeconomic Monitoring to Marikana Microfinance Mashonisas', *Third World Quarterly*, 34(4), 2013, pp. 569-92.

12   Sam Ashman and Ben Fine, 'Neoliberalism, Varieties of Capitalism, and the Shifting Contours of South Africa's Financial System', *Transformation*, 81/82, 2013, pp. 144-78.

13   Data from the Industrial Development Corporation, Stats South Africa and the Department of Mineral Resources.

14   Simon Roberts, 'Big steel? The South African Experience of Competition Law and Industrial Policy in Influencing Corporate Strategy and Outcomes in the Steel Industry', unpublished manuscript, 2010.

15   Neil Coleman, 'Towards New Collective Bargaining, Wage and Social Protection Strategies in South Africa – Learning from the Brazilian Experience', Global Labour University Working Paper, No. 17, 2013.

16   In May 2014, in the midst of the strike, Amplats announced that bonuses for its top 12 executives would be worth up to R76.5 million. In response to media criticism, CEO Chris Griffith said: 'I am not on strike. I'm not demanding to be paid what I am not worth'.

17   Andrew Bowman and Gilad Isaacs, 'Demanding the Impossible? Platinum Mining Profits and Wage Demands in Context', Research on Money and Finance Occasional Policy Paper, No. 11, June 2014, available at http://www.researchonmoneyandfinance.org.

18   See Nicolas Pons-Vignon and Aurelia Segatti, '"The Art of Neoliberalism": Accumulation, Institutional Change and Social Order Since the End of Apartheid', *Review of African Political Economy*, 40(138), 2013, pp. 507-18; and Carlos Oya 'Ambiguities and Biases in the Definition and Identification of the "Poor": Who is Missing? What is Missing?', *Afriche Orienti*, Special Issue on Poverty II, 2009, pp. 34-51. The latter contrasts residual with relational approaches to poverty reduction: the former entail the idea that the poor lack something (capital or education typically) which should be provided to them, while orthodox policies will allow them to thrive. The latter focuses on relations of exploitation and inequality as constitutive of poverty.

19   On mining rights see Gavin Capps, 'A Bourgeois Reform with Social Justice? The Contradictions of the Minerals Development Bill and Black Economic Empowerment in the South African Platinum Mining Industry', *Review of African Political Economy*, 39(132), 2012, pp. 315-33.

20   Karl Von Holdt, 'South Africa: The Transition to Violent Democracy', *Review of African Political Economy*, 40(138), 2013, pp. 589-604.

21   See 'Mining minister's platinum shares', available at http://mg.co.za.

22   Karl Von Holdt, 'Social Movement Unionism: The Case of South Africa', *Work, Employment and Society* 16(2), 2002, pp. 283-304.

23   Ben Fine, *Labour Market Theory: A Constructive Reassessment*, London: Routledge, 1998.

24   Mark Hunter, 'The Post-Fordist High Road? A South African Case Study', *Journal of Contemporary African Studies*, 18(1), 2000, pp. 67-90.

25   Keith Hart and Vishnu Padayachee, 'A History of South African Capitalism in National and Global Perspective', *Transformation*, 81/2, 2013, pp. 55-85 (quote on p. 56).

26   Interestingly, Thomas Piketty's much discussed book *Capital in the Twenty-First Century* begins its examination of global inequality with a discussion of the Marikana massacre.

27   Kally Forrest, 'Rustenburg's Fractured Recruitment Regime: Who Benefits?', *African Studies*, published online 23 June 2014, available at http://www.tandfonline.com; Sam Ashman and Ben Fine, 'The Meaning of Marikana', Global Labour Column, No. 128, March 2013, available at http://column.global-labour-university.org.

28   Alan H. Jeeves, *Migrant Labour in South Africa's Mining Economy: The Struggle for the Gold Mine's Labour Supply, 1890-1920*, Montreal: McGill-Queens University Press, 1985; T. Dunbar Moodie, *Going for Gold: Men, Mines and Migration*, Berkeley and Los Angeles: University of California Press, 1994.

29   Rob Davies et al., *The Struggle for South Africa: A Reference Guide*, Volumes I and II, London: Zed, 1988.

30   Jonathan Crush, 'Mine Migrancy in the Contemporary Era', in J. Crush and W. James, eds., *Crossing Boundaries: Mine Migrancy in a Democratic South Africa*, Johannesburg: IDASA, 1995, pp. 14-32.

31   Bateman, 'From Magic Bullet to Marikana'; Bond, 'Debt, Uneven Development and Capitalist Crisis'.

32   Forrest, 'Rustenburg's Fractured Recruitment Regime'.

33   Andries Bezuidenhout and Sakhela Buhlungu, 'From Compounded to Fragmented Labour: Mineworkers and the Demise of Compounds in South Africa', *Antipode*, 43(2), 2011, pp. 237-63.

34   Luke Sinwell, '"AMCU by Day, Workers' Committee by Night": Insurgent Trade Unionism at Anglo Platinum (Amplats) Mine, 2012-2014', *Review of African Political Economy*, forthcoming.

35   NUMSA, to its credit, has reflected openly on whether it too could face problems associated with bureaucratization, passing a resolution at its Special Congress in 2013 which said, 'as NUMSA we sincerely believe that as a union we are not immune from the mass desertion by members of a traditional union to a new union'. The union also condemned the massacre as 'a well-planned and orchestrated strategy by the state to defend the profits of the mining bosses'.

36   At present there are four union federations in South Africa. Alongside COSATU, which is the biggest (with approximately 1.8 million workers affiliated), there is FEDUSA (500,000), NACTU (400,000) and CONSAWU (290,000). NACTU, to which AMCU is now affiliated, has its roots in the

black consciousness movement and it has links to the (politically marginal) Pan Africanist Congress.

37   Terry Bell, labour analyst, radio interview, June 2014.

38   NUMSA demonstrations in July 2014 saw workers carry placards saying 'We demand 15 per cent – Marikana 2' ; 'Fifteen percent or Marikana is on the way'; and 'Prepared to continue for six months fighting'.

39   Karl Cloete, NUMSA Deputy General Secretary, interview, Johannesburg, 30 May 2014.

40   Kally Forrest, *Metal That Will Not Bend: The National Union of Metalworkers of South Africa, 1980-1995*, Johannesburg: Wits University Press, 2011.

41   Leonard Gentle, 'Forging a New Movement'; and see also Leonard Gentle, 'What About the Workers? The Old is Dead, the New is Emerging', The South African Civil Society Information Service, 12 June 2014, available at http://www.sacsis.org.za.

42   See for instance Peter Evans 'Counter-Hegemonic Globalization: Transnational Social Movements in the Contemporary Global Political Economy', in T. Janoski, A. Hicks and M. Schwartz, eds., *Handbook of Political Sociology*, New York: Cambridge University Press, 2005, pp. 655-70; and for a critique see Michael Burawoy, 'From Polanyi to Pollyanna: The False Optimism of Global Labor Studies', *Global Labour Journal*, 1(2), 2010, pp. 301-13.

43   Guy Standing, *The Precariat: The New Dangerous Class*, London: Bloomsbury, 2011; and for a critique see Jan Breman, 'A Bogus Concept?', *New Left Review*, 84(November/December), 2013.

44   Nicoli Nattrass and Jeremy Seekings, *Race, Class, and Inequality in South Africa*, London: Yale University Press, 2005.

45   For a historical discussion see M. Wuyts, 'Inequality and Poverty as the Condition of Labour', paper presented at UNRISD workshop on 'The Need to Rethink Development Economics', Cape Town, 7-8 September 2001.

46   Giovanni Arrighi, 'Labour Supplies in Historical Perspective: A Study of the Proletarianization of the African Peasantry in Rhodesia', *Journal of Development Studies*, 6, 1970, pp. 197-234.

47   Franco Barchiesi, *Precarious Liberation: Workers, the State, and Contested Social Citizenship in Postapartheid South Africa*, Albany, New York: SUNY Press, 2011.

48   John Sender, 'Women's Struggles to Escape Poverty in South Africa', *Journal of Agrarian Change*, 2(1), 2002, pp. 1-49.

49   Claire Ceruti, 'A Proletarian Township: Work, Home and Class', in Peter Alexander et al., *Class in Soweto*, Scottsville: UKZN Press, 2013, pp. 96-126 (quote on p. 123).

50   NALEDI (National Labour and Economic Development Institute), 'Identifying Obstacles to Union Organizing in Farms: Towards a Decent Work Strategy in the Farming Sector', report for the Department of Labour, 2011; see also Jesse Wilderman, 'Farm Worker Uprising on the Western Cape: The Spark, Spread, and Structure of Spontaneous Collective Action', Masters research report, Johannesburg: University of the Witwatersrand, 2014.

51   Interview with Karl Cloete.

52 Concomitantly, the ANC knows the gains it could make were Vavi to remain within the Alliance, and rumours abound that he has already been offered a senior ANC post to try to ensure this.

53 Aurelia Segatti and Nicolas Pons-Vignon, 'Stuck in Stabilisation? South Africa's Post-apartheid Macro-economic Policy Between Ideological Conversion and Technocratic Capture', *Review of African Political Economy*, 40(138), 2013, pp. 537-55.

FROM GEZI RESISTANCE TO SOMA MASSACRE: CAPITAL ACCUMULATION AND CLASS STRUGGLE IN TURKEY

FUAT ERCAN AND ŞEBNEM OĞUZ

On 31 May 2013, a local demonstration against the destruction of Gezi Park in Taksim, İstanbul as part of an urban renewal project turned into a spontaneous countrywide uprising. In the course of a few weeks, 2.5 million people filled the streets of 79 Turkish cities, with the slogans 'everywhere is Taksim, everywhere is resistance', and demanding the government resign. The Gezi resistance can be considered as part of the global wave of uprisings that started in 2009, centred in countries around the Mediterranean, as reactions against various facets of the deepening of capitalist social relations and the corresponding rise in the authoritarianism of the state. The Gezi resistance started in response to a plan to transform a public park into a shopping mall, a mosque and a historic military barrack. This was, then, a resistance against the commodification of urban space, nature and everyday life for the reproduction of capital, as well as the conservative authoritarianism of the party in power, the AKP (*Adalet ve Kalkınma Partisi* – Justice and Development Party).

The uprising was unexpected, not in the sense of a lack of previous struggles leading up to May 2013, but in the sense that the various types and fields of social struggle (such as those by public employees, professionals, students, feminist and ecological movements) came together for the first time. However, certain sections of the working class, especially of industrial labour, remained politically underrepresented among the Gezi protesters. This was a result of how the neoliberal policies advanced under AKP rule disorganized the working classes through deunionization,[1] low wages, precarization, intensification of workloads, erosion of social benefits and increasing workers' debts.[2] These developments contributed to eliminating the political channels through which workers could express their opposition.

Furthermore, urban regeneration projects in Istanbul sought to transform the inner city into a financial centre and shift manufacturing industries to the outer edges of the city. This led to the eviction of most of the workers living in inner-city squatter areas, cleansing the working class from the city centre of Istanbul. In the words of the former Chairman of the Mass Housing Administration, Erdoğan Bayraktar, 'We should find a way to keep poor people from the city of Istanbul'.[3]

Analyses of the class character of the Gezi resistance generally miss these points. On the one hand, postmodern analyses argue that the resistance had no class content. According to Ali Akay, for instance, *the* Gezi resistance was based on a micropolitics of desire rather than a macropolitics of class: Gezi was transversal, classless, non-hierarchical, disorganized and rallying.[4] On the other hand, much analysis has contended that Gezi had a middle-class character, basing the arguments on empirical observations of the class composition of protesters in Gezi Park. Çağlar Keyder, for example, argues that the protestors were predominantly members of a new middle class of professionals who have extensive economic power and cultural capital, and demand a corresponding political power to limit the policies of a conservative and authoritarian AKP government.[5] In a different take, Korkut Boratav argues that the working class may not have joined the resistance with its own organizations and programmes, but the Gezi resistance was still a 'matured class reaction' of 'highly qualified and educated workers, together with their future class comrades (students), and with the inclusion of professionals; confronting a massive urban plundering attempt by the bourgeoisie and the political power unified with it'.[6] Boratav's argument has the merit of showing that the majority of protestors belonged to the working class, in the sense of non-owners of means of production. In that sense, it is a necessary corrective to middle-class analyses. His thesis of a 'matured class reaction', however, leaves the question of why industrial labour was largely absent from the protests unanswered, as well as the broader issues of class formation.

There are two main problems, as we see it, of the middle-class thesis. First, it focuses on the individual class positions of the protestors, defined narrowly as a place in production relations or in the consumption sphere. What differentiates Marxist class analysis from other theories of stratification, however, is its analytical priority on the dynamics of capital accumulation and class struggle as the determinants of classes as a social process. In this context, classes can be defined in terms of their objective and subjective relations to the *totality of the capital accumulation process*, including all three of its constituent dimensions – production (including extraction of surplus value); realization (transformation of commodities into money by the act of exchange); and revalorization (allocation of surplus value to new production).

It is thus necessary to analyze the *political content of the demands* expressed by the protest in relation to the moments of capital accumulation in Turkey today. Protests related to *production* still take the form of struggles against low wages, poor working conditions or labour flexibility; protests related to *realization* usually take the form of struggles against the commercialization of public services; and protests related to *revalorization* increasingly take the form of struggles against the commodification of nature.

Moreover, in late neoliberalism, as certain parts of the state themselves start to act like capital in commercializing their operations to attain revenues under the pressure of financial constraints, struggles over accumulation often take the form of protests directed against the state itself rather than capital. Since these are struggles against the reproduction by the state of various facets of capital accumulation, these protests always have working-class content. In that sense, the class struggle is inscribed in all three types of protests that emerge in relation to the dynamics of accumulation *and* the practices of the state. And that was very much the case with the Gezi resistance, which erupted as an example of the third category of protest: that is, as a struggle against commodification of nature in the context of the revalorization of capital and the reproduction of the state.

The other major problem with the middle-class thesis is that it turns attention only to the beginning of the events and the nature of the protests at Gezi Park; the uprising is reduced to a *moment* rather than a *process*.[7] But if we take into account the class composition and political demands of 2.5 million people who protested in all but two cities of Turkey over the month of June 2012, as well as the ongoing struggles before and after the Gezi resistance, a quite different image emerges. This is a picture which can only be grasped through what Ellen Wood has called 'class as a relationship and process'.[8] This larger setting for class struggle revealed itself in the grim reality of the mine explosion that took place in Soma, a small town in the Aegean province of Manisa. On 13 May 2013, almost one year after the Gezi protests, 301 workers were killed in the largest work-related massacre in Turkish labour history. The carnage of the mineworkers reveals, much more than numeric counts of occupational categories, the changing class relations in the current phase of capital accumulation in Turkey. The Soma tragedy helps uncover the reasons why industrial labour was not visible as the politically leading force in the Gezi resistance.

THE SOMA MASSACRE AND CLASS RELATIONS IN TURKEY

The Soma massacre exposes the bigger picture of class relations in Turkey today. The first aspect is the changing form and pace of privatization in the

2000s as a result of the increasing financial constraints of the state, elimination of the legal-institutional obstacles against privatization, as well as the new orientation of Turkish capitalism towards productive capital accumulation. In this process, new forms of symbiotic relationships between capital and the state have emerged, one of them being the system of 'redevance' (the French for a royalty fee). In the case of Soma, the lignite mines were formerly a state-owned property in the hands of Turkish Coal Enterprises (TKİ), and were privatized in 2005 in line with the 'redevance' system, first introduced into Turkey in the late 1980s as a means to prevent unlicensed mining. It became a widespread practice during the 1990s, and was made an explicit part of the mining law by AKP in 2004. In the system, the state keeps the property rights of the mines while transferring their operating rights to private companies. These companies then sell their monopolistically priced products to the state-owned thermal power plants. In the case of Soma, the operating rights of the mines were transferred to Soma Holding, the parent company of Soma Coal, which had close ties with AKP. Since the state sets the price of coal (which provides just under 30 per cent of Turkish electricity production), Soma Holding had a guaranteed source of profit and a commitment on its part to decrease its production costs. In an interview in 2012, Ali Gürkan, the owner of Soma Coal, proudly stated that they decreased production costs from US $130-140 to US $23.80 per ton, including the 15 per cent royalty share. When asked how, Gürkan simply answered, 'the business style of the private sector came into play, that's all'.[9]

What Gürkan meant by 'business style of the private sector' included various elements of the new control mechanisms established over labour in the 2000s. Among these mechanisms, the subcontracting of unskilled mining labour was one of the main factors in reducing costs. The workers were not employed directly by Soma Coal, but recruited from the countryside through subcontractors, known as 'head uncles', who led teams of 30 to 60 workers. The 'head uncles' reproduced pre-capitalist mechanisms of control over labour within a capitalist setting. Besides their wages, they received informal bonuses based on the amount of coal their team produced; so the work-teams were severely pushed to extract more coal. Therefore the workers had to endure long working hours and take more risks to increase output. The workers were deprived of the most basic occupational safety rights. Their trade union, the Mine Workers' Union of Turkey (Maden-İş), moreover, was collaborating with the mining company rather than protecting the safety of workers. The slack enforcement was made easier by the fact that Turkey did not sign the ILO's Convention No.176 on Security and Health in Mines, the ILO being an important social pressure on labour rights in Turkey; and the Council of Public Inspection was dissolved by government decree in 2011. Following the catastrophe, when asked why the mine did not have a safe room stocked with oxygen masks, Gürkan could just say that the company had planned to complete one in the next few months, but that it wasn't legally obliged to do so.

A second part to the picture revealed by the Soma massacre is the role of subcontracted labour, which increased by 300 per cent between 2002-07, and by 50 per cent between 2007-11 in the overall economy.[10] With higher worker turnover and less training in safety issues, the total number of work-related deaths during the same period rose tremendously. Between 2000 and 2012 alone, 12,686 workers lost their lives due to work accidents across the whole economy.[11] According to a 2012 ILO report, Turkey is the third worst in the world for deaths on the job, and number one in work-related accidents in Europe. Every day in Turkey 172 work accidents take place, with on average three workers losing their lives and five others rendered permanently disabled. The highest proportion of these deaths, accounting for one-third of all work accidents reported, is in the construction industry, where the rate of subcontracting system is among the highest.

The Soma massacre shows, thirdly, the particular ways in which the AKP has managed to maintain its hegemony through the deployment of the economic, ideological and repressive apparatuses of the state. The Soma Coal Company provided the charity coal bags distributed by the AKP during the previous local elections. Charity distribution is the Turkish version of poverty reduction strategies suggested by the World Bank since the early 2000s, and one of the most important political tools of the AKP in recruiting support from the working class. However, charity distribution does not automatically translate into support for the AKP on the part of workers. The repressive and ideological apparatuses also play their roles. In the case of Soma, the management actually threatened to fire the workers if they refused to participate in AKP rallies. After the explosion, Prime Minister Recep Tayyip Erdoğan transferred troops to Soma to repress the protests of his own 'supporters'. Erdoğan's words in response to the Soma disaster – 'these things happen in coal mines' – was a typical example of how he uses fatalism as a major ideological tool for justifying neoliberalism and work-related deaths as the natural order of things rather than as a direct consequence of government policies.

A fourth revelation of the Soma massacre is with respect to the current phase of industrialization in Turkey. The coal sector is crucial to the current pace and form of productive capital formation in Turkey, which in the 2000s has required an eight per cent annual increase in energy resources for a four per cent annual growth rate. Energy imports are a key source of current account deficits, and the Turkish state has encouraged private companies to invest in both renewable and non-renewable energy sources such as coal, petroleum, wind, hydro and even nuclear energy.[12] The energy sector is not only a crucial sector in the total reproduction of capital; it is also a new area of revalorization for the leading capital groups in Turkey. This has meant an intensification of the commodification of nature, as exemplified by recent government plans to construct 1,738 dams and hydroelectric power plants by 2023. Soma Holding's corporate structure illustrates well the particular sectoral combinations involved in capital accumulation in Turkey in the 2000s. In 2006, Soma Holding's purchased Tilage, a construction firm in İstanbul. Through Tilage, Soma Holding transfers the profits it obtains in the mining sector to investments in the high-profit real estate and construction sectors in İstanbul. The construction sector is a major area for the revalorization for capital in itself, as well as spurring growth because of its backward linkages with varying sub-sectors of manufacturing. What occurred in Soma was not an event on the margins of Turkish capitalism, but at the core of its class relations.

Finally, the occupational composition of the workers who were killed in the Soma mines provides two important further insights into the recent pattern of class formation in Turkey. Many of the unskilled workers were previously tobacco farmers from neighbouring villages who had to give up agriculture after the privatization of TEKEL, the former state-owned alcohol, cigarettes and tobacco monopoly; others were farmers from all parts of Turkey who have left their lands due to the neoliberal transformation of agricultural policies in recent years. The continuing process of dissolution of the peasantry, which still forms 25 per cent of Turkish population, is one of the peculiarities of Turkish capitalism. Also, the simultaneous presence of unskilled, semi-skilled and skilled workers in the mines illustrates the differentiation within the working class in the process of transition from labour-intensive to capital-intensive production. But even with the increased differentiation of the working class, both unskilled workers with the equivalent of US $500 monthly wages and engineers with US $5,000 were killed in the catastrophe, suggesting how the fates of all waged labourers are united.

THE CHANGING MECHANISMS OF CONTROL OVER LABOUR

Due to the late development of capitalism in Turkey, the process of capital accumulation is at the same time the *formation and internationalization* of the circuits of productive, commercial and money capital. In the nineteenth century, the Ottoman economy was inserted into the commercial circuit of West European capital; and following the Great Depression of the 1930s, the transition from commercial to productive capital started through state-led industrialization substituting domestic production for the imports of basic consumer goods. In the 1950s, sections of domestic commercial capitalists turned to production of durable consumption goods in cooperation with foreign capital. From the 1960s on, some of the domestic productive capital groups that grew through the import substitution strategy started to gain control over commercial and money-capital through the ownership of banks, eventually forming conglomerates known as 'holding companies'. By the end of the 1970s, these big holding companies, which had absorbed the potential of inward-oriented accumulation, sought new market openings through integration into the world market and export-oriented accumulation. In the post-1980 period, the capital accumulation process went through three main phases: accumulation through export promotion in the 1980s; accumulation through the inflow of money-capital in the 1990s; and global integration on the basis of productive capital accumulation from the 2000s onwards.

The key strategy in the 1980s was export promotion through specialization in the production of labour-intensive goods and suppression of wages, which led to a phenomenal growth in Turkish exports. But by the end of the 1980s, the failure to achieve an investment boom as well as the new wave of labour militancy made wage suppression polices unsustainable as the means to competitiveness. As a result, the momentum of the export drive slowed. At this point, external financial liberalization was seen as an opportunity to overcome the difficulties faced by domestic capital and the state. Throughout the 1990s, financial liberalization worked as a mechanism of resource transfer to the major capital groups, as the holding banks directed the money-capital they derived from financing state debts to the expansion of their holding companies. The orientation of Turkish capital towards the accumulation of money-capital, however, resulted in a decline in the production of new surplus value through fixed investments in new plant and equipment. This was the basis for the series of crises in 1994, 1998 and 2000-01. From the late 1990s onwards, a new phase of capital accumulation was therefore directed at increasing productive capacity for exports.

In this latest phase, the economic policies of the Turkish state centred on the capacity of large domestic companies to expand internationally and engage in partnerships with global capital. This meant that the capital groups which previously relied on the extraction of absolute surplus value, or the redistribution of surplus value by the state, would have to reorient themselves towards relative surplus value production through higher technology and increasing labour productivity. Five major polices were adopted. First, the relations between banking and industry were reconfigured to shift money-capital from state debts into fixed capital investments through comprehensive banking reforms in 1999.[13] Second, the legal-institutional barriers to private investment were gradually removed through the 'reform program for the improvement of the investment climate' that was adopted in 2001. Third, new industrial policies were adopted for the purpose of improving global competitiveness through a shift in the sectoral composition of investments from labour-intensive to capital-intensive sectors. However, this did not mean that labour-intensive sectors would be totally eliminated. Instead, the companies in these sectors were encouraged to relocate to cheap labour regions in eastern and southeastern Anatolia. In the famous phrase of former State Minister Kürşat Tüzmen, 'Turkey should create its own China'.

Fourth, and following from this, there was a fundamental change in regional development policies. Subnational regional economies would be conceived as spaces with strong inter-sectoral linkages and thus as the key nodes benefiting from the global capital flows. With this rationality, the government adopted a new incentive package for promoting regional investment. In its latest 2012 version, six regions are defined on the basis of their development levels. In the western provinces, high and medium-technology based investments are to be supported; and in the south and eastern provinces, labour-intensive sectors are promoted. The most labour-intensive sectors were encouraged to move to the least developed region, composed almost solely of Kurdish provinces, thereby accentuating the regional inequalities between these provinces and the rest of Turkey. The regional differentiation strategy implicitly meant, moreover, the establishment of different mechanisms of control over labour at the different socio-spatial scales of production and the state so as to enhance competitiveness.

This brings us to our final point on the new economic policy regime. The new competitiveness agenda required the establishment of new and variegated control mechanisms over labour. In the 1980s and 1990s, labour was mostly controlled through policies of absolute surplus value production and wage suppression, which was made possible through a series of restrictions on trade unions. From the late 1990s onwards, policies towards increasing labour productivity through relative surplus value production required more qualified labour power, i.e., 'active labour policies' for the creation of a flexible labour power capable of adapting to the rapidly changing conditions of global capital accumulation. Lifelong training programmes, for example, were introduced, although the burden of paying for these programmes was largely assumed by the workers themselves. An important effect of this was the creation of a direct link between education and employment, thereby decreasing the importance of formal education and increasing the importance of short-term vocational training.[14] A radical step in this direction was the introduction in 2012 of a law known as the '4+4+4 education model'. This law divided the eight years of primary education into two stages, each lasting four years, and allowing for distance education and apprenticeship training starting in stage two. This effectively reduced compulsory education to four years and enabled vocational training to start at the age of 10.

The focus on higher skilled production and relative surplus value extraction did not mean, however, any lessening of the significance of absolute surplus value extraction. Rather, the policies towards increasing global competitiveness of Turkish economy necessitated the intensification of both absolute and relative surplus value extraction through the establishment of new mechanisms of control over labour as well as the diversification of these mechanisms at both the sectoral and work-site levels.[15] If policies towards relative surplus extraction through re-skilling strategies came to the fore in high-technology sectors and regions, it was strategies based on absolute surplus value extraction that predominated elsewhere. In brief, the change in the orientation of Turkish capitalism towards productive accumulation in the 2000s meant more exploitation, labour flexibility and significant changes in the pattern of class formation in Turkey.

CLASS FORMATION IN THE 2000s

It is possible to identify several specific features of the processes of class formation in Turkey in the 2000s: a dissolution of the peasantry and the growth of waged labour, with opposing effects on Kurdish and women labourers; the transformation of the public sector and proletarianization of professionals; and a precarity of work and income as a uniting force across all sections of the working class.

Dissolution of the peasantry and the massive growth of waged labour

In his panoptic survey of the twentieth century *The Age of Extremes*, Eric Hobsbawm observed that 'Only one peasant stronghold remained in or around the neighbourhood of Europe and the Middle East – Turkey, where the peasantry declined, but, in the mid-1980s, still remained an absolute majority'.[16] The continuing presence of peasant labour power in the Turkish countryside carries the implication that the process of the formal subsumption of labour continues to operate, despite the dominance of the commodification of labour power into waged labour across the rest of the economy.[17] The reason why dissolution of the peasantry has been such a slow process is related both to the strength of traditional relationships between peasants and landowners, and the necessity for the export of agricultural goods in order to purchase the import goods for industrialization. With the transition from inward to outward-oriented accumulation processes in the 1980s, and especially from the 2000s onwards, however, the Turkish state has encouraged the dissolution of the peasantry, in order to make labour power plentiful at a low wage, and to enlarge the potential circuit of capital by incorporating former commons.[18] To this end, support purchases of agricultural products by state institutions were largely abandoned. The government initiated an income support programme which was supposed to recover at least a part of the lost income of peasants. But only peasants with some land holdings could benefit from the payments, geared according to the size of the land owned, cultivated or not. As a result, many peasants left their lands uncultivated and moved to the cities.[19]

The rapid dissolution of the peasantry resulted in a massive growth of the working class. The share of urban working-class households rose from 49.58 per cent in 2002 to 56 per cent in 2010. Moreover, there was also a slight increase in the share of rural workers in the same period. In 2010, six out of every ten households in Turkey was of working-class origin. The combined share of the petite bourgeoisie, rural propertied classes and landed subsistence peasants declined from 22.93 per cent in 2002 to 15.68 per cent in 2010. Turkey's class structure had never before witnessed such a great transformation in such a short period, with quite different effects for different sections of the population.[20]

The patterns of participation of Kurdish peasants in the labour force

The dispossession of the Kurdish peasantry has been taking place through both economic and political mechanisms. Dispossession through economic means is not unique to the Kurds, but part of the overall change in the agricultural polices described above. Dispossession through political means, in contrast, refers to the process by which Kurds were forced to leave their lands and migrate to cities, particularly between 1993-99, in response to the evacuation of their villages and destruction of their houses by the Turkish military.[21] As a consequence, it is estimated that more than 378,000 people were internally displaced. The deterioration of economic conditions in the Kurdish regions due to the Gulf and Iraq Wars also accelerated this process.[22] The participation of Kurdish migrants in the labour force has taken five main forms. Some have migrated to the western provinces and participate in the regular labour force either temporarily or permanently. These workers face low wages, social exclusion and poor conditions in housing, transportation and health. As such, they put pressure on the living conditions of the working class as a whole. A second group has moved to what Ferda Koç calls 'reservoir cities' in the big Kurdish provinces such as Diyarbakır, where workers join the passive labour force waiting to be employed in other cities or countries, such as Germany, Russia, the Arab countries and recently South Kurdistan (Iraq).

A third group is employed as seasonal agricultural workers in both the Kurdish and western provinces. These workers start their trips with their entire family in overcrowded trucks in a harrowing journey. Once they arrive, they live in tents under extremely unhealthy conditions. The majority of these workers are women and children. They find jobs through so-called 'intermediaries' ('head uncles') based on family connections. Seasonal agricultural work forms another significant proportion of the subcontracting system in Turkey. In terms of class formation, the relationship between Kurdish seasonal agricultural workers and Turkish farmers depends on whether the Kurdish workers are directly employed by them or work together. In both cases, there are ethnic tensions. In the first case, the tension reveals itself in the methods of labour control used by the landowning medium-sized Turkish farmers over Kurdish seasonal workers; in the second case, small Turkish farmers and Kurdish migrants directly compete for seasonal work.[23]

A fourth group of Kurdish migrants work as informal labourers in the dirtiest jobs of the construction sector in the major cities, again largely through subcontracting firms which pay extremely low wages and avoid any other labour costs. It is politically very important for the Turkish and Kurdish segments of the working class to unite in the struggle against these working conditions rather than compete along the chasm of ethnic division. The trade unions have an important role here in organizing a unity through anti-nationalist policies.

Finally, an increasing proportion of Kurdish rural migrants are employed in the low-wage, labour-intensive sectors such as textiles and mining in the Kurdish provinces. The number of workers in this category is expected to increase rapidly in line with the new regional investment incentive package. On 24 November 2013, in a press release on the outcomes of this package, Zafer Çağlayan, the past Minister for the Economy, announced that the proportion of new investments has been highest in southeastern Anatolia (i.e. the region comprised of the Kurdish provinces) in the last 16 months.[24] This might have significant political implications for the Kurdish movement, as class divisions in the Kurdish provinces might increasingly come to the fore. It is striking to note, in this context, that while only five per cent of the labour force is employed in the Kurdish provinces, 10 per cent of labour protests in 2013 took place in this region.[25]

Participation of women in the labour force

In contrast to the experience of Kurdish migrants, the participation of women in the labour force has decreased partly as a response to the transformation of the peasantry into workers, with the notable exception of the high participation rates of women as seasonal agricultural workers. This is a peculiarity of Turkish development, too: the so-called 'feminization of labour' which has been the general trend in response to neoliberalism in other countries has not taken place in Turkey. According to an ILO Report in 2008, the female labour participation rate in Turkey is 22.2 per cent (falling from 34.3 per cent in 1988), in comparison to a global participation rate for women in 2008 of 49.1 per cent and an EU-25 rate of 58.6 per cent. Of the women in Turkey employed in 2008, 49 per cent were in agriculture, 13 per cent in industry and 35 per cent in the service sector.[26] The rates of informal employment were 66 per cent and 42 per cent for females and males, respectively.[27] All these numbers show that the female employment rate in the formal sector is far from absorbing the women who have left peasant-based agriculture. This situation is associated with the particular fusion of neoliberalism and conservatism in Turkey. Women are expected to participate in the informal sector through flexible and low-wage jobs in line with the neoliberal policies. But they are also expected to assume more responsibility in the private sphere through unpaid domestic labour, including housework as well as various forms of care work (of children, the sick and elderly in the family), in line with the conservative values gaining ground under AKP rule.[28] Accordingly, the position of women within the Turkish working class is defined more on the basis of their role in the reproduction of labour power, rather than their role in the production process. This has important political implications for the socialist feminist movement. The specific form of articulation of capitalism and patriarchy in Turkey brings out private forms of patriarchy to the fore, finding its most grim expression in the increase in the murder rate of women by 1,400 per cent between 2002 and 2009, and in the Turkish feminist slogan that 'male love is killing three women per day'.

Another peculiarity of the Turkish case, in comparison to Southeast Asia and Latin America, is the lower proportion of export-oriented production jobs in women's employment.[29] Yet, in the limited cases where women have been employed in export-processing zones in Turkey, they have been in the frontlines in the struggle against the working conditions there. The most famous example of this is the Novamed strike (known as the 'women's strike'), which was the first strike launched in a Turkish export zone in 2006 in Antalya against a medical equipment manufacturing factory owned by a German-based MNC. Novamed employed 320 workers, of which only 15 were men, with all the workers employed on the production line being women. In 2005, factory workers applied to the Petrol-İş union to improve their working conditions. In September 2006, 85 women workers went on strike due to Novamed's refusal to recognize the union. The main reasons for women to join the union were poor working conditions and harassment by their superiors. The employer's permission was required to get married; the time workers spent in the toilet was monitored; and pregnancy schedules were introduced in order to prevent several women on the same line from simultaneously taking maternity leave. Those who did not comply with these rules were insulted by supervisors and eventually forced to quit their jobs. After 15 months of resistance, the strike ended with the recognition of the workers' right to a collective agreement. It turned out to be a victory both on the part of the union and 'The Women's Platform for Solidarity with Novamed Strikers', founded in September 2007 by the coalition of 27 women's organizations across Turkey.[30]

Transformation of the public sector and proletarianization of professionals

In Turkey, the class position and political organization of professionals has been historically shaped by the nation-state building process of late development, and directly influenced by the changing conditions of public employment. However, the professional strata have started to lose their protected positions in response to the neoliberal policies adopted since the 1980s. This process has occurred across three stages of neoliberal transformation of the public sector in Turkey. In the initial stages in the 1980s, under the financial constraints resulting from the tax revolt of Turkish capital, the state rapidly withdrew from the provision of public services and opened them up to the revalorization of capital through *privatization*. In the 1990s, as the state's financial difficulties deepened in response to the loss of export capacity and a consequent decline in revenues, it resorted to external borrowing from private capital markets. This eventually forced the state to take a further step of *commercializing* public services, that is, through the sale of state services to citizens at a price (the process of realization turning citizens into customers). Finally, in the 2000s, as financial constraints deepened, the state resorted to the *commodification* of public services at the production level, that is, through the change in the production relations and labour process of public employees. This meant the commodification of the labour power of public employees (particularly of the professional strata), increasing labour flexibility, the introduction of performance criteria that increase relative surplus production, Taylorist methods of deskilling and so forth, all in order to decrease the costs of public sector provision.

This was a critical turning point in terms of the class nature of the state because it started acting like capital not only at the realization level, but also at the production level. In this process, the lines between state and capital become blurred, as the economic apparatuses of the state themselves participate in the circuits of capital for the institutional self-reproduction of the state as a whole.[31] It was this phase that accelerated the process of differentiation and proletarianization among public employees and professionals.

The case of physicians is a good example. As the state started to introduce capitalist production methods in the provision of public services, it needed more waged labour as variable capital in its own production process. The state not only made plans to add to the number of future physicians through increasing the number of medical schools, but also encouraged the existing self-employed physicians to work as wage earners. In order to do so, in 2004, it adopted a performance-based wage system to encourage physicians who had their own private clinics and also worked as part-time wage earners in hospitals, to close down their clinics and totally shift to full-time wage-earner status in public hospitals, operating like private companies. In this process, the proportion of physicians working in full-time status increased from 11 per cent in 2002 to 92 per cent in 2010.[32] At the same time, as more and more capitalists invested in the health sector, small private clinics were replaced by nationwide chains of large-scale private hospitals belonging to either the big Turkish holding companies or multinational chains. Some of the physicians who owned small private clinics were also forced into wage-earner status through employment in these hospitals. These developments led to an active struggle against commercialization and commodification of health services by the physicians' main organization, the Turkish Medical Association (TTB).

The proletarianization of nurses took another form, and was mainly accomplished through the expansion of contract labour and transformation of their labour process. This meant a deskilling of nursing labour power through the introduction of Taylorist methods of dividing qualified nursing service into components not requiring qualifications, to be assumed by different types of health workers with different – lower – educational backgrounds and wages.[33] The Health and Social Service Workers Union (SES), which organizes in the public sector, assumed an active position in the fight against these developments.

Teachers experienced a similar process. With the extension of contract labour in the education sphere, and particularly the introduction of a central nationwide test in 2001 for choosing public personnel, teachers lost their right to get automatically appointed as teachers in public schools upon graduation from university. This regulation led to a tremendous increase in the number of unemployed teachers, some forming the 'Platform of Non-Appointed Teachers' in 2009. The introduction of the 4+4+4 education model has also had the effect of forcing teachers to renew their own labour power in order to train the future skilled labour power needed by the system. This entailed a serious loss of autonomy and control over their labour process.[34] The Union of Education and Science Workers (Eğitim-Sen) in the public sector was very active in the fight against these developments.

For lawyers, the increasing incorporation of the legal sphere into the laws of capitalism and the commodification of legal services led to the transformation of legal offices and their working procedures. Lawyers also confronted proletarianization through the fragmentation, loss of control and deskilling of their labour process. This led to their increasing participation in the labour force as wage earners rather than small office owners, and the relative decline in their earnings.[35]

Finally, engineers, who had a privileged status until the 1970s amidst the active role of state planning agencies and public enterprises in industrialization, lost this status with the downsizing in the public sector.[36] From 1976 to 2006, the share of public sector waged employees within the overall employment of engineers fell from 63.1 per cent to 44.9 per cent; private sector waged employees rose from 16.3 per cent to 36.6 per cent; and the self-employed/ entrepreneurs fell from 20.6 per cent to 18.5 per cent of the total. In the same period, the unemployment rate for engineers rose from 1.3 per cent to 17.5 per cent.[37] This process has also led to tensions between the older and younger generations of engineers. As practical experience is seen as a more important merit than theoretical knowledge (as with physicians and lawyers), young engineers now have to choose between long-term unemployment and low-wage, unskilled jobs that reduce their role to technicians. At the same time, as with the health sector, the boom for private engineering companies seems to be ending as the state transfers public works and inspections to the private sector; therefore, we can expect another wave of proletarianization for engineers, too. This process is reflected in the policies of the Union of Chambers of Turkish Engineers and Architects (TMMOB), which is actively playing its part in social struggles and trying to protect the integrity of the engineering occupation.

Precarization among all sections of the working class

Policies of labour flexibility were adopted in the 2000s as part of the new mechanisms of labour control that cut across all sectors. In the private sector, the main step in this direction was the adoption of a new Labour Law in 2003, which legitimized flexible work through the legal recognition of part-time, temporary and contract labour, as well as increased working time and the right of employers to discharge workers collectively 'in times of crisis'. The most important effect of this was the creation of a new generation of workers whose first jobs in the labour market were precarious. The decline in importance of formal university education, and the increase in the importance of short-term vocational training, also accelerated this process, by increasing the unemployment rate among new university graduates. They are being pushed into work in areas unrelated to their own training – generally in unskilled, part-time white-collar jobs in the service sector, such as call-centres, fast-food chains, shopping malls, etc. Even if they find jobs in areas related to their training, they do not have job security, so they internalize the potential of precarity into their consciousness. Generally, they do not identify themselves as workers because this is a term, for them, associated with industrial workers. And since they did not have any union experience, individualism animates their behaviour. However, some gain consciousness of a class identity in the course of struggle against the new, flexible work conditions. An interesting example of this is the 'Association of Call Centre Workers', founded in 2004 as an internet site named 'the call for truth'. Although it turned into an association in 2006, it continued to work informally to avoid dismissal of its members. Another example is the 'Plaza Action Platform', formed by the weekly gathering of various precarious skilled white-collar workers in front of the IBM Plaza in Istanbul to show their solidarity with the unionization struggle of IBM workers. Both of these groups, along with other members of the new generation of precarious workers, were active in the Gezi resistance.

In the public sector, labour flexibility was introduced within the framework of public personnel reform. From the late 1990s onwards, many civil servant positions were transferred to the contractual personnel category, especially in the education and health sectors. Besides the contractual personnel employment, the temporary staff category also increased rapidly in this period. Temporary staff were originally used only in exceptional cases where provisional services were needed in areas that did not require specific skills. With the introduction of new legislation in 2004, however, workers who lost their jobs from privatization were also categorized as temporarily employed. These jobs were to be provisional for up to one year with salaries tied to the legal minimum wage. The new jobs would not necessarily be related to the workers' expertise, and workers could be relocated anywhere.

After its privatization in 2008, for example, 12,000 workers at TEKEL were transferred into this category. In December 2009, TEKEL workers resisting the legislation marched to Ankara from 21 provinces, and set up tents in the heart of Ankara, where they continued their struggle for two more months. The TEKEL resistance drew on the class identity of an older generation of workers who entered the labour market through full-time secure jobs in the industrial sector and had years of union experience. A sense of collective struggle was already part of their workplace experience; but, in contrast to the younger generation of workers, they had no experience of precarity. In the course of their struggle, the TEKEL workers gained a common consciousness of their own precarity, as well as the precarity of other sections of society. Indeed, the tent city in Ankara served as a place of direct encounter with other sections of society and their struggles. Students, young precarious white-collar workers, public employees such as teachers and doctors, could all see that the TEKEL workers' demands reflected issues confronting all labourers under the threat of precarious work. The following words of a TEKEL worker are telling in this regard: 'I learned when I came here that doctors and teachers are also workers and we share the same problems'.[38]

Flexibility and precarity, Metin Özuğurlu argues, have opposite effects on working-class formation. Flexibility divides and heterogenizes the working class on the basis of different types of employment, such as part-time, temporary or contract labour; while precarity homogenizes and reunites them at the level of consciousness through a common sense of insecurity and uncertainty.[39] In E.P. Thompson's terms, precarity can be seen as a class phenomenon that unifies workers both 'in the raw material of experience and in consciousness'.[40] However, this unity can only reveal itself through experience and struggle, through social interactions between different sections of labourers as well as through their interaction with broader sections of society – a process Thompson identified with class formation. The TEKEL resistance can be seen, in this sense, as a significant instance of class formation, and a precursor to the Gezi resistance in articulating different labour practices to a common struggle.

CLASS AND POLITICS TODAY

Class formation cannot be conceived apart from the specific dynamics of capital accumulation and the state in a social formation. The specific pattern of capitalism in Turkey in the 2000s has brought to the fore particular aspects of the accumulation process, as pertains to production, realization and revalorization, as salient issues of class struggle. At the level of production, for instance, it is possible to see an inherent link between the transformation of the sectoral composition of investments and the nature of labour protests. In terms of the sectoral composition of labour protests in the private sector in 2013, 68 per cent of all labour protests took place in construction, metal, health, textile, local government and energy sectors, in that order.[41] This is related both to the growing importance of these sectors in the accumulation process and the introduction of new control mechanisms over labour such as the subcontracting system. It is not a surprise, therefore, that 15 per cent of the protests took place in the construction sector, where 79 per cent of subcontracted employment across the economy is located. These protests can be considered as examples of resistance against absolute surplus value production, as one of the facets of capital accumulation. On the other hand, 13 per cent of the labour protests took place in the metals sector, and can be seen as examples of struggles against relative surplus value production, and explained by the high degree of unionization as well as the militancy of a specific union in this sector.[42]

In terms of the public sector, the most militant protests at the production level took place against precarization, as exemplified in the TEKEL resistance in 2009. At the level of realization, the resistance of Eğitim-Sen and SES, the major public employee unions in the education and health sectors, against commercialization of public services can be considered as a good example. Finally, the ongoing struggles of villagers living in the Black Sea regions against the construction of hydroelectric power plants, most of whom are elderly women making their living working on tea plantations and being forced to abandon their valleys, are not only parts of ecological struggles against the commodification of nature but also against the revalorization of capital in the energy sector.

How can all these struggles be brought together in the subjective experience and consciousness of workers? According to Mario Candeais, neoliberalism involves two types of precarization: in the working conditions of labourers on the one hand, and in the conditions of social reproduction (such as health, housing, daycare) of broader sections of society on the other.[43] In that sense, the struggle against precarity under neoliberalism has become the intersection point between interests of the working class and the interests of society in general. In his 1985 book *Towards 2000*, Raymond Williams argued that the main problem with the relationship between class and politics today is that the intersection between the interests of the working class and that of society as a whole cannot be shown as easily as in the past.

In order to defend socialism as a project, 'a practical and possible general interest, which really does include all reasonable particular interests' has to be found, and this general interest must be related to the labour movement.[44] In the current historical moment, the working class has the general interest, in the complex sense Williams invokes, to eradicate precarity for the whole of society through eradicating its own precarity – the potential to lead a general human emancipation through its own self-emancipation.

In Turkey, this can be seen most clearly in the struggle of public employees against the commodification of public services. When physicians struggle against the commodification of health services, for instance, they do not only struggle against the commodification of their own labour power. They also struggle for the access of broader sections of society to decent health services and thereby protect the general social interest while pursuing their own. Similarly, when teachers struggle against the neoliberal 4+4+4 education model, they do not only struggle to protect their own professional dignity, but also the rights of all sections of society to decent education. It is in this sense that the TEKEL and Gezi resistances have been turning points in terms of working-class formation in Turkey.

The increase in the number and militancy of labour protests since the Gezi resistance bears notice. The most interesting example of this has been the Kazova textile workers' strike, which had begun in January 2013 well before the Gezi resistance. Spurred on by the Gezi uprising, the workers occupied the factory, and began to produce and sell sweaters under workers' control. The same spirit of resistance could be seen in the workers' protests after the Soma massacre, too. A week after the disaster, the surviving miners of Soma stormed the headquarters of both the mining company and the company union, calling for the resignation of the union leadership and pursuing affiliation with a more left-wing union. The spirit of freedom sparked by Gezi resistance is increasingly encompassing industrial workers.

The Gezi resistance reflects, as well, a general shift in protests from the anti-globalization protests of the late 1990s against supranational institutions to anti-government protests targeted at national states. The shift in discourse of these ongoing protests in Turkey, now directed against class power concentrated in the Turkish state, mark a huge leap forward in class struggle from the national-developmentalist discourse of the late 1990s against external forces such as the IMF and the World Bank. What we have termed 'a nation-based anti-capitalist politics that does not fall into the pitfalls of either nationalism or abstract internationalism' is gaining in resonance.[45] In the words of a Gezi slogan, 'the empire of fear has collapsed' and the class struggle escalates.

NOTES

We would like to thank İbrahim Gündoğdu for commenting on an early draft of this paper.

1   Between 2000 and 2011, the Turkish unionization density rate fell from 10 per cent to 5.9 per cent, making Turkey the OECD nation with the lowest level of trade union organization. See Aziz Çelik, 'Trade unions and deunionization during ten years of AKP rule', available at http://www.tr.boell.org.

2   The total of consumer loans and credit card debt increased sharply from 1.8 per cent in 2002 to 18.7 per cent in 2012. Over 2009-11, two-thirds of consumer loans went to wage earners and low-income households. See Elif Karacimen, 'Financialization in Turkey: The Case of Consumer Debt', *Journal of Balkan and Near Eastern Studies*, 16(2), 2014, pp.161-80.

3   Quoted in Ibrahim Gündogdu and Jamie Gough, 'Class-cleansing in Istanbul's world-city project', in Libby Porter and Kate Shaw, eds., *Whose Urban Renaissance? An International Comparison of Urban Regeneration Strategies*, London: Routledge, 2009, p. 16.

4   Ali Akay, 'Transversal Struggle: Gezi Park', *Eurozine*, 11 June 2013.

5   Çağlar Keyder, 'New Middle Class', in *Gezi Park Events from Sociological and Political Perspectives,* Turkish Academy of Sciences, Ankara, 2013 (in Turkish).

6   'Korkut Boratav evaluates the gezi resistance: a mature class-based contumacy', available at http://www.sendika.org.

7   Cenk Saraçoğlu, '2013 Uprising in Turkey: The Reversal of the Process of Ideological Dispossesion', Paper presented at the Conference on the June Uprising: Background, Dynamics and Perspectives, University of Kassel, 15-16 May 2014.

8   Ellen Meiksins Wood, *Democracy Against Capitalism*, Cambridge: Cambridge University Press, 1995.

9   *Hürriyet Daily News*, 30 September 2012.

10   Serkan Öngel, 'The Dimensions of Subcontracting in Turkey', 21 March 2014 (in Turkish), available at www.kesk.org.tr.

11   DİSK-AR Report on Work-related Murders in Turkey, 26 May 2014 (in Turkish), available at www.disk.org.tr.

12   Derya Gultekin-Karakas and Fuat Ercan, 'Financialization in Turkey: A Form of Dependency or an External Financing Strategy of Productive Capital?', Paper presented at IIPPE, the Fourth Annual Conference in Political Economy, Netherlands, 9-11 July 2013.

13   Derya Karakaş, *Global Integration of Turkish Finance Capital: State, Capital and the Banking Reform in Turkey*, Berlin: VDM Verlag Dr. Müller, 2009, p. 82.

14   Fuat Ercan and Ferda Uzunyayla, 'A Class Perspective on the New Actors and Their Demands from the Turkish Education System', in Dave Hill and Ellen Rosskam, eds., *The Developing World and State Education: Neoliberal Depredation and Egalitarian Alternatives*, London: Routledge, 2008, pp. 109-24.

15   That is why using the word 'savage capitalism' for the Soma massacre is quite problematic. It disregards the simultaneous operation of relative

surplus production along with absolute surplus production and pre-capitalist mechanisms of labour control by 'head uncles'. It also leads to the politically misleading conclusion that what we need is a more humane capitalism against what Ayse Kadıoğlu and Fuat Keyman call 'merciless growth' based on subcontracted labour. See Fuat Keyman, 'From Gezi to Soma: Merciless Growth', *Radikal*, Daily Newspaper, 17 May 2014 (in Turkish).

16   Eric Hobsbawm, *The Age of Extremes: A History of the World, 1914-1991*, New York: Vintage, 1994, p. 291.

17   As Raju Das argues, the transition from absolute to real subsumption is not automatic, but is a protracted process, mediated by class struggle and state interventions which vary from place to place. See: 'Reconceptualizing Capitalism: Forms of Subsumption of Labor, Class Struggle, and Uneven Development', *Review of Radical Political Economics*, 44(2), 2012, pp. 178-200.

18   Serdal Bahçe and Ahmet Haşim Köse, 'The Effects of the New Welfare System on the Inter- and Intra-Class Distribution of Income in Turkey', Paper presented at Global Labour University, Berlin, 2014.

19   In this process, seven agricultural producers' unions came together in 2008 to establish the Farmer Unions Confederation (Çiftçi-Sen) to defend the rights of small-scale farmers and food security against neoliberal agricultural policies.

20   See Bahçe and Köse, 'The Effects of the New Welfare System', for a class-based analysis of all the other figures on income distribution in this period.

21   Ferda Koç, 'Kurdish Segment of Proleterianization Process or the Problem of Kurdish Labour', in Özay Göztepe, ed., *Precarization: Process, Delusion, Opportunity*, Ankara: Notabene, 2012 (in Turkish).

22   Özgür Müftüoğlu, 'Academy Disregards the Kurds in Labour Studies', *Tiroj*, 60(January/February), 2013 (in Turkish).

23   Koç, 'Kurdish Segment of Proleterianization Process'.

24   *Dünya Gazetesi*, Daily Newspaper, 24 November 2013 (in Turkish). For the list of provinces included in this new region since 2012, see http://www.incentive.gov.tr.

25   İrfan Kaygısız, 'An Evaluation of 2013 Labour Protests', Paper presented at the Association of Sociology Graduates, 2014 (in Turkish).

26   International Labour Organization, *The State of Women's Employment in Turkey*, Geneva: ILO, 2008.

27   Gülay Toksöz, *Women's Employment Situation in Turkey*, Ankara: International Labour Office, 2007, available at http://www.oit.org. The participation of women in the informal sector mainly takes four forms: home-based work related to industrial production, paid domestic work, unpaid rural work and production of handicraft. See Saniye Dedeoğlu, *Women Workers in Turkey: Global Industrial Production in Istanbul,* London: Tauris, 2008, p. 52.

28   Melda Yaman Öztürk, 'Women's Labour on the Axis of Waged Labour and Unwaged Care Labour', in Saniye Dedeoğlu and Melda Yaman Öztürk, eds., *Capitalism, Patriarchy and Women's Labour*, İstanbul: SAV, 2010 (in Turkish).

29   Öztürk, 'Women's Labour'.

30   Aysen Ustubici, 'Export-processing Zones and Gendering the Resistance: "Women's Strike" in Antalya Free Zone in Turkey', *London School of Economics, Gender Institute, New Working Paper Series*, Issue 24, March 2009.

31   Fuat Ercan, 'What Does a Commodity Consist of? Commodification of Health Services', in Osman Elbek, ed., *Capitalism is Harmful for Health*, İstanbul: Haykitap, 2013 (in Turkish).

32   Çağla Ünlütürk Ulutaş, *Transformation of the Labour Process in the Turkish Health Sector*, Ankara: NotaBene, 2011, p. 220 (in Turkish).

33   Özlem Özkan, 'Is Flexible Labour a Trap, or an Opportunity for Nurses?', in Melda Yaman et al., eds., *The Book of Labour*, İstanbul: SAV, 2014 (in Turkish).

34   Gizem Şimşek, '4+4+4 Discontinuous Education Model and the Transformation of Teachers' Labour as Human Capital: Capitalism that Expands through Creating Difference', *Praksis*, 33(3), 2013 (in Turkish).

35   Kasım Akbaş, 'Gilded Collars Between Class and Middle-Class Debates: Are the Lawyers in the Process of Proletarianization?', *Praksis*, 32(2), 2013 (in Turkish).

36   Ahmet Haşim Köse and Ahmet Öncü, 'A Class Analysis of the Professional and Political Ideologies of Engineers in Turkey', in Sungur Savran and Neşecan Balkan, eds., *The Ravages of Neo-Liberalism: Economy, Society and Gender in Turkey*, New York: Nova Publisher, 2002.

37   Serdal Bahçe, 'The Myth of the Middle-class and the Engineer's Nemesis', *Praksis*, 32(2), 2013 (in Turkish).

38   Deniz Yıldırım, 'Interview with Tekel Workers', *Bulletin of Education and Science Workers Union*, February/March 2010 (in Turkish).

39   Metin Özuğurlu, 'The TEKEL Resistance Movement: Reminiscences on Class Struggle', *Capital & Class*, 35(2), 2011, pp. 179-87.

40   E.P. Thompson, *The Making of the English Working Class*, London: Penguin, 1963, p. 9.

41   Kaygısız, 'An Evaluation of 2013 Labour Protests'.

42   Kaygısız, 'An Evaluation of 2013 Labour Protests'.

43   Mario Candeias, 'Double Precarisation of Labour and Reproduction: Perspectives of Expanded (re)Appropriation', Paper presented at the World Social Forum, Porto Allegre, 2005.

44   Raymond Williams, *Towards 2000*, London: Penguin, 1983, p. 165.

45   Fuat Ercan and Şebnem Oğuz, 'Rethinking Anti-Neoliberal Strategies Through the Perspective of Value Theory: Insights from the Turkish Case', *Science and Society*, 71(2), 2007, p. 200.

THE EGYPTIAN WORKERS' MOVEMENT BEFORE AND AFTER THE 2011 POPULAR UPRISING

JOEL BEININ AND MARIE DUBOC

Continuing a cycle of contention over economic demands that began in the late 1990s, Egyptian workers sharply escalated the pace of their strikes and collective actions in early 2014. The movement has been in large measure a response, albeit for the most part not articulated in these terms, to the neoliberal transformation of the Egyptian economy.

In January and February 2014, about 100,000 workers participated in strikes and other collective actions. The pace of protest escalated further in March when thousands of public sector doctors, dentists and pharmacists declared a full strike, as did thousands of Alexandria Public Transport workers. During the year's first quarter there were a total of 240 labour actions.[1] Projected to an annual basis, this is a significant decline from the high point of 2011-12, but still far more than any year during the decade before the demise of former President Hosni Mubarak in 2011. The upsurge followed a relatively quiescent six-month period after the ouster of President Muhammad Morsi of the Muslim Brothers-sponsored Freedom and Justice Party. Morsi was removed by a combination of massive popular demonstrations on 30 June 2013 – even larger than those that had led to the demise of Mubarak two and a half years earlier – followed by a military coup on July 3 after serving just one year in office as Egypt's first democratically elected president.

Like the majority of Egyptians, most workers and trade unions hoped the new government installed by the military on 16 July 2013 would end Morsi's escalating undemocratic practices and political incompetence, stabilize the country and address their economic needs. Six months after the coup it was evident that none of this had happened. The two post-Morsi interim governments, in which Minister of Defence and Commander in Chief of the Armed Forces, Field Marshal Abdel Fattah el-Sisi was the strong man, soon began restoring major elements of the Mubarak regime.

Repression of all forms of opposition (not only the Muslim Brothers), detention without charges, filing manifestly false charges against prominent opposition figures, beating and torture of prisoners, intimidating and jailing journalists, restricting the activities of legal opposition political parties and disciplining workers rather than addressing their pressing economic needs were the order of the day.

In the wake of campaigns by workers and their allies going on since 2008, the post-coup government announced that the monthly minimum basic wage for state employees would be almost doubled (while the minimum wage for the private sector remained unchanged), effective 1 January 2014. Notably, however, the increase did not apply to the 2,846 enterprises (employing 835,000 workers) comprising the 'public business sector'; nor did it apply to workers in publicly owned utilities, nor to many others (like non-professional staff at public universities). Hoda Kamel, a member of the Executive Board of the Egyptian Federation of Independent Trade Unions, criticized this limited application:

> For the past six months, the people waited for the government to be the government of the revolution – as they had promised … But when January came, people realised it was a trick because the minimum wage is just for a very small part of people working in the government, not for the private-sector or most government workers.[2]

Workers at Egypt's largest industrial enterprise, Misr Spinning and Weaving Co. (known as Ghazl Mahalla after the central Delta city where it is located), which employs some 22,000 workers, over 20 per cent of all public sector textile workers, were prominent in the protests demanding broader application of the minimum wage. On February 10 they struck for the fourth time in nine months to demand inclusion in the minimum wage, payment of an overdue annual bonus and removal of the CEO of the public sector textile holding company they denounced as corrupt. They were joined by some 20,000 public sector textile workers from a dozen other firms as well as workers in Cairo public transport, railways, post, telephone, telegraph and garbage collectors – all demanding that the new minimum wage be applied to them.[3] Publicly employed professionals – not only doctors, dentists and pharmacists mentioned above, but also nurses, veterinarians and teachers – engaged in partial strikes, thereby continuing the protest campaigns they had begun in the last years before Mubarak's overthrow.

Adding to this upsurge of collective action were strikes and sit-ins demanding renationalization of ten public sector enterprises that were privatized in the last years of the Mubarak era. The struggle has been sharpest in three firms with a total workforce of about 10,000 – the Indorama Spinning (known as Ghazl Shibin), Tanta Flax and Oils and Steam Fittings companies, where court rulings ordered renationalization because the private investors failed to uphold their contractual obligations to the workers. Delegations from those factories sat-in for over a month at the state-sponsored Egyptian Trade Union Federation (ETUF) offices in central Cairo to demand implementation of the court orders before being joined by representatives of seven other privatized firms.

At the same time, independent trade unionists and their supporters renewed their demand that the government promulgate the 'Trade Union Freedoms Law' which, as first drafted in August 2011, would permit forming independent unions and federations. Indeed, the ETUF's legal monopoly on representation of workers had been increasingly challenged well before the 2011 uprising. The failure of both Morsi and the generals to implement the court decisions on renationalization or to enact the 'Trade Union Freedoms Law' most clearly indicate that the overthrow of Mubarak did not alter the Egyptian elite's commitment to neoliberalism.

THE EGYPTIAN WORKERS' MOVEMENT BEFORE 2011

Perhaps unsurprisingly in the era of global neoliberal hegemony, the significance of the workers' movement has been underestimated in both Western and Egyptian explanations for Mubarak's overthrow. Egyptian workers had participated significantly in the burgeoning culture of protest that delegitimized the Mubarak regime during the decade before his ouster on 11 February 2011. From 2004 to 2010, there were over 3,400 strikes and other collective actions, involving somewhere between 2 and 4 million workers (see Table 1). This was a substantial escalation compared to previous mobilizations. From 1998 to 2003, there was an average of 118 collective actions a year by workers, compared to only 33 for the 1986 to 1993 period.[4]

This extraordinary social movement placed the issue of social justice on the public agenda more forcefully than at any time since anti-IMF bread riots erupted in 1977, repudiating policies adopted after President Anwar al-Sadat's proclamation of the 'Open Door' economic policy in 1974. During the Mubarak era (1981-2011), successive governments, albeit some more reluctantly and haltingly than others, set about restructuring the economy following what became known in the 1980s as the 'Washington Consensus' model. This was enshrined in the Economic Restructuring and Structural Adjustment Program Egypt signed with the International Monetary Fund and the World Bank in June 1991, immediately followed by new legislation (Law 203) that established the framework for no less than 314 privatizations.

Table 1

Collective Actions and Participants, 1998-2010[8]

	Strikes, Sit-ins, Demonstrations, etc.	Workers Participating
1998	114	n/a
1999	164	n/a
2000	135	n/a
2001	115	n/a
2002	96	n/a
2003	86	n/a
2004	266	386,346
2005	202	141,175
2006	222	198,088
2007	614	474,838
2008	609	541,423
2009	432	318,967
2010	371	145,671
TOTAL	**3,426**	**2,206,508**

Workers' contestation increased exponentially and adopted a more militant character after the installation of Prime Minister Ahmad Nazif's 'government of businessmen' in July 2004, which was charged with accelerating the neoliberal restructuring of the economy. Rather than sitting in at their workplaces and maintaining production – a tactic from the limited repertoire of contention during Gamal Abdel Nasser's authoritarian-populist 'Arab Socialist' regime (1954-70) – strikes, some lasting for months, became increasingly common.[5] A high proportion of workers' grievances were rooted in their opposition to the consequences of the privatization of public sector enterprises. It was also related to the impact of new legislation (the Unified Labour Law No. 12 of 2003) to encourage foreign direct investment by authorizing employers to sign 'temporary' contracts with workers that could be terminated unilaterally and without cause. The ETUF leadership accepted the Unified Labour Law in exchange for securing greater prerogatives in decision-making processes. But far from 'expand[ing] the political space that labour institutions enjoy', as some observers of Egyptian state-labour relations in the neoliberal era have argued,[6] these very limited state concessions, in fact, expanded the state's means of co-optation of the ETUF, which remained largely unaccountable to its members.

Because the Unified Labour Law required approval of local strikes by the ETUF national leadership, strikers throughout the 2000s mobilized illegally and independently of the ETUF.[7] In 2004 alone, the number of collective actions more than doubled the annual average from 1998 to 2003 (Table 1). Although initially concentrated in the textile industry (a declining sector particularly affected by the privatization programme), by 2007 the strike movement encompassed nearly every economic sector and extended beyond workers to include publicly employed professionals – doctors, health technicians, teachers and university professors.

This did not constitute a classical, western-style workers' movement animated by trade unions, cooperative associations, labour parties and alliances with left intellectuals. But it certainly fits Tarrow and Tilly's definition of a social movement as 'a sustained campaign of claim making, using repeated performances that advertise the claim, based on organizations, networks, traditions, and solidarities that sustain these activities'.[9] Egyptian workers mobilized under highly constrained conditions. They confronted an authoritarian regime fully supported by the United States (unlike the case of Solidarity in Poland); an official trade union structure (ETUF) that functions as a state institution; and an extreme paucity of independent organizational resources. Alliances with left intellectuals were weak or non-existent; indeed, most workers distrusted the Cairene intelligentsia and what passed for 'politics' in the Mubarak era.

Moreover, the most substantial oppositional political force throughout the Mubarak era was the Muslim Brothers, who have long been regarded by the left as strikebreakers.[10] Since 1996, their members or supporters have won elected offices in ETUF affiliated local unions. Although individual Brothers sometimes supported strikes and other forms of contestation, the leadership consistently maintained a corporatist view of society and denied the existence of class distinctions among Muslims while embracing neoliberal policies.

The paucity of Egyptian workers' organizational resources and capacities was exemplified by the fact that in the 2000s, during a strike wave of unprecedented proportions, there were only two NGOs working on labour issues with less than half a dozen paid staff between them. One was the Center for Trade Union and Workers Services (CTUWS, Markaz al-Khadamat al-Niqabiyya wa'l-'Ummaliyya), which had been established in 1990 following two exceptionally violent strikes at the public sector Helwan Iron and Steel Company. Kamal 'Abbas, one of the fired strike leaders, has served as

CTUWS General Coordinator since then. The other was the Coordinating Committee for Trade Union and Workers Rights and Liberties (al-Lajna al-Tansiqiyya li'l-Huquq wa'l-Hurriyat al-Niqabiyya wa'l-'Ummaliyya), which was established to monitor the 2000 trade union elections and which continued as a monthly forum for exchange of information and advice until it was folded into the Egyptian Center for Economic and Social Rights (ECESR, al-Markaz al-Misri li'l-Huquq al-Iqtisadiyya wa'l-Ijtima'iyya) in 2010.

The ECESR's energetic director, the labour lawyer Khalid 'Ali, ran for president as an independent in 2012. Although widely respected by workers, he won less than 1 per cent of the first-round votes – in large measure due to the limited organizational capacity of Egypt's subaltern strata. The other highly regarded 'workers' candidate' in the race, Abu al-'Izz al-Hariri, running on the Socialist Popular Alliance Party ticket, did even worse. In fact, political groups have rarely been directly involved with workers' collective actions.[11] Only a handful of journalists, urban intellectuals and political activists have provided sustained support. Consequently, even the most militant workers commonly defined themselves as 'natural leaders' (qiyadat tabi'iyyin) to indicate their distance from formal political parties. As one labour activist put it:

> Strike leaders used to be members of political parties, but now they are created during the strikes. They are called natural leaders because they come from the ranks of the workers and the workers gather around them, spontaneously.[12]

To discredit labour action, the Mubarak regime regularly accused strikers of advancing the agenda of political opposition groups – Muslim Brothers or Communists – rather than representing workers' demands. In this context, workers' insistence on presenting themselves as independent from political groups was both factually correct and tactically efficacious. It legitimized their demands and increased the likelihood of winning economic gains.

The authoritarian social pact of the Mubarak era relied on a certain level of redistribution backed by what Béatrice Hibou terms 'powerful mechanisms of inclusion'.[13] These mechanisms confirmed workers' belief that the state and ultimately the president were responsible for resolving their grievances. Consequently, workers were reluctant (and remain so even today) to be associated with opposition political groups. If strikes had been associated with political demands they would have been seen as a challenge to the regime and risked harsh repression. Hence, while calling on the state and its representatives to meet their demands, striking workers very rarely called for the overthrow, or even significant reform, of the Mubarak regime.

For example, even in the important 2009 Ghazl Shibin strike, workers' demands were formulated as calls on the government, and as a last resort the president, to pressure the privatized company's new management to pay a bonus which had been one of the benefits provided under their contract with the former public enterprise. Since the company was located in the home province of Mubarak's family, workers carried posters, along with pictures of him, proclaiming: 'Hosni, son of Minufiyya rescue the workers of Shibin'.

Workers' expectations that the state owes them something has generally led demands to be framed as 'rights' (*huquq*) rather than as overt opposition to the regime. This differs from E.P. Thompson's concept of 'moral economy', which he used to show how protests by the emergent English working class were fuelled by a growing sense of injustice in the face of ruling elites who were no longer adhering to the norms of mutual reciprocity and responsibility that had structured the old class society.[14] In contrast, the most prominent and typical demands that emanated from recent Egyptian labour protests were cast in terms that reflected a sense that rights secured by law rather than custom were being violated. While demands for workers on temporary contracts to be given permanent status might be considered closer to Thompson's 'moral economy', even these types of demands by Egyptian workers reflected the expectation that the state owes workers a secure job, although the 2003 Unified Labour Law definitively eliminated this 'right'. Consequently, some workers employed on permanent contracts see these demands as 'meaningless'.

The fraying of the distinction between demands for 'rights' and opposition to the regime was already evident in the high profile and successful strikes of 2006-07 at Ghazl al-Mahalla. A third strike was planned for 6 April 2008 to secure a minimum monthly basic pay of EGP 1,200 and other wage supplements. The strike call acquired national political resonance and the minimum wage demand was subsequently widely adopted. Some Cairo-based political parties and opposition groups, including the widely touted April 6 Youth Movement, announced their solidarity with the workers and called for a general strike.

The Mubarak regime properly understood the demands emanating from this local strike and the attempted political mobilization around them as a challenge to its national economic policies. Before the strike date, the head of the ETUF summoned seven local workers' leaders to a meeting in Cairo to intimidate them into calling off the strike. Five agreed to cancel the strike in exchange for a higher food allowance, while two refused to back down. Intense repression and deployment of security forces throughout the city intimidated the majority of the Mahalla workers who remained on the job on April 6. However, there were large demonstrations in the streets of Mahalla that day, mostly by women and children, against the high price of bread.[15] In response to attacks by police and regime thugs on the demonstrators, two days of popular riots erupted, which some consider a dress rehearsal for the 2011 uprising. Two young men were killed and hundreds were wounded in the clashes between protesters and the police. Three workers from Ghazl al-Mahalla were arrested and several faced arbitrary transfers or pay cuts to intimidate them from taking part in future protests.

The call for a national strike was not heeded, nor did any coordinating bodies of workers or sustained alliance between workers and oppositional intellectuals emerge during and after the events of 6–7 April 2008. However, in October 2008, forty NGOs and opposition political parties launched a 'Campaign for the Freedom, Independence, and Democratization of Labour Unions'.[16] Meanwhile, the struggle for a monthly minimum wage continued, but rather than being based on local workplace action it was advanced mainly by the small pro-labour NGOs mentioned above and by supportive intellectuals. Therefore, Egyptian workers arrived at the 25 January 2011 uprising with no national organization and no political or economic programme beyond the demand for a substantial increase in the monthly minimum wage.

WORKERS AND THE 2011 UPRISING

Workers deserve more credit for Mubarak's ouster than they are typically given. Despite their inability to take the lead, they were quick to mobilize in the early stages of the groundswell that eventually unseated the president. As Khalid 'Ali explained:

> The workers did not start the January 25 movement because they have no organizing structure …. [But] one of the important steps of this revolution was taken when they began to protest, giving the revolution an economic and social slant besides the political demands.[17]

Facilitated by the government's closure of all public sector workplaces in early February, many workers participated in the popular uprising as individuals. Just two days after work was resumed on February 6, tens of thousands of workers – including those employed at large and strategic workplaces like the Cairo Public Transport Authority, Egyptian State

Railways, the subsidiary companies of the Suez Canal Authority, the state electrical company and Ghazl al-Mahalla – went on strike, demanding both the resolution of local grievances and the ouster of Mubarak. There were some sixty strikes and protests in the final days before Mubarak's fall on February 11. The exact weight of these strikes in the decision of the Supreme Council of the Armed Forces (SCAF) to push Mubarak aside in what was as much a soft military coup as a revolution is uncertain. However, one Egyptian NGO asserted that the economic paralysis created by this strike wave 'was one of the most important factors leading to the rapidity of ... Mubarak's decision to leave'.[18]

Mubarak's removal satisfied the majority of demonstrators, at least during the first half of 2011. But workers continued to protest. At least 150,000 participated in 489 strikes and other collective actions during February 2011.[19]

One of the less noticed events of the popular uprising was the formation of the Egyptian Federation of Independent Trade Unions (EFITU) – the first new institution to emerge from the revolt. Its existence was announced on 30 January 2011, at a press conference in Cairo's Tahrir Square – the epicentre of the popular movement. The initiative to establish the new federation was launched by the pro-labour NGO, CTUWS, the Independent General Union of Real Estate Tax Assessors, established in 2009, and the much smaller independent unions of healthcare technicians and teachers.[20] They were joined by the recently established 8.5 million member retirees association and representatives of textile, pharmaceutical, chemical, iron and steel and automotive workers from industrial zones in Cairo, Helwan, Mahalla al-Kubra, Tenth of Ramadan City and Sadat City.

Forty EFITU leaders and labour activists met on February 19 and adopted a proclamation of 'Demands of the Workers in the Revolution', including the right to form independent trade unions, the right to strike and the dissolution of ETUF, 'one of the most important symbols of corruption under the defunct regime'. Reflecting a widespread sentiment among workers and the poor, they asserted:

> If this revolution does not lead to the fair distribution of wealth it is not worth anything. Freedoms are not complete without social freedoms. The right to vote is naturally dependent on the right to a loaf of bread.[21]

After a decade of struggle around economic and trade union issues, the participation in the popular uprising followed by the removal of some (but far from all) of the repressive constraints of the Mubarak regime gave trade union activists the confidence to assert political demands that they had previously mostly avoided. However, many revolutionary activists – especially young liberals with little political experience who had been prominent in the occupation of Tahrir and other urban squares – regarded these as 'special interest' (*fi'awi*) demands rather than proper 'national' demands, and refused to support them during February and March 2011, when the opportunity for change was greatest.[22]

Independent trade unionists vehemently opposed the SCAF's appointment of ETUF treasurer Isma'il Ibrahim Fahmi as Minister of Manpower and Migration (i.e., Labour) and proposed instead Ahmad Hasan al-Bura'i, a professor of labour law at Cairo University who had been publicly advocating trade union pluralism for several years. Under pressure, the generals replaced Fahmi with al-Bura'i. On March 12, the newly installed minister, in a previously unimaginable scene, participated in a panel discussion at the Press Syndicate along with EFITU president Kamal Abu Eita and CTUWS general coordinator, Kamal 'Abbas. The event, entitled 'Know your Role', was moderated by the Trotskyist labour journalist, Mustafa Basyuni. The daily *al-Ahram* reported:

> With tears in his eyes, El-Borai [al-Bura'i] stated with resolve that workers would soon have the right to establish, form and join any trade union of their choice – trade unions which would remain completely independent of the ministry. These unions would be able to independently conduct their domestic affairs, develop regulations, allocate their funds and choose their own leaders.[23]

Al-Bura'i did indeed recognize EFITU and scores of newly established independent enterprise-level trade unions. In doing so he interpreted Egypt's ratification of the International Labour Organization conventions guaranteeing freedom of association and the right to organize and bargain collectively as international treaty obligations that superseded national legislation establishing the ETUF as Egypt's only legal labour union. For their part, the EFITU and the CTUWS, the two-decade old pro-labour NGO, felt empowered enough by the new political legitimacy of their organizations, as well as the popular uprising, to submit memoranda to the Ministry of Manpower and Migration proposing a new trade union law. Their briefs drew on materials first drafted in 2008 by the 'Campaign for the Freedom, Independence, and Democratization of Labour Unions'.[24] The EFITU and its allies also received support from the international trade union movement, including the Solidarity Center of the AFL-CIO, several European trade union federations and the International Trade Union Confederation.

The EFITU and the Egyptian Democratic Labour Congress (EDLC), which split from the EFITU and held its founding congress in April 2013, claim that some 1,800 new unions independent of the ETUF have been established since the uprising against the Mubarak regime.[25] Some have no affiliations; others belong to regional confederations in Upper Egypt or the Permanent Congress of Alexandria Workers (PCAW); but many hundreds are affiliated with either EFITU or the EDLC.

Despite the promise of this independent union formation, the establishment of the EDLC divided the fledgling independent labour movement and weakened it as a national force. The roots of the split, which had both personal and political dimensions, go back to the summer of 2011 when the CTUWS and the unions in its orbit broke off from EFITU. The CTUWS has generally prioritized grassroots organization over participation in national politics. In contrast, EFITU President Kamal Abu Eita, a veteran Nasserist political activist, sought to seize the moment of Mubarak's demise to assert the national political presence of the independent workers' movement. Abu Eita, running on a joint electoral list with the Muslim Brothers, was the only worker elected to the first post-Mubarak parliament.

Beyond its internal divisions, the independent federations and their constituent local unions have limited organizational capacity and operate on uncertain legal ground, as the Trade Union Freedoms Law has not been adopted. Nonetheless, despite the continuing legal limitations on the right to strike, collective action, strikes and labour protests skyrocketed to 1,377 in 2011 and to 1,969 in 2012, thereby doubling and then tripling the previous highs of 614 in 2007 and 609 in 2008 (see Table 1). Estimates of the total number of workers participating in these actions in 2011 range widely – from 593,000 to 1,308,000.[26] There is no reliable estimate for the number of participants in collective actions in 2012 or for the number of collective actions or participants in 2013.

Since 2011, independent unions – representing municipal real estate tax assessors, teachers, Cairo bus and Metro workers, iron and steel, ceramic, port workers in Alexandria and 'Ayn Sukhna and many others – have continually mounted high-profile strikes that have forced the demands for workers' freedom of association, collective bargaining rights and a living wage onto the political agenda. Alongside the independent trade union movement, public sector industrial workers in large enterprises like Eastern Tobacco, Egyptian Aluminum and Ghazl al-Mahalla have sought to gain control of their ETUF-affiliated unions rather than join the new independent union movement, since leaving the state-run federation would endanger their pension, health and vacation benefits.

The post-Mubarak upsurge of labour protest was motivated by many of the same demands as most collective actions over the previous decade. One notable change in the pattern of collective action since 2011 is the relative decline in the participation of the private sector, possibly due to the closure of as many as 4,000 private firms whose investors fled Egypt's unstable conditions and harsh repression of efforts to organize independent trade unions in hitherto mostly nonunionized workplaces.[27] One high point in the first period after Mubarak's fall was the national teachers' strike in September 2011. Another outburst after Morsi's election as president, during the summer and fall of 2012, tested his intentions towards workers and found him lacking. Then, the December 2012 strikes at Ghazl al-Mahalla, Eastern Tobacco, the Egyptian Aluminum Co. and the 'Ayn Sukhna port – altogether nearly 40,000 workers – signalled growing opposition to Morsi's rule.

Both the SCAF and the Muslim Brothers attempted to repress the new labour movement as well as to exercise continued state control over the ETUF. They largely failed in the former, but had greater success in the latter. The SCAF responded to the surge of workers' collective action unleashed by Mubarak's demise by issuing a military decree (revised as Law 34 of 2011) establishing a fine of up to EGP 50,000 (then about US $7,200) for anyone participating in or encouraging others to join a sit-in or any other activity that 'prevents, delays or disrupts the work of public institutions or public authorities'. The penalty increased tenfold to EGP 500,000 and at least a year's imprisonment in the event of violence or property damage that may lead to 'destruction of means of production' or harm 'national unity and public security and order'.[28]

Moreover, less noticed than President Morsi's 22 November 2012 'Constitutional Declaration', granting himself wide-ranging powers subject to no judicial review, was a presidential decree issued three days later amending the Trade Union Law (No. 35 of 1976). Its effect was to allow the Muslim Brothers to take over large parts of the ETUF apparatus by removing all executive board members over 60 years old and replacing them with candidates selected by the Minister of Manpower and Migration.

This post under Morsi was occupied by Khalid al-Azhari, a member of the Muslim Brothers' Freedom and Justice Party. In December 2012, al-Azhari installed Gibali al-Maraghi, a Mubarak-era union apparatchik, as ETUF president, while Morsi at the same time appointed al-Maraghi to the upper house of parliament (the Shura Council). This was widely viewed as an offer by the Muslim Brothers to share control of the ETUF with former Mubarak supporters. But if this was designed to help keep Morsi in power, it had little effect, especially once his 'constitutional decree' provoked the fear and resistance that ultimately led to his downfall.

THE POST-MORSI WORKERS' MOVEMENTS

All the independent trade union federations – EFITU, EDLC and the Permanent Congress of Alexandria Workers (PCAW) – as well as the pro-labour NGOS, the CTUWS and ECESR, enthusiastically supported the Tamarrud (Rebel) campaign which turned out millions of demonstrators on 30 June 2013 to express 'no confidence' in President Morsi and demand early presidential elections. Thus when the Egyptian military seized the opportunity this presented to depose Morsi on July 3 it could claim with some validity that this military coup was the will of the people. But the army soon invoked its supposed popular mandate to justify increasingly repressive and anti-democratic actions, including not only the killings of some 1,000 pro-Morsi demonstrators in August, but also the muzzling of the press, the arrest of opposition figures across the political spectrum and numerous trials on spurious charges.

Nevertheless, many workers hoped that their demands would receive a more attentive hearing with Morsi gone, particularly since the founding president of the EFITU, Kamal Abu Eita, accepted an appointment as Minister of Manpower and Migration in the interim cabinet. As if to assure the military of his acceptability, Abu Eita proclaimed that 'Workers who were champions of the strike under the previous regime should now become champions of production'.[29] A sharp debate ensued among independent trade unionists over Abu Eita's acceptance of the ministry and the military's transitional 'road map'. A majority of the EFITU leadership and many others believed that his presence in the cabinet represented a victory and would ensure that workers' demands were met. Expressing the minority view, EFITU executive board member Fatma Ramadan believed that 'the military and the remnants of the old regime (*fulul*)... kidnapped' the movement with Abu Eita's appointment, and criticized him for not consulting with other EFITU leaders before suggesting that workers would abandon the strike weapon:

> As a union federation our role must be to uphold all workers' rights, including the right to strike .... We cannot possibly call on workers to protect the interests of businessmen by forfeiting labour rights under the pretext of bolstering the national economy.[30]

Abu Eita would surely never have been appointed were it not for the mass social movement in which he had risen to leadership. But it should have been obvious that neither the military nor any government that relied on its support would countenance the decentralized direct action from below that has been the strength of the workers movement throughout the current cycle of contention. Moreover, given that the military had already blocked enactment of the Trade Union Freedoms Law in 2011, the majority of the business-friendly cabinet installed on July 16, with its Mubarak-era retreads, was most unlikely to support it. Any questions about the balance of forces within the post-coup government were clarified when Abu Eita stood by while security forces crushed a militant strike at the Suez Steel Company, located in the Suez Canal city whose protesters were the first to target police stations and the local headquarters of the ruling National Democratic Party during the January 25 uprising.

When on 6 July 2013 interim President 'Adly Mansour issued a constitutional declaration to govern the period until adoption of a new constitution, the pro-labour NGO, ECESR, openly attacked this as a 'Constitutional Coup Against the Principles of the Revolution'.[31] It protested that there was no consultation with the political forces that mobilized the June 30 demonstrations over its contents, while pointing out that Mansour's declaration ignored

> economic and social rights, such as the right to housing, health, medical treatment, food, drink, clothes, insurance, pensions, social security and the minimum and maximum wage. It failed to link wages to prices or to specify the right to worker representation on corporate boards and in profit sharing.[32]

For its part, the CTUWS, which was at first more reserved in its criticism of the military-installed regime, issued several reports documenting the Muslim Brothers' anti-worker policies, which could be interpreted as an oblique indication of some degree of support for the military. However, its annual report for 2013 firmly asserted that 'there was no improvement' in workers' conditions since Morsi's overthrow.[33]

When Minister of Defence Abdel Fattah el-Sisi called for nationwide demonstrations on July 26 to give him a mandate to confront 'violence and terrorism' – a thinly veiled reference to the Muslim Brothers – the ECESR joined several human rights NGOs in issuing a declaration expressing concern about Sisi's intentions. In contrast, the EFITU released a statement affirming workers' rights to freedom of expression, to demonstrate peacefully and to strike, but simultaneously supporting 'all the security apparatuses of the Egyptian state in confronting terrorism and the forces of darkness [i.e. the Muslim Brothers]'.[34] Those same apparatuses were breaking strikes and attacking demonstrators during the Morsi administration and continued to do so after his demise.

The July 26 demonstrations were massive – as were counter-demonstrations by supporters of Morsi. Among those who answered Sisi's call was the ETUF, which pledged to mobilize all its members. Independent trade unionists who supported military intervention to oust Morsi thus found themselves uncomfortably close to the key labour institution of the Mubarak regime. The new cabinet soon announced a series of measures that aimed at reducing contestation by appearing to respond to Egyptians' expectations of social justice. Most importantly, in September 2013 the interim government raised the monthly minimum wage for state employees. Given the widespread consensus in favour of the military, these measures temporarily succeeded in halting labour protests. But by reviving the remnants of a social contract, they also raised expectations that the government would deliver on its promises.

Of the 38.6 per cent of eligible voters who participated in the January 2014 referendum on a new Egyptian Constitution to replace the one Morsi had forced through in December 2012, 98 per cent voted 'yes'. A majority of political parties and religious institutions, including al-Azhar and the Coptic Church, supported the Constitution and encouraged their members to participate in the vote. Having been declared a terrorist organization by the government in December 2013, the Muslim Brothers boycotted the referendum.

A relatively small minority who rejected both the Brothers and the military-sponsored regime, including the Strong Egypt Party, which is led by a former Muslim Brother with a more democratic orientation than the Brothers' leadership, also boycotted or voted no. Thus despite the extreme polarization of the Egyptian political field since July 2013, some of the intelligentsia and labour activists reject the Brothers/military dichotomy. Some of them are organizationally represented by the Road of the Revolution Front, which was established by urban, middle-class leftists, secular liberals and moderate Islamists in September 2013. A few labour leaders have similar views, but they are isolated and their organizational links to the Front are uncertain. In any case, the Front has limited influence; several of its leaders were jailed in November–December 2013.

Article 77 of the 2014 Constitution reiterates the provisions of Article 53 of the 2012 Constitution, which independent trade unionists had denounced for permitting only one syndicate per profession. The article appears to apply only to professional syndicates (i.e., the bar and medical associations, etc.), not labour unions. But unclarity in the language of the article may serve to limit the growth of labour unions independent of the state and permit continuation of the ETUF's legal monopoly over trade union representation in most industries.[35]

The upsurge of strikes and labour protest in early 2014 indicated that although most workers and publicly employed professionals, like the great majority of Egyptians, continued to support the military-installed post-July 3 government, they were unwilling to put their pressing economic needs on hold despite repeatedly being urged to do so since 2011. This may eventually provide a basis for challenging the mindless ultra-patriotism, xenophobia and demonization of the Muslim Brothers that substituted for political discourse after July 2013. On 24 February 2014, the entire government of Prime Minister Hazem al-Beblawi resigned. Some believed that the principal reason for this was the rash of strikes and labour protests. Others cited the government's general incompetence. Like many aspects of contemporary Egyptian politics, it is impossible to know for certain.

What is certain is that the government of Prime Minister Ibrahim Mahlab, a former member of the National Democratic Party's Policies Committee, the political apparatus of Mubarak *fils* and leading neoliberal promoter, Gamal Mubarak, which was sworn in on March 1, proved even less friendly to labour than its predecessor. Most of the ministers in al-Beblawi's government retained their posts; only those identified as liberals were removed. Kamal Abu Eita was replaced as Minister of Manpower and Migration by Nahid al-'Ashri, who headed the Dispute Resolution Bureau in the ministry during the Mubarak era. In that capacity she oversaw the privatization of Ghazl Shibin, Tanta Flax and Oils and other firms. Hisham al-'Uql, who was forced to resign from his job at Tanta Flax and Oils in 2010, was among the many workers and leftists who criticized al-'Ashri's appointment saying, 'She's the worst person who could possibly be chosen to fill the post of Minister of Manpower'.[36] Only a week after her appointment al-'Ashri proposed banning strikes for one year. Unsurprisingly, Gibali al-Maraghi, the Mubarak-era figure retained (after some to and fro) as head of the ETUF, welcomed al-'Ashri's appointment. Thus at both the ETUF and the Ministry of Manpower and Labour there appears to be a complete restoration of the Mubarak regime, with the promotion of former second level figures to leadership positions.

On June 8, Abdel Fattah el-Sisi was sworn in as Egypt's president following his predicted landslide electoral victory. Sisi faced only one opponent, Hamdeen Sabahi, leader of the Nasserist al-Karama (Dignity) Party and the somewhat broader Popular Current. Sabahi reached an unexpected third place in the first round of the 2012 presidential elections (in which a dozen candidates participated). But the political context of the 2014 race was radically different.

The state media relentlessly promoted Sisi as the man of the hour who had rescued Egypt from the Muslim Brothers and whose military credentials were essential to governing Egypt. Sisi's campaign stressed stability and security over civil liberties and justified the increasingly repressive environment since July 2013, which intimidated most credible opponents from challenging him. In addition to the more than 1,000 demonstrators killed by the police, 16,000 have been detained. A law enacted in November 2013 criminalizes protests, allows security forces to use lethal violence to disperse protesters and authorizes the Ministry of Interior to ban protests on grounds including 'threats to security and peace'.[37]

Sisi won less than a million more votes in 2014 than Morsi in 2012. Hence, Sisi's mandate is not as solid as he anticipated. An embarrassingly low turnout during the mandated two days of balloting (May 26 and 27) indicated lack of enthusiasm for the race and its ill-defined issues. In response, the state media hysterically pleaded for greater participation and the government extended voting for a third day, proclaiming a national holiday and offering free transportation to the polls. Official sources (whose reliability must be suspect) assert that 47 per cent of those registered voted, somewhat less than in the 2012 presidential election and far less than Sisi hoped for.

Both the ETUF and the independent trade union federations supported Sisi's candidacy. There is no reason to believe that workers diverged significantly from the other 97 per cent of Egyptians who voted for the retired field marshal. However, endorsement of Sisi's candidacy exacerbated tensions among labour activists. After the election EFITU executive board member Fatma Ramadan froze her membership in the body. She accused several other members of contravening a previous decision to refrain from endorsing a candidate and reaching a secret agreement with Sisi's campaign to support him as well as signing a no strike agreement with the other union federations and the government, abandoning the demand that workers fired for organizing be returned to their jobs, and ceasing to press for the adoption of the Trade Union Freedom Law.[38] CTUWS General Coordinator Kamal 'Abbas, who was personally neutral in the presidential election, was expelled from the EDLC in April 2014 despite being the leading personality in its establishment.[39] The extent to which political differences with EDLC leaders over support for Sisi were the main issue is unclear.

In Mahalla al-Kubra, according to a reliable report, most workers supported Sisi, although the most militant leaders saw his election as a restoration of the Mubarak regime.[40] Unsurprisingly, the president of the ETUF-affiliated National Union of Textile Workers 'Abd al-Fattah Ibrahim announced his union's unequivocal support for Sisi. Ibrahim gave the new president a pass on immediately addressing workers' demands and called for suspending strike action.[41]

In contrast, many workers who voted for Sisi expect him to deliver social and economic, as well as physical, security. If he does not do so, labour protests will likely continue. As an activist and former worker at Ghazl al-Mahalla observed: 'Workers in cities like Mahalla are supporting Sisi, but if he fails to achieve social justice, they will return to the streets against him'.[42]

The presidential election has left the workers' movement and the left divided and dispirited. The political arena and the mass media are toxic. Most Egyptians are weary after more than three years of upheaval, and desperately hope that Sisi can stabilize Egypt's economy, suppress the Islamist insurgency based in the Sinai Peninsula and restore 'normalcy'. These expectations are a legacy of the Mubarak regime's claim to deliver 'security'. Through a combination of repression and populist rhetoric, Sisi has rehabilitated this claim as his basis of legitimacy, presenting himself as the sole figure able to restore economic and physical security. The challenges faced by labour activists to organize a national movement beyond sectoral grievances and the commonly asserted dichotomy between economic and political demands derive from the character of politics under Mubarak, and in different ways also Sadat and Nasser, which aimed to 'depoliticize' workers' actions. This also explains workers' continuing distrust of most activists and intellectuals, who they mainly perceive as representing dysfunctional political parties or groups with programmes limited to variants of restoring Nasserist populism.

Sisi, encouraged by the United Arab Emirates, Saudi Arabia and Kuwait, which have fronted Egypt over $12 billion since Morsi's ouster, has authorized the government to consult with the global management firm Strategy& (formerly Booz and Co.) and the Lazard investment bank to prepare new 'reforms' that would pave the way for receiving a loan from the IMF: that is, restoration of the *status quo ante*. This will likely ensure that the root causes of workers' grievances will not be addressed and lead to more labour protest. During the last three years many – though still too few – Egyptians have learned that real change comes from the bottom up and that politics can be about something more than empty rhetoric, personalities and a choice between Mubarakist, Islamist or military capital. But absent a reconfiguration of relations among the oppositional intelligentsia, workers and the ruling elite and an autonomous opposition movement with a programme beyond the limits of Nasserism, no radical political change is likely in the short term.

NOTES

1   Egyptian Center for Economic and Social Rights, 'Protests in 2014', available at http://ecesr.org.
2   Quoted in Patrick Kingsley, 'Egyptian army runs Cairo buses amid ongoing strikes; Around 100,000 workers have taken industrial action this year over demands for minimum wage to be rolled out nationwide', *The Guardian*, 27 February 2014.
3   Jano Charbel, 'Strikes in public sector textile companies reach new high', *Mada Misr*, 18 February 2014, available at http://www.madamasr.com; AbdelHalim H. AbdAlla, 'Spinning and weaving workers at Kafr Al-Dawar strike in solidarity with Mahalla workers', *Daily News Egypt*, 16 February 2014, available at http://www.dailynewsegypt.com.
4   For 1986-93 see the somewhat conflicting figures of Hishaam D. Aidi, *Redeploying the State: Corporatism, Neoliberalism, and Coalition Politics*, New York: Palgrave Macmillan, 2009, pp. 142-3; Omar El Shafei, 'Workers, Trade Unions, and the State in Egypt: 1984-1989', *Cairo Papers in Social Science*, 8(2), 1995, p. 19; Marsha Pripstein Posusney, *Labor and the State in Egypt: Workers, Unions, and Economic Restructuring, 1952-1996*, New York: Columbia University Press, 1997, p. 139; Nicola Christine Pratt, *The Legacy of the Corporatist State: Explaining Workers' Responses to Economic Liberalisation in Egypt*, University of Durham: Centre for Middle Eastern and Islamic Studies, 1998, p. 70; Huwayda 'Adli Ruman, 'Al-Haraka al-ihtijajiyya lil-tabaqa al-'amila al-misriyya, 1982-91', in Ahmad 'Abd Allah, ed., *Humum misr wa-azmat al-'uqul al-shabba*, Cairo: Markaz al-Jil lil-Dirasat al-Shababiyya wa'l-Ijtima'iyya, 1994, pp. 173-96.
5   Mustafa al-Basyuni and 'Umar Sa'id, *Rayat al-idrab fi sama' misr: 2007, haraka 'ummaliyya jadida*, Cairo: Markaz al-Dirasat al-Ishtirakiyya, 2007, pp. 13, 15, 19.
6   Agnieska Paczyńska, *State, Labor, and the Transition to a Market Economy: Egypt, Poland, Mexico, and the Czech Republic*, State College, PA: Pennsylvania State University Press, 2009, p. 30.
7   Any strike had to be approved by two-thirds of the members of the board of directors of the national sectoral union to which all ETUF local unions are affiliated, rather than by the local leadership. The 2009 strike at Tanta Flax and Oils over abuses of the Saudi investor who bought the formerly public sector firm was the only strike to receive ETUF sanction during the entire decade. It was authorized for five days and continued for five months.
8   The table is based on data presented in selected numbers of the bulletins from 2004-11 of *Markaz al-ard li-huquq al-insan, Silsilat al-huquq al-iqtisadiyya wa-l-ijtima'iyya* (Land Center for Human Rights, Series on Economic and Social Rights).
9   Charles Tilly and Sidney G. Tarrow, *Contentious Politics*, Boulder, CO: Paradigm Publishers, 2007, p. 8.

10   Joel Beinin, 'Islam, Marxism and the Shubra al-Khayma Textile Workers: Muslim Brothers and Communists in the Egyptian Trade Union Movement', in Edmund Burke III and Ira M. Lapidus, eds., *Islam, Politics and Social Movements*, Berkeley: University of California Press, 1988, pp. 207-27.

11   Some local strike leaders during the workers' movements of 1974-76 and 1986-93 were members of the Tagammu' (National Progressive Unionist Party), the only legal leftist party under Mubarak, in which members of the Communist Party of Egypt participated. In the mid-1990s, the Tagammu' was co-opted by the regime and became discredited.

12   Interview with Marie Duboc, Mahalla al-Kubra, 21 June 2009.

13   Béatrice Hibou, *The Force of Obedience: The Political Economy of Repression in Tunisia*, Cambridge: Polity Press, 2011, p. xiv.

14   E. P. Thompson, 'The Moral Economy of the English Crowd in the Eighteenth Century', *Past and Present*, 50(1), 1971, pp. 76-136.

15   For details of the events of 6-7 April 2008 see Joel Beinin, 'L'Egypte des ventres vides', *Le Monde Diplomatique*, May 2008.

16   Khalid 'Ali, *Hamlat ma'an min ajl itlaq al-hurriyat al-niqabiyya wa-istiqlal al-niqabat al-'ummaliyya wa-dimuqratiyyatiha*, Cairo: Hisham Mubarak Law Center, 2009.

17   Quoted in Raphaël Kempf, 'Racines ouvrières du soulèvement égyptien', *Le Monde Diplomatique*, March 2011.

18   Mu'assasat Awlad al-Ard li Huquq al-Insan (Sons of the Land Center for Human Rights), '186 i'tisaman wa-77 idraban wa-151 tazahuratan wa-48 waqfa ihtijajiyyatan wa-27 tajamhuran wa-fasl wa-tashrid 4205 'amilan - hisad al-haraka al-'ummaliyya fi shahr fibrayir', March 2011, available at http://www.e-socialists.net.

19   Mu'assasat Awlad al-Ard li Huquq al-Insan, March 2011.

20   Jean Lachapelle, 'Lessons from Egypt's Tax Collectors', *Middle East Report*, 264, Fall 2012.

21   Kamal Abu Eita et al., 'Matalib al-'ummal fi al-thawra', 19 February 2001, available at www.e-socialists.net.

22   See Joel Beinin, 'Revolution and Repression on the Banks of the Suez Canal', *Jadaliyya*, 12 July 2011, available at http://www.jadaliyya.com/pages/index/2116/revolution-and-repression-on-the-banks-of-the-suez; Kempf, 'Racines ouvrières du soulèvement égyptien'.

23   Yassin Gaber, 'Egypt Labour Minister Declares the End of Government Domination of Trade Unions', *Ahramonline*, 14 March 2011, available at http://english.ahram.org.eg.

24   'Ali, *Hamlat ma'an min ajl itlaq al-hurriyat al-niqabiyya wa-istiqlal al-niqabat al-'ummaliyya wa-dimuqratiyyatiha*.

25   Center for Trade Union and Workers Services, 'Trade Union Freedoms Report of 2013', January 2014, p. 3.

26   Monthly reports of The Land Center for Human Rights for 2011; Ilhami al-Mirghani et al., *Ihtijajat al-'ummaliyya fi misr, 2012*, Cairo: al-Markaz al-Misri li'l-Huquq al-Ijtima'iyya wa'l-Iqtisadiyya, 2013, pp. 1, 7, 12, 34, 5; '70 cases of labour protests over 5 months: Manpower Ministry', *Egypt Independent*, 5 December 2013; al-Markaz al-Misri li'l-Huquq al-Ijtima'iyya wa'l-Iqtisadiyya, 'al-Ihtijajat wa'l-nidalat al-'ummaliya allati tab'aha al-markaz khilala 2013', 31

December 2013, available at http://ecesr.org; al-Markaz al-Misri li'l-Huquq al-Ijtima'iyya wa'l-Iqtisadiyya, 'Taqarir 'ummaliyya', 15 February 2014; Kingsley, 'Egyptian army runs Cairo buses'.

27 According to data collected by the ECESR there were 393 collective actions in the private sector in 2012, about 20 per cent of the total, while they comprised about one-third of the protests in the second half of the 2000s.

28 Amnesty International, 'Egyptian Authorities Must Allow Peaceful Protest and the Right to Strike', 30 April 2011, available at http://www.amnesty.org.

29 Jano Charbel, 'And where do the workers stand?', Mada Misr, 15 July 2013, available at http://www.madamasr.com.

30 Email correspondence with Fatma Ramadan, 'Raddan 'ala bayan al-ittihad al-misri li'l-niqabat al-mustaqilla', 10 July 2013.

31 Egyptian Center for Economic and Social Rights, 'Constitutional Coup Against the Principles of the Revolution', 11 July 2013, available at http://ecesr.org.

32 Egyptian Center for Economic and Social Rights, 'Constitutional Coup …'

33 Center for Trade Union and Workers Services, 'Trade Union Freedoms Report of 2013', p. 1.

34 'Bayan al-ittihad min fadd al-i'tismat, 14-8-2013', available at http://www.efitu.com.

35 Both the ETUF and independent trade unionists criticized the 2014 Constitution for removing the 50 per cent quota of farmers and workers in the lower house of parliament in effect since 1956. On the positive side, the 2014 Constitution specifies significant increases from the Mubarak era in the proportion of the state budget to be allocated to health, primary and secondary education, higher education and research. However, health professionals regard the healthcare allotment as insufficient to address the deficit of resources in that sector or to sufficiently enhance the low wages of health sector employees. They have demanded enactment of the Medical Staff Law drafted in coordination with their representatives and the relevant ministries to enhance working conditions in the public healthcare sector. In early March public sector physicians escalated the two-day per week strike they had been engaged in since January to a full strike. In May they suspended their strike to allow the ministry time to address their demands.

36 Jano Charbel, 'New gov't announces aim to limit labour unrest', Mada Masr, 4 March 2014, available at http://madamasr.com.

37 Amnesty International, 'Egypt: New protest law gives security forces free rein', 25 November 2013, available at http://www.amnesty.org.

38 Fatma Ramadan, 'I'lan tajmid 'udwiyya', email, 4 June 2014.

39 Mu'tamar 'Ummal Misr al-Dimuqrati, 'al-Intihaziyya al-siyyasiyya li-dar al-khadamat', email, 11 April 2014.

40 Jano Charbel, 'Mahalla highlights high expectations of Sisi', Mada Masr, 27 May 2014, available at http://www.madamasr.com.

41 Sharif al-Baramuni, 'Niqabat al-nasij … nad'am al-sisi', al-Tahrir, 6 June 2014, available at http://tahrirnews.com.

42 'Defiant workers pose a challenge to next president', Daily News Egypt, 24 April 2014, available at http://www.dailynewsegypt.com.

TRANSNATIONAL SOLIDARITY? THE EUROPEAN WORKING CLASS IN THE EUROZONE CRISIS

ANDREAS BIELER AND ROLAND ERNE

European labour movements are under severe pressure as a result of the global financial and eurozone crises, which have been used by capital to attack unions and workers' rights. In this essay, we will assess the response of European labour movements to this attack and discuss to what extent relations of transnational solidarity have been established in this process. Germany has been at the core of discussions about the eurozone crisis. While peripheral European Union (EU) member states have run into severe problems, the German economy appears as the clear winner, the example to follow due to its booming exports. As it is the largest national economy within the EU, what happens in Germany has also wider implications for the rest of the EU. Hence, we will specifically focus on the response by the German labour movement to the crisis. What has been more important for German unions – solidarity with workers elsewhere or solidarity with one's own employer? The analysis of German unions will be complemented by brief discussions of struggles in Europe's southern periphery. In the conclusion we will reflect on the response by labour movements at the European level to establish whether unions have been able to go beyond their traditional national environment in the search for new strategies against the attack of capital.

THE EUROPEAN UNION'S UNEVEN AND COMBINED DEVELOPMENT

The global financial crisis triggered the sovereign debt crisis in Europe, but the real cause of the crisis was the uneven and combined development underlying the European political economy over the last decades. In the words of Ray Kiely, 'capitalist expansion is a dynamic but also an uneven process, and in contrast to the neo-liberal (and pro-globalization) positions, this unevenness is not seen as a result of market imperfections, but is in fact a product of the way competitive markets work in the real world'.[1] Development was highly uneven in that 60 per cent of German exports go to eurozone members, 85 per cent including the other EU members, resulting in large account surpluses. 'The net trade in goods between Germany and [Portugal, Ireland, Italy, Greece and Spain] amounted to some 2.24 per cent of GDP in 2007, accounting for 27.5 per cent of Germany's trade account surplus'.[2] Nevertheless, development was also combined as these profits needed new points of investment to generate more profits. The EU's periphery, be it the construction booms in Spain and Ireland or the focus on individual consumption in Greece and Portugal, seemed to be ideal locations in this respect. Thus, 'Germany has been recycling its current account surpluses as FDI and bank lending abroad'.[3] In turn, these credits to the periphery were used to purchase more goods in the core. The recurrent distinction between credit- and export-led economies, it follows, is misleading. Firms in core countries would not have been able to pursue export-led growth strategies if global aggregate demand had not been supported by the real estate and stock market bubbles that occurred in the periphery.[4] Germany's export successes crucially hinged on the credit-led solutions to neoliberalism's aggregate demand problem.[5]

The quest for national competitiveness and corresponding policy adjustments played an ever increasing role in the EU policy discourse during the period of eastward enlargement to Central and Eastern Europe (CEE) from the early 2000s onwards, while the EU's transfer payments failed to counter economic disparities even at a distributional level.[6] In fact, West European corporations have benefited greatly from this unevenness between the old EU member states and the new members from CEE. By integrating suppliers from low wage CEE countries in their transnational production networks they reduced their wage costs considerably through whipsawing tactics that put subcontractors and workers from different locations in competition with each other. German multinationals profited most from the availability of a cheap and well-trained industrial labour force in its Eastern hinterland. But whereas German firms established themselves predominately in the Czech Republic, Poland, Hungary and Slovakia, and used relocation threats to obtain concessions at home,[7] a notable part of Southern Europe's low-cost industry moved to the EU's Southeast,[8] where wage-levels are as low as in China.[9] Between 2003 and 2008, the flow of Italian and Greek direct investments in Romania and Bulgaria (US $12.89bn), for example, exceeded German investments in these two countries ($11.08bn) by far, especially if one bears in mind that the German GDP figures were about

40 per cent higher than the combined Italian and Greek numbers.[10] As long as credit guaranteed the necessary aggregate demand despite ongoing wage moderation, the relatively high growth rates between 2000 and 2007 in Europe's southern and eastern periphery seemed to indicate a catching-up process with core EU countries. In 2008, the global financial crisis put an end to this and revealed the underlying unevenness in the European political economy.

From the very beginning, the institutional bias of

the eurozone has directed the pressures of economic adjustment to the labour market: competitiveness in the internal market would depend on productivity growth and labour costs in each country, while labour mobility would be in practice relatively limited. As a result, a 'race to the bottom' for wages and conditions has emerged in the eurozone benefiting large industrial capital.[11]

Until 2007, Europe's business elites almost unanimously opposed any further centralization of Economic Governance at the EU level,[12] most likely because they believed that the Economic and Monetary Union (EMU) would automatically lead to the desired 'race to the bottom' in wages and labour standards.[13] But as national adjustment processes induced by the Maastricht Treaty arguably did not progress quickly enough, EU leaders used the eurocrisis to impose radical adjustment programmes on peripheral countries in exchange for emergency loans. Additionally, EU state-like structures were further strengthened in 2011 after European Commission President Barroso triggered a 'silent revolution' that led to an unprecedented centralization of economic governance at the EU-level.[14] Most EU countries signed the Treaty on Stability, Coordination and Governance in the EMU that is formally not part of EU law, but among other things made the access to further European rescue packages conditional upon the inclusion of severe debt brakes in national law. At the same time, all EU member state governments and a large majority of the European Parliament adopted the so-called 'six pack' of EU laws on European Economic Governance of November 2011 and the 'two pack' on the strengthening of economic and budgetary surveillance of Member States of May 2013.[15] As a result, eurozone countries with 'excessive deficits' or 'excessive macroeconomic imbalances' can be sanctioned by the European Commission with a yearly fine equalling 0.2 per cent or 0.1 per cent of GDP respectively.[16]

The EU's new 'macroeconomic imbalance procedure' is organized in several, ever more intrusive stages. First, the Commission assesses the performance of all EU member states according to a 'scoreboard consisting of a set of eleven indicators covering the major sources of macroeconomic imbalances' it designed.[17] If the Commission notes that scoreboard figures for a particular country are problematic, then it initiates an in-depth review. Subsequently, on a recommendation from the Commission, the Council that is representing national governments may issue country specific recommendations or binding corrective action plans that will be monitored through surveillance visits.[18]

The EU's new Country Specific Policy recommendations are increasingly shaping national policy.[19] Even in countries such as Belgium, France and Denmark, which belong to the core rather than the periphery of the European economy, have relatively strong union movements and are led by social democratic prime ministers, the increasing convergence between national government policy and EU policy guidelines is striking. In April 2013, for example, the Danish government pushed an emergency law through Parliament that ended a nationwide lockout of teachers by the Danish schools' municipal employers and unilaterally enforced employers' demands for a 'new working-time agreement with no limits to the teachers' working hours'.[20] This incident is remarkable also because one of the only five 'country specific policy recommendations' the government received from the EU for the period 2012 to 2013 clearly stated that Denmark must 'without delay implement the measures announced in order to improve cost efficiency in the education system'.[21] Although this Troika-style intervention against the teachers' unions in Denmark would hardly have been possible without the collusion of important national actors, the popular view according to which the Commission's new economic governance regime would only affect countries in Europe's periphery is wrong.

The Commission also singled out the French government for censure. The Commission insisted that the French government's 'reform programme' around a draconian €50bn austerity plan and the €20bn reduction in employers' social security contributions announced early 2014 would not be going far enough 'in restoring private companies' profitability … in particular, it will be insufficient to compensate for the contrasted wage developments seen in France and Germany between 2000 and 2008'.[22] The Commission maintained that France would require specific monitoring and decisive policy action, including further tax cuts for business, curbs to health care and pensions spending and a flexibilization of its 'rigid' wage setting system.[23]

In sum, austerity in the form of wage cuts in the public sector, cuts in services, pensions and social benefits has in fact not only been imposed on countries struggling with sovereign debt, but across the whole EU.[24] The crisis has been used by capital to carry out further restructuring. As a result, the balance of power between capital and labour has been shifted towards capital and the Commission at the expense of labour and national legislators. Unsurprisingly, workers and trade unions as their representatives have come under severe pressure.

EUROPEAN LABOUR AGAINST NEOLIBERAL RESTRUCTURING

From the inception of the EMU, European unions had not been unaware of the dangers implied in an institutional set-up in which wages were the only adjustment mechanism to remain competitive. They recognized that 'the logic of "regime competition" … has become a main feature and a driving force of current industrial adjustments within the European Union'.[25] Nevertheless, it was hoped that economic union would only be a step towards political union, including a strong social dimension across the EU. It was the presence of Jacques Delors as President of the Commission and his emphasis on the necessity of a social dimension to economic integration, including the participation of unions in EU politics, which convinced them to support the Internal Market. The small gains of the Social Chapter at Maastricht, and the relative weakness of unions across the EU due to the economic recession in the early 1990s, led unions to accept the EMU.[26] This support was not uncritical. European integration was supported as such, but additional social policy measures were demanded. In short, the support for the EMU did not imply that European unions had accepted the principles of neoliberalism.[27]

Nor did support for the EMU imply that European unions had not tried to counter the negative impact on wage formation. The European Metalworkers' Federation (EMF), which organizes workers in one of the most transnationalized sectors in Europe, including many TNCs in consumer electronics, car manufacturing and machinery production, became aware of these dangers in the early 1990s. The EMF realized that wage bargaining was no longer a national issue in its sector, characterized by an increasing transnationalization of production. Plans for the EMU implied the danger of social dumping through the undercutting of wage and working conditions between several national collective bargaining rounds. In response, the EMF approved the European-level co-ordination of national wage bargaining in 1998 and it tried to ensure that national unions pursued a common strategy of asking for wage increases along the formula of productivity increase plus inflation rate. In summer 1999, the European Trade Union Confederation

(ETUC) as a whole adopted the co-ordination of collective bargaining as one of its four main tasks and established an ETUC Collective Bargaining Committee.[28]

And yet the implementation of the co-ordination strategy was unsuccessful. In 2006, the ETUC published (for the last time) data on whether the various national collective bargaining rounds had been in line with the ETUC guidelines of wage increases along the formula of productivity increase plus inflation. The findings make clear that not only had no country managed to achieve this target except for Finland, but also that German unions, which had been a driving force behind developing the strategy, were actually the ones that missed it by the largest amount insofar as cumulative productivity growth exceeded the total real wage over the 2003-06 period by 8.6 per cent.[29] Indeed, for the whole period from the adoption of the euro in 2000 right up to 2012, the average negotiated salary increase in Germany was 5.5 per cent below productivity increase; and even more drastic, the effective average salary increase was a further 9.3 per cent below the negotiated average salary.[30] As these figures indicate, German workers have not benefited from the export boom. Highlighted by the Hartz IV Reform of 2003, which led to the largest cut in, and restructuring of, the German welfare system in the postwar era,[31] the eurozone has amounted to 'a "beggar-thy-neighbour" policy for Germany, on condition that it beggars its own workers first'.[32] In short, downward pressure on wages and working conditions of German workers was actually the cause of the export boom. In turn, these wage developments, while ensuring that Germany could emerge from the crisis with an export boom, have put downward pressure on wages and working conditions elsewhere and become a problem for other unions in Europe.

German unions under pressure

German unions have lost considerable power from the 1990s onwards and some argue that they were simply too weak to obtain larger wage increases. Later than elsewhere in Europe, German production structures became increasingly transnationalized during the 1990s. Outward FDI increased significantly in key industrial sectors including especially chemicals, road vehicles and electrical and mechanical engineering.[33] Germany's proximity to the EU's new member states in CEE provided capital with a vast array of options to cheapen product prices or threaten exit from Germany's postwar class compromise. The share of CEE in German automotive component imports, for example, rose from 9 per cent to 37 per cent between 1995 and 2005.[34] The import of low-cost components has, in turn, increased the competitiveness of German companies. Additionally, with the upgrading of production processes in CEE, Western European companies have increasingly started to threaten relocation in discussion with unions. 'In particular in Germany, automobile companies use the relocation "option" to demand higher work and employment flexibility, longer working times and lower wages.'[35]

Hence, the overall balance of power in Germany has been shifted towards capital at the expense of labour. German unions' defensive, protectionist reactions to EU eastward enlargement, moreover, proved to be counterproductive.[36] By insisting on a seven-year-long suspension of CEE migrant workers' right to work in Germany, German unions virtually forced CEE workers to become self-employed entrepreneurs, as Germany's free movement restrictions obviously did not restrict the free movement of capital and services, including self-employed entrepreneurs. Nevertheless, self-employed entrepreneurs are, of course, extremely difficult to organize.

Furthermore, German unification put additional pressure on unions. There was a decline in the coverage of collective bargaining with wage levels in East Germany being generally lower than in the West, in turn putting downward pressure on West German wage levels and the bargaining system overall. 'The East German transformation became the central catalyst for re-commodification in Germany on the whole.'[37] Moreover, the IG Metall, organizing workers in manufacturing and being the most important industrial union in Germany, lost a strike in 2003 over the equalization of conditions in the metal industry between East and West Germany, i.e. precisely at the moment when the controversial Hartz IV reforms, mentioned above, were imposed on German unions. Defeating the IG Metall took priority for German employers over social peace.[38]

The restructuring of the social relations of production has not helped either. Traditionally, temporary agency work was highly regulated in Germany and mainly used by companies to respond flexibly to short-term challenges in the production process. It was the 2003 change in legislation by a coalition government of Social Democrats and the Green Party, deregulating temporary agency work, which facilitated the change in employers' strategy. The EU's fixed-term work directive and the preceding Business Europe-ETUC social partnership agreement on fixed-term work both forbid employers to treat fixed-term workers less favourably than permanent workers. But the German government made use of the EU directive's opt-out clause that allows derogations for fixed-term workers if they have been agreed in collective bargaining agreements. The German Trade Union Confederation (DGB) also supported the government's use of this opt-out clause, arguably as it would give temporary work agencies a powerful incentive to enter into collective bargaining.

Such hopes, however, only partially materialized, as employers successfully used contracts with yellow unions and intra-union rivalries to enforce lower wages and working conditions for temporary workers. Several key companies in turn moved towards employing a significant number of their workers through temporary work agencies in order to be able to contain wage costs and respond flexibly to changes in the economy and thereby to secure their short-term financial profits. 'By employing a certain share of their permanent workforce through agencies, client firms bypass statutory dismissal protection and binding collective agreements in order to establish a "security net" for their short-term profits or rate of return.'[39] To date, only four per cent of the overall German workforce are temporary agency workers. However, the fact that between 10 to 20 per cent of the overall workforce in large manufacturing companies are temporary agency workers signifies the overall importance of this type of worker for German industrial relations.

The increasing use of temporary agency workers has had drastic implications for workers and unions. First, being a temporary agency worker becomes less and less a route into permanent employment. Companies have to some extent stopped employing new workers directly. Second, the fact that temporary agency workers are employed on lower salaries than their colleagues, although they are doing the same jobs, and that they face the constant threat of dismissal should there be an economic recession, has a disciplining effect on permanent workers. 'Looking at the temporary agency workers, the regularly employed workers of the client firm sense that, in case they would lose their job, their chances of re-entry into regular employment would be equally low'.[40] This will affect their position on whether to criticize management and, unsurprisingly, it has become more difficult for unions to organize strike action.[41]

German unions have to some extent regained influence since the onset of the global financial crisis in 2008. Against the background of global recession, union leaders were suddenly once again consulted by the state and employers. However, as Klaus Dörre points out, this type of

crisis corporatism only intensifies the declining power of unions in the labour market, which will ultimately also come to haunt the core workforce in stable, full-time employment. If employment risks are systematically referred to informal workers, already existing divisions will be furthered, and will also erode unions' organisational and institutional power resources. This, in turn, will eventually affect negatively the core workforce.[42]

Therefore, union incorporation into crisis corporatism should not be mistaken for regaining their traditional power and influence over policymaking.

German unions and transnational solidarity

In what way has this weakening at home impacted on German unions' efforts of transnational solidarity with workers elsewhere in Europe? Some have accused German unions of consciously putting the interests of German workers above the interests of workers elsewhere in Europe. After their 'competitive corporatist' wing had won the internal battle against their Euro-Keynesian opponents following the defeat and resignation of Oscar Lafontaine as German finance minister in the spring of 1999, German unions did not implement the co-ordination strategy at home from the early 2000s onwards.[43] Confirmation of German unions' lack of solidarity with other European unions and workers was apparently given by Berthold Huber in 2012, then General Secretary of IG Metall. First he blamed Spanish unions for the fate of the Spanish economy. Having obtained 'too high wage increases' they would be responsible for undermining the competitiveness of Spanish companies. Then, he argued that the Spanish labour market should be restructured to regain competitiveness. Finally, he criticized the planned strikes in some Southern European countries for the European-wide trade union mobilization of 14 November 2012 as 'voluntaristic nonsense'.[44] By arguing that wage formation is responsible for competitiveness and supporting labour market deregulation, Huber placed himself well within the dominant understanding of the crisis and its required solutions.

This understanding of the role of wage formation, in fact, may have underpinned unions' engagement with employers. While there has been a significant weakening of German unions, which may partly explain the wage increases below productivity increases noted above, German unions may have at least some responsibility for this development. Indicative here is also the fact that the increase in effective average wages is below the negotiated average wages, resulting not only from the decline in bargaining coverage, but also the increasing use of opening clauses since 2003, as highlighted in an EU report that is informed by studies of Bispinck and Schulten from the union-related Institute of Economic and Social Research (WSI). The so-called Pforzheim Agreement of 2004, the Commission document points out, also allowed deviations from collectively agreed standards in certain cases in order to maintain and improve competitiveness, innovative capability and investment. Hence, opening clauses are now possible for companies in acute economic difficulties as well as in response to general competitive pressures. Unsurprisingly, there was an increase in company-level derogation agreements from 70 in 2004 to 730 in early 2009. 'Around 70% of these agreements include derogations concerning wages.'[45] These opening clauses are part of collective bargaining and were thus agreed upon by trade unions in line with the understanding that wage formation is responsible for national competitiveness.

And yet it would be dangerous simply to write off German unions as a potential part of resistance to austerity. First, the IG Metall and German unions in general should not be understood as homogenous actors. Huber's statements led to heavy criticism from within the labour movement.[46] Second, within the IG Metall different fractions can be identified. Hans-Jürgen Urban, a left-wing member of the Executive Board of the IG Metall, has a rather different position and is fully aware of the problems resulting from German wage developments for other European unions. In order to counter capital more successfully, the European labour movement would need to develop a European strategy, and in view of the need for more solidarity in Europe, he argues that unions should pursue a double function: (1) they need to purse an offensive redistribution policy in collective wage bargaining; and (2) they should operate as political pressure groups mobilizing against the Troika's austerity policies.[47]

Moreover, the current General Secretary of the IG Metall, Detlef Wetzel, recently criticized the negotiations for a neoliberal Transatlantic Free Trade Agreement. While the potential benefits are either unclear or small at best, the planned investor-state dispute settlement mechanism would undermine popular sovereignty and potentially also include downward pressure on working conditions and workers' rights.[48] In fact, in its October 2012 declaration, 'Change of course for European solidarity', the IG Metall Executive Board not only demanded radical medium-term institutional reforms towards a political and social EU as well as an active, co-ordinated and democratically legitimate economic and industrial policy, but also explicitly mentioned the important role of unions in co-ordinating collective bargaining: 'The trade unions must also contribute to the management of a common currency union. This particularly applies to wage coordination.'[49] In short, the nationalist assessment, visible in Huber's competitive corporatist position on Spanish competitiveness, is not necessarily predominant within the IG Metall.

In general, it is often assumed that areas of transnational production, in which IG Metall organizes workers, are those most easily susceptible to strategies of transnational solidarity. Unions in these sectors are the first to recognize that organization at the national level is no longer enough to keep wages and working conditions outside capitalist competition. And there are positive examples of transnational solidarity. In 2001, unions and works councils organized a successful one-day strike of 40,000 General Motors (GM) workers across Europe against the closure of the GM plant in Luton in the UK. This did not only lead to a pioneering European labour agreement that prevented forced redundancies in all European sites from 2001 to 2008; it also showed that competition for investments does not necessarily pre-empt transnational collective action.[50] Nevertheless, transnational solidarity in transnational production structures is hardly automatic. When GM established a new production site in Poland in the late 1990s, this new site 'entered a competitive race with the German plant in Rüsselsheim over the distribution of new Opel Zafira capacities'.[51] Moreover, in view of GM's decision to close down the production of Opel in Bochum/Germany towards the end of 2014, the German chairman of the European Works Council (EWC) from Rüsselsheim, as well as the chair of the works council at Opel in Bochum, tried to save local jobs by highlighting the higher quality and productivity of their production sites.[52]

Perhaps it is actually in the service sector that co-operation between unions and social movements may provide a better platform for resistance against austerity as well as the establishment of solidarity across borders. Ver.di organizes workers in the service sector, and in 2010 had already blamed German wage policy for causing 'unfair competition' and downward pressure on wages of workers in other eurozone countries. 'The wage policies of the EU Member States must be geared to national productivity and inflation indicators, so that as a minimum, they make full use of the cost-neutral scope for redistribution of wealth.'[53] The union also demanded a transnational minimum wage policy. Of course accomplishing these goals in practice has been difficult for Ver.di, too. In the most recent round of collective bargaining Ver.di was unable to catch up with private industry.[54] While its rhetoric is more radical, in understanding that low wage increases in industry affect its members negatively, Ver.di's concrete power has been weakened by the fragmentation of the public sector due to decentralization and privatization.[55]

Nevertheless, Ver.di has demonstrated some concrete actions of transnational solidarity. For example, the union developed a global dimension in its current struggle over collective bargaining rights with the retail giant Amazon. While Ver.di members went on strike in several Amazon depots in Germany in December 2013, the union sent a delegation to Seattle to protest together with several US unions in front of the company's headquarters.[56] In turn, Ver.di supported striking workers at one of Amazon's depots in

France and started to develop this into a fully international campaign. While this does not yet constitute the organization of a transnational strike against a particular TNC, it nonetheless indicates how unions can successfully support each other across borders in industrial conflicts. Furthermore, Ver.di supported Turkish workers, who were made redundant by the Deutsche Post DHL company for joining a trade union. First, they sent a fact-finding and solidarity mission to the striking workers in Istanbul; then they lobbied the General Meeting of Deutsche Post DHL in May 2013. Moreover, Ver.di was heavily involved in the European Citizens Initiative, '*Water and sanitation are a human right!*' The significance of this example for transnational solidarity is returned to below, but the various aspects of struggles in Europe's Southern periphery will first be assessed.

Struggles in Europe's southern periphery

It is countries in Europe's southern periphery that have been hit particularly hard by the eurozone crisis, being subjected to austerity programmes by the Troika. For example, 'the fiscal cuts imposed on Greece amount to 10.5 per cent of GDP for 2010 and 2011, and another 9.9 per cent until 2014. The consequence of this austerity is a drop in real GDP in Greece of more than 4 per cent in 2009 and 2010.'[57] But imposed austerity went also beyond direct cuts. 'At the same time [Greece] has been forced to introduce new legislation in labour markets and to engage in ambitious privatisation.'[58] These measures were clearly directed against trade unions' involvement in social and economic decision-making at the national level and meant to shift the balance of power towards capital. Unsurprisingly, resistance against austerity erupted predominantly in Europe's southern periphery with 35 out of 36 general strikes having taken place in Southern Europe and France.[59]

Interestingly, resistance to austerity brought new types of movements to the fore. In Spain, the M15 movement was launched on 15 May 2011, and is primarily made up of various other groupings of progressive social movements. The movement coalesced around the slogan of 'real democracy', whilst also attempting to assemble various 'citizen coalitions' to resist the targeted government actions of austerity.[60] A prominent member is the Plataforma de Afectados por la Hipoteca (PAH; Mortgage Victims Platform). They have successfully been involved in stopping evictions through direct and legal action, whilst also relocating those who are evicted.[61] Spanish unions initially hesitated, while there was still a social democratic government in power. Only after the electoral victory of the right-wing Popular Party in November 2011 and anti-union labour market reforms did unions start to organize mass demonstrations and a general strike on 29 March 2012.[62] In turn, the social movements distrusted the unions, and regarded them as implicated in the crisis and part of the establishment due to their focus on 'social pacts' and dialogue with employers and government. Nevertheless, at the local and sectoral levels, campaigns based on alliances between unions and social movements have been established. In defence of public education, for example, the so-called Green Tide movement, including unions, parents' organizations and neighbourhood assemblies, has been formed in Madrid from August 2011 onwards.[63]

In response to the first bailout package in May 2010, the initial resistance in Greece was led by the big unions, which called dozens of general strikes. Over time, however, partly as a result of close links between the union bureaucracy and the social democratic PASOK party, deeply implicated in the crisis, rank–and–file members and the wider Greek population took over in setting the pace of resistance.[64] The so-called Greek Indignados were 'awoken' by M15 after a Greek news story reported a banner being held up in Puerta del Sol, Madrid (the main occupied square in Spain), stating 'Shhhhh … keep it quiet, we might wake up the Greeks'.[65] Whether the banner existed or not, on the very next day, 25 May 2011, more than 20,000 people had gathered in Syntagma Square, although unlike in Madrid there was not a popular unified assembly there. Spatially the square became divided, not only along the lines of ideology, but also the pursuit of particular actions. Progressive voices linked the struggle to the experience of occupation during the Second World War, along with the struggles against military dictatorship in the postwar period. Strong nationalist sentiments were, however, also present. They drew on the struggles of independence from the Ottomans of 1821. This highlights the unprecedented heterogeneity of the protestors' identities.[66] Importantly, parallel to these developments, and alongside the emergence of Syriza on the left, and to a lesser extent Golden Dawn on the right, as strong electoral forces, Greek citizens increasingly organized collectively the provision of basic services ranging 'from social clinics and pharmacies to social groceries, and from the movement to cut out the intermediaries in agricultural production to various cooperative ventures'.[67] Overall, however, there is still too much mistrust between trade unions and social movements in both Greece and Spain, preventing the emergence of a more permanent and powerful force of resistance.

In Italy, trade unions have to a large extent accepted capital's offensive around the hollowing out of the collective bargaining system.[68] Resistance against austerity and neoliberal restructuring, however, evolved around struggles against water privatization. The Italian water movement, a broad alliance of social movements and trade unions, successfully mobilized around a discourse of water as a human right and a commons to be jointly administered and enjoyed by all, achieving a referendum against the privatization of water in June 2011. Developed over a period of ten years, this broad alliance included Catholic and secular organizations dealing with labour issues, environmental groups, consumer groups as well as local citizens' initiatives. On the union side, Funzione Pubblica – CGIL, the largest Italian federation organizing public sector workers, was the most important actor. Nevertheless, the rank-and-file unions Cobas and Unione Sindacale di Base (USB) also had become actively involved.[69] When the referendum took place on 12 and 13 June 2011, the victory of the water movement was overwhelming. For the first time in 16 years it had again been possible to secure the quorum of at least 50 per cent plus one voter participating. In fact, just over 57 per cent of the electorate cast their vote. The majorities on the questions against the forced privatization of water services and against the right to make a profit with water were even more impressive: '95.35% yes (4.65% no) on the first question; 95.80% yes (4.20% no) on the second'.[70]

The victory could not have been more decisive. The successful referendum, however, did not prevent the European Central Bank leaders, Draghi and Trichet, on 3 August 2011 from making any ECB help for the Italian state conditional on a long list of 'business friendly' measures, including 'the full liberalisation of local public services ... through large scale privatizations'.[71] Nonetheless, precisely because the victory in the national referendum did not stop the privatization pressures, the Italian water movement arguably paved the way towards the broader, European-level European Citizens' Initiative (ECI) on water as a human right. Building on the success of the Italian water movement, the European Federation of Public Service Unions (EPSU) was crucial in launching this ECI, collecting almost 1.9 million signatures between May 2012 and September 2013. The demands of the ECI were threefold: '(1) For the EU to recognise the UN right to water and sanitation into EU law; (2) not to liberalise water services in the EU; and (3) to contribute to achieving access to water and sanitation for all across the world'.[72] On the one hand, there is the interest of trade unions in keeping water provision in public hands, as working conditions are generally better in the public sector. On the other, user groups are supportive of universal access to affordable clean water. It is the inclusion of issues beyond the workplace, the right to access clean water, which has allowed the EPSU to link up with other social movements and thereby broaden the social basis for resistance and form bonds of solidarity.

Returning to the role of German unions in transnational solidarity, it was unsurprisingly Ver.di which most strongly supported this initiative in

Germany and was at least partly responsible for the fact that out of the almost 1.9 million signatures, 1.38 million were collected in Germany.[73] In turn, observing the hearing in the European Parliament of the ECI through a video link gave water activists in Thessaloniki, Greece the confidence to go ahead with their plans of holding an independent referendum on water privatization in their city. The EPSU and the European water network supported this initiative through sending international observers to monitor the referendum on 18 May 2014, when proposals to privatize the company were overwhelmingly rejected with 98 per cent of votes against.[74]

THE RISK OF BEING PUSHED ASIDE

When analyzing the response by European unions to neoliberal austerity it remains important to remember that this is not a struggle between different countries such as Germany on the one hand, and Greece, Portugal, Spain and Ireland on the other. Rather, this is about class struggle between capital and labour. At the European level, unions have been unable to converge around a strong counter-austerity strategy. It proved impossible to organize a European-wide strike as a result of uneven political and economic conditions in the various member states, different levels of union power resources and traditions as well as a missing common discursive frame of reference.[75] While several Southern European unions are more supportive of general strikes, most Nordic unions tend to favour not doing anything at the European level, as they are confident that they can still contain austerity at the national level. Some unions also try to secure their position nationally through concession bargaining,[76] whereas others proposed an ECI against austerity, following the successful ECI on water as a human right.[77]

What has ultimately emerged from these discussions was first a European-wide day of action on 14 November 2012, which combined general strikes in Greece, Portugal, Italy and Spain with solidarity demonstrations in other countries. Moreover, an ETUC initiative for a European investment programme was adopted at the meeting of the ETUC Executive Committee on 7 November 2013[78] and an ETUC demonstration of 40,000 workers took place in Brussels on 4 April 2014, causing a security 'lock down' at the US permanent representation to the EU.[79] Interestingly, in its recommendations for a European investment programme the ETUC follows closely the 'Marshallplan für Südeuropa' initially proposed by two Euro-Keynesian Ver.di economists[80] and the DGB's subsequent 'Marshall Plan for Europe', published in December 2012.[81] It also includes the idea that interest bearing bonds, intended to raise the necessary money for investment, should be partly financed and secured through the receipts from a Financial Transaction Tax and a one-off tax on wealthier people. There is, however, also a national dimension in the ETUC's plan when it argues that individual countries should identify for themselves how to raise the necessary finances for investment. There is thus still the danger of a nationalist, competitive corporatist strategy, reflecting ultimately the position of many of the ETUC's national members.

As we have seen, the most high profile and successful strategy of concrete transnational solidarity was organized in the service sector against water privatization. While manufacturing unions in transnational production networks often found it difficult to prioritize transnational solidarity over national competitiveness, and the European labour movement has been unable to agree on joint anti-austerity actions through the ETUC, service sector unions across Europe, together with social movements, managed to organize a truly transnational solidarity campaign at national and European levels.

Finally, we should not overlook developments from below. While unions often struggle to identify strategies of transnational solidarity, at times workers take the initiative into their own hands as in the case of recent factory occupations by workers in Greece, Italy and France.[82] Unions have to be careful to appreciate this new reality if they do not want to run the risk of being pushed aside by more active forces in the wider labour movement.

NOTES

We are grateful to Oliver Nachtwey and Daniel Behruzi for their assistance with material on German unions. Many thanks also to colleagues from the *Transnational Labour Project* at the Centre for Advanced Study in Oslo (see http://transnationallabour.wordpress.com) for the necessary time and space to complete this essay.

1   Ray Kiely, *The New Political Economy of Development: Globalization, Imperialism, Hegemony*, London: Palgrave, 2007, p. 18.

2   Christos Laskos and Euclid Tsakalotos, *Crucible of Resistance: Greece, the Eurozone and the World Economic Crisis*, London: Pluto Press, 2013, p. 86.

3   Costas Lapavitsas et al., *Crisis in the Eurozone*, London and New York: Verso, 2012, p. 31.

4   Roland Erne, 'European Unions after the Global Crisis', in L. Burroni, M. Keune and G. Meardi, eds., *Economy and Society in Europe: A Relationship in Crisis*, Cheltenham: E. Elgar, 2012, pp. 124-43.

5   Riccardo Bellofiore, Francesco Garibaldo and Joseph Halevi, 'The Global Crisis and the Crisis of European Neomercantilism', *Socialist Register 2011*, Pontypool: Merlin Press, 2011, pp. 120-46.

6   Donnacha Ó'Beacháin, Vera Sheridan and Sabina Stan, eds., *Life in Post-communist Eastern Europe After EU Membership: Happy Ever After?*, London: Routledge, 2012, p. 227.

7   Guglielmo Meardi, *Social Failures of EU Enlargement: A Case of Workers Voting with Their Feet*, London: Routledge, 2013; Dorothee Bohle and Béla Greskovits, *Capitalist Diversity in Europe's Periphery*, Ithaca: Cornell University Press, 2012.

8   Devi Sacchetto, 'Isolani dell'arcipelago. Delocalizzatori e forza lavoro in Romania', in F. Gambino and D. Sacchetto, eds., *Un arcipelago produttivo. Migranti e imprenditori tra Italia e Romania*. Roma: Carocci, 2007, pp.133-170.

9   Sabina Stan and Roland Erne, 'Explaining Romanian Labor Migration: From Development Gaps to Development Trajectories', *Labor History*, 55(1), 2014, pp. 21-46.

10 UNCTAD, *Bilateral FDI Statistics 2014*, Geneva: UNCTAD, 2014, available at http://unctad.org.

11 Lapavitsas et al, *Crisis in the Eurozone*, p. 158.

12 Evelyne Leonard, Roland Erne, Stijn Smismans and Paul Marginson, *New Structures, Forms and Processes of Governance in European Industrial Relations*, Luxembourg: Office for the Official Publications of the European Communities, 2007.

13 Roland Erne, *European Unions: Labour's Quest for a Transnational Democracy*, Ithaca: Cornell University Press, 2008, p. 54.

14 Roland Erne, 'European Industrial Relations after the Crisis: A Postscript', in S. Smismans, ed., *The European Union and Industrial Relations – New Procedures, New Context*, Manchester: Manchester University Press, 2012, pp. 225-35.

15 Vote Watch, 'Enforcement measures to correct excessive macroeconomic imbalances in euro area, Vote of the European Parliament, 28 September 2011', 2014; available at http://www.votewatch.eu.

16 Erne, 'Postscript', p. 228.

17 Despite its far-reaching policy implications, however, the scoreboard's indicators (e.g. maximum Unit Labour Cost increases) and the indicators' acceptable benchmark levels have not been selected by the EU's legislators, but by a sub-group of the EU's Economic Policy Committee (EPC). The EPC comprises two Commission officials, two officials from each Member State (e.g. from the Finance Ministry and the Central Bank) and two officials from the ECB. See http://europa.eu.

18 Erne, 'Postscript'.

19 Anne Dufresne and Jean-Marie Pernot, 'Les syndicats européens à l'épreuve de la nouvelle gouvernance économique', *Chronique Internationale de l'IRES*, No.143-4, 2013, pp. 3-29.

20 Education International, 'Denmark: Union dismay as Government intervention ends teachers' lock-out', 2013, available at http://www.ei-ie.org.

21 Danish Government, 'National reform programme: Denmark', April 2013, available at http://ec.europa.eu.

22 European Commission, 'Macroeconomic Imbalances. France 2014', *European Economy, occasional papers*, 178, March 2014, available at http://ec.europa.eu.

23 European Commission, 'Recommendation for a COUNCIL RECOMMENDATION on France's 2014 national reform programme and delivering a Council opinion on France's 2014 stability programme', 2 June 2014, available at http://ec.europa.eu.

24   Erne, 'Postscript', p. 227; Michael W. Bauer and Stefan Becker, 'The unexpected winner of the crisis: the European Commission's strengthened role in economic governance', *Journal of European Integration*, 36(3), 2014, pp. 213-29.

25   Hans-Jürgen Bieling, 'European Constitutionalism and Industrial Relations', in A. Bieler and A.D. Morton, eds., *Social Forces in the Making of the New Europe: The Restructuring of European Social Relations in the Global Political Economy*, Houndmills: Palgrave, pp. 94, 103.

26   Bieling, 'European Constitutionalism', pp. 100-5.

27   Andreas Bieler, *The Struggle for a Social Europe: Trade Unions and EMU in Times of Global Restructuring*, Manchester: Manchester University Press, 2006.

28   Roland Erne, *European Unions*, pp. 80-90. Thorsten Schulten, 'A European solidaristic wage policy?', *European Journal of Industrial Relations*, 8(2), 2002, pp. 173-96.

29   Erne, *European Unions*, p. 97.

30   Steffen Lehndorff, 'Un géant endormi? Le rôle des syndicats avant et pendant la crise européenne', *Chronique Internationale de l'IRES*, 143(4), 2013, p. 56.

31   Ian Bruff, 'Germany's Agenda 2010 reforms: Passive revolution at the crossroads', *Capital & Class*, 34(3), 2010, pp. 414-16.

32   Lapavitsas et al., *Crisis in the Eurozone*, p. 30.

33   Bieler, *Struggle for a Social Europe*, pp. 78-9.

34   Ulrich Jürgens and Martin Krzywdzinski, 'Changing East-West Division of Labour in the European Automotive Industry', *European Urban and Regional Studies*, 9, 2009, p. 32.

35   Jürgens and Krzywdzinski, 'Changing East-West Division of Labour', p. 40.

36   Dorothee Bohle, 'Neoliberal hegemony, transnational capital and the terms of the EU's eastwards expansion', *Capital & Class*, 30(1), 2006, p. 74.

37   Ulrich Brinkmann and Oliver Nachtwey, 'Industrial Relations, Trade Unions and Social Conflict in German Capitalism', *La nouvelle revue du travail*, 3, 2013, p. 5.

38   Damien Raess, 'Globalization and why the "time is ripe" for the transformation of German industrial relations', *Review of International Political Economy*, 13(3), 2006, pp. 449-79.

39   Hajo Holst, Oliver Nachtwey and Klaus Dörre, 'The Strategic Use of Temporary Agency Work – Functional Change of a Non-standard Form of Employment', *International Journal of Action Research*, 6(1), 2010, p. 110.

40   Holst, Nachtwey and Dörre, 'Strategic Use of Temporary Agency Work', p. 133.

41   German unions have, however, started to respond to this situation. The more union officials realized that the growing vertical disintegrated labour relations are also increasingly affecting the apparently secure core workforce, the more they emphasized the need for inclusive trade union strategies and policies. See Hajo Holst, '"Commodifying institutions": vertical disintegration and institutional change in German labour relations', *Work, Employment & Society*, 28(1), 2014, pp. 3-20.

42   Klaus Dörre, 'Funktionswandel der Gewerkschaften. Von der intermediären zur fraktalen Organisation', in T. Haipeter und K. Dörre, eds., *Gewerkschaftliche Modernisierung*, Wiesbaden: VS Verlag, p. 284.

43   Erne, *European Unions*, pp. 99-103.

44   Stephan Krull, 'IG Metall: Vorsitzender Huber auf Abwegen!', *LabourNet Germany*, 28 October 2012, available at http://www.labournet.de.

45   European Commission, *Industrial Relations in Europe 2010*, Luxembourg: Publications Office of the European Union, 2011, available at http://ec.europa. eu.

46   See, for example, 'Offener Brief an den Vorsitzenden der IG Metall', *LabourNet Germany*, 2012, available at http://labournet.de.

47   Hans-Jürgen Urban, 'Strohfeuer oder Wendepunkt? Gewerkschafliches Comeback in Zeiten der Krise', *Blätter für deutsche und internationale Politik*, 5, 2013, p. 90.

48   Detlef Wetzel, 'Freihandelsabkommen sofort stoppen', Frankfurter Rundschau, 4 March 2014, available at http://www.fr-online.de.

49   IG Metall, 'Change of course for European solidarity', IG Metall Executive Board, 9 October 2012, available at http://www.igmetall.de.

50   Erne, *European Unions*, p. 34; Ann Cecilie Bergene, *Preaching in the Desert or Looking at the Stars? A Comparative Study of Trade Union Strategies in the Auto, Textile and Garment, and Maritime Industries*, PhD Thesis, Department of Sociology and Human Geography, University of Oslo, 2009, pp. 151-222.

51   Magdalena Bernaciak, 'West-East European labour transnationalism(s): rivalry or joint mobilisation?', in A. Bieler and I. Lindberg, eds., *Global Restructuring, Labour and the Challenges for Transnational Solidarity*, London: Routledge, 2010, p. 37.

52   Wolfgang Schaumberg, 'General Motors is attacking European workers. Is there no resistance? The example of Opel Bochum', *Interface: a journal for and about social movements*, 6(1), 2014, pp. 412-15.

53   Ver.di, *European Policy Manifesto*, 2-3 December 2010, Berlin: Ver.di, p. 20.

54   Wolfgang Günther, 'Zur Tarifrunde im Öffentlichen Dienst', 21 May 2014, available at http://www.linksnet.de.

55   Bernd Riexinger and Werner Sauerborn, 'Ver.di goes FLUPO', Interview by Express Redaktion, 2012, available at http://archiv.labournet.de.

56   For this and the following instances of Ver.di's transnational solidarity see http://www.verdi.de.

57   Elmar Altvater, 'From Subprime Farce to Greek Tragedy', *Socialist Register 2012*, Pontypool: Merlin Press, 2011, p. 277.

58   Lapavitsas et al., *Crisis in the Eurozone*, p. 120.

59   Nico Weinmann and Stefan Schmalz, 'Zwischen Macht und Ohnmacht: Gewerkschaftliche Krisenproteste in Westeuropa', *Kurswechsel*, 1, 2014, pp. 26, 28-9.

60   *The Guardian*, 15 October 2013.

61   *The Guardian*, 28 April 2013.

62   Holm-Detlev Köhler and José Pablo Calleja Jiménez, *Trade Unions in Spain: Organisation, Environment, Challenges*, Bonn: Friedrich-Ebert-Stiftung, 2013,

pp. 14-7, available at http://library.fes.de; Murray Smith, 'Europe: Greece, Spain, Portugal – the arc of resistance to austerity hardens', *LINKS: international journal of socialist renewal*, 2012, available at http://links.org.

63   Sophie Béroud, 'Une mobilisation syndicale traversée par le souffle des Indignés ? La «marée verte» dans le secteur de l'éducation à Madrid', *Savoir/ agir*, 27, 2014, pp. 52-3.

64   Lina Filopoulou, 'The resistance movement in Greece: challenges and alternatives', Corporate Europe Observatory, 2012, available at http:// corporateeurope.org.

65   Nikos Sotirakopoulos and George Sotiropoulos, '"Direct democracy now!": The Greek *indignados* and the present cycle of struggles', *Current Sociology*, 61(4), 2013, p. 446.

66   Marilena Simiti, 'Rage and Protest: The Case of the Greek Indignant Movement', Hellenic Observatory Papers on Greece and Southeast Europe, GreeSE Paper, 82, 2014, available at http://www.lse.ac.uk.

67   Laskos and Tsakalotos, *Crucible of Resistance*, p. 143.

68   Davide Bradanini, 'Common Sense and "National Emergency": Italian Labour and the Crisis', *Global Labour Journal*, 5(2), 2014, pp. 176-95, available at http:// digitalcommons.mcmaster.ca.

69   Emanuele Fantini, 'Catholics in the Making of the Italian Water Movement: A Moral Economy', *PArtecipazione e COnflitto*, 7(1), 2014, pp. 35-57, available at http://siba-ese.unisalento.it.

70   Tommaso Fattori, 'Fluid Democracy: The Italian Water Revolution', *transform!*, 9, 2011, available at http://transform-network.net.

71   Erne, 'Postscript', p. 229.

72   See http://www.right2water.eu.

73   See http://www.verdi.de.

74   Jan Willem Goudriaan, 'Resisting austerity in Greece: The Thessaloniki water referendum', 13 May 2014, available at http://andreasbieler.blogspot.no.

75   Julia Hofmann, 'Auf dem Weg zu einem europäischen Generalstreik? Erste Annäherung an eine grosse Frage', *Kurswechsel*, 1, 2014, pp. 37-40.

76   Roland Erne, 'Let's accept a smaller slice of a shrinking cake. The Irish Congress of Trade Unions and Irish public sector unions in crisis', *Transfer: European Review of Labour and Research*, 19(3), 2013, pp. 425-30.

77   Corinne Gobin and Roland Erne, 'Des défis sans précédents mais des réponses faibles. La Confédération européenne des syndicats dans un contexte de crise financière et économique', under submission with *Revue internationale de politique comparée*.

78   ETUC, 'A new path for Europe: ETUC plan for investment, sustainable growth and quality jobs', 7 November 2013, available at http://www.etuc. org.

79   *Reuters*, 'Union protest against unemployment turns violent in Brussels', available at: http://www.reuters.com.

80   Dirk Hirschel und Klaus Busch, 'Marshallplan für Südeuropa', *Blätter für deutsche und internationale Politik*, 8, 2011, pp. 5-8.

81 DGB, 'A Marshall Plan for Europe. Proposal by the DGB for an economic stimulus, investment and development programme for Europe', 2012, available at http://www.fesdc.org.

82 Markos Vogiatzoglou, 'Workers' trans-national networks in austerity times: The case of Italy and Greece', under submission with *Transfer: European Review of Labour and Research*.

THE NEW MORPHOLOGY
OF THE WORKING CLASS
IN CONTEMPORARY BRAZIL

RICARDO ANTUNES

Contemporary capitalism is bringing profound changes to the composition of the working class on a global scale. While the industrial proletariat is declining in many parts of the world due to the new international division of labour, particularly in the advanced capitalist countries, new cohorts of male and female workers in the service industries sector are expanding significantly, alongside employment in agribusiness and manufacturing, especially in many countries in the Global South.[1] The enormous expansion of work in *call centres* and telemarketing in information and communication technology (ICT) companies, ever more involved in the valuation process of capital, has also across the globe spawned the birth of a new proletariat of services, the infoproletariat or cybertariat. Thus, in the era of *computerization of work* in the mechanical-digital world, we see also an adversarial process developing, marked by the increasing *informalization of labour* (workers without rights) in the growth of outsourced/subcontracted, flexible part-time teleworkers, expanding the universe of insecure work.[2]

In this essay we will present certain distinguishing features that characterize the working class in Brazil, drawing attention to core elements of what I have called labour's new morphology. We start from a broad definition of the working class. The working class, especially since the changes that have taken place within contemporary capitalism, should not be seen as encompassing manual workers only, but rather should be seen to extend to the entirety of social work, the whole of collective labour, selling their work as a commodity in exchange for wages and paid by money-capital, regardless of whether their activity is predominantly material or immaterial. Although centrally composed of *the group of productive workers who produce surplus value and participate in the process of capital accumulation*, through the interaction between living labour and dead labour, between human labour and scientific-technological machinery, it also incorporates all *unproductive workers*, those whose activities are used as services, either for public *use*, such as traditional public services, or for capitalist *use*. In fact, in contemporary capitalism there exists a substantial overlap between the productive and the unproductive. Suffice to remember that in the world of production today a job may have both productive and unproductive dimensions, in that the same workers who produce have simultaneously to check the quality of what they have produced.[3]

An expanded notion of the working class must include not only productive workers in industry, agriculture and the service sector – privatized according to the prevailing logic of financial capital – but also the wide range of unproductive wage earners, who do not generate surplus value, yet are nevertheless essential in the capitalist labour process, and whose work experience closely parallels that of productive workers. As all productive work tends to be paid work, but not every wage earner is productive, an expanded notion of the working class must articulate these two dimensions. That is what we will try to do when dealing with the Brazilian reality.

ECONOMIC AND CLASS TRANSFORMATIONS IN BRAZIL

The changes that took place in late capitalism in Brazil, driven by the new international division of labour, particularly in the 1990s, were of great intensity and triggered a series of transformations, especially in the world of work. The way Brazil's economy was structured before this followed a dual production pattern. One side was geared towards the manufacture of durable consumer goods such as cars, electrical appliances, etc., targeting a limited and selective internal market. The other side, dependent on advanced capitalism, developed production for the export market for both primary products and manufactured goods. Internally, the dynamics of the pattern of capitalist accumulation were based on the presence of a process of workforce exploitation, characterized by low wages, intensified rates of production, long working hours and by extracting surplus value in both absolute and relative terms. During the military dictatorship of 1964-85, and especially its 'economic miracle' phase of 1968-73, this pattern generated high rates of accumulation, with the tripod of state production and national and international capital as its basic pillars.[4]

But it was really only from the 1990s, with the victory of neoliberalism in Brazil, a decade after the fall of the dictatorship, that the process of productive restructuring of capital intensified. The new organizational and technological standards, new forms of social organization of labour and new 'participatory' methods which companies adopted were mainly the result of: (1) impositions by transnational companies on their Brazilian subsidiaries (to a greater or lesser degree inspired by Toyotism and by flexible forms of accumulation); (2) the need for Brazilian companies to adapt to the new phase of strong 'international competitiveness'; and (3) the reorganization carried out by both MNCs and Brazilian companies in response to the confrontation created by the 'new unionism' (starting with the historic strikes that took place in 1978 in São Paulo, and especially its ABC industrial region).[5]

As a result of these mutations, a symbiosis was generated between elements inherited from the period of Fordism (which are still effective in various productive sectors and branches) using new tools characteristic of forms of flexible accumulation (lean production). The combination of the most technologically advanced production standards, the quest for a more highly qualified workforce and the practice of intensified workforce exploitation, have become characteristic of capitalism in Brazil. The implementation of total quality programmes, and the just-in-time and *kanban* systems, along with the introduction of wages linked to profitability and productivity (e.g. the Profit and Income Sharing Program (PLR)), combined with a pragmatism that strongly suited neoliberal objectives to enable an intensified expansion of productive restructuring in Brazil that led to flexibility, informality and a growing precariousness of the Brazilian working class. If informality (which occurs when the employment contract fails to observe social protective labour legislation) is not directly synonymous with precariousness, it amounts effectively to forms of work that are devoid of rights and thus closely similar. And making labour more flexible in Brazil has been, as we shall see throughout this essay, an important tool used by companies to cheat social labour legislation. These changes within the dynamics of capitalist accumulation ultimately affected the composition of the workforce. While between 1950 and 1980 the agricultural and industrial sectors actually increased their positions in terms of total employment, from 1980 to 2008 employment in agriculture fell rapidly from 32.9 per cent to 18.4 per cent. Industrial employment, accounting for almost one quarter of the total remained relatively stable, but services began to grow systematically, contributing heavily to the reconfiguration of the Brazilian working class. If until the 1980s the distinctive feature of the Brazilian economy was its strong industrial expansion, in recent decades the tertiary sector has registered an increase in relation to GDP. Between 1980 and 2008, the service sector 'increased its relative weight by 30.6 per cent, currently accounting for two thirds of all domestic production, while the primary and secondary sectors lost 44.9 per cent and 27.7 per cent, respectively, of their relative shares in GDP'.[6]

THE ROLE OF THE STATE

The restructuring process during the 1980s was limited and localized in some sectors, but from the 1990s it gained momentum, first during the period of Collor de Mello's government (1992-94) and later in that of Fernando Henrique Cardoso (1994-2002), a time when neoliberalism was developing rapidly. Brazilian production facilities, particularly in industry, were significantly altered by the privatization of the state production sector, directly affecting steel, telecommunications, electricity, banking, etc., sectors with a previously strong state presence that passed into private capital, both transnational and national. This process disrupted the tripod that supported the Brazilian economy (national, foreign and state capital), significantly reducing the state production sector and changing the very structure and composition of the ruling classes. With greater internationalization of the Brazilian economy, broad sectors of the national bourgeoisie and the state production sector were incorporated in or associated with external capital.

The first acts of Luiz Inácio (Lula) da Silva's Workers' Party (*Partido dos Trabalhadores*, PT) government (2003-10) signalled continuity with Cardoso's economic policy, albeit with social-liberal nuances. His government preserved the interests of finance capital by maintaining the primary surplus (budget resources allocated to the payment of interest on the public debt). With regard to labour legislation, initially the Lula government took very unpopular measures such as taxing pensioners and, at the end of his first term, he tried to carry out union and labour reforms that were strongly opposed, as much by employers associations as by unions and union federations.[7] The most negative element of this labour reform was that it allowed negotiation to prevail over legislation, so that an agreement between unions and companies might trump existing labour laws. Although the agrarian structure remained highly concentrated, it provided a great incentive to agribusiness (with important consequences for the working class), along with liberalized use of genetically modified organisms in agricultural production approved by Lula.

While the Lula government passed numerous measures that greatly benefited financial, industrial, agribusiness and services capital, it also allowed a relative appreciation of the national minimum wage compared to the Cardoso government. Social welfare policy also became quantitatively speaking much more comprehensive. The main social policy of the Lula government – the so-called Bolsa-Familia – was one of welfare, although of great reach, affecting in 2014 some 13 million poor families with low incomes and who therefore received a salary supplement. This social policy, much praised by the World Bank, significantly expanded the social support base that Lula lost in his first term. It benefited not the organized working class, Lula's natural constituency, but especially the most impoverished sectors of the population that live in the most distant peripheries of urban areas and that usually depend on state welfare to survive.

But while decreasing the level of social pauperism in Brazil, the Lula government also strengthened big capitalists, maintaining a level of inequality that is among the highest in the world. In reconciling these clearly conflicting interests, the Lula government did not confront any of the key features of Brazilian social inequality, with wealth still highly concentrated and the most acute levels of social misery only partly addressed. When the global crisis hit the core capitalist countries, the Lula government took steps to encourage a return to economic growth by means of tax cuts in key economic sectors such as automotive, domestic appliances and construction, all of them major employers. This encouraged the expansion of the Brazilian domestic market as a means to offset the contraction in the export market, which reduced demand for Brazilian commodities. By adopting a privatization policy based on public-private-partnerships (P3s), his government has also considerably encouraged the transnationalization of Brazil's economy, whether by opening the domestic market to international capital, or by giving impetus to the internationalization of various sectors of the Brazilian bourgeoisie (such as construction, for instance), which began investing in various parts of the world, always with the strong backing of PT governments.

Creating continuity with the Lula government, the PT government of Dilma Roussef (2010-14) is following the same paths: (1) economic growth based on the expansion of the internal market; (2) encouraging the production of export commodities, to the benefit of capital linked to agribusiness; (3) a financial policy that ultimately ensures the support of the financial system; and (4) reduction of capital taxes to the benefit of the automotive industry, construction, and so forth – in order to minimize the effects of weakening commodity exports. The effects of the international crisis spreading to intermediary countries like Brazil, however, greatly changed the economic, social and political situation. The riots that began in June 2013 are emphatic examples of the enormous social discontent that has built up against the government, a crisis that worsened during the eventful period between the Confederations Cup of 2013 and the FIFA World Cup of June-July 2014.[8]

If the Lula and Dilma governments managed to increase the number of workers in formal employment, and thus reduce joblessness, they also failed to eliminate the vulnerable conditions currently present within informal employment, outsourcing and workforce casualization in Brazil. Deregulation of labour, the expansion of outsourcing (subcontracting) and the duration of informality all remain, albeit at a lower level compared to

1990, a period characterized as the most acute in Brazil's social neoliberal desertification. The most significant result of this complex and contradictory process, with its advances and retreats, was the expansion of the new services proletariat that developed as a result of the significant process of privatization of state enterprises and public services. Since the beginning of the 1990s the number of outsourced workers (subcontractors) increased significantly, reaching in 2014 approximately 15 million workers in Brazil that were often without official employment or formal registration, and sometimes outside labour law, constituting a significant process of workforce casualization in Brazil.

The 1990s saw a sharp decline in formal jobs. According to Pochmann, '11 million jobs were created, of which 53.6 per cent of the total were unpaid. In the income range of up to 1.5 of the minimum wage there was a net reduction of nearly 300,000 jobs'.[9] Over the following decade, 21 million jobs were created, of which 94.8 per cent were poorly remunerated at barely 1.5 times the minimum monthly wage. Services activity generated 6.1 million jobs, followed by trade workers with 2.1 million; construction with 2 million; office workers with 1.6 million; the textile and garments industry with 1.3 million; and the public sector with 1.3 million. These professions totalled 14.4 million new jobs, comprising 72.4 per cent of all occupations and also paid up to only 1.5 times the minimum monthly wage. It is worth adding, moreover, that there was a significant growth of female labour, reaching almost 60 per cent of all occupations and mostly concentrated in the 25-34 age range.[10]

THE OUTSOURCING EPIDEMIC

Among all the changes in the structure of the Brazilian working class, outsourcing and subcontracting were some of the most harmful. In the last decade, the growth of outsourcing as a way to manage, organize and control labour in the corporate world brought with it a new type of instability, one that began to influence the ratio of capital to labour.[11] In a world where financial capital dominates the economy, companies seek to ensure high profits by transferring the pressure to workers by means of time optimization, high productivity rates, reduction of labour costs and increased flexibility in employment contracts. Outsourcing has also come to play a central role in employer strategy since social relations between capital and labour are disguised as inter-company relations, based on fixed-term contracts designed to suit the contracting companies and further damage the rights and livelihoods of the working class.[12] Moreover, the explosion of outsourcing companies has been an important driver of businesses generating added value that were formerly state-owned companies providing services on a non-profit basis. With privatization these became directly or indirectly involved in the appreciation of capital, increasing and expanding methods of extracting surplus value, both direct and indirect.

In the case of Brazil there has been a real epidemic of outsourcing in the last two decades, one that has contaminated industry, services, agriculture and public service, and that has affected production as well as support activities. In the various forms of outsourcing, one observes new working conditions that define workers in 'primary' and 'secondary' categories, and reveal distinctions or conditions of inferiority and inequality. These differences are yet more apparent in long shifts, the pace and intensity of the work, high levels of turnover, low wages, unsafe conditions and health hazards, among many others. Thus, outsourcing further increases fragmentation, heterogeneity and divisions within the working class, and increases competition among those who work in the same production area.[13] Outsourcing also tends to fragment unions, so that often within the same company different outsourcing sectors (such as cleaning, security, supply, maintenance, etc.) all have their own union representation, further weakening their ability to achieve organization, unity, solidarity and class resistance.

In the various sectors surveyed in *Riqueza e Miséria do Trabalho no Brasil (Wealth and Poverty of Labour in Brazil)*,[14] including banking, call centres and telemarketing, oil and petrochemicals, electrical power, communications and health, among many others, multiple forms of differentiation can be observed between contract workers, in terms of different types of contracts, remuneration, working conditions and union representation.[15]

In a relatively recent study by DIEESE, the sectors considered to be 'typically outsourced' accounted for 25.5 per cent of formal jobs in Brazil, their remuneration being 27.1 per cent lower than the rest. Regarding working shifts, outsourced employees worked on average three hours at most, and the time they remained in employment was 55.5 per cent lower than others. Their turnover rate was 44.9 per cent compared with 22.0 per cent in other companies.[16]

These insecure working conditions have had a major impact on occupational health and safety in Brazil. Several case studies reveal how outsourced contractors are the most vulnerable and the most likely to suffer accidents. This is the case in strategic sectors such as electricity, mining, steel and oil refining.[17] A significant example concerns workers in the oil industry, where the process of outsourcing has intensified enormously over the past two decades: in 2012 the proportion of contract workers compared with those hired directly by Petrobras was four to one. The giant state-owned company at that time had 85,065 employees and 360,372 contractors.[18] The growth of outsourced workers in the electric power company Eletrobras is also alarming: in 2011 there were 8,248 contractors rising to 12,815 the following year, an increase of 55 per cent, while the number of employees grew over the same period by only 13 per cent.[19]

A study conducted in 2010 found that between 2006 and 2008, 239 workers died in an accident at work, among whom 193 (80.7 per cent) were outsourced workers. In the same period the average mortality rate among formalized workers was 15.06, while among outsourced workers it was 55.53.[20] Another study showed that from 1995 to 2010, 283 deaths were recorded from industrial accidents, of which 228 were of outsourced workers.[21] According to statements by union leaders:

> The inequality of security conditions in big companies is well known by all employees … often the contractors, although they are in the same industrial plant, and sometimes involved in activities that expose them to higher risk, are completely unprotected whether collectively or individually. When accidents occur, the main contracting companies disclaim responsibility, arguing that they have nothing to do with the worker, who is employed by contract and is not a member of company staff…. The number of victims is increasing among outsourced workers.[22]

Business discourse justifies outsourcing as part of the 'modernization' of companies in the globalization era, one that brings greater 'expertise' to production activities. It has indeed greatly expanded opportunities for making previously unproductive work productive for capital, generating surplus value and participating directly in the productive value chain. But it is clear that companies also outsource in order to transfer the risk to workers, releasing themselves from the need to fulfil legislation requirements or respect workers' rights, both of which become the responsibility of the outsourcing firms. Outsourcing has thus become a central element of the current process of labour casualization in Brazil. And the phenomenon is present in virtually all branches, sectors and areas of work, a management practice that discriminates against the workforce by making contracts more flexible and, in the process, evading responsibility for labour protection.

Familiar business fallacies – 'outsourcing creates jobs', 'outsourced employees receive wages' and 'enjoy rights' and 'outsourcing is positive' since it provides opportunities for 'specialization and skills training' – seek to conceal something quite fundamental: that outsourcing has as its central objectives wage reduction, higher profits, a diminution of workers' rights and an increase in the fragmentation and disorganization of the working class, as much in the weakening of trade unions sphere as in the various other forms of collective solidarity that flourish in the workplace. In summary, it favours the exploitation of labour and trade unions, and the political fragmentation of the working class. Characterized by lower wages, long working hours and the daily trials brought about by the cheating of social protective labour legislation, outsourcing is becoming the main cause of work processes becoming corroded, and is expanding on a global scale. It is therefore a key component of the following section, which deals with the over-exploitation of labour in Brazil.

THE PHENOMENOLOGY OF OVER-EXPLOITATION OF LABOUR

The new morphology of labour in Brazil, and especially the principal features of the over-exploitation of labour in Brazil, will be examined here in relation to three distinct sectors. We will begin with the metallurgical industry where the industrial proletariat is heir to the period when Taylorism and Fordism held sway in Brazil. Then we will describe dimensions of labour exploitation in agribusiness, and finally the proletariat of the call centre services that has expanded exponentially in the era of neoliberal financialization and privatization in Brazil.[23]

The metallurgical sector

As shown by Luci Praun's survey of workers at the General Motors of Brazil (GMB) production plant in the city of São José dos Campos/SP, there was a clear link between different forms of labour exploitation caused by the sharp acceleration of activity in terms of pace and intensity that resulted in a high incidence of occupational accidents and illnesses. This was especially the case after 2008, when GM, in the throes of a deep crisis, triggered a new phase of deployment of its so-called Global Manufacturing System. In the context of this crisis, the company stepped up the integration of manufacturing processes within its various units globally. The immediate results of this 'rationalization' process were to close down manufacturing plants and lay-off workers, besides the relocation and transfer of activities among the various production units of GM.

This process was achieved through: layoffs, imposed directly or by means of voluntary redundancy schemes; new reduced salary levels; an increased pace and intensity of work, with the introduction of new mechanisms for measuring and standardizing activities, aimed at cutting the duration of operations; increased automation of manufacturing processes; an intensification of targets and results systems, with an emphasis on profit sharing; and greater control over evaluation systems, individuals, work teams and others.

Differentiation of wages and working conditions has also been, as Luci Praun has highlighted, an important feature of the metallurgical sector, not only among countries that make up GM's global supply chain, but also within Brazil, in terms of regional differences, size of organization, union resistance, etc. Table 1 below shows the significant wage differences in three industrial complexes GM has in Brazil for manufacturing cars: São Caetano do Sul (in operation since 1930), São José dos Campos (opened in 1959) and Gravataí/RS (organized from its inception in 2000 according to the Modular Consortium model).

TABLE 1

Average income of General Motors'workers (in R$)[24]

	São Caetano do Sul	São José dos Campos	Gravataí
2012	5.996,19	4.813,21	2.505,43
2011	6.223,66	4.928,22	2.549,64
2010	6.883,78	4.851,84	2.643,27
2009	6.725,46	4.751,31	2.569,74
2008	5.906,93	4.628,50	2.666,82
2007	6.434,58	4.767,54	2.592,50

As well as wage differentiations, GM also increasingly reorganized production to reduce 'dead time'. An example can be found in the actual length of the operational cycle (known in lean manufacturing terms as 'takt time') for the attachment of antilock brakes on S10 pickup trucks: this had already been only 175 seconds, but following reorganization was sped up further by almost 30 per cent. Similarly, a change in computerized systems of projection and implementation of manufacturing processes was carried out by GM, resulting in greater intensity of work. According to the vice president of manufacturing of GM South America, the impact of these procedures on the implementation of new projects can be clearly measured: 'Thanks to technology and the process of continuous improvement we can gain an extra second or two on each vehicle cycle. To get an idea of the importance of this, in Gravataí, which has a capacity of 360,000 units per year, to gain a second, just within operations that cause production bottlenecks, results in 7,000 more cars a year'.[25]

The effects on workers of this enhancement can be understood from the testimony of Alex Gomes, the worker representative on the Internal Commission for Accident Prevention in the São José dos Campos plant:

> With this increase in internal pressure in the factory, the worker is in fear of being fired, he works all the time with this dread, a climate of terror. We live in a constant climate of terror. After 2011 it just got worse. A guy comes into the factory every day thinking he will be fired. It distracts him from doing his job, it increases the number of incidents, it creates a greater risk of accident.

In relation to performance evaluation, he adds:

> Once a year each employee is called by the management to do a performance analysis, which involves a series of quality and attendance assessments. If the guy over the course of the year has an issue of producing less, it all goes into the evaluation. And that triggers a conversation between his supervisor and his time coordinator. He's called in. The supervisor passes it all over to him: 'you're no good at this, you're no good at that', and gives it to him to sign.

GM also conducts reviews of the work team, where results are presented by means of coloured balls affixed to the side of each team: *green ball* means that production is normal; *yellow ball*, you need to improve; and *red ball* means that production is lower than expected. And this form of performance evaluation, besides requiring a greater intensity and pace of production, causes an even greater division between workers themselves (those that are more productive and those that are less productive), including bullying. A worker in a foundry sector where five employees had been injured due to the accelerated pace of work and type of work recounted that:

> One day [the supervisor] took those five employees and locked them in a room, an office, turned off the light, went and turned off the main switch and locked the door from the outside so that those injured people could not leave, as if it were a punishment. He left them there for three or four hours locked in the room.

The many repetitive strain injuries (RSI) that working men and women suffer end up permanently incapacitating them for work, as in the automotive industry these lesions tend to be located mostly in the upper limbs, especially in the shoulders, and in the lumbar and cervical spine region. And besides physical harm, there are also significant indications of distress and mental illness that result from work and are treated by the use of antidepressants. Feelings of disposability and worthlessness as a result of sickness are also endemic, as another worker put it: 'Work is important. Work is everything. I feel like crap. The company used me for 25 years and then threw away the husk. I was always a good worker.'

Agribusiness

Another sector that is emblematic for understanding the new morphology of labour in Brazil is agribusiness. A sugar mill plant based in Cosmopolis, São Paulo, in the region of Campinas, for example, had about 1,000 rural workers in 2010 employed to cut sugar cane (which has become central to the production of ethanol, a fuel that is widely used in Brazil as a substitute for gasoline).[26] A payment-by-production remuneration system already adopted by a number of mills before the 1970s has become the predominant form of remuneration in the biofuels industry. As workers' wages are generally linked to the amount of cane harvested daily, this led to a significant intensification of labour. This framework means that the *average daily production* required by companies in cane cutting presents the most serious picture of over-exploitation of labour in agribusiness. According to the one excellent study: 'in 1980, the average required in cutting cane hovered around 6-8 tonnes daily; in the 1990s, these figures reached 10, and from 2000 between 12 and 15 tonnes'.[27]

Through productive restructuring in the biofuels sector, mills seek to make workers not just more productive, but also more controlled and disciplined in their activities. But there is one more element in the over-exploitation of labour in agribusiness: the way the production level is calculated. Because it is not the workers who account for the production – this is done by the employees of the mills – this calculation has frequently been a means by which the total is fraudulently reduced, routinely measured as less than the actual amount.

Illnesses, maimings and premature aging all become part of the daily work in agribusiness, as one worker called Maria attested: 'I myself got into their way of payment and already in the first month of work I had to get a certificate because I hurt my wrist. … I actually sprained the wrist … I was trying to keep up with the others and injured my wrist.' Another worker called Osvaldo described the consequences of his contract job (synonymous with working for production) this way:

Today you work by contract job and it has rules, you have time off for lunch and rest, but no one takes time off for lunch… if you do you won't make money … you finish eating and go straight back to work … some eat early the morning and stay the whole day without eating, they just have a coffee.

As each worker earns in accordance with the amount that he or she produces daily, managers can take account of those who produce more and those that are considered unproductive, keeping on the former and dismissing the latter. As long as wages are tied to production, rural workers end up exhausting their physical energies while trying to produce more and more in order to increase their earnings. This leads to the extension of their long working hours, further reinforcing the over-exploitation of labour as well as increasing competition among workers.

Cheating and over-exploitation of labour have become the daily reality in the cane fields of the ethanol agribusiness. The result is devastating for cane cutters: made to share responsibility for production volumes they push themselves to their absolute physical limits in terms of the intensity with which they work, the number of breaks they take or how much they will earn. In addition to significantly increasing profit and surplus value, an increase in illnesses resulting from overwork is to be observed, along with innumerable work-related maimings, injuries and deaths.

Another survey was carried out in in Toledo in the region of Paraná, at one of the world's largest producers of poultry meat and its derivatives, where approximately 6,500 workers are employed and a shift system is maintained continuously, 24 hours a day for seven days a week. The shift is eight hours and 48 minutes with an hour for lunch.[28] The organization of work in the sector is predominantly Taylorist and Fordist, through a fixed belt that carries the product to be boned. By combining elements of Taylorist/Fordist labour organization together with targets and development plans based on the Quality Control Circles typical of Toyotism, agribusiness in poultry has been able to leverage a greater degree of exploitation of the workforce that brings with it a daily risk of physical and mental illnesses, helping to shape the new morphology of labour dominated by insecurity and by the over-exploitation of labour.

The pace of work varies, but the average number of movements needed to debone a leg of chicken (drumstick plus thigh) is 18 performed in 15 seconds. The temperature is maintained at between 10 and 12 degrees; the humidity and noise are intense, along with the strong smell that is peculiar to this type of activity. The most frequent result is physical and emotional exhaustion of the workers, frequent illnesses and work accidents, as noted in the statement below on the subject of time and intensity of production. One 27-year-old worker, who has been employed there for 9 months, describes this as follows:

> At the start it was 25 seconds [the time required], now it's 20 seconds … The [speed of] the conveyor belt increased, the minimum is 19 seconds, but we still can't manage it… Every 20 minutes one sits down, but most of the time one is standing … it's tiring sitting on those chairs … then your back starts to hurt … the most I managed to stay on those chairs was an hour … then you start getting pain in the back, pain in the shoulder.

Besides the intense pace and adverse temperature conditions, a 20-year-old worker who had ben employed there for eight months described the system of targets, which makes it even more strenuous work: 'There's a target that has to be achieved, and a production [unit] is allowed a maximum of six mistakes … the whole [unit] has to achieve this target. If there are more than six mistakes the target is blown and the supervisor has to account for anomalies.'

Telemarketing and call centres

The telemarketing sector is also emblematic for understanding the new morphology of labour in Brazil, with 96 per cent of call centres created after 1990, and most of these after the privatization of the state utility company Telebras in 1998. The Brazilian Association of Teleservices (ABT), which represents the major call centre companies (Contax and Atento being the largest), estimated in 2012 that more than 1.4 million workers were employed in the sector, in a type of job that requires low qualifications and has limited experience of union activity. Of these, a large portion are youths and women, working at wages that are among the lowest in the world in this sector, surpassed only by those of Indian workers.[29]

Atento-Brasil, in the city of São Paulo in Campinas, is a company that provides customer care services through what are known as 'contact centres'.[30] It began operations in April 1999, with just over 1,000 employees, and by 2003 had grown to almost 30,000 and by 2013 to over 84,000, making Atento-Brasil one of the largest private companies in telemarketing and call centres. In the course of her work, the telemarketer (over 70 per cent of this group is female) remains seated for 85 per cent to 90 per cent of her six-hour daily shift, giving full attention to the computer screen, keyboard and headset, with only one five minute personal break to go to bathroom and one 15 minute break allowed for a snack. According to the testimony of one former operator called Ignez:

> I worked from 2pm to 8pm, I was sitting down for six hours, I only had 15 minutes for coffee and to go to the bathroom. … For six hours I was sitting down talking on the phone. … I do not want to sit in one place for six hours per day without being able to move.

A supervisor is constantly present to check the operators' work, requiring greater productivity by controlling their TMO (average operating time), a process that can lead more rapidly to the operator contracting an occupational illness. On this point one operator called Luiza testified as follows:

> You have a target. When you are giving out information [to a customer] you are watching your TMO, the average time to give out the information. For example, they ask for 29 seconds, and there are people who want not just that information, but also want to talk about something else, so you end up attending badly to that person. For example, you will not pay attention to her because you know that your TMO is going up, and that's what makes people tense in the service. Plus they are also saying that productivity fell and, because of that, we can't even have our personal break. Because they say: we're going to lower the TMO. I'm going to lower the TMO. How? People want information; they don't want a robot.

As Luiza also explained:

> There are very few breaks. It's just five minutes to go to the bathroom, which they call a personal break, and lunch would be about 15 minutes. I mean anyone who brings food or something doesn't chew, she swallows. Because otherwise it's not possible. Often I don't manage to have my personal break, I try to contain myself, but some people don't manage it because they've got this business of urinary retention or are taking medicine. So it's difficult. … Those people have no respect. There are people who need to go to the bathroom and can't.

The work control is intense, largely facilitated by the advanced technology present in this sector. The machine in turn becomes so dominant that the possibility of interpersonal relationships is almost nil. Another operator called Fernanda described this:

It's funny, when people arrive, it's a glance at the other person's face and 'Bye!' There's no time for us to talk. You have to talk before you go in, because once you've gone in it's impossible to talk any more. And when your day finishes you're so exhausted that you get in the lift and keep quiet: 'Another day', and the other person only manages to answer, 'Another day'.

The time control is extremely rigid, and this intensification of the working day means a lack of freedom for telemarketing operators, where scripts and service flowcharts are predetermined. Many telemarketing companies have standardized dialogues, prescribing behaviour standards that even cover the tone of voice, since this often determines whether or not the answer given to the customer is accepted. The control of operators' emotions by the company is another important factor, clearly showing how profoundly this workspace affects workers' personal outlook. The operator must exercise self-control, having to cope with situations of aggression and even harassment that frequently occur. Regardless of the aggression shown by some customers, she must maintain service standards with regard both to tone of voice and sticking to the predetermined script. 'All this control goes through a hierarchy: the directors cover the managers, who cover the supervisors, who in turn cover the telephone operators. The considerable sufferings, embarrassments and even psychological illnesses in this workspace are easy to imagine.'

Supervision with regard to real-time call duration aims for calls to be answered within the allotted time, which makes it a means of control and of cost-reduction since it avoids the need to hire a larger number of workers. Here is the testimony of telephone operator Maria about this effective vigilance:

Once companies have been contracted to monitor us, every day they are monitoring. There are other supervisors from other sites supervising also, even apart from the quality of the telephone calls which people are also monitoring, so I think it worsens the working atmosphere. It's a lot of supervision, it's a lot, they demand a lot from you, you sacrifice a lot for the company and the company doesn't acknowledge it, it doesn't give you any incentive, that's what it's like.

In addition to this control there are sanctions against delays and absenteeism, with campaigns developed by the company as a means to encourage discipline among the telephone operators. Telephone operator Havana testified:

> Just this month they were holding a 'work day ...', I don't remember the exact title, but it's like this, if you have no absenteeism and don't arrive late, at the end of the month you can win a bicycle, a DVD, a television, a mobile phone. So it's an incentive for not being absent.

Another important element in telemarketing work, from the point of view of the owners, are campaigns to boost productivity, usually promoted by the sector in charge of quality. These campaigns, known as a 'motivational incentive', are about stimulating competition among workers in order to increase productivity by intensifying the pace of work, while using mechanisms that may disguise that intention from the workers.

Nor should the illnesses routinely experienced in telemarketing workplaces be ignored. The statement below confirms this problem:

> The problem I have is with my arm. It hurts a lot, mainly when the weather changes, but this happened because of repetitive strain. I went to the doctor, but he didn't say it was RSI/ WMSD, those things. He told me to do physiotherapy, but I never manage to book physiotherapy because there are no appointments available. You have to be on a waiting list and it's only provided by two hospitals in the city. And so I keep on doing my job and it just keeps getting worse. He (the doctor) did not ask for sick leave for me, he only prescribed injections, and that's it. By now I've taken five injections and it eases the pain. But then it comes back again.

At the Atento Campinas site where this survey of operators was carried out, among of a contingent of 1,863 workers (396 men and 1,467 women), some 136 (the vast majority of them female) were off work because of sickness or work-related accidents.

Telemarketing and call centre work are characterized by intense exploitation aimed at achieving productivity targets within the times and standards imposed by the company.[31] Beyond the apparent objectives of 'ensuring quality of service' and 'customer satisfaction', telemarketing operators experience a significant process of exploitation of their labour, which becomes visible when research is carried out into their health conditions, time, 'quality', 'motivation', alienation, heteronomy of the work process, among many elements that the testimony above indicates. Targets, routinization of labour, despotism on the part of coordinators and supervisors, low salaries, illnesses and ailments resulting from working conditions – all these characteristics typify the new service proletariat that is growing in Brazil and in many other parts of the world as a result of the growing importance of information in global financial capitalism. They are a new constituent in the expansion and diversification of the new morphology of labour in Brazil and in various parts of the world.

A FINAL NOTE

Against theories advocating the loss of relevance of labour in the contemporary world, the challenge is to understand its new morphology, whose most visible element is its multifaceted profile, the result of the powerful changes that capitalism has undergone in recent decades. In Brazil, this new morphology encompasses not only the classic industrial and rural proletariat but also waged service workers, those new contingents of outsourced, subcontracted, temporary workers that are growing in number. It is a new morphology that represents the expansion of new proletarians in the worlds of industry, of services and of agribusiness, examples of which are telemarketing and call centre operators, along with the digitizers who work – and are injured – in banks and who have burgeoned in the digital and tele-information age, of wage earners in fast food, the young workers in hypermarkets, the couriers who die on the roads and streets using their motorbikes to transport goods, etc.

They constitute part of the social labour forces involved directly or indirectly in the generation of surplus value and capital appreciation. They are workers who oscillate between, on the one hand, great heterogeneity in terms of gender, ethnicity, generation, environment, qualifications, nationality, and so on, and on the other, a tendency towards strong homogenization that results in the insecurity currently present in different types of work. This is an insecurity that is growing on a global scale. And these different working arrangements are playing a prominent role, not just by creating new ways of generating added value, but also by triggering new social struggles in which the wage earners in industry, agribusiness and services are heavily involved. With an economically active population approaching one hundred million workers, Brazil offers a particularly useful snapshot of this new reality, and the emerging class struggles.

NOTES

1   We will always use the term 'workers' while being conscious of its gender
     dimension, as indicating both female and male workers, since an unequal and
     differentiated socio-sexual division often exists in the world of labour. So when
     we use the word 'workers' we hereby clarify that we also conceive it in its
     gender dimension.

2   Ursula Huws, *The Making of a Cybertariat: Virtual Work in a Real World*,
     New York: Monthly Review Press, 2003; Ricardo Antunes and R. Braga,
     Infoproletários: Degradação Real do Trabalho Virtual, São Paulo: Boitempo,
     2009; R. Antunes, 'Freeze-dried flexibility: a new morphology of labour,
     casualisation and value', *Work organization, labour and globalization*, 5(1), 2011,
     pp. 148-59; R. Antunes, 'Who is the Working Class Today?', *Workers of
     the World: International Journal on Strikes Social Conflicts*, 1(2), January, 2013,
     available at http://workersoftheworldjournal.net

3   Ricardo Antunes, *The Meanings of Work: Essay on the Affirmation and Negation of
     Work*, Leiden: Brill, 2013.

4   Ricardo Antunes, 'Trade Unions, Social Conflicts, and the Political Left in
     Present-Day Brazil: Between Breach and Compromise', in Jeffery R. Weber
     and Barry Carr, eds., *The New Latin American Left: Cracks in the Empire*, Lanham,
     New York: Rowman & Littlefield Publishers, 2013, pp. 255-76.

5   Giovanni Alves, *O novo (e precário) mundo do trabalho*, São Paulo: Boitempo.
     2000.

6   M. Pochmann, *Nova Classe Média? – o trabalho na base da pirâmide social brasileira*,
     São Paulo: Boitempo, 2012, pp. 16-7.

7   R. Antunes, *Riqueza e Miséria do Trabalho no Brasil* [Wealth and Poverty of
     Labour in Brazil], Vol. I, São Paulo: Boitempo, 2006; A. Galvão, *Neoliberalismo
     e reforma trabalhista no Brasil*, São Paulo: Ed. Revan/FAPESP, 2007.

8   Ricardo Antunes, 'Die Revolten von 2013', *Emanzipation, Zeitschrift für
     sozialistische Theorie und Praxis, (Vom Recht auf Stadt zur urbanen Revolution)*,
     3(2), 2013.

9   Pochmann, *Nova Classe Média?*, p. 27.

10   Pochmann, *Nova Classe Média?*, p. 32.

11   In this section we present ideas written in partnership with Grace Druck to
     be published in *Riqueza e Miséria do Trabalho*, Vol. III, São Paulo: Boitempo,
     forthcoming, October 2014.

12   G. Druck, 'Trabalho, Precarização e Resistências', *Caderno CRH (UFBA)*, 24,
     2011.

13   Research among petrochemical and chemical companies in Bahia, where 358
     workers directly contracted by 52 companies in the sector were interviewed
     in 2000, reveals how outsourcing is seen by workers. Asked if they would like
     to be outsourced, 93 per cent answered 'no'. Among these, the main reasons
     for not being outsourced were: loss of rights, benefits, rewards and wages (47
     per cent); instability and insecurity (11 per cent); poor working conditions (7
     per cent). The remainder indicated various reasons that can be summarized

as: discrimination, humiliation and devaluation. See the Report of the Wage Campaign Survey issued by the Center for Human Resources/UFBa and Union of Chemical and Oil Workers, 2000.

14   R. Antunes, *Riqueza e Miséria do Trabalho*, Vol. I; and Vol. II, São Paulo: Boitempo, 2013.

15   G. Druck, *Terceirização: Desfordizando a fábrica – um estudo do complexo petroquímico da Bahia*, São Paulo: Boitempo, 1999.

16   DIEESE-CUT, *Terceirização e Desenvolvimento: uma conta que não fecha – Dossiê sobre o impacto da terceirização sobre os trabalhadores e propostas para garantir a igualdade de direitos*, São Paulo: DIEESE, 2011.

17   One study conducted in 2010 found that between 2006 and 2008, 239 workers died in an accident at work, among whom 193 (80.7 per cent) were outsourced workers. In the same period the average mortality rate among formalized workers was 15.06, while among outsourced workers it was 55.53. (DIEESE, *Terceirização e Desenvolvimento*, subsection in Sindieletro Minas Gerais). And data presented by FUP – United Federation of Oil Companies of CUT – shows that from 1995 to 2010, 283 deaths were recorded from industrial accidents, of which 228 were of outsourced workers

18   Petrobras, Relatório de Sustentabilidade, 2012, p. 160.

19   Eletrobras, Relatório de Sustentabilidade, 2012, p. 184.

20   DIEESE, *Terceirização e Desenvolvimento*, subsection in Sindieletro Minas Gerais.

21   Data presented by FUP – United Federation of Oil Companies of CUT, cited in Antunes and Druck, in *Riqueza e Miséria do Trabalho*, Vol. III.

22   SINDIQUÍMICA, 2001, p. 7, cited in G Druck and T Franco, 'Terceirização e precarização: o binômio anti-social em indústrias', in Druck and Franco, eds., *A Perda da Razão Social do Trabalho: Precarização e Terceirização*, São Paulo: Boitempo, 2007.

23   All the research information contained in this section is the result of the collective research project under R. Antunes, 'The Metamorphosis in the World of Work', at Universidade Estadual de Campinas (UNICAMP) and published in *Riqueza e Miséria do Trabalho*, Vol. I, II and III. The material here on General Motors in the Metallurgical Sector draws on the PhD Thesis by Luci Praun, 'Não sois máquina! Reestruturação produtiva e adoecimento na General Motors do Brasil', Sociology Department, Instituto de Filosofia e Ciências Humanas da (IFCH/UNICAMP), 2014. Its main results will be published in *Riqueza e Miséria do Trabalho*, Vol. IV, São Paulo: Boitempo, forthcoming 2015.

24   The source for this table is Praun, 'Não sois máquina!, p. 13.

25   Praun, 'Não sois máquina!' pp. 113; the following quotations from workers are at pp. 72, 59, 144-5 and 123.

26   The material here on agribusiness draws on research by Juliana Guanais.

27   M. M. Silva, 'Trabalhadores Rurais: A Negação dos Direitos', *Raízes*, 27(1), 2008.

28   The material here on agribusiness draws on research by Vera Navarro and Marcos Neli.

29   See Antunes and Braga, *Infoproletários*.

30   The material here on telemarketing and call centres draws on research by
     Claudia Mazzei Nogueira.
31   The following discussion on telemarketing and call centres draws on research
     by Ruy Braga.

CLASS TRANSFORMATIONS
IN CHILE'S CAPITALIST REVOLUTION

TIMOTHY DAVID CLARK

As in much of Latin America, the history of capitalism in Chile is one of profound unevenness and halting advance. One of the chief reasons for which capitalist social relations expanded in such a faltering manner was the absence of clas0s forces and institutional configurations conducive to the acceleration and deepening of capitalist development.[1] In response to the revolutionary capitalist pressures emanating from the foreign owned nitrate fields in the north and the world market of the late nineteenth century, the dominant segment of Chilean landlords and industrialists sought to contain and control pressures for capitalist transformation by retreating into the state to defend individual and sectoral interests against foreign competitors and domestic opposition. For Chilean capitalists, the competitive impulses and class transformations of capitalist modernity were as much threat to entrenched power as they were opportunity. Marx's discussion of the French bourgeoisie of the mid–nineteenth century is apt: 'Instinct taught them that while, indeed, the republic completes their authority, it at the same time undermined their social foundation … It was a sense of weakness that caused them to recoil before the unqualified demands of their own class rule, and to retreat to the less complete, less developed, and, for that very reason, less dangerous forms of the same'.[2]

It was the state-based middle class, represented by the Radical Party, and the organized working class, represented by the Socialists and Communists, that emerged in the 1920s and 1930s to push for a more aggressive and state-led industrialization. The prior assimilation of Chilean capitalists into the state, however, impeded the kind of state autonomy and capacity required to discipline capitalist investors and construct a dynamic capitalist economy, the result of which was that the character and trajectory of industrialization were guided not by state officials according to a coherent developmental programme but from within peak associations and elite social clubs according to the short-term interests of a narrow segment of property owners.[3] Indiscriminate protectionism and no-strings public credit resulted in cycles of import-substitution boomlets, monopolization and under-utilization, and the formation of low-productivity and uncompetitive industrial and agricultural sectors. At the same time, the expansion of an inefficient industrial structure resulted in the rapid growth of a working class radicalized by the incapacity of political and economic systems to meet their demands, which fuelled the battle over a stagnant economic base that would drive inflation and demands for expropriation. From the mounting pressures of a restricted capitalist development emerged revolutionary socialism.

The election of Salvador Allende in September of 1970 was a watershed moment in Chilean and Latin American history. The standard reading of these tumultuous years opposes Allende, the socialist revolutionary who sought to place the economy under state control, and Augusto Pinochet, the neoliberal counterrevolutionary who freed the market from its state shackles. Although Allende and Pinochet were indeed historical adversaries, their opposition was dialectical, wedded by the common objective of deploying the power of the state to transcend the frustrated transition to industrial modernity via the radical reconstruction of state and society. And in one of history's great ironies, it was the mass expropriations of the Allende years that made possible the depth of the subsequent capitalist reforms of the military regime by enervating the chief obstacle to rapid capitalist development: Chilean capitalists. In Chile, the midwife of capitalist modernity was socialist revolution.

As revolutionary socialism gained momentum over the 1950s and 1960s, moreover, bourgeois-revolutionary forces began to emerge on the right, led by a young generation of economists who gradually gained footholds in the political, economic and academic spheres. The product of an agreement between the Catholic University of Chile and the University of Chicago, itself part of the Mutual Security Program of 1957, the Chicago Boys and their policies were consistently rebuffed by the owners of the major conglomerates and the rightist political elites. Under the patronage of the powerful Edwards family, however, the Chicago Boys gradually began to extend their influence into the financial, media and political spheres, as well as into the military via former naval officer and Edwards confidante Roberto Kelly, who spearheaded the drafting of the infamous economic blueprint for the military government, *The Brick*, and who transformed the National Planning Office (ODEPLAN) into a bourgeois-revolutionary beachhead within the state apparatus following the coup of 11 September 1973.

When the Chicago Boys were elevated by Pinochet to the top economic policymaking portfolios in mid-1975, they had a very clear sense of historical mission: to carry out a state-led capitalist revolution. For José Piñera, one of the central architects of policy under Pinochet, the chaos unleashed by the Allende government bestowed upon the military regime a 'revolutionary legitimacy ... to carry out profound transformations'.[4] The mission of the Chicago Boys was not to reverse the statist expansion of previous decades but to reconstruct Chilean society so that the state itself would be seen as largely superfluous, a sort of historical inversion of the prediction of Engels that the state would 'wither away' in communist society. In yet another ironic twist, however, the power of the state would be central to the planning of its obsolescence. For the Chicago Boys the state was 'decisive in the socio-economic development of the country' precisely in order to construct a market society, inspired by the Hayekian vision of a 'catallaxy' in which 'the community expresses itself through market prices', as former Finance Minister Sergio de Castro remarked.[5] The construction of a new society was the job not of reactionary but of revolutionary forces, as Former Minister of Finance Hernán Büchi recognized when he wrote that the dictatorship initiated 'an authentic revolution in the productive and social structure, in the orientation of its development, and in the perceptions of the people'.[6]

This analysis of the reconstruction of the class foundations initiated by the military dictatorship will begin with an examination of the reconstitution of the capitalist class, on the one hand, and the working and middle classes, on the other. The essay will conclude with a brief consideration of the faultlines that threaten the political and economic stability and reproduction of the neoliberal order, as well as the social movements that have emerged to challenge the legacies of the dictatorship and the prospects for a deeper transformation of Chilean society. Although the bulk of the analysis focuses upon the Pinochet dictatorship, public policies and processes of class transformation will be traced through the post-authoritarian period to the present. The underlying assumption is that the centre-left coalition that controlled the presidency from 1990 to 2010 represented continuity with the public policies and class transformations of the dictatorship to a far greater degree than it did change.[7] Although there were certainly policy divergences, such as the capital controls of the 1990s, and policy improvements, such as the substantial increases in social expenditures, the centre-left governments reproduced – and in some cases even deepened – the basic macroeconomic and social policies of the Pinochet years and their concomitant effects on the processes of class formation.

RECONSTRUCTING THE CAPITALIST CLASS

After being consistently rebuffed by the entrenched capitalist elite for much of the 1960s, the Chicago Boys knew full well that one of the chief obstacles to their radical agenda was these same industrial and agrarian interests that, in the words of de Castro, 'cultivate close relationships with politicians and state officials' and 'whose actions run contrary to the general interest'.[8] Although Allende in many ways facilitated the implementation of the revolutionary project by expropriating many of the traditional capitalists, the Popular Unity years left the Chicago Boys without a stable and defined social foundation through which to carry out their reforms, that is to say capitalists not only capable of but willing to lead the restructuring project from civil society. The dictatorship thus faced the same fundamental problem that had haunted governments from the 1920s onwards: how do you construct a dynamic capitalist society without a powerful and dynamic capitalist class? The answer of the economic planners, as it turns out, was to construct a new capitalist class, and financial reform and privatization were the initial mechanisms.[9]

Over the course of the 1960s, numerous Chicago Boys and their graduates had established an economic toehold in the financial sector, taking advantage of low stock valuations following decades of financial repression. In mid-1974, Chicago Boys within the state and the financial sector drafted and implemented financial reform, whose first step was the creation of a new class of non-bank financial institutions (*financieras*) with no interest rate restrictions and low reserve requirements. The Chicago Boys in the financial sector were able to use their insider information to jump the gun on financial reform, quickly setting up *financieras* to purchase the soon-to-be-privatized banks and take advantage of the reduction of restrictions on foreign liabilities.[10] As foreign loans trebled in the last years of the 1970s, the percentage captured by the financial sector rose from 4 per cent in 1976 to 73 per cent by 1981 and two Chicago-Boy-dominated financial firms – BHC-Vial and Cruzat-Larraín – controlled over 60 per cent of all domestic credit.[11] These firms used their control over credit and their connections to state planners to snap up a vast array of productive assets during the privatizations of the 1970s, whose rules and timing greatly favoured financial firms, as well as initiate a wave of mergers and acquisitions. Between 1970 and 1979, BHC-Vial and Cruzat-Larraín increased the number of firms under their control from 28 to 174.[12]

As their power grew, the Chicago Boy conglomerates became the bearers of the new hegemonic rationality, substituting for the coordinating function of the state and transforming Chilean capitalism. These new nodal firms used cross investments and new forms of corporate organization, such as holding companies and indirect forms of control, to constitute interlocking alliances between economic groups that transcended firm or sectoral interest and diffused new patterns of corporate organization and investment. At the same time as power and control were centralized in the hands of holding companies, the productive structure was decentralized via specialization and externalization, which in turn facilitated the introduction of Taylorist principles into the factory and a flexibilization of labour relations.[13] The Chicago Boy firms similarly played a central role in the development of the new exports industries such as forestry, fisheries and agribusiness through direct investment and the provision of credit to a new generation of middle-class entrepreneurs who were founding many of the earliest export firms. From their positions in the public and private sectors, moreover, the Chicago Boys increasingly influenced the ideological realm, from universities to a host of media fora and right-wing think tanks that propagated a new vision of private enterprise and individualism as the motive force and fundamental value of growth and progress.[14]

The revolutionary project, however, was not without contradictions and crisis. The early 1980s witnessed unsustainable levels of speculation and consumption punctuated by a severe financial crisis and de facto nationalizations at a tremendous cost to the Chilean public. Yet the unprecedented surge in private fixed-capital investment in machinery and equipment (concentrated in the emergent exports sectors) in the second half of the 1970s laid the foundations for the extraordinary export expansion from the mid-1980s.[15] What is more, state planners were able to build upon the economic, organizational and ideological transformations of the capitalist class during the 1970s to fortify the remaining internationally oriented conglomerates by means of debt-for-equity swaps and privatization. With the aid of privatized pension funds, large conglomerates and connected state officials directed resources towards a reconstructed and powerful segment of capitalist investors, linked to foreign firms via joint ventures in the non-traditional export sectors and domestic monopolies. By the second half of the 1980s, the dominant fraction of the Chilean capitalist class had been reconstituted into three subsets: non-financial and export-oriented groups, such as Matte, Luksic and Angellini; the new groups that emerged from the privatization process of the 1980s, such as Pathfinder and Sigdo Koppers; and foreign groups, such as Nestlé in agribusiness, ENDESA in electricity, Telefónica in communications and Citicorp, Santander and Aetna in banking, pensions and insurance.[16]

In addition to the reconstitution of urban capitalists, the state constructed a new agrarian bourgeoisie. In control of the majority of arable land at the time of the military coup, state officials quickly dashed the hopes of traditional landlords for a return to the old agrarian order when a senior junta official declared to the National Agricultural Society, 'We consider the latifundio socially and economically retrograde'.[17] Instead, the military regime deployed a variety of mechanisms to constitute a new agrarian capitalist class and transform the social value of land. On the one hand, an agrarian bourgeoisie was resuscitated from the modernizing elements of the old agrarian elite via the restitution of approximately 30 per cent of expropriated land, up to a limit of 80 hectares to prevent the reconstitution of the great landed estates. And on the other hand, the Chicago Boys slashed state support for peasant producers (who had received more than 50 per cent of expropriated land) while opening agricultural markets to foreign products, squeezing smallholders and generating a supply of available land. Shortly after, state planners legalized the sale of land and removed the size restrictions on landholdings and the prohibition of the sale of land to corporate entities, fomenting demand. The result was a dramatic concentration of landholdings and the rise of powerful agribusiness companies that exerted control over land via direct investments and product contracts.

The reforms of the military regime fundamentally revolutionized the relationship between land and class power. In the pre-land reform period, the social purpose of land was in no small part as a source of political power and prestige, and processing industries were founded and controlled primarily by large landlords. Agrarian reform, however, severed the traditional nexus between agriculture and political power, on the one hand, and agriculture and industry, on the other. Land ceased to provide reliable votes and new urban agro-industrial and commercial firms not linked to the countryside were concentrated in the hands of the financial and urban conglomerates via privatization. According to the new rationality, the value of land ownership was related less to farm size than to relative levels of capitalization and profitability. In the post-land reform countryside, therefore, the social purpose of land was primarily as an instrument for the reproduction and expansion of private capital accumulation and landowners were increasingly subordinated to urban agro-industrial and retail-distribution interests.[18]

As part of the construction of a powerful capitalist class, and contrary to the neoliberal imaginary of non-interference in the market, the state lavished the private sector with supports throughout the 1970s and 1980s. Organizations such as ProChile and Chile Foundation were set up to connect producers to foreign markets and develop new product lines, including the extraordinarily successful salmon and wine industries. Sales tax and tariff rebates were approved for exporters, in addition to special lines of credit refinanced by the Central Bank at a reduced cost, while the 1980s witnessed the implementation of the successful simplified drawback of input costs for exporters. In addition to vertical supports, numerous sectoral subsidies were provided. Decree Law 701 provided a subsidy for the planting and management of forestry plantations up to 75 per cent of cost. Large-scale agricultural capitalization was similarly favoured, with public-sector credit exploding from US$30 million in 1974 to nearly $170 million by 1979, focused on agroindustry, vines and fruit.[19]

Supported by the continuation and deepening of pro-business policies under the centre-left coalition, the reconstruction of Chilean capitalists resulted in the emergence of a handful of powerful conglomerates that represent the axis around which the capitalist class and the national economy orbit. Large firms that comprise 1.4 per cent of all firms now account for an extraordinary 81.6 per cent of sales and approximately 1,500 firms control 74 per cent of all domestic sales. The large firms that dominate the economic landscape of Chile are in turn controlled by a small number of conglomerates, a mere sixteen of which account for 80 per cent of GDP. At the sectoral level, three companies control 92 per cent of the pharmaceutical industry, two companies control nearly 70 per cent of electricity generation, and one firm controls 78 per cent of the sugar market, 88 per cent of airline traffic, and 89 per cent of the beer market.[20] Because the main conglomerates cut across numerous activities and much of the national economy, their vision and leadership transcend the firm or sectoral levels towards a global political-economy perspective and their power and influence over state and civil society is unprecedented in Chilean history.

RECONSTRUCTING THE WORKING AND MIDDLE CLASSES

The reconstitution of the Chilean capitalist class upon the export and service sectors provided the foundation for the reconstruction of the working and middle classes. Cast from the import-substitution industries and public sector that had bred collective organization and demands for state redistribution and public provision, Chilean workers were integrated into a rapidly expanding market economy that would drive unprecedented declines in poverty and indigence over the course of the 1990s and 2000s. As private sector employment grew, moreover, consumption was shifted from the public to the private realm via real wage increases, the greater availability of low-cost goods and services, and an unprecedented explosion of consumer credit. This individualization, privatization and marketization of the working and middle classes was reinforced by the so-called modernizations of labour, social security, education, health care and social assistance that individualized, privatized and marketized social services and stigmatized public provision.

The past three decades have witnessed an unprecedented increase in market output, driven in large part by rapid growth in the wage-labour force, which expanded at nearly triple the rate of population growth between 1970 and 2012.[21] Unlike many countries in the region, however, newly proletarianized workers in Chile were integrated into formal employment, which by 2010 had risen to 61.7 per cent of the labour force, compared to 47.4 per cent in Argentina and 33.2 per cent in Peru, and more than 70 per cent of labour contracts in Chile are permanent.[22] Even informal employment was transformed by the rise of productive decentralization and subcontracting, with an estimated 45 per cent of informal employment concentrated in the two top income quintiles.[23] As formal employment expanded, moreover, real average and minimum wages rose 3.5 per cent and 5.8 per cent per annum between 1986 and 2010, while marginality declined. The World Bank estimates that only 25 per cent of the Economically Active Population (EAP) in Chile work in 'vulnerable' forms of employment, comparable to South Korea, and the percentage of low-wage workers in the EAP, defined as earning less than two-thirds the median wage, is similar to Belgium and half that of Argentina and Uruguay.[24]

Although the outcomes in terms of the individualization, privatization and marketization of social subjectivities were similar, the working and middle classes were differentially reinserted into capitalist markets. Following an intense period of repression, macroeconomic and fiscal policies initiated a profound transformation of the organized working class. Trade liberalization and fiscal austerity provoked widespread industrial bankruptcy and a sharp decline in blue-collar employment, precipitated by the collapse of employment in industry and construction, from 25.8 per cent of the EAP in the 1970s to less than 10 per cent by early 2014.[25] Workers in highly unionized industries moved into emergent sectors such as commerce and services, agroindustry and forestry, where productive decentralization, subcontracting and geographical dispersion mitigated collective organization. The rate of unionization and the percentage of workers covered by collective bargaining agreements correspondingly collapsed from averages of 29 per cent and 26 per cent, respectively, under Allende, to a mere 14 per cent and 12 per cent under the right-wing government of President Sebastian Piñera.[26]

The middle class underwent similarly profound transformations. Salaried employment in the public sector fell dramatically from 18.4 per cent of the EAP in the early 1970s to 6.8 per cent by 1995, under the weight of fiscal austerity. As middle-class workers were pushed out of their traditional base in the state, they were incorporated into the private sector dominated by the economic conglomerates, as salaried professionals and small and medium-sized business owners providing inputs and services into national and global supply chains. The private-sector salaried middle class saw its numbers swell from 20.3 per cent of the EAP in 1980 to more than 30 per cent by 2014, while the number of business owners in the EAP more than doubled and the share of small business owners in the top 40 per cent of income earners increased by nearly 50 per cent.[27] As an illustration, in 1970 two US firms controlled 70 per cent of Chilean exports; by 2011, however, there were nearly 2,000 Chilean firms exporting to the United States alone. This entrepreneurial middle class, moreover, is sociologically and culturally distinct from capitalists of the past, with business experience and educational achievement rather than family name or inherited wealth as the principal determinant of success.[28]

As employment opportunities were individualized and privatized, so was consumption, driven in significant part by an explosion of consumer credit. Facilitated by the greater formality of employment and rising real wages, consumer credit increased sharply from the early 1990s, more than quadrupling its share of GDP to 14 per cent by 2012, with the volume of consumer credit rising from $34 billion to $159 billion between 2002 and 2012 alone.[29] Credit growth was fuelled by the extraordinary expansion of credit cards, whose numbers swelled from 2.6 million in 1993 to 23.7 million by 2007 to more than 30 million by 2013, led by retail firms whose share of cards in circulation exceeds 80 per cent.[30] The rise of the 'credit-card citizen' has played a central role in the reconstruction of social subjectivities. Consumer credit plays a potent constructivist role in capitalist society, as a powerful tool for social transformation and control whose disciplinary mechanism is unique because it is completely commodified. Because of its purely commodified nature, credit serves to individualize, privatize and marketize forms of social identity, social consumption and social advancement: 'Credit, much more than trade unions, appears as the instrument of progress'.[31] Retail firms are particularly significant in the integration of labour into the privatized and marketized social world because they cater to low-income populations through the practice of 'sowing', whereby individuals with low or no income access small quantities of credit, whose amounts increase not as incomes rise but on the basis of their consumer behaviour, i.e., the frequency of card usage and repayment habits.[32]

As the structures of employment and consumption underwent tectonic shifts, the Labour Plan of 1979 transformed unions from vital sites in the formation of class consciousness and political mobilization to the intermediaries between localized market actors. The plan restricted collective bargaining to the plant level and limited strike activity and coordination while instituting a host of measures to discourage unionization and the reconstitution of ties between organized labour and party politics. The labour 'modernization' was followed by social security in 1980, which established an individual capitalization scheme administered by private investment firms. The heavy hand of the state was again visible: the legislation made contributions compulsory for all workers with permanent contracts and the state guaranteed minimum rates of return for contributors and fund administrators, as well as maintaining responsibility for the pensions of those who remained in the previous pay-go system and providing a public-assistance pension for the destitute. The constructivist character of the pension reform was laid bare by Hernán Büchi, one of its principal architects, when he predicted 'the day will arrive when individual responsibility is so rooted in the population that compulsory contributions … will no longer make sense'.[33]

The decentralization and privatization of public and social services further evidenced the deeper objectives of individualization and marketization of subjectivities and pathways of social advancement via the introduction of private and for-profit schools and healthcare providers that has resulted in deeply segregated systems of service provision. Social assistance programmes, while undoubtedly benefiting many of the poorest members of society, had similar intentions and effects. For example, the flagship welfare initiative of the early post-transition years, the Solidarity and Social Investment Fund, was designed not to address the structural origins of poverty, provide a buffer against unemployment and destitution, or develop and articulate a sense of common welfare and social rights. On the contrary, the programme seeks first and foremost to integrate marginalized populations into precarious positions within stratified labour markets and pit groups and communities against each other in the process of competitive bidding for scarce resources.[34]

One of the foundational objectives of the military regime was the displacement of identity formation and social advancement from the collective-political realm to the individual-market realm. Prior to the coup of 1973, social identities were formed, interests were organized and aggregated and opportunities for advancement were channeled through participation in labour unions and political parties. From 1973, however, state repression, economic restructuring and the social modernizations have disarticulated the organized working and middle classes, rendered employment and wages dependent upon levels of private-sector investment and productivity, and conditioned access to services such as education to levels of income obtained in the private marketplace.

These processes of individualization, privatization and marketization have in turn resulted in a significant level of de-alignment and depoliticization within civil society. Since 1990, non-identifiers on the left-right continuum and non-partisanship have risen, as have those who never read political news, watch political forums or discuss politics.[35] At the same time, voter turnout has declined precipitously. Between 1989 and 2013, the percentage of the Voting Age Population that votes in elections declined from 86 per cent in congressional and presidential elections to barely 42 per cent in the most recent presidential run-off election. Voter turnout in municipal elections, moreover, fell from 80 per cent in 1992 to a mere 41 per cent in 2012, the first election since the electoral system was reformed to make registration mandatory but voting voluntary.[36] Declining electoral participation is in turn strongly impacted by socioeconomic strata and age. Recent studies have found a strong positive correlation between income and electoral participation. What is more, the positive correlation between income and voter turnout is stronger among youth, the result of which is that the 'class bias' of voter turnout is in fact increasing over time as a result of the dynamic replacement of older cohorts in the voter universe by younger ones.[37]

In this individualized, privatized and marketized Chile, approximately 50 per cent of the population defines itself as 'middle class'.[38] This 'middle-classization' of the country reflects two interrelated processes. On the one hand there is the aforementioned decline of collective forms of identity formation and interest aggregation and the privatization and stigmatization of public provision. Indeed, a central component of what it means to be 'middle class' is precisely non-reliance upon state provision. On the other hand there is trade liberalization, the rapid expansion of private-sector employment and the 'democratization of consumption' via credit that have made social status signifiers like cars and cell phones available to an unprecedented swath of the population. Things that used to be luxuries of the top decile, such as foreign travel, are now widely available to middle and lower-middle income earners. This new 'middle class' is the highly individualized, atomized and privatized representative of the 'neoliberal citizen'. It is the socioeconomic counterpart and complement to the dominant economic conglomerates, a disorganized and depoliticized centre that sustains a political and economic system dominated by a small minority.

CONTRADICTIONS OF THE REVOLUTIONARY PROJECT

This essay has contended that the Pinochet dictatorship is best thought of not as a neoliberal counterrevolution but rather as a state-led capitalist revolution that reconstructed the class foundations of Chilean society and institutionalized a profound capitalist hegemony.[39] The particular manner in which this hegemony was institutionalized, however, created a series of profound fault lines. For one, Chilean society remains plagued by deep inequalities of power, income and opportunity. By 2010, income inequality had barely declined from a Gini coefficient of 0.57 in 1990 to 0.55. The growth of formal employment did not necessarily entail, moreover, high wages and job security for the majority of workers. Despite the significant increases in real and minimum wages from the mid-1980s, wages were in the 1990s still catching up to pre-coup levels. What is more, there is a strong concentration of incomes towards lower levels. Nearly two-thirds of Chilean households have a monthly income of under $600 and Zahler found that approximately 60 per cent of the Chilean population lives on incomes at or below the average income of Angola.[40] Even the comparatively 'secure' workers in the formal sector often find themselves in precarious conditions. Half of 'permanent' work contracts last fewer than three years and 20 per cent are terminated within one year.[41] The trend towards greater formality in the economic and contract structure, therefore, has been counterbalanced by the growing precariousness of the formal economy and the downward redefinition of 'permanent' contracts, with workers largely disorganized and at the whim of private-sector investment and employers.

Transformations in the socioeconomic structure have also exacerbated the disparities between the private-sector middle class in salaried positions and small and medium-sized businesses connected to the conglomerates, on the one hand, and the working class in precarious employment and informal businesses in marginalized neighbourhoods, on the other, to the detriment of left and working-class protagonism. Over the past four decades, the share of private-sector salaried employees and independent contractors in the top four income deciles increased sharply while the shares of public-sector employees and blue-collar workers collapsed.[42] As the fates of the middle and working classes diverged, the privatization of social services ensconced a deep socioeconomic segregation. For all the discussion of education as the silver bullet for inequality, it is ancestry and parental income that determine salary and wage levels in Chile.[43] University graduates from high-income families earn on average 50 per cent more than similar graduates from poor families, and the 'class earnings gap' is nearly twice as large as the gender gap and more than three times the racial gap. The inequalities produced by this network of ancestry and income are compounded by profound levels of socio-geographical segregation. In Santiago, the isolation index is 90 per cent, meaning that families from poor neighbourhoods have only a 10 per cent chance of interacting with families from different socioeconomic strata.[44]

Not surprisingly, Chile has comparatively low levels of intergenerational mobility.

It is the centrality of the privatized system of social services in the reproduction of social, economic and geographical inequality and segregation that resulted in the meteoric rise of the student movement as the principal social force opposed to the extant order, first with the secondary student 'Revolution of the Penguins' in 2006 and then with the larger protests and occupations by post-secondary and secondary students in 2010-11, the so-called 'Chilean Winter'. The chronic underfunding of public schools, when combined with the 'shared financing' reform of 1994 that allowed private, subsidized primary and secondary schools to charge parents additional fees, has transformed the education system into a mechanism for the reproduction of inequality and segregation. Primary and secondary schools in Chile demonstrate characteristics of 'hyper segregation' and segregation levels have risen since 2000, despite expenditure increases, while the high cost of university education, where 80 per cent of the cost is born by families and the share of the family budget dedicated to university fees is between three to four times higher than in Europe, serves to constrain both the entrance and retention rates for students from low-income families.[45] In response, the student movement sought to reframe education as not a commodity but a social right, demanding free education up to and including post-secondary studies and an end to for-profit schools, among other demands. Backed by enormous public support, leaders of the student movement were recently elected to congress in the Communist and Autonomous Left parties, and newly elected Socialist President Michelle Bachelet has prioritized an ambitious education reform aimed eliminating school fees and profit in universities and primary and secondary schools that accept public resources.

The problems of inequality, low incomes and restricted social mobility are exacerbated, moreover, by the absence of a more aggressive industrial policy, the result of which is that primary and natural resource-based products continue to represent nearly 70 per cent and more than 90 per cent of all exports.[46] In the case of copper, diversification has regressed, with the share of refined copper in total copper exports falling from 97 per cent in the early 1970s to barely 50 per cent. As the most recent commodity supercycle unwinds, Chile will face significant pressures on its trade and payments balances. Despite the strong growth and low unemployment of the past several years, inequality and resource dependence have fuelled popular unease, with only 21 per cent of the country characterizing the economy as 'good' or 'very good' and 60 per cent stating the country is either stagnating or declining.

As the socioeconomic pressures for change mount, the rigid and exclusionary political system inherited from the military regime and perpetuated by the centre-left coalition further limits the possibilities for change. In addition to the power of the capitalist class to block reform, the institutionality of the state itself acts as an impediment to policy change, whether through the internal hegemony of the neoliberal Ministry of Finance or the series of constitutional protections of the principal reforms of the dictatorship. The transformation of political parties from vehicles for popular mobilization to bulwarks of the dictatorial order, in turn, has fuelled the deligitimization of the political process, with nearly 94 per cent of the population registering little or no confidence in political parties.

None of this should be taken to mean, however, that more radical change is impossible. Rather, we must be clear as to the nature and depth of the reforms implemented by the Pinochet dictatorship and maintained by the centre-left governments, and the challenges they represent, if we are to transcend them. As one of the principal architects of policy under Pinochet observed, 'One has to recognize that the process of modernization in Chile, apart from a series of sectoral reforms, included a serious attempt to modify the analytical and judgemental criteria of public opinion and to change the forms of thought in the society'.[47] The upsurge of social mobilization and protest over the past decades, on a range of issues from subcontracting and hydroelectricity to reproductive rights and education, provide evidence of the deep fissures that threaten the fragile and ever-shifting equilibrium of the neoliberal order. And yet, these same social movements and mobilizations evidence the scale of the challenges posed by the processes of individualization, privatization and marketization initiated by the military regime. Even the wildly successful student movement has failed to generate sustained linkages with other social movements in order to articulate a more ambitious and far-reaching challenge to the principles and policies of neoliberalism, let alone one capable of reconstituting class identities and alternative political parties and mass movements. As such, students and other social movements in Chile have yet to crack the individualized, privatized and marketized shell of the new 'middle class' that will represent the ultimate battleground in which the direction of the country, and the aspirations of those who desire a more radical break from the legacy of the dictatorship, will be determined.

NOTES

1   For a more detailed discussion of this process, see Timothy David Clark, 'The State and the Making of Capitalist Modernity in Chile', PhD Dissertation, York University, 2013, Chapters II and III.

2   Karl Marx, *The Eighteenth Brumaire of Louis Bonaparte*, New York: Mondial, 2005, p. 26.

3   Constantin Menges, 'Public Policy and Organized Business in Chile: A Preliminary Analysis', *Journal of International Affairs*, 20(2), pp. 343-65.

4   José Piñera, 'Dar Un Golpe de Timón, Crear Esquemas Nuevas', *Qué Pasa*, 454, p. 7.

5   ODEPLAN, *Eficiencia Económica para el Desarrollo Social: Plan Nacional Indicativo de Desarrollo, 1976-1981*, Santiago: ODEPLAN, p. 8; DIPRE, *Somos Realmente Independientes Gracias al Esfuerzo de Todos Los Chilenos*, Santiago: Ministro de Hacienda, 1978, p. 324.

6   Hernán Büchi, *La Transformación Económica de Chile: El Modelo de Progreso*, Santiago: El Mercurio-Aguilar, 2008, p. 237.

7   See Marcus Taylor, *From Pinochet to the 'Third Way': Neoliberalism and Social Transformation in Chile*, London: Pluto Press, 2006.

8   Sergio de Castro and Juan Carlos Méndez, eds., *El Ladrillo: Bases de la Política Económica del Gobierno Militar Chileno*, Santiago: Centro de Estudios Públicos, 1992, pp. 33, 47.

9   For a detailed discussion of the reconstruction of Chilean capitalists, see Clark, 'The State and the Making', Chapter IV.

10   Eduardo Silva, *The State and Capital in Chile: Business Elites, Technocrats, and Market Economics*, Boulder: Westview Press, 1996, pp. 107-8.

11   Andrea Mizala, *Segmentación del Mercado de Capitales y Liberalización Financiera*, Santiago: CIEPLAN, 1985, p. 6; Sebastian Edwards and Alejandra Edwards, *Monetarism and Liberalization: The Chilean Experiment*, Chicago: University of Chicago Press, 1991, p. 76.

12   For data on economic concentration in the 1970s, see Fernando Dahse, *Mapa de la Extrema Riqueza: Los Grupos Económicos y el Proceso de Concentración de Capitales*, Santiago: Editorial Aconcagua, 1979.

13   Patricio Rozas, *Elementos de un Diagnóstico Sobre la Situación del Empresariado Nacional Durante el Régimen Militar (1973-1983)*, Santiago: Centro de Estudios del Desarrollo, 1984; Álvaro Díaz, *La Industria Chilena Entre 1974-1994: De la Sustitución de Importaciones a la Segunda Fase Exportadora*, Santiago: CEPAL, 1995.

14   Marcelo Pollack, *The New Right in Chile, 1973-1997*, New York: St. Martin's Press, 1999.

15   Banco Central de Chile, *Indicadores Económicos y Sociales de Chile, 1960-2000*, Santiago: Banco Central, 2001, pp. 856-9.

16   Alex Fernández Jilberto, 'The Origin and Formation of Economic Groups in Chile', *Journal of Developing Societies*, 20(3/4), 2004, pp. 189-206.

17   Cited in Verónica Ortiz de Zárate, *El Golpe Después del Golpe: Leigh vs. Pinochet, 1960-1980*, Santiago: LOM Ediciones, 2003, p. 47.

18   Harry Díaz and Rigoberto Rivera, *Notas Sobre la Estructura Social Agraria en Chile*, Santiago: Grupo de Investigaciones Agrarias, 1986, pp. 53-4.

19   Ministerio de Agricultura, *La Agricultura Chilena Durante el Gobierno de las Fuerzas Armadas y de Órden: Base del Futuro Desarrollo*, Santiago: MINAGRI, 1989, pp. 227-9.

20   See José Cademartori, 'Growing Disparities and the Extreme Concentration of Wealth in Chile', in X. de la Barra, ed., *Neoliberalism's Fractured Showcase*, Leiden: Brill, 2011, pp. 113-34; and Carlos Ruiz and Víctor Orellana, 'Panorama Social de Chile en el Bicentenario', *Revista Análisis*, 2011.

21   Drawn from various editions of the 'Economic and Social Indicators' of the Central Bank of Chile.

22   Roxana Maurizio, *Labour Informality in Latin America: The Case of Argentina, Chile, Brazil, and Peru*, Manchester: Brooks World Poverty Institute, 2012, p. 11; Carlos Ruiz and Giorgio Boccardo, 'Problemas Sociales de la Concentración Económica', *Revista Análisis*, 2009, pp. 41-2.

23   Catalina Amuedo-Dorantes, 'Work Contracts and Earnings Inequality: The Case of Chile', *The Journal of Development Studies*, 41(4), 2005, p. 596.

24   Dante Contreras and Ricardo Ffrench-Davis, 'Policy Regimes, Inequality, Poverty and Growth', UNU-Wider Working Paper No. 2012/04, Helsinki: World Institute for Development Economics Research, 2012, p. 3; data on vulnerable employment drawn from the online database of the World Bank; ILO, *Global Wage Report 2010/2011*, Geneva: International Labour Organization, 2011, p. 36.

25   Arturo León and Javier Martínez, *La Estratificación Social Chilena Hacia Fines del Siglo XX*, Santiago: CEPAL, 2001, pp. 18-20; 2014 data calculated by author from information in the 'National Employment Survey' of the National Statistical Institute of Chile.

26   Valentina Doniez, *El Modelo Laboral: La Deuda Pendiente*, Santiago: Instituto de Políticas Públicas, 2012, p. 1.

27   Giorgio Boccardo, 'Cambios Recientes en la Estructura Social de Argentina, Brasil y Chile', *Revista de la Carrera de Sociología*, January/June, 2012, p. 63; 2014 data compiled by author from the information in the 'National Employment Survey' of the National Statistical Institute of Chile.

28   José Miguel Benavente, 'Empresario Chileno Durante Los Noventa: ¿A Self-Made Man?', *Economía y Administración*, 148, p. 13.

29   The Abraaj Group, *View on Latin America*, London: The Abraaj Group, 2013, p. 26.

30   Juan Pablo Montero and Jorge Tarziján, *El Éxito de las Casas Comerciales en Chile: ¿Regulación o Buena Gestión?* Santiago: Banco Central de Chile, 2010, p. 3; 'Impacto Económico', TeleSurTv, 10 May 2013, available at http://multimedia.telesurtv.net.

31   Tomás Moulian, *Chile Actual: Anatomía de un Mito*, Santiago: LOM Ediciones, 1997, p. 105.

32   José Ossandón, 'Sowing Consumers in the Garden of Mass Retailing in Chile', *Consumption, Markets, and Culture*, 2013, pp. 13-4.

33   Büchi, *La Transformación Económica*, p. 117.

34   Taylor, *From Pinochet*, pp. 190-5.

35   Ryan E. Carlin, 'The Decline of Citizen Participation in Electoral Politics in Post-Authoritarian Chile', *Democratization*, 13(4), 2006, pp. 632-51.

36   Electoral data drawn from the website of the International Institute for Democracy and Electoral Assistance (IDEA), available at http://www.idea.int.

37   Alejandro Corvalán and Paulo Cox, When Generational Replacement is Class Biased: Voter Turnout in Chile', unpublished manuscript, 2011.

38   Ruiz and Boccardo, 'Problemas Sociales', p. 49.

39   This thesis and its supporting arguments were profoundly influenced by Javier Martínez and Álvaro Díaz, *Chile: The Great Transformation*, Washington, DC: Brookings Institution, 1996.

40   Andrés Zahler, '¿En Qué Pais Vivimos Los Chilenos?, *CIPER*, 2011, available at http://ciperchile.cl.

41   Ruiz and Boccardo, 'Problemas Sociales', pp. 41-2.

42   León and Martínez, *La Estratificación Social*, pp. 22-4.

43   Javier Núñez and Roberto Gutiérrez, *Classism, Discrimination and Meritocracy in the Labor Market: The Case of Chile*, Santiago: Departmento de Economía de la Universidad de Chile, 2004; Javier Núñez and Graciela Pérez, 'Díme Cómo te Llamas y te Diré Quién Eres: La Ascendencia como Mecanismo de Diferenciación Social en Chile', Santiago: Departmento de Economía de la Universidad de Chile, 2007.

44   Dionysia Lambiri and Miguel Vargas, 'Residential Segregation and Public Housing Policy: The Case of Chile', unpublished manuscript, 2011.

45   Gregory Elacqua, Matías Martínez and Humberto Santos, *Lucro y Educación Escolar*, Santiago: Instituto de Políticas Públicas, 2011; Juan Pablo Valenzuela, Cristian Bellei and Danae de los Ríos, 'Socioeconomic School Segregation in a Market-Oriented Educational System: The Case of Chile', *Journal of Education Policy*, 29(2), 2014, pp. 217-41.

46   The next two paragraphs draw upon Clark, 'The State and the Making', Chapter V.

47   Büchi, *La Transformación Económica*, p. 237.

THE OLYMPIC RULING CLASS

GEORGE WRIGHT

The International Olympics Committee's main functions consist of overseeing National Olympic Committees (NOCs) and Olympic Games Organizing Committees (OGOCs), cooperating with affiliated international sports federations (IFs), selecting the host city for the Olympic Games and enforcing the operational guidelines for organizing the Games.[1] The formation and institutionalization of the International Olympics Committee (IOC) and the modern Olympic Games in the 1890s was carried out by European aristocratic and capitalist elites at a time when industrialization, monopoly capitalism and the republican-democratic project were coalescing. They were motivated by a commitment to educational reform involving physical education and sport so as to establish domestic equilibrium among the social classes and military preparedness for future wars. While incorporating their nineteenth century elite ideals (classical liberalism, volunteerism, philanthropy, amateurism, etc.) into the 'Olympic Movement', the founders hoped to use the Olympic Games – and the promotion of sport more generally – to ameliorate the domestic class struggles as well as inter-imperial rivalry.

Despite the growing chasm between those ideals and twentieth century historical realities the IOC leadership clung to its ideals from its founding in 1894 until the early 1970s, above all its commitment to a non-profit approach based on amateur competition and opposition to the commercialization and commodification of the Olympic Games. This was reinforced by those who joined the IOC between 1945 and 1972 from Communist and Third World states. Given the extent to which the IOC had always resembled an exclusive Western 'Gentlemen's Club', it was no little shock to its system when after World War Two the composition of the IOC membership was altered with the inclusion of individuals from the Soviet Union and the East European Communist-ruled countries, the newly independent Third World nations, as well as some sportswomen and other representatives of the Olympic Movement's broader constituency. These new representatives somewhat altered the class composition of the IOC; however, rather than changing the IOCs character and political orientation they were, in point of fact, assimilated into that body.

What did radically alter the character of the Olympic Movement was how the IOC leadership, beginning in 1972, transformed its economic orientation and structures to generating unprecedented sums of revenue. This was not just a matter of IOC presidents Lord Killanin, Juan Antonio Samaranch and Jacques Rogge being themselves capitalists or closely affiliated with capitalist interests. There was nothing new in this. What determined the change was the institutional imperative to survive the structural crisis of capitalism beginning in the 1970s and how the IOC learned to promote neoliberal globalization and operate and prosper within it. By the new millennium, the total amount of revenue the IOC garnered during the Salt Lake City and Athens quadrennial cycle (2001-04) was $2.3 billion; the Torino and Beijing (2005-08) cycle garnered $3.4 billion; while the Vancouver and London (2009-12) total was $4.8 billion.[2]

Clearly this is no trivial aspect of global capital accumulation via the commodification of international sport. What is less apparent is that the IOC needs to also be seen as an important place of ruling class formation. The significance of this today is especially marked in terms of what the Olympic Games in Beijing and Sochi represent in terms of the rise of the BRICS (Brazil, Russia, India, China and South Africa) and their ruling classes within global capitalism. But no less significant, as can especially be seen with respect to the run up to the 2016 Rio Games in Brazil, may be the contradictions this is throwing up.

THE MAKING OF THE IOC

When Pierre Fredy, Baron de Coubertin, brought 78 delegates, representing thirteen countries and 37 sporting societies, to the International Congress of Amateurs in Paris in 1894 to discuss the status of 'amateurism' in international sport, his guiding thought was that the revival of the Olympic Games might ease inter-imperial rivalry and conflict and bring the youth of the world together into a spirit of 'brotherhood'.[3] Born into a long line of aristocrats going back to the late fifteenth century, which had maintained their monarchist loyalties into the late nineteenth century, Coubertin had been inspired as a boy by reading Thomas Hughes' *Tom Brown's School Days* which emphasized the role of sport in the moulding of young men in the English public school system. Believing the lack of physical fitness was a major factor in France's defeat in the 1870-71 Franco-Prussian War, Coubertin had for many years advanced physical education as part of French school reform, contending that a curriculum including physical education and sports would contribute to domestic social equilibrium in an increasingly urbanized, industrial society.

The first modern Olympic Games in Athens in 1896 were presided over by Coubertin's friend, Demetrious Vikelas, who after having made his fortune in his family business as a London merchant by the age of 35 had retired to Paris where he lived the life of a scholar, poet and philanthropist. Coubertin then took the IOC presidency himself, and for the next three decades oversaw the Olympic Movement. After the Olympics in Paris in 1900, St. Louis in 1904, London in 1908 and Stockholm in 1912, the Games scheduled for Berlin in 1916 were cancelled, but were successfully resumed in Antwerp 1920 and Paris in 1924. By the late 1920s, the Olympic Games had become the world's premiere international sporting festival.

The traditional class composition of the IOC was established when Coubertin chose the original all-white male grouping of aristocrats, wealthy capitalists (bankers, investors, industrialists), retired military officers and sports educators from elite institutions, mainly from Europe, with a few selected individuals from the United States, Argentina and New Zealand. Their common worldview consisted of adherence to classical liberalism, tethered to a belief in European racial and cultural supremacy, contempt for working-class self-organization and agitation, fear of the influence of the radical ideas of socialism, communism and anarchism, and opposition to women's equality. Significantly, the members contributed dues to the IOC, paid their own way to meetings and volunteered their time without expecting remuneration.

All the original IOC members had some association with sport, either as patrons, administrators, advocates or propagandists, physical education reformers, enthusiasts, educators or coaches. From Coubertin's perspective, the national origins of the members would reflect the universality of the Olympic Movement as well as provide coordination and cooperation with sports administrators and relevant political and economic interests in their respective nations or regions. By 1901, there were 25 members; 48 in 1914; 65 in 1930; and 73 in 1939. Of the 73 members in 1939, 44 were from Europe; five from North America (with two from Canada); ten from Latin America; eight from Asia (including two from Australia and one from New Zealand); and three from Africa (two from South Africa and one from Egypt). Even though the regional diversity of the membership had increased somewhat, the social background, gender, class composition, political orientation and their relationship to sport remained the same.

Financially exhausted from subsidizing the Olympic Movement,

Coubertin retired the year after the 1924 Paris Olympics and was succeeded by Count Henri Baillet-Latour, a Belgian aristocrat with a lineage that went back to the eleventh century who oversaw the Olympic Games in Amsterdam in 1928, Los Angeles in 1932 and Berlin in 1936 – the largest and most dramatic Olympic spectacle of the modern era. Baillet-Latour worked closely with Avery Brundage, the President of the Amateur Athletic Union and the American Olympic Association, to successfully prevent a threatened boycott of the Nazi propaganda extravaganza that marked Berlin Olympic Games.[4] Baillet-Latour's reasoning in opposing the boycott was that the IOC would not interfere in the internal politics of a host nation. Of that period, Michael Real has observed: 'Gradually, the "Old Boy" network of support was giving way to support from cities, which spent increasing amounts in hosting the games, reaching the apex with the Berlin Games in 1936'.[5] Notably, with the Olympics being by now lavishly publicly financed, both national and local capitalist interests (land developers; construction companies; building material producers and suppliers; food and beverage possessors and suppliers; public relations and advertising firms; and local hotels and restaurants) benefited considerably, whether through transparent contracts or backroom deals.

Tokyo, which was slated to host the 1940 Olympics, withdrew from the Games in 1938 owing to the Sino-Japanese War. Those Games were then given to Helsinki; however, they were cancelled due to the Second World War. After Baillet-Latour died in German-occupied Brussels in 1942, the Swedish IOC Vice-President Sigrid Edstrom was selected Acting-President; he was elected President in 1946 and oversaw the first two postwar Olympic Games, which were held in London in 1948 and Helsinki in 1952. Edstrom was an engineer who, after starting his career with Westinghouse in the US, eventually came to head the General Swedish Electric Company and chair the International Chamber of Commerce between 1939 and 1944. He had been involved in sports administration since the early twentieth century and was a staunch defender of amateurism.

This proved important for the way the Cold War was played out in the IOC from the outset of the postwar period.[6] Immediately after the war, the IOC allowed National Olympics Committees from Eastern Europe (Bulgaria, Czechoslovakia, Hungary, Poland, Romania and Yugoslavia) back into that body, and they remained on it even as they became Communist regimes.[7] In April 1951, the Soviet Union's recently formed National Olympic Committee requested to join. Russia had been active in the Olympic Movement prior to the 1917 Bolshevik Revolution, having participated in the 1900, 1908 and 1912 Games. However, the Soviet leadership withdrew from the Olympic Movement, viewing the Games as bourgeois, elitist and opposed to the working class.[8] Although most of the IOC members were staunchly anti-Communist, they voted to admit the Soviet Union, 31 in favour, with no opposition, and three abstentions, on the grounds that the commitment to universality meant including any country eligible for the movement regardless of its internal politics.

But the IOC was also impressed that the Soviet NOC President, Konstantine Andrianov, was 'a true sportsman', and was co-opted onto the IOC (the vote for Andrianov was 24 in favour, five opposed and five abstentions).[9] A mill operator who had worked his way up the precarious party-state bureaucracy through sports administration, starting in the Komsomol, then as chair of the Moscow City Sports Committee, and finally as vice-chair of the All-Union Committee on Physical Culture and Sport. In general the Communist states' IOC members had been former athletes, sports enthusiasts and/or national sports administrators, integral to the state-party bureaucracy that formed what Milovan Djilas called 'the new class' in the postwar Communist states. In fact, Djilas commented, 'The ownership privilege of the new class and membership in that class are the privileges of administration. This privilege extends from state administration and the administration of economic enterprises to that of sports and humanitarian organizations'.[10]

The Soviet IOC members' agenda included increasing the number of members from the Communist-ruled countries and the newly emerging Third World. In 1948, there were two sportsmen from Communist-ruled East European countries in the IOC; steadily growing to six by 1960, which was the number of members they still had in 1972. And as the post-Second-World-War dismantlement of the European and Japanese empires led to 64 former colonies and territories in Asia, Africa, the Caribbean, Latin America and the Pacific gaining national independence, this also had the effect of altering both the membership of the Olympic Movement and the class composition of the IOC. Prior to 1945, there were 18 Asian, African and Latin American NOCs in the Olympic Movement. Between 1945 and 1972, of the 77 NOCs that joined the Olympic Movement, 73 were from the Third World. In 1939, the 16 IOC members were from Asia (4), Latin America (10) and Africa (2). By 1955 there were 19 Third World members; 24 in 1965; and 28 in 1972.

Africa experienced the largest increase in IOC membership during this period. In 1950 there were only two IOC members from Africa, both from apartheid South Africa, and even in 1960 there were only three IOC members from Africa, with one each from South Africa and colonial Kenya, and the other member from Egypt. However, by 1965 the number of African members of the IOC increased to seven; and by 1972 to ten.

The new African IOC members had close ties with their governments, generally as political officials, judges or bureaucrats.[11] However, not unlike their IOC counterparts, all of them had elite backgrounds: some had degrees from European universities, many were medical or legal professionals, and all of them had a history of involvement in national and/or international sports federations. Most were generally from 'privileged' social layers during the colonial period, which allowed many of them to receive education in the West, acquiring what Robin Cohen calls 'European skills'.[12] Nevertheless, their class backgrounds did differ from the Western IOC members; since a national capitalist class did not exist at independence, the African IOC members were drawn from various petty-bourgeois or comprador interests who functioned in or around the state. African IOC members working closely with Andrianov secured the banning of South Africa from the 1964 and 1968 Olympic Games, as well as expelling South Africa in 1970 and Rhodesia in 1972 from the Olympic Movement.

The changing class composition of the IOC was facilitated by Avery Brundage, who succeeded Edstrom to become the first non-European to be elected IOC President. Brundage's social background was entirely different from his predecessors. While, like Edstrom, trained as a civil engineer, Brundage was born into a working-class family and already by age 30 epitomized the 'self-made' millionaire. After losing his first fortune in the 1929 crash, he had amassed another fortune and served as the Vice-President and Director of the Chicago Association of Commerce. An ardent believer in Coubertin's vision of the transformative power of amateur sport, Brundage led the IOC when the Olympics became a Cold War arena with the United States and Soviet Union counting medals to determine which country 'won' the Olympic Games – and by implication, which economic system was superior. Brundage could not prevent this, but consistently maintained that the 'Olympic Games were for individuals only [and] not for national teams'.[13]

THE MAKING OF THE NEOLIBERAL OLYMPICS

By 1972, 121 nations and 7,134 athletes were at the Munich Games. Sixty-nine nations and 4,955 athletes had attended the 1952 Helsinki Games. Over the intervening two decades the Olympics (Melbourne in 1956, Rome in 1960, Tokyo in 1964, Mexico City in 1968) experienced tremendous growth in scale and global reach. With the advent of television the Olympics became a worldwide phenomenon. In the mid-1960s, Brundage allowed the organizing committees to negotiate broadcast rights as well as distribute the revenue based on an agreed upon formula whereby the OGOCs received two-thirds and the rest equally divided among the IOC, the International Sports Federations it recognized and the NOCs.

The 1972 Munich Olympic Games were Avery Brundage's last as IOC President. The hostage-taking and violence that shook those Games, with eleven Israelis, five Black September militants and one German policeman killed, meant he did not have a triumphant exit.[14] He was succeeded as IOC President by Lord Killanin (Michael Morris), who not only had the unenviable task of dealing with the fallout from the Munich violence, but also addressing boycotts of the successive Montreal and the Moscow Games. Despite aristocratic Irish roots and an education at Eton, the Sorbonne and Cambridge, Killanin was not independently wealthy. He worked as a journalist on Fleet Street before the war, and after being knighted as a Member of the Order of the British Empire for his service, moved to Ireland, where he wrote screenplays for film productions, authored six books and served on the board of directors of no less than fifteen companies, including Irish Royal Shell, Ulster Bank and Northern Electric, as well as being President of the Olympic Council of Ireland. Recognized for his commitment to bringing the Irish Republic's and Northern Ireland's sports federations together, he was co-opted into the IOC in 1951; as Killanin put it: 'My Olympic life began not through any prowess at sport, but by trying to resolve disputes and squabbles'.[15]

Although he was inspired by Courbertin's ideals, Killanin was practical regarding contemporary sporting realities, believing that 'the concept of amateurism was, by 1952, fundamentally different from the concept set forth by Coubertin'.[16] Soon after becoming President, he was able to change the Olympic Charter's eligibility code, with the intention of retaining 'the principles of amateurism, but at the same time move with the changing times'.[17] This was also his guiding motto when it came to coping with the stagflation and fiscal crises of the 1970s and the subsequent shift to the neoliberal mode of accumulation. For example, the Denver Olympic Organizing Committee backed out of hosting the 1976 Winter Olympics for fiscal (and environmental) reasons, causing the IOC to transfer the Games to Innsbruck.[18] Also, the Montreal Committee had to deal with triple digit inflation and national and provincial governments that were financially exhausted. The project, which combined operating and infrastructure budgets, produced a billion dollar deficit.[19] Further, owing to the fiscal crises cities were facing worldwide, Los Angeles was the only city that bid to host the 1984 Olympic Games.

It was the Los Angeles Olympic Games Organizing Committee that first fully implemented a 'for-profit' model to finance those Games utilizing television revenues, corporate sponsorships and revenue from ticket sales.[20] Killanin facilitated this, while changing how television broadcast rights were negotiated so as to gain IOC control over the distribution of broadcast revenue. After the IOC received only $150,000 rather than the estimated $4.4 million it had expected from the Munich Olympics, Killanin insisted that the IOC would participate in joint-negotiations (starting in 1977) for the 1984 Los Angeles Olympic Games' television rights. Killanin thus oversaw the first steps towards making the IOC/Olympic Movement a 'for profit' organization.

But it was Killanin's successor, Juan Antonio Samaranch, who would become most recognized for remaking the Olympic Games into a privatized corporate franchise. Born in 1920 into a wealthy Catholic family that owned a textile factory in Barcelona, he was a member of the pro-Franco Youth Front and had a brief career as a boxer known as 'Kid Samaranch'. But it was his involvement with the pro-Francoist Real Club Deportivo Espanol Roller Hockey Club and his membership of the Spanish Roller Hockey Federation and then the International Roller Hockey Federation (including financing the 1951 World Roller Hockey Championships in Barcelona which Spain won) that led to his involvement in the Olympic Movement, serving as Chef de Mission for Spain's Olympic teams from 1956 to 1964 before being co-opted onto the IOC in 1966. (The year before he was appointed Spain's Minister of Sport, while simultaneously sitting on the boards of several real estate firms, banks and manufacturing companies.) He was elected the IOC's Chief of Protocol in 1968; Chief of the Press Committee in 1971; a member of the Executive Board in 1973; and Vice-President in 1974, before taking the IOC presidency in 1980.[21]

Dealing with Samaranch, like other surviving Francoist politicians, proved to be problematic for the new Spanish government after Franco's death. In fact, on 23 April 1977, while Samaranch was in the President's office at the Catalonia Regional Council, over 100,000 people protested outside chanting, 'Samaranch, Get Out!'[22] At first, Samaranch was offered the ambassador's post to Austria. He instead requested that he be assigned to the Soviet Union. While in Moscow, Samaranch shed his Francoist past and reinvented himself as a liberal-internationalist sportsman. After 40 years of being staunchly 'anti-Communist', Samaranch ingratiated himself with the Moscow Olympic Organizing Committee in his bid for the IOC presidency, while in turn cajoling the Spanish Olympic Committee, of which he had been President, to attend the 1980 Moscow Olympic Games in face of the US-led boycott. Samaranch at the same time worked closely with the Adidas sporting goods mogul, Horst Dassler, especially to provide Joao Havelange, the President of the International Federation of Football Associations, with the financial and political resources to expand the 1982 World Cup Championships, which were to be held in Spain, from 16 to 24 teams. In return, Havelange guaranteed that the African, Asian and Latin American IOC members would vote for Samaranch to succeed Killanin.[23]

The first major change Samaranch made was co-opting women into the IOC in 1981. Samaranch made this decision to move the IOC into the twentieth century, but also as a response to the increasing demands by women around the world to participate in traditionally male-controlled public and private institutions. The women who were brought into the IOC had social and class backgrounds that were very similar to the male members. Several were from European royalty, many had been Olympic athletes and almost all had served in some capacity as national or international sports administrators and/or teachers. Nevertheless, the inclusion of women moved glacially. Only six women were co-opted during the 1980s, while 41 men were co-opted; only eight women were co-opted in the 1990s while 62 men were co-opted; and only thirteen women were co-opted during the first decade of the new century, while 60 men were co-opted. [24]

Samaranch's main concern was to make the IOC financially self-sufficient and thus gain even greater control over the Olympic Movement. This was achieved by gaining control over the negotiations for television rights and selling the Olympic 'brand' to corporate sponsors. In 1986, to make the marketing of the Olympic Games more lucrative for television broadcasters, the IOC removed the final restrictions on professional athletes participating in the Olympics. With Richard Pound, a Montreal-based corporate tax lawyer, as IOC negotiator with United States networks for the television rights to the 1988 Calgary Winter Olympic Games and the Seoul Summer Olympic Games, the IOC 'sought maximum revenue from United States television networks'.[25] The Seoul Olympic Games garnered $300 million from NBC, while Calgary garnered $309 million from CBS, with a worldwide total of $728 million. These sums were enormous in light of the fact that the IOC had only received $150,000 from the Munich organizers and $33 million from the Los Angeles organizers. The revenue increased incrementally over the next three Olympic quadrennial cycles.

As for the corporate sponsorship programme, the IOC, along with the Seoul and Calgary OGOCs and the United States Olympic Committee, signed an initial contract with Dassler's marketing firm for Adidas, International Sport and Leisure. This seeded The Olympic Program I (TOP I), whereby the IOC would provide worldwide licensing rights to corporations to use the Olympic 'brand' when they signed a contract. The TOP I plan, which covered the 1985-88 period (Calgary and Seoul Olympic Games), had nine companies sign contracts, which paid the IOC $106 million; while TOP 2 (1989-92: Albertville and Barcelona) garnered $192 million from twelve firms; Top 3 (1993-96: Lillehammer and Atlanta) earned $376 million from ten companies; and TOP 4 (1997-00: Nagano and Sydney) raised $579 million.

Once the increased revenue began to pour in, the IOC began to be restructured under Samaranch. This process entailed expanding or developing departments that facilitated the accumulation, management and distribution of the television and sponsorship revenue. The IOC staff was also increased. In 1980 there were only 27 staff members; by 1982, there were 48; 78 in 1987; 139 in 1994; and 208 in 2001.[26] The IOC was, thereby, restructured into a corporate configuration, with Samaranch functioning as its CEO. The increased revenue also deepened the integration of the Olympic Movement constituents (NOCs, IFs and Olympic athletes) while minimizing long-term tensions over its distribution. This implies that as the constituents received increasing amounts of revenue they became ever more dependent on the IOC. The television revenue was still dispensed based on the formula established in the mid-1960s. The revenue generated from the TOP programme was based on the following formula: 60 per cent went to the OGOCs, with the Summer Games organizers receiving two-thirds and the Winter Games organizers receiving one-third; the NOCs receiving 30 per cent with approximately 15 per cent of that amount going to the United States Olympic Committee and 10 per cent going to the IOC. Olympic Solidarity, which had originally been formed in 1971, was expanded so as to distribute the television and TOP revenue to the NOCs. Olympic Solidarity's budget included funding for technical assistance, sports administration, sports medicine courses, marketing development, scholarships for coaches and athletes and subsidies for airfares to competitions and workshops.

Notably, the IOCs neoliberal model created conditions for new levels of corruption in the Olympic Games bidding process. The underlying reason for this was that more and more cities were bidding to host the Olympic Games because of how lucrative they were becoming for local organizers, politicians and capitalists. In December 1998, Chris Vanocur, a local television reporter in Salt Lake City, reported that the SLCOOC Bidding Committee had bribed an IOC member by providing his daughter's college tuition.[27] Over the next several weeks, evidence emerged that a number of IOC members had been bribed by the SLCOOC as well as by other cities' bidding committees. These revelations severely threatened the credibility of the Olympic Movement, particularly among corporate sponsors. The IOC, the Salt Lake City Olympic Committee, the USOC and the United States Department of Justice formed separate committees to investigate the scandal. The United States Congress also introduced legislation that potentially would cut off United States corporate sponsorship money going to the USOC unless the IOC instituted reforms – which it was in any case already being heavily pressured to do by corporate sponsors directly.

Citing 'behavior unfitting IOC members', the IOC expelled six members and reprimanded 24 others, while four more resigned.[28] A number of reforms claimed to prevent such behaviour from occurring again were introduced (including limits on gifts, banning site visits, establishing term limits and mandatory age limits) while the IOC membership was restructured. In Richard Pound's words, 'Up to 1999, members were always chosen solely for their personal qualities, but we decided that we should make sure, on a structural basis, that the membership reflected the principled constituencies within the Olympic Movement'.[29] This reorientation of the IOC membership, as Chappelet and Kubler-Mabbott have written, 'constitutes a fundamental change to the very nature of the IOC, in which all members were once supposed to represent the IOC and Olympism in their countries and not their organization in the IOC'.[30]

To boost the IOCs credibility, Samaranch was succeeded in 2001 by Jacques Rogge, who had been an IOC member since 1991, and now became the eighth IOC President since 1894, the second Belgian and the second former Olympian to hold the office. As Olympic historian David Miller has put it: 'In the post-scandal environment, [Rogge] was the ideal palliative: orthopedic surgeon, former Olympian yachtsman, with some commercial background from his involvement in the development of the Belgian NOC finances, yet free of any politico-social labels or private agendas that might be difficult baggage'.[31] The first IOC President to represent the postwar generations (he was born in 1942 into an upper-middle class family), Rogge earned a degree in sports medicine from the University of Ghent, played Rugby on the national level and competed in the 1968, 1972 and 1976 Olympics. He then attended the Free University Medical School in Brussels and began a very successful career as an orthopaedic surgeon. He was chosen to be the Belgian Chef de Mission for the Moscow Games, and when Belgium complied with the United States-orchestrated boycott, Rogge opposed this, arguing that 'politics should not interfere with sports matters' and that athletes should not be 'deprived of the fruits of four years of training'.[32] Also the Belgian Chef de Mission for the Los Angeles,

Innsbruck, Calgary and Seoul Olympic Games, Rogge became President of the Belgian NOC in 1988 and the following year President of the European Olympic Committee. Co-opted onto the IOC in 1991, he was elected to the Executive Board in 1998 and chaired the Coordination Commission between the IOC and the Sydney Olympic Organizing Committee.

'There can be no doubt that the arrival of Jacques Rogge as the IOC President constituted a major turning point for the IOC on a management level, with the introduction of more solid structures and procedures', as Chappelet and Kubler-Mabbott have noted. He evinced 'a more technocratic style of management that [was] far more sensitive to questions of governance and risk management, yet less entrepreneurial and paternalist than [Samaranch]'.[33] Assessing Rogge's twelve-year tenure, Norwegian IOC member Gerhard Heiberg concluded, 'We had a lot of turmoil. We had to get out of that. We had to get another image. [Jacques Rogge] brought that stability to the organization'.[34]

As we noted at the outset of this essay, each of the three Summer Olympic Games (Athens, 2004; Beijing, 2008; and London, 2012) and three Winter Olympic Games (Salt Lake City, 2002; Turin, 2006; and Vancouver, 2010) generated increasing amounts of income for the Olympic Movement, reaching over $8 billion in television and TOP revenue during the quadrennial cycle starting in 2009 through the 2012 London Olympic Games. That amount includes broadcast rights ($3.850 billion); TOP revenue ($950 million); domestic sponsorships arranged by the OGOCs ($1.838 billion); ticket revenue ($1.238 billion); and license fees ($170 million). The prospect of future revenue beyond Rogge's tenure seemed also to be secure. In September 2011, the IOC signed a television contract with NBC, where that company agreed to pay the IOC $4.38 billion for the broadcasting rights for four Olympic Games.[35] The amount included $775 million for the 2014 Sochi Winter Olympics; $1.226 billion for the 2016 Rio de Janeiro Summer Olympics; and $993 million for the 2018 Winter Olympics and $1.418 billion for the 2020 Summer Olympics. Rogge announced, as he prepared to depart in 2013, that the IOC had $900 million in reserves, compared to $105 million in 2001. Obviously, the Olympic Movement constituency would agree with Rogge's understated assessment of his legacy: 'I received an IOC in good shape from Samaranch. And I believe I will leave an IOC in good shape for my successor'.[36] Rogge was succeeded by Thomas Bach, a former German Olympian Gold Medal-winner in Fencing, who had been an IOC member since 1991, and, notably, a former Adidas executive. His mandate was to maintain the stability and profitability of the IOC.[37]

THE CONTRADICTIONS OF OLYMPIC GLOBALIZATION

The overall composition of the IOC was by now considerably changed from what it had been thirty years earlier. Women were increasingly being placed in prominent administrative positions in the IOC,[38] while the reforms introduced in the aftermath of the Salt Lake City 'scandal' were institutionalized, and the mission of the so-called 'stakeholders' – members representing the NOCs, the IFs, and Olympic athletes – defined as to articulate and safeguard the financial, technical and political interests of their respective constituencies. Nonetheless, long-promised policies pertaining to 'transparency' and 'accountability' in IOC governance still were far from being completely implemented.[39] The number of countries in the Olympic Movement had increased from 147 in 1981 to 204 by 2010, over which period the IOC board membership itself increased from 83 to 113.[40] Europe still had the most members (38 in 2013, including 10 from the former Communist countries), but it was the increased IOC membership from South America, Africa and Asia that was most notable.

The 2008 Beijing Olympic Summer Games were the coming-out party for the rapidly developing capitalist states of the global south, ostensibly marking the beginning of the shift of global capitalism away from the IOC's former Western European and North American heartlands. As Olympic historian Michael R. Real noted of Beijing's selection in 2001: 'The bid of a wealthy authoritarian country with the largest population in the world and an active history in Olympic competition [was] virtually irresistible to an organization with the priorities of the IOC'.[41] Coming at the same time as the US's decision to allow China's admission to the WTO, and amidst the deeper and broader economic engagement of US and Chinese capitalism, the IOC's embrace of China withstood extensive criticism of Beijing's selection, as it did the subsequent calls for a boycott of the 2008 Olympics in light of alleged human rights abuses.[42]

The Beijing Olympic Games were financed by both private and public revenue.[43] The organizers utilized IOC-generated funds (television revenue, corporate sponsorships) and tickets and merchandise sales as well as a national lottery to finance the $2.8 billion operating budget, which covered expenses on such things as the global torch relay, broadcasting accommodations, medical services, transportation and the opening and closing ceremonies. On the other hand, 85 per cent of the nearly $3 billion budget for capital expenditures, covering the construction of the athletic and training facilities, was financed by the national, regional and local levels of the Chinese state. The Beijing Olympics also provided the opportunity to develop Beijing's regional infrastructure, including highways, subway expansion, renovating the Capital International Airport and building a high-speed train to neighbouring Tainjin. These long-term capital investments, funded mainly by state revenues, amounted to some $40 billion, contributed greatly to making the Beijing Olympics a huge aesthetic as well as athletic success. They effectively projected the image of China as the rising world power just as the financial crisis of 2008 was about to explode in the US.[44]

The preparations for 2012 London Olympic Games spanned the 2009 global fiscal stimulus coordinated among the G20 states as well as the subsequent turn to global, and especially European, neoliberal austerity. The London Olympic Games – the epitome of a neoliberal mega-sporting spectacle – were conducted while the David Cameron-led Conservative-Liberal coalition government was actively slashing funding for the UK's national and local public sector, targeting welfare; pensions; education, including physical education; and the National Health Service. This stood in sharp contrast to the $3.17 billion operating costs to host the Games. These were financed by exorbitant ticket prices and massive merchandise sales, as well as IOC-generated television revenue and international and domestic corporate sponsors.[45] The British government provided $14.61 billion for the clean up and preparation of the East London Olympic site, installing infrastructure and constructing the athletic venues. That amount also included $7 billion for security and surveillance involving 49,000 military, police and security personnel, carried out in concert with the United States.[46] While the British public was being put through severe austerity, the London Olympic Games made only a tiny contribution to pulling the UK economy out of its prolonged slump.[47]

When it came to the 2014 Sochi Winter Olympic Games, the Russian government also saw this in terms of being taken seriously as a world power, as well as an opportunity to transform that Black Sea region into both a winter and summer tourist destination. The financial outlays for operating costs were largely covered by IOC generated revenue and ticket sales, while the Olympic infrastructure and athletic venues, which totalled approximately $7 billion, were financed by public funds. The regional development projects, which included infrastructure, port facilities, rail lines, apartment buildings and hotels, were financed by the national and provincial governments and public owned corporations and banks and private investors. The total amount for the Sochi project is estimated to be $51 billion.[48]

There is no question that there was corruption involved in the organizing of the Sochi Olympic Games, although the actual scale of that corruption is difficult to ascertain. Prior to the Sochi Olympics, Russian dissidents and the Western corporate media (i.e. critics who were themselves not politically disinterested) continually reported that $25–30 billion of that total had been stolen by Russian oligarchs, cronies of Russian President Vladimir Putin, and state bureaucrats.[49] There were also protests in the West calling for a boycott of those Games, in response to Russian domestic legislation restricting public display of 'Gay propaganda'.[50] Like the allegations of corruption, the protests against anti-gay legislation conveniently complemented the United States' ongoing demonization of Putin. The historical context for this was what Stephen Cohen has called the 'New Cold War' in the wake of the US expansion of NATO to Estonia, Lithuania and Latvia on Russia's border a decade earlier.[51] President Obama did not attend the Sochi opening ceremonies, sending instead an official White House delegation with several openly gay athletes. But this hardly put a dent in the Sochi Olympics, which were widely regarded as yet another athletic and aesthetic success, and were completed before the confrontation with the US over the Ukraine.[52]

Given US geostrategic tensions with China and Russia, the 2016 Rio de Janeiro Olympic Summer Games might be expected to provide a more conducive venue for the Olympic ruling class. Rio was selected by the IOC in 2009 to bring the Games to South America for the first time now that Brazil was thought to be able to afford the Olympics, as one of the largest and most successful of the developing capitalist countries known as the BRICs. Not an insignificant additional factor was that Rio's time zone would also be perfect for the United States television market.[53] The IOC decision to select Rio came on the heels of Brazil having been selected by FIFA to host the 2014 World Cup, and in fact, the two mega-sporting events have been proverbially 'joined at the hip'. But if they were initially hyped together, the serious problems the organizers for both events have experienced with construction delays, cost overruns, labour shortages, shoddy work and corruption has led to their images being increasingly tarnished in tandem. During FIFA's Confederation Cup football tournament in June 2013, there were massive daily demonstrations in cities throughout the country involving upwards of two million people critical of spending billions for the World Cup and the Olympic Games, while neglecting widespread poverty, a severe housing crisis, inadequate health care and education and high public transportation costs as well as police violence and political corruption. As the 'anti-World Cup/Olympic Games' protests have continued into 2014, they vividly exposed the limits of Luiz Ignacio Lula da Silva and Dilma Rousseff's Worker's Party 'new populist' strategy.[54]

In April 2014, IOC Vice-President John Coates stated that the Rio preparations were 'the worst I have ever seen'.[55] The IOC then set up a task force in an attempt to speed up the preparations. Whatever happens over the next two years, however, a few things seem certain. First, the 2016 Rio Olympic Games will be held as scheduled. Second, police and military mobilization, surveillance and repression at those events will be massive. Third, the thousands of wealthy foreign visitors attending the World Cup and the Olympics will wine and dine and watch in insulated comfort. Fourth, the social and economic crises in Brazil will continue and deepen, provoking more class struggle. Fifth, every economic and political interest linked to the Olympic Games will profit handsomely. Indeed, already looking beyond the 2018 Winter Olympics in Pyeongchang, South Korea and the 2020 Summer Olympics in Tokyo, the IOC announced on 7 May 2014, that it had signed a contract with NBC/Universal for $7.65 billion, giving NBC/U the rights to televise the six Olympic Games between 2022 and 2032. This is designed to assure the IOC ruling class that, short of a world war, the overthrow of capitalism and/or environmental collapse, its long-term economic future will be bright, however many managerial headaches it will have to cope with in an increasingly turbulent world.

NOTES

1   The main secondary sources used in this essay, unless otherwise indicated, are: Jean-Loup Chappelet and Brenda Kubler-Mabbott, *The International Olympic Committee and the Olympic System: The Governance of World Sport*, London: Routledge, 2008; John E. Findling and Kimberley D. Pelle, *Encyclopedia of the Modern Olympic Movement*, Westport, Connecticut: Greenwood Press, 2004; Allen Guttmann, *The Olympic Games: A History of the Modern Games*, 2nd Edition, Chicago: University of Illinois Press, 2002; Christopher R. Hill, *Olympic Politics*, Manchester: Manchester University Press, 1992; David B. Kanin, *A Political History of the Olympic Games*, Boulder: Westview Press, 1981; Arnd Kruger, 'The Unfinished Symphony: A History of the Olympic Games from Coubertin to Samaranch', in Jim Riordan and Arnd Kruger, eds., *The International Politics of Sport in the Twentieth Century*, New York: Routledge, 1999; John Lucas, *The Modern Olympic Games*, New York: Barnes and Company, 1980; David Miller, *The Official History of the Olympic Games and the IOC: Athens to London, 1894-2012*, Edinburgh: Mainstream Publishers, 2012.

2   Tripp Mickle, 'TV Rights Push IOC Revenue to Record', *Sports Business Journal*, 26 August 2013; *Olympic Marketing Fact File*, 2014, p. 8, available at http://www.olympic.org.

3   John Hoberman, *The Olympic Crisis: Sport, Politics, and the Moral Order*, New Rochelle, New York: Aristide D. Caratzas, 1986, p. 33. See also F. Lee Benns, *Europe, 1870-1914*, New York: Appleton-Century Croft, 1965, pp. 90-124.

4   For an interesting account of an attempt by the internationalist left to stage an alternative games in Barcelona in 1936 see 'The Olympics That Never Was', available at http://uncomradelybehaviour.wordpress.com.

5   Michael Real, 'Who Owns the Olympics? Political-Economy and Critical Moments in the Modern Games', in Vassil Girginov, ed., *The Olympics: A Critical Reader*, London: Routledge, 2010, p. 224.

6   See Jenifer Parks, 'Red Sport, Red Tape: The Olympic Games, the Soviet Sports Bureaucracy and the Cold War, 1952-1980', Unpublished Ph.D. Dissertation, Department of History, University of North Carolina, 2009; Jenifer Parks, 'Verbal Gymnastics: Sports, Bureaucracy, and the Soviet Union's Entrance into the Olympic Games', in Stephen Wagg and David L. Andrews, eds, *East Plays West: Sport and the Cold War*, London: Routledge, 2007, pp. 27-44.

7   The IOC refused to accept the German Democratic Republic into the Olympic Movement, so East Germany was unable to participate in the 1952 Olympics. The GDR agreed to compete as part of a united team with West Germany in the 1956, 1960 and the 1964 Olympics. The IOC recognized the GDR's NOC in 1968 and East Germany competed as a separate team in Mexico City.

8   See James Riordan, *Sport in Soviet Society: Development of Sport and Physical Education in Russia and the USSR*, Cambridge: Cambridge University Press, 1977, pp. 82-152.

9   Parks, 'Verbal Gymnastics', p. 35.

10   Milovan Djilas, *The New Class: An Analysis of the Communist System*, 2nd Edition, New York: Harcourt, Brace, and Jovanovich, 1985, p. 46.

11   See 'Obituary: Sir Adetokundo Ademola', *The Independent*, 12 February 1993; 'One of the Pillars of African Football Dies at 99', Confederation of African Football, 16 April 2009; 'Madagascar and Olympism', *Olympic Review*, 150, April 1980, pp. 180-3, Digital Library Collection, LA 84 Foundation.

12   Robin Cohen, 'Class in Africa: Analytical Problems and Perspectives', *Socialist Register 1972*, London: Merlin Press, 1972.

13   Vera Tikander, 'Helsinki 1952', in *Encyclopedia of the Modern Olympic Movement*, p. 143.

14   Among many see David Clay Large, *Tragedy, Terror, and Triumph at the Olympic Games*, New York: Rowman and Littlefield Publishers, 2012.

15   Lord Killanin, *My Olympic Years*, London: Secker and Warburg, 1983, p. 23.

16   Kathy L. Nichols, 'Michael Morris/Lord Killanin', in *Encyclopedia of the Modern Olympic Movement*, p. 483.

17   Lord Killanin, *My Olympic Years*, p. 81.

18   John J. Kennedy, Jr with Morgan Patrick, 'Innsbruck 1976', in *Encyclopedia of the Modern Olympic Movement*, p. 483.

19   See Nick Auf der Maur, *The Billion Dollar Games: Jean Drapeau and the 1976 Olympics*, Toronto: James Lorimer and Company, 1976; George Wright, 'The Political-Economy of the Montreal Olympic Games', *Journal of Sport and Social Issues*, 2(1), 1978, pp. 13-8.

20   See Peter Ueberroth with Richard Levin and Amy Quinn, *Made in America: His Own Story*, New York: William Morris and Company, 1985.

21   See John E. Findling, 'Juan Antonio Samaranch', in *Encyclopedia of the Modern Olympic Movement*, pp. 487-94; Andrew Jennings, *The New Lords of the Rings: Olympic Corruption and How to Buy Gold Medals*, London: Pocket Books, 1996; David Miller, *Olympic Revolution: The Biography of Juan Antonio Samaranch*,

London: Trafalgar Square, 1992; Vyv Simpson and Andrew Jennings, *The Lords of the Rings: Power, Money and Drugs in the Modern Olympics*, Toronto: Stoddart, 1992.

22   Simpson and Jennings, *Lords of the Rings*, p. 79.

23   Simpson and Jennings, *Lords of the Rings*, pp. 80-3.

24   Joanna Davenport, 'Breaking into the Rings: Women on the IOC', *The Journal of Physical Education, Recreation, and Dance*, 64(5), 1996; Juliet Macur, 'Samaranch Pushed for Inclusion of Women', *New York Times*, 21 April 2010; *Fact Sheet: Women in the Olympic Movement: Update*, International Olympic Committee, March 2013, available at http://www.olympic.org.

25   Stephen R. Wenn, 'Appendix C: The Olympic Games and Television', in *Encyclopedia of the Modern Olympic Movement*, p. 514. See also Richard Pound, *Inside the Olympics: A Behind-the-Scenes Look at the Politics, the Scandals, and the Glory of the Game*, Toronto: John Wiley and Sons, 2004, pp. 160-1; Scott G. Martyn and Stephen R. Wenn, 'Juan Antonio Samaranch's Score Sheet: Revenue Generation and the Olympic Movement, 1980-2001', in Gerald P. Shaus and Stephen R. Wenn, eds., *Onward to the Olympics: Historical Perspectives on the Olympic Games*, Montreal: Wilfrid Laurier University Press, 2007, esp. p. 311.

26   The figures here are drawn from Chappelet and Kubler-Mabbott, *International Olympic Committee*, pp. 33-58.

27   See Alicia C. Shepard, 'An Olympian Scandal', *American Journalism Review*, April 1999; Helen Jefferson Lenskyj, *Inside the Olympic Industry: Power, Politics, and Activism*, Albany: State University of New York Press, 2000, pp. 9-17; Pound, *Inside the Olympics*, pp. 206-25.

28   'Six Members Out: IOC Upholds Expulsion in Secret Ballot Vote', *CNN/Sports Illustrated*, 17 March 1999. See also 'List of Approved IOC Reforms', *CNN/Sports Illustrated*, 12 December 1999; and 'The Olympic Crisis in Perspective', *The Olympic Marketing Newsletter*, June 1999, pp. 5-6.

29   Pound, *Inside the Olympics*, p. 199.

30   Chappelet and Kubler-Mabbott, *International Olympic Committee*, p. 21.

31   Miller, *Official History*, p. 349.

32   Miguel Tasso, 'Jacques Rogge, In the Name of Sport and Ethics', *Olympic Review*, 27(August/September), 2001, Digital Library Collection, LA84 Foundation, p. 37.

33   Chappelet and Kubler-Mabbott, *International Olympic Committee*, p. 34.

34   'Jacques Rogge to Leave the IOC', *ESPN.com*, 13 September 2013.

35   'NBC Retains Olympic TV Rights', *ESPN.com*, 7 June 2011.

36   'Jacques Rogge to Leave', *ESPN.com*.

37   Owen Gibson, 'Thomas Bach Elected to Succeed Jacque Rogge as IOC President', *The Guardian*, 10 September 2013.

38   IOC, *Factsheet: Women in the Olympic Movement: Update*, October 2013, p. 2/5.

39   James Christie, 'Conference Hears Complaints About IOC's Slow-paced Reforms', *Toronto Globe and Mail*, 21 May 2009; updated 23 August 2012.

40   Miller, *Official History*, pp. 474-9.

41   Real, 'Who Owns the Olympics?', p. 232.

42   See Michael Klare, '"Congagement" with China?', *The Nation*, 12 April 2001; and Allison Welch, 'Human Rights in China: 2008 Beijing Summer Olympics', *Human Rights & Human Welfare*, 2008, pp. 211-20.

43   See Paul Pennay, 'Beijing Olympics: Over Budget but Still Profitable', *Economic Observer News*, 19 June 2009; as well as Ferran Brunet and Zuo Xinwen, 'The Economy of the Beijing Olympic Games: An Analysis of the First Impact and Prospects', Centre d'Estudis Olimpics, Barcelona, Spain, 2008.

44   KimEng Tan, 'Beijing Olympics -- Too Large, Too Costly? Maybe Not', *Bloomberg Business Week*, 18 June 2008.

45   'London Olympics 2012: Where Does the Money Come From -- and Where's It Being Spent?', *The Guardian*, 26 July 2008.

46   Patrick Martin, 'The Police State 2012 Olympics', *World Socialist Web Site*, 12 July 2012.

47   See Larry Elliot, 'Olympics: Why the British Economy Isn't a Winner', *The Guardian*, 2 August 2012; and Ari Dhapiro, 'Did London Get an Economic Boost from the 2012 Olympics?', National Public Radio, 3 February 2014, available at http://www.npr.org.

48   Paul Farhl, 'Did the Winter Olympics in Sochi Really Cost $50 Billion: A Closer Look at the Figures', *The Washington Post*, 10 February 2014.

49   Nic Robertson and James Masters, 'Sochi 2014: Do the Numbers Add Up?', *CNN.com*, 14 January 2014.

50   'Russia's LGBT Propaganda Law', *Wikipedia*.

51   Stephen F. Cohen, 'The New American Cold War', *The Nation*, 10 July 2006. See also Zbigniew Brzezinski, 'A Geostrategy for Eurasia', *Foreign Affairs*, (September/October), 1997.

52   Israel Shamir, 'Ukraine in Turmoil: Putin's Hard Choices', *Counterpunch*, 19 May 2014.

53   Juliet Macur, 'Rio Wins 2016 Olympics in a First for South America', *New York Times*, 2 October 2009.

54   Sharda Urger, 'Sporting Mega-events: What the Protesting Brazilians Learnt from the BRICS Competitions', *Economic and Political Weekly*, 13 June 2013; David Goldblatt, 'Brazil's World Cup Party Can't Hide the Country's Tensions', *The Observer*, 24 May 2014. See also Lise Alves, 'Anti-World Cup Protests Erupt in Brazil Daily', *The Rio Times*, 16 May 2014; Rosa Maria Marques and Aquilas Mendes, 'Lula and Social Policy: In the Service of Finance Capital', *Monthly Review.org*, February 2009; and David Rohde, 'Party's Over: How did Brazil's Economy Get So Bad So Fast?', *The Atlantic.com*, 28 September 2012.

55   Owen Gibson, 'Rio 2016 Olympic preparations damned as "Worst Ever" by IOC', *The Guardian*, 29 April 2014.

THE MIDDLE CLASS IN HOLLYWOOD: ANXIETIES OF THE AMERICAN DREAM

JOHN MCCULLOUGH

In American liberal political discourse, the middle classes are routinely portrayed as foundational to democratic order and economic growth. It is argued that they extol virtues such as individual drive, humility and social conformity that are crucial for building strong communities. Thus, 'crises' in the middle classes engender a variety of strong responses and are taken note of as though they impact on everyone. This is reinforced by the many middle-class crises represented in mass media, including popular films and television. In what follows, I provide an admittedly anecdotal overview of the expansive history of Hollywood's representations of middle-class characters, settings and stories, and I also discuss the significance of its century-long love affair with the middle classes.

As ubiquitous as it seems, the middle class is a difficult social formation to describe and theorize. Its contradictory relations to the means of production engender confusion about its relationship to social activism and transformation. From a Marxist perspective, middle classes are both an agent of the bourgeoisie and a victim of the same. If it is difficult, from a left perspective, to theorize the role of the middle classes, Hollywood film and television can help us in this task. By representing the variety of ways that the middle class suffers dispossession and proletarianization, Hollywood sets the table for an animated discussion about class struggle.

The primary exploitation in capitalism is, of course, that of the capitalist over the worker.[1] But in depicting the crises of the middle class as analogous to all workers, Hollywood films and television seem to signal a common class struggle. It's as though Hollywood came up with the tag line: workers of the world unite! But Hollywood's radical potential is always kept in check, significantly blunted by countervailing reactionary tendencies that privilege capital in its contest with workers. This includes showcasing the elevated and privileged status and power of the middle class and professionals.

In the popular imagination, the American middle class is strongly associated with the post-Second World War period, especially as captured in the image of the American Dream. The dominant archetypes of the period include nuclear households as a separate sphere marked by white picket fences, racial segregation, bomb shelters and black lists. Conformity, paternalism, consumerism and American 'exceptionalism' provide the thematic guidelines. To the extent that the middle class served an important function in consensus culture and the rise of post-industrial society, substantial attention was directed to understanding and managing it.[2] This was reflected in all aspects of American society and culture, from self-help guides for successful middle-class living to sociological studies of the 'organization man'.[3] Hollywood's representations of middle-class characters as protagonists increased in the 1950s – we can immediately think of *Rebel Without A Cause* (and many of director Nicholas Ray's other films, as well) as a high water mark.[4]

This impetus to engage the attention of the middle classes had in fact been a prominent business plan in Hollywood since the 1920s, most conspicuously in the creation of movie palaces that demarcated the movies from nickelodeons and other early forms of exhibition, which were routinely understood to be working class and *lumpen* spaces and cultural forums.[5] Also, the creation of the Academy Awards in 1928 and the enforcement in the thirties of the Production Code (i.e., the industry's self-censorship mechanism) indicate Hollywood's interest in 'professionalizing' the industry, legitimizing the movies in preparation for expansion to middle-class markets.[6] But, through the economic crises of the thirties and in stride with the New Deal, the working class and a working-class perspective came to the forefront in Hollywood films. We see this in the popularity of Chaplin, for instance, but also the success of labour friendly genres like the backstage musical, screwball comedies, gangster films and social issue dramas. This trend carried through the decade and into the beginning of the war with *The Grapes of Wrath* (1939) and *Citizen Kane* (1941), for example.[7]

By the late forties and throughout the fifties, there is a significant rise in the numbers and popularity of stories that feature middle-class characters and plot crises – their isolation from other classes becomes particularly clear, as though the middle class was the totality of the world. This effect has two sources, both stemming from fundamental changes in the American political economy after the Second World War. On the one hand, deindustrialization expanded the service sector and thus, by replacing the archetype of the worker as coterminous with the industrial shop floor, undermined the identity of working class people and organized labour. As a category, then, the working-class became a less coherent and identifiable social formation. Also, the intensified control of the workplace in deindustrialization, through technological innovation and new techniques of workplace rationalization, made even upper management jobs highly instrumentalized. These trends encouraged a perception that the old working class was disappearing, being replaced by salaried white-collar office employees, who were understood to be part of the middle classes. In Hollywood, it is this group that suffers the seeming relentless onslaught of social crises: betrayal, exile, loss, injury and death. While there are only a few popular Hollywood films about the working class after the thirties, the endless stream of images of the beleaguered middle provide stark lessons about the nuts and bolts of labour relations in capitalism.

The Hollywood middle class, consequently, represents a broad swath of occupations and lifestyles and we can appreciate the common-sense perception that, in America, everyone is middle class. Or, alternatively, in America, there is no such thing as class. So, All-American good guy, Jimmy Stewart, in *It's a Wonderful Life* (1947), is heir to a small town savings and loan company; his nightmare visions include an America run solely for profit by Dickensian-style capitalists who ruin Main Street and the centrist ideological formations that anchor populist, consensus society of the period. Our sympathies go out to this heir with a heart of gold, but this is a highly contradictory ideological achievement because, from a working-class perspective, its championing of the moral authority of entrepreneurial spirit is fully reactionary. In the period, such nightmares as Jimmy Stewart's George Bailey has – the middle class haunted by dispossession – are the primal scenes of middle class crises. In *Mildred Pierce* (1945), for example, the 'nightmare' of being a working-class single mother motivates the protagonist to climb into the upper middle class *via* ruthless sublimation and entrepreneurialism. And, the enduring popularity of Arthur Miller's play *Death of a Salesman*, which opened on Broadway in 1949, and has had various film and television versions since, also suggests the extent to which Americans are sensitive to crises in the middle classes, and are highly sympathetic to middle-class characters and their problems.[8]

The middle classes' tendency to encounter crisis in the midst of consumer paradise is refined into highly ironic commentaries in Douglas Sirk's fifties mannerist melodramas, including *All That Heaven Allows* (1955) and *There's Always Tomorrow* (1956), in which middle-class characters suffer emotional turmoil dealing with conformist society represented in part by judgmental, gossipy neighbours and co-workers. In *All That Heaven Allows*, the audience is encouraged to disdain the snooty middle-class neighbours and family members who criticize and ostracize widow Cary Scott (Jane Wyman) who has started dating Ron Kirby, played by Rock Hudson, who is judged by Cary's friends to be too young and too far below her social station. In *There's Always Tomorrow*, Fred MacMurray plays a toy manufacturer who is bored with his privileged life and pursues an affair with a former employee played by Barbara Stanwyck. While the two fall in love, it is the need to conform to middle-class values and norms that pushes MacMurray's character back into his suburban family home. In these films, and across the field of domestic melodramas in general, including most of Sirk's work, middle-class crises are driven by confusion and regret deriving from complications in class identity and social status. These 'tear-jerkers' provocatively suggest that the world has become meaner and colder in the process of advancing middle-class values and they routinely posit working-class identity as redemptive and foundational.

A more virile approach to superseding middle-class crisis in the midst of modernity is seen in *The Fountainhead* (1949), featuring Gary Cooper, which turned Ayn Rand's novel and ethos into a working ideology for the leadership-driven and conformist middle classes seeking a place in American consensus culture. During the fifties, Cooper, Humphrey Bogart, Gregory Peck, Jimmy Stewart, Fred MacMurray, Rock Hudson and Richard Widmark developed significant profiles as professionals and middle-class characters in crises. Katherine Hepburn, Barbara Stanwyck and Doris Day stand out as female stars of the period who consistently escaped the domestic sphere as middle-class women. The stereotypes of gender and class representation in the period have been recently remediated in the hit cable TV series *Mad Men* (2007-), which provides contemporary audiences with a slightly ironic and glib depiction of the class and gender relations of the later fifties and early sixties.

A more radical approach to similar material is Billy Wilder's hugely popular and Oscar-winning *The Apartment* (1960), which is rich in comic depictions of the stratified office place, the proletarianization of white-collar labour and workplace exploitation. Jack Lemmon's C.C. Baxter is a lowly white-collar worker when his superiors discover he has a downtown apartment. They coerce him to make his apartment available for their trysts (including providing alcohol and snacks and cleaning up after them) by implying that his compliance will help him gain an advantage against the 32,000 other cogs who work at Consolidated Life. He is ultimately rewarded with a promotion from a cog to professional with an office. The film's crisp black and white visual design includes low, wide angle shots of the expansive, dropped ceiling, fluorescent lit, modern office, emphasizing the rigidity of hierarchy and the extreme level of proletarianization of the workplace. Baxter's hope is that he has now moved fully out of the competitive drudgery of office work into professional autonomy and security. Nonetheless, the extortion continues. Bitter about his continued dispossession, Baxter begins to question his allegiance to his superiors, and gradually recognizes himself as an exploited employee, not an ascendant bourgeois.

Wilder's film can be seen, then, as a film about class consciousness and it reveals that, as important as Baxter's awakening to his own exploitation is in his process of transformation, the cast of workers and neighbours who befriend him serve the crucial role of providing an example of the benefits of communitarian living. For instance, the neighbour physician and his wife, who not only provide aid and cover for Baxter, but guidance as well, fully evoke images of upper-west side Jewish professionals, radicalized by the New Deal, running counter to the dominant strains of the Cold War. Fran Kubelik (Shirley MacLaine) is the catalyst for Baxter's transformation; she is an elevator operator at Consolidated's Manhattan office and she gets involved with both Baxter and the last man between him and what he imagines as freedom from class struggle, head of personnel, Jeff Sheldrake (Fred MacMurray). Wilder mercilessly ridicules the thin, pretentious layers that stratify the middle classes, portraying this stratification as a series of petty privileges and benefits (e.g., keys to the executive washroom) doled out to 'meritorious' individuals. The film suggests that, by contrast, only communities of workers have recuperative and redemptive powers.

As is evident from this brief sampling of films, the constitutive identity of the middle class is diverse and difficult to delimit. If this has been an enduring theoretical problem in Marxist methodology, we see some of that problem represented in the movies – everyone from narcissistic industrialists to sad-eyed Savings & Loan officers, from doctors to low ranking office workers – the American middle class is a grab bag of identities, associations and social formations. But in the movies and on television, we tend to recognize the middle classes by the things they own, if not immediately by the power they wield. C.C. Baxter's apartment, for instance, signifies his middle-class status, and it is its dispossession by his superiors that proletarianizes him. Moreover, if we recall Marx's observation that bourgeois social relations feature the exchange of commodities, it is apparent that, in the movies and on TV, middle classes are intended as representatives of bourgeois values and perspectives, because they are routinely shown to be surrounded by commodities (including product placement). One of the accomplishments of these types of images of the middle classes is the promotion of class identities based on lifestyle and consumerism, not work or labour relations.

In the sixties and seventies, middle-class crisis was often represented as a highly personal and internalized reaction to a variety of anti-Establishment challenges to the status quo (e.g., racial, class, gender, sexuality). In films like *The Graduate* (1967) and *The Swimmer* (1968), middle-class protagonists go on an often humiliating journey of self-discovery that is motivated by the legitimacy crisis associated with attacks on normative middle-class ideals. This self-critical mode sometimes leads to increased visibility of the non-normative when middle-class characters intersect with marginalized or working-class characters (e.g., *Guess Who's Coming to Dinner* (1967), *Zabriskie Point* (1970), *A Woman Under the Influence* (1974), *Alice Doesn't Live Here Anymore* (1974), *One Flew over the Cuckoo's Nest* (1975) and *Taxi Driver* (1976)). But rather than developing stories from a working-class perspective, the approach that Hollywood subsequently pursued emphasized the individualistic aspects of middle-class crises.

This approach is seen in the work of Steven Spielberg, for instance, whose preference for stories featuring suburban middle-class settings and characters has come to define Hollywood success from the seventies to today. This tendency leads to extensive representations of middle-class characters breaking down in the face of profound disruptions in their personal and family relations and, in the late seventies and early eighties, eventuates in the unexpected success, in the late seventies and early eighties, of such 'therapy' films as *Kramer v. Kramer* (1979), *Ordinary People* (1980) and *Terms of Endearment* (1983).

As seen in the fifties films discussed above, by transcoding social and political problems into individual and family crises, melodramas often address struggles in class, gender and racial relations. But, even more importantly, films in the late seventies and throughout the eighties humanized the middle class in the face of broad-based populist derision and criticism of middle-class identity as phony and spiritually bankrupt. With no debt to nuance, popular film and TV in the eighties redeemed the middle classes by championing suburbia and consumerism. Reflecting the ascendency of the conservative right and Reagan's victory, the image of fifties suburban middle-class lifestyle was retrofitted as an ideal of middle-class identity.[9]

But these stories were all about white people and mostly white men. When we look for images in popular film and TV of non-white middle-class characters and settings, we find that, while such characters were not invisible, they were limited (as they are now), both in numbers and range of characterization. Looking at the history of representations of African-Americans, for example, we can think of the majority of characters – well-mannered, highly-educated and professional – played by Sidney Poitier as foundational. As were those played by Bill Cosby, who played over-achieving spy Alexander Scott in the TV series *I, Spy* (1965-68), and then played obstetrician Dr. Heathcliff Huxtable, living in eighties' Manhattan with attorney wife Claire and five model consumer citizen children. But this spotty record of prominent middle-class African-American characters is countered by a more significant trend that emphasizes correspondences between racialized minorities and working-class identities, implying by association that in America there are fundamental connections between racial identity and class position.

The concept of systemic racism thus finds fertile ground in this kind of popular culture. Nonetheless, this allows for a wide range of characters, settings and plots within which to represent African-American experiences. These characters are rarely intended as role model heroes for the mainstream, and do not share the middle-class milieu and expectations of Poitier and Cosby, and are thus spared their kind of over-compensation. As a result, these characters tend to have a life and vigour that evades mainstream stars. The sixties and seventies produced a series of African-American-centric films and TV series that link expressions of class and racial identity. Far ranging examples can be seen in satire and comedy (e.g., Richard Pryor's standup routines, 'ghetto comedies' on network TV including *Sanford and Son* (1972-77), *Good Times* (1974-79) and *The Jeffersons* (1975-85)), urban action films (e.g., *Sweet Sweetback's Badasssss Song* (1971), *Shaft* (1971) and *Superfly* (1972)), as well as the extraordinary work in documentary, fiction and experimental forms by African-American filmmakers (including Charles Burnett, Larry Clarke, Julie Dash, Haile Gerima, Barbara McCullough and Billy Woodberry) that emerged from UCLA between the mid-sixties and eighties in what was called the LA Rebellion.[10]

To move through this vast terrain of class and racially inflected settings, characters and plots is to see America as the complex socio-economy that it is. These films and TV series routinely address the audience as if in discussion about issues of racial, class and gender identities in modern capitalism and hence contribute to complex understandings of the relationships between labour and social relations.[11]

In eighties' and nineties' media culture, youth and entrepreneurship are dominant themes, and teen comedies and yuppie horror are exemplary of this trend.[12] The teen comedy was almost single-handedly revived by John Hughes, whose films privileged the coming-of-age stories of whitebread suburban middle-class youth. Yuppie horror allegorically represented a variety of crises encountered by the young and upwardly mobile financial and entrepreneurial set favoured by neoliberalism. In films like *Fatal Attraction*

(1987) and *Pacific Heights* (1990), the horror at the centre of the stories typically has its source in mundane middle-class life. In *Fatal Attraction*, the central character has an office romance that goes dreadfully off the rails, and in *Pacific Heights*, the innocent new homeowners have to defend themselves against a terrifying and manipulative tenant. Even at the time, it was possible to read the monstrous co-worker or tenant as reactionary responses to progressive changes (e.g., affirmative action hiring policies and tenants rights legislation) that, in popular culture, are routinely represented as oppressive interventions by the state and hence impediments to individual achievement.

Highlighting the importance of individualism in the period, several films and TV series created central characters who hyperbolically embodied the core individual traits of the neoliberal personality: narcissism, self-aggrandizement and zero-sum competitiveness. The most famous of these have gained iconographic status: Tom Cruise as Joel Goodsen in *Risky Business* (1983), Ferris Bueller (Matthew Broderick) in *Ferris Bueller's Day Off* (1986), Gordon Gekko (Michael Douglas) in *Wall Street* (1987) and Patrick Batemen in Bret Easton Ellis's 1991 novel *American Psycho,* played by Christian Bale in the film adaptation released in 2000.[13] As seen in *Pacific Heights*, homeownership remains a central concern for middle-class characters and we see this trope in a variety of types of films including, for instance, *Poltergeist* (1982), *Indecent Proposal* (1993) and *Bamboozled* (2000), all of which characterize home owning as a battleground for middle class status. The image of the middle class in perpetual contestation was fully literalized by *Fight Club* (1999) and, not surprisingly, its story really begins when the central character's home is blown up.

Fight Club inspired some imitators, especially in terms of plot innovation, but the film is most interesting as a summary of all that had been going bad for male white-collar workers and professionals in America since the seventies. Based on the novel of the same name by Chuck Palahniuk, the film tells the story of the mental breakdown of an office worker played by Ed Norton, who is remarkably similar in gesture and physical appearance to *The Apartment*'s C.C. Baxter. Whereas Baxter musters the will to resist his superiors, Norton's character develops a disorder that includes multiple personalities, schizophrenia and dissociation. Depressed and suicidal, he conjures a *doppelgänger* named Tyler Durden (Brad Pitt) who sets out on a mission to bring capital to its knees. He forms collectives of dispossessed males and trains them in fight clubs. These clubs evolve into the paramilitary operation 'Project Mayhem' that aims to subvert the US banking industry by destroying the debt record through a series of carefully coordinated bombings of financial institutions. Durden is everything that Norton, like

Baxter, cannot be.

In both *The Apartment* and *Fight Club*, the protagonists become increasingly conscious of their exploitation and their common cause with other workers. *Fight Club* powerfully evokes the disenchantment that characterizes young workers in neoliberalism, and it found its fan base among them. But its association of worker consciousness with paramilitary violence and terrorism was much too radical for mainstream audiences. It has remained a cult favourite, which is not surprising given its uncanny symmetry to, and seeming pre-mediation of, events associated with 9/11, the financial and housing crises and Occupy Wall Street.

From the perspective of the American middle class, 9/11 can be understood as an attempt to destabilize the project of modernity, and thus an attempt to destabilize American entrepreneurs and professionals – the heart of the middle class. Hollywood films and TV series overflowed with images of professionals and the middle class under siege during the first decade of the 2000s.[14] And, with the housing crises of 2008, this effect has only been amplified. The increased interest in spies and counter-intelligence is a predictable impulse to position American professionals as agents of containment culture and redeemers of modernity and US empire.[15] Also, TV news spectacles of terror and disaster, including coverage of 9/11 and Hurricane Katrina, and the wars in Afghanistan and Iraq, include numerous scenarios in which the middle class and professionals are privileged as victims of crisis, and crisis managers, at the same time.

The interesting anomaly here, and instructive because of its class and racial implications, is Katrina. The narrative of professional state and military forces mobilizing to contain the victims in New Orleans – their racial identity conflated with their homelessness – resonated with other TV images that are powerfully inflected by racial identity and struggle: from sixties' TV images that include riots, war and civil rights activism to the OJ car chase and the LA riots. Ultimately, when FEMA's incompetent leadership was exposed, the theme of 'professionals in crisis' naturally enough took on the appearance of a legitimacy crisis wherein a white-centric power elite was perceived as alternately indifferent and confrontational in its dealings with the city's most vulnerable. The media event represented a densely complex series of screens to negotiate, the social implications of which were not lost on the American viewing audience. Politicians, academics, artists and pundits weighed in. Rapper Kanye West, for instance, gained notoriety for challenging President George W. Bush's indifference to the plight of dispossessed residents of the Crescent City, igniting a media storm by charging that: 'George Bush doesn't care about black people'. West's political posturing effectively transformed the post-Katrina narrative from bureaucratic negligence, speculative real estate development and the state's abandonment of the dispossessed and working classes, into a story about racism. In the split second it took Bush to deny being racist, the poor in New Orleans had essentially fallen through the cracks, and off the media's radar.[16]

Nonetheless, if we consider the disaster victims sequestered in downtown New Orleans as figures of dispossession rather than solely racialized figures, those TV images emerge as powerful indicators of the extent to which the American state and its elites revile the dispossessed. George Bush and FEMA, it might be said, didn't care about poor people. Moreover, these TV news images remind us that homeownership is one of the core metrics of perceived middle-class status in America, and the representation of the destruction of homes, and the spectre of homelessness, rattles the confidence of the middle class about its own dreams. This sets in motion a variety of containment strategies that are often cast as fantasies, long before they take shape as a reality. For instance, post-Katrina New Orleans was an almost perfect restaging of John Carpenter's *Escape* films: *Escape from New York* (1979) and *Escape from L.A.* (1996). In these films, Carpenter facetiously ridicules the American elite's paranoia about the dispossessed by depicting future worlds in which underclasses are contained by the state on islands that allegorically refer to the urban crises in seventies Manhattan and nineties Los Angeles, respectively.

Watching New Orleans on the news, we witnessed a contemporary containment narrative that was eerily similar to Carpenter's films. This containment was racialized to be sure, but the real threat wasn't Black Nationalism or the Black Panther Party; it didn't have a form, it was the disorganized rise of the immiserated poor – just as in Carpenter's films. And its stage was New Orleans, where Bush had partied as a young man, a city that is increasingly seen as a curio in the global system, teetering between destination city and third world slum. Bush's hesitation did not need to be fuelled by racism, but it most definitely aligned with neoliberal prioritization and austerity strategies that would all recommend containing the threat of dispossession.

David Simon's HBO series *Treme* (2010-13) attempts to realistically depict social and political life in post-Katrina New Orleans, but, distracted by touristic tangents and the fetishization of authenticity, the series misses the opportunity to fully comment on the neoliberal agenda that influenced disaster relief for post-Katrina victims. The series provides none of the critical insights that distinguish Simon's previous HBO series *The Wire* (2002-08) in which dispossession and proletarianization in Baltimore are portrayed as connected to the advancement of global capitalism and the neoliberal state. Instead, *Treme* celebrates a variety of African-American musical traditions that consequently focuses on the history of black culture in America and New Orleans as tourism destination.[17] Moreover, even while the characters include a young musician from the Netherlands, a Japanese jazz fan and a Vietnamese immigrant family of fishers, the series tends to emphasize New Orleans' isolation from the rest of the world. This reinforces the impression that the dispossession following Katrina was a moral outrage and a governmental disaster, to be sure, but not necessarily associated with dispossession as tailor made for and by neoliberalism.

If we look at post-network TV generally, we note that middle-class identity regularly serves as a pathway to America's underside of difference (racial, sexual, criminal, regional): in a way, it is a form of 'disaster tourism'. We see it especially in therapy and talk shows, that format of reality TV programming that situates a professional character as our point of access to deviance and the playing out of non-middle-class values (e.g., *Intervention* (2005-), *Celebrity Rehab with Dr. Drew* (2008-), *16 and Pregnant* (2009-). But this tendency is also seen in fictional work that features a central character who is a model of middle-class identity (or was previously) now effectively slumming it on our behalf. This is the case in *Oz* (1997-2003), *Weeds* (2005-12), *The Riches* (2007-08), *Breaking Bad* (2008-13) and *Orange is the New Black* (2013-). Also referred to as boutique programming, featuring 'quality TV', post-network TV typically requires a degree of middle-class privilege to even participate, as it is usually accessible only with a cable subscription.[18] Thus there is a distinct social status associated with cable viewing – for instance, HBO once used the tag line 'It's not television' as a way to distinguish its prestige product from network TV that anybody could watch. Notably, Simon's HBO series *Treme* gained some distinction as a progressive project by not only featuring the Katrina disaster and bringing work to the region through extensive use of location shooting, but also because the producers arranged weekly community screenings of the telecast for residents of the Treme neighbourhood who could not afford HBO subscriptions.

In American TV series generally, the workplace has served as a prominent setting for a vast array of representations of social relations, including illuminating depictions of class relations. In contemporary TV series, this continues to be true and we see hospitals, precincts, schools, lawyer's offices, media outlets, restaurants and government offices as backdrops for a range of stories about daily working life. But the emphasis, typically, is on middle-class identity, especially professional middle-class characters. In the situation comedies *The Office* (2005-13), *Parks and Recreation* (2009-), *Silicon Valley* (2014-) and Larry David's 2013 HBO movie, *Clear History*, we are provided caustic depictions of the humiliating instrumentalization of white-collar labour. In these films and TV series, the characters' actual and potential achievements are so minimal, and the workplace torment so extreme, that the viewer is constantly provoked to wonder if the grind is worth it. In *Silicon Valley*, for instance, the central character is running a start-up that is developing software that will achieve the 'highest rate of loss-less compression'. The goal is for their software to become the industry standard with the long-term goal being the purchase of the start-up by a major ICT firm. In these instances, the logic of neoliberalism drives even the most empowered workers to dispossession and it is worth noting the extent to which this dispossession fully proletarianizes even those workers that seem furthest from the shop floor – indeed, the start-up operates out of the central character's home.

As a consequence of Hollywood's reliance on crises-oriented stories and its unabashed advancement of the middle classes, we have seen how popular film and TV tends to hyperbolize middle-class crises. This is particularly acute when seen against the relative lack of representation of working-class characters and stories. But, as we have also seen, middle-class crises provocatively depict struggles about work in general, routinely representing the ways that workers across the class spectrum suffer proletarianization and dispossession. Although they often identify with owners and regularly do their bidding by managing the workforce, we are also told that professionals experience destabilizing levels of degradation, humiliation and precarity in their jobs. To take a recent example, in *Up In The Air* (2009) we first meet George Clooney's Ryan Bingham when he is at the height of his power. He is confident; he is successful; he terminates workers for downsizing companies. Almost before the movie has begun, though, Bingham loses his own job and the rest of the story involves recuperating his humanity after he finds himself on the other side of the neoliberal paradigm.

In Woody Allen's *Blue Jasmine* (2013), Cate Blanchett plays a wealthy New York socialite whose husband Hal (Alec Baldwin) suffers a Madoff-scale fall from grace. The movie follows Jasmine on her own path toward recovery; brilliantly, the plot never allows her to shake the past and never provides a sense of redemption for her complicity in her husband's white-collar crimes. The point is that, far from repressing representations of class relations and class struggle, Hollywood film and TV proliferate such images, but always from the perspective of middle-class ideals of conformity and compliance. While Hollywood rarely tells stories about socialism, many of its characters suffer through crises of dispossession and proletarianization that lead them to the brink of worker consciousness. But always only to the brink.

NOTES

1   I take my lead from Bryan Palmer who, in the *Socialist Register 2014*, argued that attempts to theorize working-class identities outside the conditions of dispossession and proletarianization are prone to obfuscation. Criticizing speculations about the precariat as a new class formation, Palmer concludes by claiming that 'all proletarians suffer precariousness, and all those constrained by precariousness in their working lives are indeed proletarians or have interests that coincide directly with this class of the dispossessed'. 'Reconsiderations of Class: Precariousness as Proletarianization', *Socialist Register 2014*, Pontypool: Merlin Press, 2013, p. 57. Regarding the role of the middle classes in processes of exploitation, I follow Erik Olin Wright's observation that capitalist societies contain a variety of forms of exploitation, and the middle classes are usefully seen as 'locations in class structure which are exploited in terms of capitalist mechanisms of exploitation, but *exploiters* in terms of one or more of these secondary mechanisms of exploitation'. 'Exploitation, Identity, and Class Structure: A Reply to My Critics', in Erik Olin Wright, ed., *The Debate on Classes*, London: Verso, 1989, p. 191.

2   Daniel Bell, *The Coming of Post-Industrial Society: A Venture in Social Forecasting*, New York: Basic Books, 1973.

3   See Sloan Wilson, *The Man in the Gray Flannel Suit*, New York: Simon and Schuster, 1955; and William Whyte, *The Organization Man*, New York: Simon and Schuster, 1956. In 1956, Gregory Peck starred in the film version of *The Man in the Gray Flannel Suit*.

4   For discussion of social and political themes in American popular film in the period see Peter Biskind, *Seeing is Believing: How Hollywood Taught Us to Stop Worrying and Love the Fifties*, New York: Pantheon, 1983; Robert Ray, *A Certain Tendency of the Hollywood Cinema, 1930-1980*, Princeton: Princeton University Press, 1985; and Stephen Powers, David Rothman and Stanley Rothman, *Hollywood's America: Social and Political Themes in Motion Pictures*, Boulder: Westview Press, 1996.

5   For an overview of early film exhibition see Douglas Gomery, *Shared Pleasures: A History of Movie Presentation in the United States*, Madison: University of Wisconsin Press, 1992, pp. 3-134.

6   See 'Motion Picture Producers and Distributors of America, The Motion Picture Production Code of 1930', in Gerald Mast, ed., *The Movies in Our Midst: Documents in the Cultural History of Film in America*, Chicago: University of Chicago Press, 1982, pp. 321-33.

7   See Robert Sklar, *Movie-Made America: A Cultural History of American Movies*, Revised and Updated, New York: Vintage, 1994.

8   In the 1951 film version of the play, Fredric March played Willie Loman; Lee J. Cobb, who defined Loman in the original Broadway performance, reprised

his role on TV in 1966; and Dustin Hoffman played the role in a 1985 TV version.

9   Michael Ryan and Douglas Kellner, *Camera Politica: The Politics and Ideology of Contemporary Hollywood Film*, Bloomington and Indianapolis: Indiana University Press, 1988; and Robin Wood, *Hollywood From Vietnam to Reagan*, New York: Columbia University Press, 1986.

10   Mark A. Reid, *Redefining Black Film*, Berkeley: University of California Press, 1993; Herman Gray, *Watching Race: Television and the Struggle for 'Blackness'*, Minneapolis: University of Minnesota Press, 1995; Ntongela Masilela, 'The Los Angeles School of Black Filmmakers', in Manthia Diawara, ed., *Black American Cinema*, New York: Routledge, 1993, pp. 107-17; Scott Forsyth, 'Hollywood's War on the World: The New World Order as Movie', *The Socialist Register 1992*, London: Merlin Press, 1991, pp. 280-3; and Douglas Kellner's chapter on 'Black Voices from Spike Lee to Rap' in his *Media Culture: Cultural Studies, Identity and Politics Between the Modern and the Postmodern*, London and New York: Routledge, 1995, pp. 157-97.

11   See Adolph Reed, Jr, 'The Underclass Myth', *Class Notes: Posing as Politics and Other Thoughts on the American Scene*, New York: The New Press, 2000, pp. 93-100.

12   See Barry Keith Grant, 'Rich and Strange: The Yuppie Horror Film', in Stephen Neale and Murray Smith, eds., *Contemporary Hollywood Cinema*, New York: Routledge, 1998, pp. 280-93.

13   Bret Easton Ellis's 1985 debut novel *Less Than Zero* and his 1987 *The Rules of Attraction* also portrayed the crises of upper-middle-class characters in the period and both were adapted as films in 1987 and 2002 respectively.

14   See Jonathan Markovitz, 'Reel Terror Post 9/11', in Wheeler Winston Dixon, ed., *Film and Television after 9/11*, Carbondale: Southern Illinois University Press, 2004, pp. 201-25; James Der Derian, '9/11: Before, After, and In Between', in J. David Slocum, ed., *Terrorism, Media, Liberation*, New Brunswick, NJ: Rutgers University Press, 2005, pp. 321-35; Douglas Kellner, *Cinema Wars: Hollywood Film and Politics in the Bush-Cheney Era*, Chichester: Wiley-Blackwell, 2010; Stacy Takacs, *Terrorism TV: Popular Entertainment in Post-9/11 America*, Lawrence: University Press of Kansas, 2012.

15   Michael Kackman, *Citizen Spy: Television, Espionage, and Cold War Culture*, Minneapolis: University of Minnesota Press, 2005; Toby Miller, *Spyscreen: Espionage on Film and Television from the 1930s to the 1960s*, Oxford: Oxford University Press, 2003; Yvonne Tasker, 'Television Crime Drama and Homeland Security: From *Law & Order* to "Terror TV"', *Cinema Journal*, 51(4), 2012, pp. 44-65.

16   For related discussions of the relationship between class and racial identity in contemporary media culture, see Manthia Diawara, 'Black American Cinema: The New Realism', in *Black American Cinema*, pp. 3-25; and Paula Massood, *Black City Cinema: African-American Experiences in Film*, Philadelphia: Temple University Press, 2003.

17   See Adolf Reed, Jr., 'Three Tremés', *nonsite.org*, 4 July 2011, available at http://nonsite.org.

18 On 'quality TV', see Jane Feuer, 'HBO and the Concept of Quality TV', in Janet McCabe and Kim Akass, eds., *Quality TV: Contemporary American Television and Beyond*, London: I. B. Taurus, 2007, pp. 145-57. On post-network TV, see Amanda Lotz, *The Television Will Be Revolutionized*, New York: New York University Press, 2007.

WHAT HAS BECOME OF THE
PROFESSIONAL MANAGERIAL CLASS?

RANDY MARTIN

The Professional Managerial Class (PMC) was once positioned to hold the promise of a knowledge-based capitalist society to resolve the deeper antinomies of social division and conflict. Accordingly, credentialized knowledge was the basis of a new category of commodities that would deliver expertise over a specialized domain. The resulting professionalization was to be meritocratically achieved and autonomously governed so as to make capital's claims for growth, progress and development mappable onto the appropriately privileged individual career. As such, the PMC was a class that was not one, comporting with a conception of class that disavowed its significance. From this perspective, self-interest would prove more compelling than mutual interdependence; collective organization would be confined to professional associations and interest groups; politics and governance would be left to the appropriate specialists rather than being the prize that a revolutionary mass party could seize and transform. Marxism itself would be relegated to a footnote in this triumphalist storyline, with the PMC democratizing capitalism from the reactionary clutches of the self-contained petit bourgeois or the violent disruptions of a universalizing proletariat on the march.[1]

The historical point of reference for this essay is the conjuncture between the emergence of a knowledge society and the access to credentializing higher education that would provide the labour for it. The justification for expanding higher education to the masses was a form of entitlement for a democratic citizenship that was meant to adhere populations to the progressive and developmental nation state. Yet this social compact posed around an ideal of meritocracy was not potent enough to overcome the translation of knowledge-for-itself into a kind of circulating asset that would be achieved through the opening of new profit-taking markets. This, as with past expansions of the horizons of capital accumulation, would require massive state intervention. Expanded governmental and regulatory engagement would be needed to construct the physical and fiscal access to what had been a privilege of the elite to higher education, and of the global regimes of finance, techno-science and culture that would industrialize knowledge through various expansions and elaborations of intellectual property.

While the PMC was to be the postwar harbinger of a post-industrial, post-conflict, post-revolutionary capitalism, much has changed over the past fifty years to complicate this social compact and remake the formation and composition of this class. The vaunted autonomy of the PMC has been disrupted by various forces of decomposition and formalized rankings and measures of performance that features managerial protocols that, rather than reflecting confidence in expertise, now promote scepticism regarding specialized knowledge. Yet, by conventional measure, the ranks of the PMC defined as an assortment of occupational categories (at over a third of the workforce, larger than any other grouping of occupations) continue to swell in places like the United States, as manufacturing employment continues to decline.[2] Concomitantly, higher education continues to expand even as it shifts emphasis and effective consequence from an engine of mobility to one of debt.

The class question newly posed by the PMC then becomes how to understand the social conditions of these massive aggregations of debt, which, if taken as a source of expansive revenue streams suggest a rethinking of the relations between labour and capital. When Marx looked at these relations during the nineteenth century he focused on the industrial proletariat not because they were the most numerous formations, but because he saw in the principle of association expressed through abstract labour the basis for a more general class politics and claim on social wealth through a re-appropriation of surplus value. Now as then, capitalism has brought hitherto existing modes of living together into ruin. It has also introduced terms of interconnection that provide the grounds for emergent political forms which make legible the horizon of a different social order within the decay and expansiveness of present conditions.

This essay will consider some of these political implications by looking at key arguments regarding the PMC. The current status of this class will be understood in the context of contemporary finance, which bears unprecedented wealth and holds the promise of a society founded on abundance as opposed to austerity in its sway. Certainly there have been other conceptions of how a knowledge-based conception of the PMC could open new social possibilities. Over two decades ago, Robert Reich, just before becoming Clinton's Secretary of Labor, pushed at the limits of liberal policy analysis by advancing the notion of symbolic analysts whose mastery of expertise would command high salaries and absorb increasing numbers of workers. Along with young urban professionals, this claim turned out to be at odds with actual wage trends, and in both cases these beneficiaries of the knowledge boom turned out to be but a small fraction of the employment demographic.[3]

In the new millennium, the rich and complex Marxist analysis in the multi-volume series from Michael Hardt and Antonio Negri picked up from the account in the *Grundrisse* of mass intellectuality (the general intellect) as a basis for socialized labour they term immaterial. They acknowledge that the affective, embodied, knowledge-making and creative dimensions of immaterial labour 'remains material ... What is immaterial is its product'.[4] But this divide between material and immaterial labour and production has sometimes been characterized as corresponding to a split between a real and a speculative economy that at once diminishes the significance of these new labour forms and smuggles back a conception of economic growth as the basis for capital accumulation as such. This unwittingly weds the immaterial to an expansion of mastery over the physical world and sits uncomfortably beside Hardt and Negri's environmental commitments.[5]

There is good reason to be sceptical that the professional managerial class, however revised, could provide the basis for a renewal of left politics, just as there are ample grounds to doubt that the formulation of a knowledge society bears the credibility to grasp how political economy might be productively rethought. The PMC and knowledge are now joined around notions of a creative class and a 'high tech' economy which have become watchwords of inequality, gentrification, competition and indifference toward those excluded from the gains of new found wealth.[6] All these dimensions are also linked, most profoundly, with contemporary finance dominated capitalism in complex ways that Marxists are only now coming to terms with.[7]

If the decomposed PMC is to be reconstituted now as a political potentiality because of the sociality it makes legible, we would need to follow the road that Marx took in analytically privileging emergent tendencies of what kinds of social wealth might arise from the ruins of the prior class order. The historical limits of the postwar PMC class project are evident in the serial crises of expertise expressed in the financial debacle, environmental disasters and governmental impasse, which have continued to unfold after 2008. If new political prospects that are not simply nostalgia or more reaction are to rise from the ruins, it will be crucial to reflect upon some of the organizational implications of this class formation that cleaves populations between those who benefit from risk and access to lines of credit and debt, and those who are at-risk and whose lives are made precarious by credit dependence and crushing obligations to debt repayment. The path taken here will lead through the kind of immanent critique of finance capital that Marx provided for the commodity form – in which what he understood as the socialization of labour can be elaborated through debt and credit instruments epitomized in the derivative, a bundling of variable attributes of commodities, such as currency or interest rates that are priced and deployed to manage the risks they engender.

The continued expansion of the PMC has disarticulated the growth of credentials from the conditions of labour. Autonomy has been replaced with market driven demands for enhanced productivity through continually measured valuations of performance where the outlier continually pushes the norm by means of an unfavourable comparison.[8] Here, specialized knowledge is taken to be non-translatable in its own terms, but fully transferable into enhancements of capital. Knowledge serves a master indifferent to its sources and yields an excess of what can be absorbed in use as the quants and professional risk managers that shouldered the blame without sharing the benefits soon found out. This evident contradiction between the reliance upon expert knowledge and a dismissal or scepticism toward its surplus product is at once the basis for further means of knowing and an endemic failure to make use of knowledge productively that references those moments where there arises the prospect of an expansive sociality that capital can neither tame nor abide.

THE FORMATION AND DECOMPOSITION OF THE KNOWING CLASS

In many formulations, the advent of a knowledge society, based upon reflexivity, risk, networks, markets or other conditions of mutual attachment, was said to displace polarizing and internally homogeneous class divisions. In a new economy based on shared information, all would manage themselves without iron-fisted bosses and help themselves without the tedious control of the nanny state.[9] Sure enough, a postwar social compact based on corporate welfare, an alignment of national and career security, entitlements and social investments in public goods that drove the expansion of the PMC in the 1960s was reconstructed by the 1980s. Consequently, the bundle of social rights organized under the banner of citizenship had to make room for a cleavage of the population between those who benefit from taking risks and those considered at-risk that needed to be contained from spreading dangerous behaviours reminiscent of Cold War anxieties over the contagion of communism. Pulled at from these extremes, outliers and peripheries, the stable centre where the secure middle resided could no longer hold and the volatile margins came to orient the way in which populations were treated in their relations to both state and markets. The technical knowledge that flowed from instrumental reason (in the Weberian and Habermasian formulations) was supposed to subordinate the life world of substantive reason or shared values. But the public sphere turned out to be less a liberated zone from market clutches then a cauldron for that very commodification of knowledge and of the labour required to produce it.[10]

More fluid than the partition between mass and elite, refusing the rigidities of owners and employees, those who could manage risk through the metrics and measures of accountability would generate their own capital, even if this meant undoing the distinction between economic, cultural and symbolic forms thought to secure credentialized self-governance.[11] On the other hand, as the rewards of disequilibrium prevailed over security-inducing distributions, those who failed to embrace risk — and this could be anyone at any time — would slide into the abyss of the at-risk, the failed state of being whose contagion needed to be targeted and contained.[12] A technics of knowing, the translation of all human relations into information driven decision making of a profit-taking market, now described as neoliberalism, would combine with a moralizing sense of being associated with a neoconservative temperament, in which the anointed deserved salvation or at least rescue in the form of moral hazard. And those incapable of profiting from the risks they bear engendered a contagion or moral panic that had to be combated pre-emptively as a series of wars on crime, drugs, culture and eventually terror.[13]

Yet the advent of the knowledge or post-industrial society was framed by its own, albeit contrary, class narratives. One is that professionals constitute a new working class and the other is that they comprise the new mandarins, a professional managerial class aligned with the highest echelons of societal command.[14] In some respects, this was a class that could not shoot straight, or one that defied notions based upon solidarity and the political problematic of how an array of objective conditions would craft common interests that would assert a collective consciousness to forge society in its image. Further confounding the understanding of professional managerials as a class was the very sociological metric of occupational status, educational attainment and income that converted a collective entity into a scalable and distributed individual datum.[15] If what distinguished the PMC as a class was its capacity for self-rule through the mastery of a knowledge domain, then in effect the principle of autonomy, as an ascendant historical project that all might aspire to and join, translated an individuated conception of class back into social terms.[16] Impatient with orderly historical formation, this was a class whose making was also its undoing, for by coming together through particular domains of self-mastery, it also came apart as an integrative social foundation.

The Ehrenreichs, in their influential work in the 1970s, argued that while the PMC were 'mental workers' without control over the means of production, they serve to reproduce capitalist culture by solving the problems of daily life, be these affective or scientific. While the PMC divided between business and non-profit services, the generalized anxieties about class reproduction or upward mobility meant that 'private life thus becomes too arduous to be lived in private; the inner life of the PMC must be continuously shaped, updated and revised by – of course – ever mounting numbers of experts: experts in childraising, family living, sexual fulfillment, self-realization, etc., etc'.[17] Paradoxically this insecurity was the basis for class expansion and hegemony over the traditional working class through self-legitimation of its own expertise, with consequent anti-working-class radicalism. The Ehrenreichs' analysis points to the emergence of the new right at the end of the seventies. While Derber notes that professionals have the power to 'enclose the mind', he also observes that the Reagan revolution was hostile to the new mandarins.[18] No longer disinterested or narrowly self-interested in expert autonomy, the professions become a field where larger social contests are played out.

Indeed, between the forces of risk and self-management that have borne upon class formation, the last thirty years have also witnessed more general class decomposition. The principle of association known as social class is forged by perpetual processes of both making and unmaking. The rise of the PMC is accompanied by an internal cleavage between compromised professionalization and rampant managerialism.[19] The utopian promises of emancipating consumerism are swallowed by unending labours of credit and debt. We see this in the complications in the once clear separation between labour power as a commodity fettered to the wage relation of employment and labour as an asset that can be tied to future wages, unpaid labour of social reproduction, social benefits or entitlements. In either case the knowledge-work tied to self-ranking and performance assessment which are part of the managerialist frameworks of both production and consumption or circulation, stage a confrontation between knowledge use and exchange value across all manner of once distinct sites and spheres. While the notion of a middle class was based upon central location within an income distribution rather than an occupational address, it was also commonly used to displace the link between class and labour by means of identifying with an expanding capacity for consumption. Middle-class anxieties are multiplied between professional services and the industry in self-help.

As Micki McGee has shown, the impulse to do-it-yourself was explicitly at odds with organized labour as a means to collective betterment, while simultaneously expanding the work of reproduction into the spheres of private lives.[20] With government mandating furloughs for public employees, corporations reaping higher productivity and profit from fewer workers, and college graduates facing the gloomiest of employment prospects in decades, the present financial crisis has had a profound impact on the lustre of professional labour even if professionals have fared better than others.[21] Still, years into the aftermath of the great recession, half of the US workforce was impacted by either job loss or cuts to their hours or wages, and shed over half a trillion dollars in consumer debt while corporations and banks declined to lend or reinvest their mounting cash reserves.[22] Expanding debt in the face of expanding magnitudes of credit driven wealth fuels austerity rather than mutuality, while governments place a lien on future wealth in order to return less by way of social benefit.

But if the crisis was an occasion for these contractions, it has been used to argue that such labour is permanently expendable. The disposability of professional expertise has been a long time in the making and while many youth may still harbour dreams of secure professional career tracts, the do-it-yourself ethos has also been aligned with student and protest movements, maker, slacker and hacker culture and a range of alternative approaches to labour that do not assume the stable structure of a job.[23] With the expanded numbers of the PMC over the past thirty years has come a concomitant rise in informality and precarity in the labour market and a valuation of the local in government policy from Reagan's devolution to Bush père's volunteerism to Clinton's communitarianism to G.W. Bush's ownership society and the privatizing initiatives of micro-credit, wiki work and YouTube self-production.

CHANGING THE INSTITUTIONS OF HIGHER EDUCATION

Higher education has been key to the fortunes of the professional managerial class. Its shift from a province of the elite in the middle of the nineteenth century to mass access during the expansion of public institutions in the 1960s met its demise as post-secondary education was reconceived as an investment in future earnings and shifted from a public to a private good.[24] On the supply side of the knowledge economy, higher education has been a leader in the new casualized professional workforce, its models of part-time and contract faculty as insourced replacement workers for long-term tenured employees are now increasingly common in other corporate sectors.[25] In the early seventies, 70 per cent of courses were taught by faculty considered permanent; now that ratio is reversed. It was the Bayh–Dole Act, passed in 1980, that enabled universities to keep money from patents they yielded from federal grants. Consequently, intellectual property increased seven-fold while universities held but five per cent of patents, effectively trading their credential-based monopoly on disciplined knowledge as a public good for a model of education as an investment that would be driven by increased debt. Following a line of shareholder value, college presidents committed their institutions to the pursuit of small changes in rankings which de-emphasized local faculty governance in favour of externally comparable metrics of excellence, achievement, a position relative to peer institutions that aligned with an emphasis on facilities construction over enhanced faculty salaries and benefits.

Along with this loss of faculty-centredness came an increase in administrative labour, discounted in value as 'service' tied genealogically to the unpaid labour of domestic and slave work while senior administrators reaped more handsome rewards. In the United States, a full-time faculty average workweek runs over fifty hours and a fifth of that is comprised of administrative tasks. This loss of disciplinary autonomy based upon a craft conception of knowledge shifted orientation toward a combination of the professional association as faculty gained expertise in how the institutions are run that launched a new wave of interdisciplinary programs. Additionally, there is a more robust relation to knowledge industries as a whole sector from culture to technology to finance affiliates faculty who circulate through projects, consultancies and collaborations inside and outside the university. When considered from an industrial perspective rather than as single craft based affiliations upon which faculties have been unionized, campus-wide responses to the plight of service workers or graduate students engage faculty and other constituencies, as was the case at Yale University during the 1990s where the treatment of food service workers animated a broader engagement. This organizational amalgamation resonant of earlier consolidations of capital in such fields as communications is referred to as convergence and results in what has been called a cybertariat.[26]

These changes were accompanied by a renewed activism amongst graduate students who not only were fighting battles against government defunding and debt, but were also in effect double majoring in their chosen fields, on the one hand, and in forms of administrative politics, activism and organizing, on the other. While this has certainly been true of student movements historically, these activists are training for labour relations very different from the job prospects of those who have trained them. At the same time, the transformations of academic labour suggest a kind of organizational binding and blending or convergence as faculty expertise is not simply for itself, but operates in and moves through organizational registers of professional associations that challenge how institutions are run, industrial unions that contend with the configuration of the knowledge economy, and political parties in which specialized area knowledge is treated as a threat to the prosecution of war as evident in the cases of Sami al Arian and Ward Churchill. Institutional and administrative knowledge accrues to professionals beyond their disciplinary specialty in a manner that has undone the separation between academic freedom and campus command from a hundred years ago when tenure emerged. At the same time the industrialization of knowledge places academics in a wider circuit of intellectual property that moves them inside and outside the university.

CAPITALIST CRISES AND ORGANIZATIONAL IMMANENCE

The selective corporate bailout of 2008 demonstrated a political will to leverage the entire tax base, some \$14 trillion, to particular ends with only a commitment to profit from the investment that effectively eviscerated the public claim on its own wealth capacities while presuming the necessity of transferring social wealth to private entities that needed to demonstrate no obligation to social purpose. The lesson of how to make a contingent claim on such massive wealth capacity – and not simply to resist the burdens of debt (as crucial as this is as a response to present constraints) – is one that remains to be learned for organizational expressions of labour and popular political movements.[27]

The failure of professionalized knowledge within capitalism is evident not only in the malfunction of risk management tools and models for the 2008 financial debacle, but also in such examples of failure as the Deepwater Horizon and Fukushima energy disasters where similar mathematical models were employed by technical risk engineers in the name of forestalling the very danger they were so ill-equipped to contain and control. These shortcomings precipitated a crisis in the legitimacy of their own forms of labour to govern and control the outcomes of their expertise. Certainly amongst financial, energy and civil engineers, their models assume a normal distribution that exposes vulnerability to the highly volatile and supposedly improbable yet increasingly frequent 'black swan' events. These professionals bore the brunt of the consequences of these various disasters as executives retained their own seats and increased their bonuses while the bearers of technical knowledge labour were laid-off and furloughed. Once stalwart professions such as law have become increasingly precarious as fewer law school graduates get hired and the opportunities to attain partnerships are diminished.[28] Even Wall Street has shed 20,000 jobs since the bailout.[29]

At first blush the consequences of financially driven knowledge failure appear to be fragmentary and haphazard, incomplete and incapable of control, features of a moment in which decision making seems doomed to come up short. But at the same time, these failures of specialized expertise sequestered in segregated spaces point to what it means to know together when the boundary conditions of disparate domains fall. Activists too have learned how to leverage the volatility that their occupations and interventions generate to more expansive effects where small movements of prices, data or bodies on the street can yield extensive consequences. Participation is organized in terms of attributes that can be ideologically inconsistent. When such knowledge making is treated as equivalent according to measures of performance ranking and measurable value added, what is referenced is an inescapable interdependence which establishes inter-commensurability among aspects of concrete particulars. If the PMC is no longer able to monopolize decision making in the name of credentialed expertise, there is a potential to renew an inquiry into what knowledge might be for if it is not assumed to serve aspirations for upward mobility or capital accumulation.

When managerialism is unmoored from professional expertise, all are potentially positioned to make a claim on how things might be run. When debt is treated as a source of liquidity, a promise is made on how the future might be decided. When credentials fail to deliver security, knowledge must reflect on its own organizational capacities. Managerialism renders organization immanent to the deployment of knowledge. It calibrates pathways by which labours of administration are affiliated across lines of expertise, industry and societal direction linked to a political party. As more time and effort is spent in the exercise of administrative deliberation, an anxious expectation of ongoing assessment, deliberation and decision presses into view. The decomposition of the professional managerial class has subjected professionals to shared protocols of performance based assessments and rankings on the basis of productivity, but lost autonomy has not created a homogeneous mass (any more than had earlier socializations of labour been without forces of division).

As professional autonomy erodes in favour of an endemic incompleteness of knowledge competence over a specialized domain, knowledge workers produce the very excess of knowledge that slips from command and control to a potent and volatile environment over which their existing ways of organizing themselves have less influence and durability. This is the uncertainty which recurs as crisis that no one can see coming, but that nonetheless bears the force of the future down on the present. Paradoxically, then, the principles of association that make for an emergent class may only be detectable on its own ruins. Unmaking, just like the unknown, are conditions of an uncertain sociality to come.

The loss of intellectual autonomy through the current data mining and information capture of cognitive capitalism invokes a securitization of expertise, which strips away the protective hull of specialization, delocalizes technical domains and bundles them together in the service of a master that can take the form of an employer or government that is indifferent to validity claims in terms other than market based performance which treats knowledge of particular risk exposures such as variations in interest or mortgage rates, or projections of future tuition increases as tradable assets. While this process can be seen as a replay in the domain of mental labour and knowledge production of the agrarian enclosures of the feudal commons that sired industrial capitalism, it is less clear that the data being mined for sale and knowledge being licensed as intellectual property once belonged to a self-sustaining knowledge commons before they were placed in circulation.[30] Certainly for those professionals who once directed their own affairs, ran their own practices or owned their own businesses, inner-directed careers might have the same nostalgic appeal as the commons. Yet this would assume that in the shift from craft to industrial production the social and material aspects of the knowledge in question remain the same, with the only salient difference being the shift to an external authority of control to which professional labour is now alienated.

The decomposition of the PMC suggests different principles for class association and organizational affiliation than the conventional social science notions of class based upon where one is located in an occupational status hierarchy. This distributional notion of class can be contrasted to a relational conception of class where the PMC is situated in a contradictory class location because of their autonomy. But what seems to now be emerging is an attributional notion of class where professionals are securitized through circulating attributes of their labour in which performance outcomes matter more than expertise. The doctor, lawyer, professor, finance engineer are assessed by metrics of productivity, customer satisfaction, portfolio contributions, rather than by measures of their expertise or knowledge per se.

This is the predicament of a professional subsumed to a managerialism that ranks their performance on a pricing model that does not recognize intrinsic value and refuses translation of specific knowledge in favour of measures of worth added to the portfolio of the enterprise. Dispersed spatially, class formation assembles disparate attributes of intelligence, profiles of identity, exposures to volatility that generate associative interdependence. The consequences are manifold: loss of security to accountability, the exchange of generalizable growth for targeted performance, the shift in reference from the norm to the outlier, the mass to the star performer. All of which seems to unmake the solidaristic experience associated with class shift to a leveraged cooperation. What appears consequently are the twin figures of a locally administered knowledge commons, a domain of non-proprietary shared endeavour, or of a much more dispersed entanglement of knowledge production and circulation whose effects can be highly leveraged and volatile, as in the case of security leaks and hacktivists. Both the autonomist and the indebtedness trajectories of what emerges from PMC ruination are entangled – as indicated by their coincident use of open source software and free labour as their guide.[31]

What was present in the earlier story that has dropped out in the more recent accounts is that enclosure, the loss of what was held in common, such as land, also fosters a socialization of labour, which in the nineteenth century was the advent of an organizationally promising industrial proletariat. The novelty of Marx's analytic and political wager is often lost when it is forgotten that factory workers were a small slice of the Victorian labour force, well overshadowed by servants and domestic labour in England. Manufacturing barely exceeded a quarter of the workforce at its height in the early part of the twentieth century, and the larger transformation was from agriculture to service – the commodification of the domestic labour of social reproduction – that then morphed into the professional and knowledge based jobs that are now the largest occupational category. Marx understood that a population is not inevitably absorbed into the workforce. Just the contrary, the hoarding and other mechanisms that render capital unproductive or in excess of what can be placed in circulation also create a relative surplus population of those who find no place within the labour market for employment. Today, relative surplus population is no longer simply a means of suppressing the costs of labour through unemployment, but is increasingly tied to sources of free labour without being fettered to employment, which can take the form of unpaid internships or the widespread free labour of the internet or other start-up ideas that seek support through crowdfunding.

Industrialization of knowledge also transforms the activities, expressions and terms of association of labour, where debt rises in pursuit of credentials, jobs and careers disappear, and knowledge makers access their own means of producing, representing and disseminating what can be assembled as their collective value. Before attending to what the PMC is becoming, it is important to say something about the changes to ways of organizing this labour, if indeed it is to pose the prospect of a larger societal shift and not simply be a reconfiguration of how labour is divided, reassembled and evaluated.

Organization once attached monogamously to class position – professionals had their associations, labourers their unions, militants their parties. The new configurations of knowledge production and the decomposition of the PMC have altered this political geography. The unknown unknowns that Donald Rumsfeld had used to justify pre-emptive strikes describe both the generalized anxieties around volatility and the excess of knowledge that can be processed and controlled.[32] This state of affairs depicts a far more decentralized but also interwoven world than imagined by the older models of imperial centres knowing the world and acting upon their interests in the name of a grand strategy.[33] Seizing upon these organizational links and the new combinations they offer of how we create bonds of debt long figured in gift exchange and now being commercially touted as a new sharing economy.[34] Beyond the straightforward commodification of spare rooms for short-term let marketed by Airbnb or music sharing sites is the bundling of debts into assets that serve as collateral as was evident in the subprime derived mortgage backed securities that whatever their baleful consequences still bind people to one another across far flung sites and circumstances but that nonetheless lacks a political language adequate to make a contingent claim on all this wealth. Crafting this language may help turn what has been imposed by the current dominance of finance back on itself without first needing to settle on a single organizational form.

BACK TO THE FUTURE

The two most intriguing tendencies to emerge from the ruins of the PMC today would be the hackers of big data and the self-conscious 'alternative makers' (in contrast to the self-designated market makers in finance). These strains to emerge from the ruins of professional expertise suggest an inversion of the individualistic investment in self of human capital and an undoing of the separation between capital based rent and labour generated surplus value, as making knowledge materializes associations, interconnections and interdependencies between producers and consumers along global supply chains amidst the processing and pricing of data or information. These represent a loose amalgamation of those who proffer their creative labour as a form of capital without benefits of a credential or a monopoly on legitimate means of knowledge. These kinds of post-professional 'creatives' (conceived very differently from the contentless creative economy used to rank one city against another in terms of their vibrancy as centres of accumulation) generate value by leveraging small differences in comparable products (such as coffee, clothing, web platforms) to make a contingent claim on the superiority of their own efforts. This is the critical labour from which small differences come to matter, connect and spread in which a small intervention acts as a decision on the market value as a whole. Critical decision making and risk taking operate by treating the attributes of a commodity – their exposures to market volatility from which derivatives are made – into a more general capacity for exchange and mutual indebtedness (in the sense of social obligation rather than financial debt). Knowledge that can be parceled and recombined stands as a token store of value and medium of exchange much like what the money form did in Marx's day as a then unrealized promise of universal exchange.[35]

The mid-twentieth century PMC morphed from the mid-nineteenth century petit bourgeoisie in that space between labour and capital; self-employment predicated on possessing small scale means of production shifted to autonomous control of specialized knowledge which promised to reward hard work of mastering expertise with upward career mobility that would ride the crest of economic growth. Now, information traders and market makers, extended beyond the financial services industry to apply to all manner of cultural practices, forms of activism and entrepreneurial endeavours, suggest a reconfiguration of the labour-capital relation. Information traders mine and harvest vast fields of information to their own collaborative enhancement that portends a form of capital as labour. The information mined by Google or Facebook is treated as proprietary, yet the collected and collective labour provided of depositing and making use of it is provided for free. The creative entrepreneurs identified as makers insert their knowledge of salient difference and bond chains of buyers and sellers, producers and consumers, supply chain providers and end-users that pose an intensive knowledge labour as a form of capital. The product differentiation amongst crafted coffees or clothing or an album of songs relies upon a consumer commitment which is underwritten by the hours of labour that makers offer as a capital input.

Financial derivatives have captured much political space while disavowing that the claims made on the wealth of society could be contested by others than a privileged few who benefit from the risks tendered as collateral by all.[36] Derivatives yield far-flung entanglements of what were once merely local units of production but nothing as clearly formed as a world wrought into two great opposing camps, unified in their interests and synchronous in their movement will lead them. The activisms to emerge from the ruins of the PMC that are advancing a language of networks, refusal, nonrepresentational consensus have expanded the terms of the political without pre-requisites of unity, yet still they must grapple with their own versions of the organizational question by which their practices and interventions are valued as sustainable and scalable. The gap opened up between these dilemmas of emergent intersections between capital and labour points to some work to be done for a renewed Marxist politics.

Both the information networks of big data and the supply chain interdependencies of 'alternative makers' can be said to be 'derivative' in the sense that neither existed prior to their invocation and circulation. They also act in anticipation of a future and bring what is far or spatially dispersed into actionable proximity. Both these traders and makers are taking risks, hedging volatility, to maintain participation or liquidity in the circuits to which they are committed. This is the case not simply for the highly profitable hedge fund managers, but for the precarious knowledge workers, do-it-yourselfers and hacktivists who cluster innovative approaches to self-production, critical self-evaluation and dissemination of their work through various social media sites.[37] The translation of these emergent class socialities into an organizational mode is by no means simple or direct. The libertarian orientation of such formations typically trumps consideration of how larger engagements with state and capital, or scaling up in spatial, temporal or geopolitical strategies might proceed.[38]

Neither 'alternative makers' nor big data free labour miners have coalesced around a coherent politics – although that may be all the more reason to seek the social foundations of one. Still, if we are to do more than decry the inauthenticity of what capitalism has become and of the emergent forms of labour that it has pressed together, our own analyses must identify the social bases for the politics we seek and recognize the organizational potential that such labour augurs. In addition to the break up and reconstitution of hitherto discrete class formations such as the PMC along the lines of the synthetic finance which disperses and reassembles attributes of various risk exposures into stores of value and a medium of exchange, we might want to consider what a synthetic politics along these lines might entail. It may now be possible to think various political trajectories together for their lateral and horizontal interrelations rather than as distinct alternatives where going down one road precludes what another has to offer. The most immediate political mobilizations to emerge from the rise of finance and the decomposition of the PMC are legible in the anarchist inspired debt refusal that resists enclosure and advocates a return of the commons as a shared resource which raised under a million dollars to purchase and effectively eliminate many millions of dollars of debt which has been named as communalism.[39] Marx's basis for socialism lay in conceiving of the 'society of producers' as the means and ends of society, such that the form that mutual association takes becomes itself an object of political struggle. Rather than a mass unity, the dispersed and distributed debts of the decomposed PMC posit the question of how social affiliation is to be constituted, of how knowledge makers could be bound together without needing to become unified as one organizational or demographic entity. Finally, any communism that emerges from the dominance of finance may entail pursuing what it means to be able to make a claim on the entirety of wealth so as to move society from the management of scarcity to the access on the abundance that is already in our midst.

The more intimate entanglements of labour and capital to emerge from the ruins of the PMC point to a lateral if still nascent movement among alternative makers (less organized but reminiscent of earlier lateral movements between organizational registers of professional association, industrial union and party). Whether a hacktivist, a locavore, a 'fair trade' coffee enthusiast or a precarious faculty, all are placing knowledge in circulation and seeing what they can make together that they could not value apart; namely, a society contingent on the claims they might make on one another. To be sure, for this to go so far as to involve taking from each according to abilities and giving back according to needs would entail configuring the social form of this mutually entangled commitment as a historical project aimed at scaling up from the commons to incorporate the entire scope of populations and scaling down from the abundance of wealth as aggregated in the precincts of finance so that these revenue streams flow back to the labour that was the source of it. It would, in other words, enlarge the demands that people can make upon one another for the 'production of society' as the means and ends of deliberative social wealth.[40]

NOTES

These ideas on a politics that would emerge from a critique of finance are being developed with a group of colleagues: Arjun Appadurai, Ben Lee, Ed Lipuma, Robert Meister and Robert Wosnitzer.

1   Fritz Machlup, *The Production and Distribution of Knowledge in the United States*, Princeton: Princeton University Press, 1962; Daniel Bell, *The Coming of Post-Industrial Society: A Venture in Social Forecasting*, New York: Basic Books, 1973; Manuel Castells, *The Rise of the Network Society, The Information Age: Economy, Society and Culture, Volume 1*, Malden: Blackwell, 1996. Because the amelioration of inequality is tied to knowledge diffusion, Thomas Piketty's *Capital in the 21ˢᵗ Century*, Cambridge, MA: Harvard University Press, 2014 might be seen as continuing this line of argumentation.

2   According to Bureau of Labor Statistics data 54,712,000 of a workforce of 143,929,000 belong to 'management, professional and related occupations' as compared to just over eight million in 'production occupations'. See Household Data Annual Averages, Table 11, 'Employed Persons by Detailed Occupation, Sex, Race and Hispanic or Latino Ethnicity', 2013, available at http://www.bls.gov. It should be acknowledged, however, that grouping by occupational category avoids consideration of the relations to surplus value, supervisory authority, or discretion over knowledge production, transmission, or application that would be features of a more robust conception of class rather than the conventional classification of jobs arrayed by imputed status.

3   See Robert Reich, *The Work of Nations*, New York: Vintage, 1991. A more bleak appraisal of this divide between those relative few who master symbolic analysis and those with diminishing prospects is Tyler Cowan, *Average is Over: Powering America Beyond the Age of the Great Stagnation*, New York: Dutton, 2013.

4   Michael Hardt and Antonio Negri, *Multitude: War and Democracy in the Age of Empire*, New York: Penguin, 2004, p. 109.

5   This dilemma has been recognized in more recent contributions to the autonomist perspective. See, for example, Christian Marazzi, *The Violence of Financial Capitalism, New Edition*, Los Angeles: Semiotext, 2011, p. 61, where 'the becoming rent of profit ... is justified as a result of the capture of value produced directly outside productive spaces'.

6   Richard Florida, *The Rise of the Creative Class – Revisited 10th Anniversary Edition*, New York: Basic Books, 2012.

7   Greg Albo, Sam Gindin and Leo Panitch, *In and Out of Crisis: The Global Financial Meltdown and Left Alternatives*, Oakland, CA: PM Press, 2010; Leo Panitch and Sam Gindin, *The Making of Global Capitalism: The Political Economy of American Empire*, London: Verso, 2013; Costas Lapavitsas, *Profiting Without Producing: How Finance Exploits Us All*, London: Verso, 2014; William K. Tabb, *The Restructuring of Capitalism in Our Time*, New York: Columbia University Press, 2012; Gerard Dumenil and Dominque Levy, *The Crisis of Neoliberalism*, Cambridge, MA: Harvard University Press, 2011.

8   Dick Bryan and Mike Rafferty, *Capitalism with Derivatives: A Political Economy of Financial Derivatives, Capital and Class*, Basingstoke: Palgrave MacMillan, 2006.

9   For an account of the special features of knowledge as non-rival and partially non-excludable after Paul Romer as the basis for the new economy of productive intellectual property see David Warsh, *Knowledge and the Wealth of Nations: A Story of Economic Discovery*, New York: W.W. Norton, 2006.

10 Max Weber, *The Protestant Ethic and the Spirit of Capitalism*, New York: Routledge, 1992; Jurgen Habermas, *The Structural Transformation of the Public Sphere: An Inquiry Into a Category of Bourgeois Society*, Cambridge, MA: MIT Press, 1989.

11 Pierre Bourdieu, 'The Forms of Capital', in John G. Richardson, ed., *Handbook of Theory and Research for the Sociology of Education*, New York: Greenwood Press, 1986, pp. 241-58.

12   Angela Mitropoulos, *Contract and Contagion: From Biopolitics to Oikonomia*, Wivenhoe: Minor Compositions, 2012; Tom Baker and Jonathan Simon, eds., *Embracing Risk: The Changing Culture of Insurance and Responsibility*, Chicago: University of Chicago Press, 2002.

13   Randy Martin, *Financialization of Daily Life*, Philadelphia: Temple University Press, 2002.

14   Noam Chomsky, *American Power and the New Mandarins*, New York: Vintage 1969; Andre Gorz, *Farewell to the Working Class*, London: Pluto, 1982; Serge Mallet, *Essays on the New Working Class*, St. Louis: Telos Press, 1975; Mike Dent and Stephen Whitehead, 'Configuring the "New" Professional', in Dent and Whitehead, eds., *Managing Professional Identities: Knowledge, Performativity and the 'New' Professional*, London: Routledge, 2002; C. Derber, W. Schwartz and Y. Magrass, *Power in the Highest Degree: Professionals and the Rise of a New Mandarin Order*, New York: Oxford University Press, 1990.

15   E. O. Wright, 'Social Class', in G. Ritzer, ed., *Encyclopedia of Social Theory*, New York: Sage, 2003, available at http://www.ssc.wisc.edu.

16   Andrew Abbott, *The System of Professions: An Essay on the Division of Expert Labor*, Chicago: University of Chicago Press, 1988; Eliot Friedson, *Professionalism: The Third Logic*, Chicago: University of Chicago Press, 2001.

17   Barbara Ehrenreich and John Ehrenreich, 'The Professional Managerial Class', *Radical America*, 11(March/April), 1977, pp. 7–31 and 11(May/June), 1977, pp. 7–22.

18   Charles Derber, *Professionals as Workers: Mental Labor in Advanced Capitalism*, Boston: C. K. Hall and Co., 1982, p. 226.

19   Stephen Brint, *In an Age of Experts: The Changing Role of Professionals in Politics and Public Life*, Princeton: Princeton University Press, 1994; Jeff Schmidt, *Disciplined Minds: A Critical Look At Salaried Professionals and the Soul-Battering System That Shapes Their Lives*, Lanham, MD: Rowman and Littlefield Publishers, 2000.

20   Micki McGee, *Self-Help, Inc.*, New York: Oxford University Press, 2006.

21   N. Schwartz, 'Industries Find Surging Profits in Deeper Cuts', *New York Times*, 26 July 2010.

22   Roger Lowenstein, 'Paralyzed by Debt', *New York Times Magazine*, 18 July 2010.

23   Stanley Aronowitz and William DiFazio, *The Jobless Future* 2nd ed., Minneapolis: University of Minnesota Press, 2010.

24   These are the broad strokes of argument made in Randy Martin, *Under New Management: Universities, Administrative Labor and the Professional Turn*, Philadelphia: Temple University Press, 2011.

25   Andrew Ross, *Nice Work if You Can Get It: Life and Labor in Precarious Times*, New York: New York University Press, 2009.

26   See Ursula Huws, *The Making of a Cybertariat: Virtual Work in a Real World*, New York: Monthly Review Press, 2003; Vincent Mosco, 'The Labouring of the Public Service Principle: Union Convergence and Worker Movements in the North American Communication Industries', *Info: The Journal of Policy, Regulation and Strategy for Telecommunications, Information and Media*, 9(2/3),

2007, pp. 57-67; Catherine McKercher, *Newsworkers Unite: Labor, Convergence, and North American Newspapers*, Lanham, MD: Rowman and Littlefield Publishers, 2002.

27   For concrete manifestations of the movement to arise from debt resistance see *The Debt Resisters' Operations Manual: A Project of Strike Debt*, Oakland: PM Press, 2014.

28   See James Moliterno, *The American Legal Profession in Crisis: Resistance and Responses to Change*, Oxford: Oxford University Press, 2013.

29   Yuval Rosenberg, 'On Wall Street, Fewer Jobs But Bigger Paychecks', *The Fiscal Times*, 12 October 2012.

30   David Harvey, *The New Imperialism*, Oxford: Oxford University Press, 2005, p. 158; Carlo Vercellone, 'From Formal Subsumption to General Intellect: Elements for a Marxist Reading of the Thesis of Cognitive Capitalism', *Historical Materialism*, 15, 2007.

31   Matteo Pasquinelli, *Animal Spirits: A Bestiary of the Commons*, Rotterdam: NAi Publishers Institute of Network Cultures, 2008; Yann Moulier-Boutang, *Cognitive Capitalism*, Cambridge: Polity Press, 2011; Tiziana Terranova, *Network Culture: Politics for the Information Age*, Cambridge: Pluto Press, 2004.

32   The notion of unknown unknowns, popularized by then Secretary of Defense Donald Rumsfeld in his apologia for the pre-emptive strike in the war on terror, bears a curious resemblance to the idea of nonknowledge conceived by Georges Bataille, which is an excess of knowledge or accursed share that cannot be absorbed but that comes to define the principle of society as such. Donald Rumsfeld, 'Press Conference at NATO HQ', 2002, available at http://www. nato.int; Georges Bataille, *The Accursed Share: An Essay on General Economy, Volume 1: Consumption*, New York: Zone Books, 1988; Georges Bataille, *The Unfinished System of Nonknowledge*, Minneapolis: University of Minnesota Press, 2001, especially the essay, 'Nonknowledge, Laughter, and Tears (February 9, 1953)'.

33   These arguments are explored more fully in Randy Martin, *An Empire of Indifference: American War and the Financial Logic of Risk Management*, Durham: Duke University Press, 2007.

34   See Richard Dienst, *The Bonds of Debt: Borrowing Against the Common Good*, London: Verso, 2011; Maurizio Lazzarato, *The Making of Indebted Man: An Essay on the Neoliberal Condition*, New York: Semiotexte, 2012.

35   This idea that knowledge in circulation or price-making decision operates with some of the features of money now stretches a range of perspectives from the concept of moneyness developed in Dick Bryan and Mike Rafferty, 'Financial Derivatives and the Theory of Money', *Economy and Society*, 36(1), 2007; to the informational technology of Jaron Lanier, *Who Owns the Future?*, New York: Simon and Schuster, 2013; as well as the perspective of the commons and money put forth by Charles Eisenstein, *Sacred Economics: Money, Gift and Society in an Age of Transition*, Berkeley: Evolver, 2011.

36   Robert Meister has articulated a derivatives based politics for reparations and justice based upon options models. See his *After Evil: A Politics for Human Rights*, New York: Columbia University Press, 2011, especially Chapter 8, 'Adverse Possession'.

37 This sensibility is expressed in MacKenzie Wark, *A Hacker Manifesto*, Cambridge, MA: Harvard University Press, 2004. Gabriella Coleman in *Coding Freedom: The Ethics and Aesthetics of Hacking*, Princeton: Princeton University Press, 2012, speaks of hacking as located between craft and craftiness, invoking at once the precursor to contemporary makers in the form of the late nineteenth century arts and crafts movement associated with William Morris and the current intersection with big data.

38 Margaret Gray, *Labor and the Locavore: The Making of a Comprehensive Food Ethic*, Berkeley: University of California Press, 2013.

39 Andrew Ross, *Creditocracy: The Case for Debt Refusal*, New York: OR Press, 2014, which details the repurchase and forgiveness of debt as a Rolling Jubilee that is a concrete if small scale exemplification of student organized debt refusal being applied to medical debt.

40 This is the reading of Marx through the three volumes of *Capital* provided by Michael E. Brown in *The Production of Society: A Marxian Foundation for Social Theory*, Totowa, NJ: Rowman and Littlefield, 1986.

CLASS THEORY AND CLASS POLITICS TODAY

HUGO RADICE

In the spring of 2013, the BBC unveiled a major survey of the class structure of modern Britain, prepared by a team of sociologists led by Professor Mike Savage of the London School of Economics. The survey sought to broaden the traditional occupational analysis of class by more fully taking into account 'the role of cultural and social processes in generating class divisions', and the authors argued that 'this new seven class model recognises both social polarisation in British society and class fragmentation in its middle layers'.[1]

These two observations – of polarization and fragmentation – will certainly strike a chord with any casual observer of social change. In recent years, in many countries around the world, inequality of income, wealth and power has undoubtedly been increasing; for example in Britain, where the rise of inequality has been widely studied, often connecting inequalities of income and wealth to those in health, housing, education and other quality of life issues.[2] At the same time, the increasingly complex configurations of class, as understood in the LSE survey, have also been evident. What has traditionally been understood as the working class has been seen by many as fragmenting into layers defined as much by social standing, spending patterns and welfare dependency as by the more traditional attributes of occupation and income.[3] Meanwhile, the middle class has remained, as it has always been, hard to define with any clarity: it includes small business owners, professionals, managers and higher-skilled or supervisory workers across all sectors of the economy, public and private.

The authors of the LSE survey identify their classes in terms of people's experiences, attitudes and lifestyles, and relate these to underlying economic and social trends. Such an approach is attractive because it roots class identity in something common to all of us, namely a life-path that can be mapped out and analyzed, and because the data generated in such a survey can then be subjected to sophisticated statistical analysis. The elements selected for recording are underpinned by a particular conceptual framework, developed some thirty years ago by Pierre Bourdieu.[4] In this approach, individuals are differentiated by their possession of economic, cultural and social capital in different quantities and proportions – the three forms of capital being in principle independent of each other. The data are then analyzed in order to identify clusters of individuals – eventually in this case, seven in number – who broadly share the same economic, social and cultural characteristics.

While such a survey provides an informative snapshot of these clusters, it leaves open the question of what social processes are shaping how we cluster in this way, and how these classes-as-clusters interact with each other.[5] Some of the forces shaping the clusters are treated as distinct, if interacting, and in the final analysis attributable to factors such as technology or resource constraints that are seen as external. However, the survey is in essence a heuristic exercise rather than one of testing distinct hypotheses about social change, and the main outcome is a mapping of how the various observable changes are compatible with each other; it remains very hard to ask really important questions about society as a whole, and how social differentiation changes through time.

But the current renewed preoccupation with class also raises important questions about whether and how we can challenge the present social order. If society is really as fragmented as it immediately appears, what chance can we ever have of once again promoting the progressive ideals of democracy, equality and solidarity pursued by socialists – in the broadest sense – for the last two hundred years? The wider political environment is hardly helpful, given ever-deepening global integration which seems to undermine any sense of local or national political agency; the pervasive fracturing of most if not all societies along lines of gender, race, sexuality and religion; and the looming problem of climate change that threatens the entire relation of humanity with nature. After decades of retreat in the face of such obstacles, the global financial crisis unfolding since 2007 has led to many disparate initiatives across the world, but not as yet to any significant renewal of the left, or at least one sufficiently unified, sustained and widespread to provide cause for real optimism.

On the contrary, whether in the supposedly more advanced rich countries or elsewhere, neither social democracy nor state socialism have been able to withstand the political consequences of the new circumstances, and we have hardly begun to respond creatively. We still too readily turn to the old playbooks, clinging to the belief that the problem does not lie in how we as socialists have translated our political ideals into an effective left politics, but rather in failures of leadership, or deficiencies in our unresponsive fellow citizens. It is indeed hard, these days, to talk about socialism as any kind of real alternative, let alone to map out a politics that can build prefigurative institutions and practices that will in turn persuade others, in meaningful numbers, of the possibility of a better world.

So where do we begin? Surely, we have to campaign on many fronts. The renewed interest in inequality (such as Piketty's *Capital*[6]) is having an impact on public debate in many parts of the world. Sadly, this is not because of a real sea-change in opinion – let alone political action – among the public at large, for they display that mix of aspiration and resentment usually attributed to them by the commentariat. Rather, it is largely because to the political élites, whether liberal, social democrat or authoritarian, the gap between rich and poor has grown so wide that they fear aspiration faltering and resentment deepening into disenchantment and revolt – as much from the 'new middle classes' as from the poor and excluded.

The starting point of this essay is the proposition that the question of class is central, as argued in the preface to last year's *Socialist Register*.[7] This is not because I want in any way to suggest that it must take precedence over other issues; on the contrary, it seems obvious that the counterposing of 'class politics' against 'social movements' has been one of the main obstacles to left renewal now for forty years or more.[8] Instead, in what follows I want to argue that the painful experiences of this whole period can only be resolved through a thorough critique of the ways class has been understood.

In order to do this, I propose first to revisit Marx's original relational understanding of class, and how that understanding was taken up by later generations in the Marxist tradition, especially in the revival of debate about class from the 1960s to the 1980s. In the following sections, I look first at the analyses of the middle classes in relation to Marx's two-class model, in which the New Left sought to respond to claims that their growth had confounded Marx's expectations of social polarization. I then examine the related question of whether in any case the working class was (or still is) a revolutionary subject capable of overthrowing the capitalist order. This, then, sets up the problem of how far class relations can really be understood in relation to labour within capitalist production alone, rather than embracing also labour and other activities taking place elsewhere in society, or what has come to be called the sphere of social reproduction. Here I suggest an alternative understanding of production and labour that can effectively integrate the sphere of reproduction, and provide a better way of deploying class as a critical concept. This approach is then applied in the last section to political practice in the contemporary world, the aim being to shed light on the changes that have taken place in the neoliberal era and the political consequences that now confront us.

Finally, this essay is deliberately open and exploratory in nature. It is futile to imagine that locked within the past contributions of scholars or activists is a key that can unlock a better future. Equally futile is the time-honoured method of argument-by-quotation, with the implicit assumption that every proposition must be justified by appeals to authority, related to the study of time-honoured questions, and deploying approved terminology. That method may safeguard a tradition, but at the cost of reducing still further its appeal to a society that has plainly rejected the failed socialisms of the past.

CLASS ANALYSIS IN THE MARXIST TRADITION

For Marx there were two great classes in capitalist societies, the capitalist class or bourgeoisie and the working class or proletariat, bound together in the social relation of capital. In this view, capitalists own the means of production, and purchase labour-power from workers with the purpose of increasing their wealth by extracting surplus-value and accumulating it as capital; workers have been dispossessed of direct access to the means of subsistence through self-activity, and therefore must sell their labour-power in order to subsist. The two classes in relation to each other constitute the relations of production in capitalism, which is a historically distinct mode of production that emerges from a pre-existing feudal order undermined by economic, social and technological change. Its own development, in turn, entails a growing economic polarization between the two great classes; this generates a political consciousness uniting the working class in collective action to overturn the capitalist order and usher in a classless society.

This core 'Marxist theory of class' has been challenged and qualified on a great variety of grounds, precisely because it stands at the heart of the political theory and practice of his followers. Theoretically, the two classes and the relationship between them are co-constituted with the concepts of mode of production, relations of production, value, capital, surplus-value, labour process, accumulation – and necessarily also the forms of law and state that ensure the political rule of the capitalist class. Practically, socialism as a political movement rests on the belief that there exists a common interest across the working class, on which a unity of action can be built, first for resistance and then for revolution; this directs attention to the empirical configurations of class, the determinants of belief and behaviour, and the strategies and tactics of political mobilization.

Before turning to the main critical challenges to the two-class model, it is worth setting out the positive case for it, and especially for the idea of the working class as agent of social change. There is no question that Marx and his successors argued repeatedly that the dynamics of capital accumulation would tend to generate increasing social polarization between capitalists and workers. Even in the first volume of *Capital*, these tendencies find empirical specification in the account of how, after its initial phase of 'primitive accumulation' in which the means of production are appropriated by the rising capitalist class, both the production of commodities and their circulation are transformed by the drive to accumulate. In production, the key argument is that the 'formal' subsumption of labour to capital, in which capitalists assume control of substantively unchanged material production processes based on handicraft methods, tends to be transformed towards a 'real' subsumption of labour, entailing the development of first a detailed division of labour in factory production, and then the application of science and technology to the development of machine-based production. As Braverman, Gorz and others reminded us in the 1970s, this transformation of the capitalist labour process tends to reduce an increasing proportion of the direct labour force within the capitalist workplace to an undifferentiated mass of unskilled (or more euphemistically 'semi-skilled') workers, subjected to the relentless discipline of mechanical or chemical processes designed and policed by capitalist managers.

At the same time, competition in the marketplace reinforces this process. In the labour market, technological change in production, appearing for capital in the form of increased labour productivity, continually leads to reductions in the demand for labour, and thereby a reserve army of labour that depresses wages and undermines attempts to organize opposition on the shop floor. In product markets, competition leads inevitably to the concentration and centralization of capital: the scale of production tends to grow faster than sales, leading to concentration in ever-larger units, while the development of credit and financial markets encourages the centralization of capital through the creation and merger of joint-stock companies.

But do these developments lay the foundations for the self-organization and growth of the working class as a collective actor? The conventional understanding within Marxism has always been that the collective experience of class struggle brings home to workers their shared class interest, encouraging self-organization and political contestation. Marx and Engels themselves left no systematic account of how this might transpire, but their writings abound in concrete analyses of the political activities of the working class, analyses which necessarily can only be undertaken by successive generations in response to the contingencies of time and place. Such contingencies evidently include a vast array of natural, social and cultural factors which stand alongside the reproduction and accumulation of capital, shaping the thinking and the actions of different groups within the working class. It is this unavoidable gap between abstract theory and concrete self-activity that later Marxists summed up in the formula that the 'class in itself' had to become a 'class for itself' equipped with a collective understanding of their circumstances.[9] This gap can only be navigated by developing and contesting political strategies for overthrowing capitalist rule and ushering in a classless society. It is in this context that the validity of the two-class model has been questioned.

THE MIDDLE CLASSES

A first important challenge to the two-class model has been the existence of social groups that appear to stand between capital and labour. The empirical existence of 'middle classes' was clear to Marx and Engels themselves, and has been the subject of periodic debates ever since.[10]

Capitalism had emerged over a long historical period from societies of a very different kind, building upon components in a social division of labour which was dominated politically by a land-owning ruling class and characterized by its own distinctive relations of production. The transition to capitalism entails the continuing coexistence of earlier institutions, cultures and practices with the emerging capitalist order, and this hybridity is remarkably persistent; but in addition, the spread of capitalism generates rapid economic growth, new patterns of international trade and continuous technological change. These transform the division of labour both in society at large and within workplaces: new occupations arise and old occupations are brought within the scope of capitalist production, not only affecting the make-up of the two new great classes, but also continually generating an ill-defined border zone between them. Furthermore, these complexities are never observable in isolation from the processes of social contestation that accompany the development of capitalism.

Thus in the late nineteenth century, socialists recognized the political importance of both a 'labour aristocracy' and a 'petty bourgeoisie'. The former was made up of workers organized both to defend the skill-based material privileges that they retained from their artisanal origins, and to establish shop-floor control within the new industries of the second industrial revolution. Their generally higher levels of education and income ensured that they played a disproportionate role in the development of trade unions and social democratic parties, but it was open to such workers to pursue their own interests at the expense of the working class as a whole. This could be achieved both individually through promotion within the workplace,[11] and collectively through maintaining separate 'craft' unions and pursuing demarcation disputes against management attempts to deskill their work.

As a result, they could be drawn into political alliances with liberal reform. The petty bourgeoisie, the small proprietors in industry and commerce, were capitalists by definition, but in the face of market competition and the development of large-scale industry and finance in this period, their position became increasingly precarious, especially at times of economic crisis. They therefore gravitated politically towards populist alliances with the working class, but on the other hand, political ideologies of nationalism, racism or imperialism could suffice to keep them loyal to the *haute bourgeoisie* and the capitalist state.

Of greater interest in more recent debates have been other intermediate groups, such as managers and technical specialists in capitalist production; independent professionals such as lawyers, accountants, doctors, artists, journalists, clergy, etc.; and managers within the public sector and the state apparatus. There is no question that the occupational groups in question expanded greatly in the twentieth century in the advanced capitalist countries, and indeed in the Soviet bloc and other state-socialist countries also. At the turn of the century, Thorstein Veblen had already identified the potential antagonism between businessmen and engineers in large-scale industry, and the work of Berle and Means and James Burnham in the 1930s launched the idea of the 'managerial revolution'.[12] By the 1960s, even mainstream economists and sociologists were heralding a 'post-capitalist' order based on technical rationality and economic efficiency, and it is hard to find much difference in this respect between the 'new industrial state' of J. K. Galbraith and the ostensibly Marxist analysis of 'monopoly capital' in the work of Baran and Sweezy.[13]

In relation to these middle-class elements, Marxists have followed two main analytical strategies. One strategy is to attribute to these groups, or even by extension the middle classes as a whole, a set of activities and beliefs that seem to define a distinct location within the class structure of capitalism, which then becomes a three-class model. The second is to argue that the various components of the middle classes have no distinct function or purpose, but instead occupy a collectively ambiguous position; rather like the traditional labour aristocracy and petty bourgeoisie, they align with either the capitalist class or the working class, most visibly in periods of crisis. Both strategies were extensively deployed in European and North American debates in the 1960s and 1970s.

A well-known example of the first strategy was the thesis of the professional-managerial class, or PMC, posited in 1977 by Barbara and John Ehrenreich.[14] They distinguished the PMC from the traditional petty bourgeoisie of small proprietors, and included in it a wide range of salaried white-collar workers, including scientists, engineers, managers, public officials, teachers, journalists, accountants, lawyers and the medical professions. Citing E. P. Thompson's view that class could only be understood as a historical relationship, they argued that the specific class role of the PMC was primarily one of reproducing capitalist social relations. The occupational, educational, social and economic diversity of the PMC was no obstacle to its identification, and in any case no greater than the diversity of the capitalist class or the working class. Its rapid expansion during the post-1945 boom years was closely linked to the consolidation of monopoly capitalism and the expansion of the state, but also to the renewal of middle-class radicalism in the form of the New Left. This allowed the possibility of the PMC becoming a 'class for itself', developing a distinct political voice and purpose, and even potentially taking over the role of revolutionary agency traditionally attributed to the working class. In all respects, this placed the putative PMC of the 1970s firmly in the American progressive tradition. It also stood alongside a growing literature in mainstream US sociology that advanced 'new class' theses,[15] as well as echoing parallel thinking among dissident Marxists in Eastern Europe on the role of the intelligentsia.[16]

In contrast to the depiction of the PMC as a distinct if related class, other writers used various arguments to claim either that the occupational groups contained within it were liable to absorption into either the capitalist or the working class, or that they remained unable to cohere into a class-for-itself and were therefore irrelevant to the prospects for revolutionary change.[17] Braverman's deskilling thesis, though much misrepresented, provided ammunition to the prediction that intermediate groups were liable to undergo the same process of polarization that the original two-class model entailed. After all, the principles that Marx applied to the appropriation of workers' skills in the development of the capitalist labour process could be applied just as well to mental as to manual workers, and therefore to the various occupations included in the PMC. Since the 1970s, many low- and mid-level technical, professional and managerial occupations have indeed become more routinized, and their workers subjected to the steady erosion of the advantages that they once enjoyed in the labour market. Elements of the process of deskilling long identified in blue-collar work now apply not only to low-level clerical or retail jobs, but also to supposedly higher level jobs. The close monitoring of work processes in graduate professions such as university teaching undermines the traditional ideology of professionalism, creates antagonism between staff and senior management, and encourages traditional responses such as trade union activism.

At the same time, in the higher reaches of the PMC, the once-fêted managerial revolution has very largely been reversed. In the private sector, the revival of shareholder power, the use of stock options and widespread privatization of state enterprises have drawn the highest levels of management firmly into the capitalist class. In the public sector also, the wholesale adoption of management techniques from the private sector has steadily undermined the traditional ideology of public service, installing instead apparatuses of strategic management based on top-down executive hierarchies and financial incentives. This has been accompanied by the outsourcing of everything from policy design through to routine service provision, overseen by growing two-way managerial traffic between the public sector and its private contractors. Today, it would be hard to argue that there exists a class, in the Marxist relational sense, that is distinct from the working class and the capitalist class. The trends that have brought about the demise of the PMC are part of the wider turn to neoliberalism in recent decades, although it could still be argued that there *really was* a nascent PMC in the period from the 1920s to the 1970s.[18]

THE FRAGMENTATION OF THE WORKING CLASS AND THE PROBLEM OF AGENCY

If the working class in Marx's sense can now be understood once more to be overwhelmingly predominant in terms of numbers, it remains the case that the concept of the middle classes is very widely accepted in public debate; and the course of the global crisis since 2008 shows all too clearly how far we are from an effective class-based socialist politics. This brings us to the second critical issue for Marxist class theory, namely the question of agency: can either side of the two-class model really be seen as a historical subject? As far as the capitalist class is concerned, this centres on the historical development of capitalism, and the economic and political processes by which the capitalist class becomes hegemonic in relation to landed interests as well as subordinate classes. There is a long tradition of debate on divisions within the capitalist class, most notably between industry and finance, as well as on the institutions and practices through which individual capitals or 'fractions' of capital overcome the antagonisms generated by their competitive struggles and arrive at some form of hegemonic strategy to sustain their class rule. Any historical inquiry into these issues unavoidably has to take fully into account the development of the capitalist state, which like class was vigorously debated in the 1970s and 1980s, but more recently has been relatively neglected; the main exception being the focus on the states system in arguments over globalization.[19]

Problematic though the relation between capital and the state remains, however, the question of working-class agency is far more challenging. As noted earlier, the standard formula for this has traditionally been to distinguish between the 'class in itself' and the 'class for itself': while accumulation expanded the ranks of the working class as a structural category and concentrated them in ever-larger production sites, it would then take the active organization of workers to transform them from victims of exploitation into agents of social transformation. This analytical distinction played a crucial part in shaping socialist politics, especially in ensuring the ascendancy of political parties, whether ostensibly reformist or revolutionary, over alternative working-class agencies such as trade unions that focused either on labour market conditions or on workplace struggles. Most damaging to the grassroots political engagement of workers at large was the concept of 'false consciousness', used to justify the elimination of rank-and-file democracy in workers' organizations of all kinds.[20] But although the in-itself/for-itself distinction appears to have been largely rhetorical, it does direct us to the fragmentation of the working class across society at large, as well as the advances that have historically been achieved through party politics.

That the proletariat is differentiated in a great variety of ways is indeed clear, not least in the empirical evidence on which Marx himself drew in analyzing capitalist production in *Capital*. The social division of labour between branches of production, coupled with the technical division of labour within the workplace, means that wage labourers are highly differentiated by location, income, skill and authority, in complex combination with dimensions of difference such as gender, ethnicity and religion whose origins appear to lie outside the capitalist production process as such. In his analysis of the evolution of capitalist production from simple co-operation to manufacture to modern industry, Marx places considerable emphasis on how in the latter two stages the drive to extract relative surplus-value entails the transfer of immediate control over production from workers to capital and its agents.[21] This leads not to the reduction of all to interchangeable general labourers, but to the decomposition of earlier forms of hierarchy and division of tasks and their recomposition as elements, no less hierarchical and diverse, within the collective labourer of developed capitalist production. At the same time, he sees the shedding of employment by large-scale modern industry as providing the basis for a continuous renewal of small-scale and less technically advanced fields of production; for example, the widespread existence of adjunct production formally outside the factory, such as homework in the textiles industry, allows factory owners to transfer to petty producers the financial consequences of periodic crises. Labour shedding constantly feeds into the broader reserve army of the unemployed, but they too are differentiated into what Marx dubs the floating, the latent and the stagnant.

Despite this obvious diversity within the mid-nineteenth century workforce, there is little doubt that traditionally the primary reference point for assessing the unity and cohesion of the working class was the large factory. In his general discussion of the development of machinery in *Capital*, Marx argues that once machine-based production takes hold of an industry, the relation between the workers and their instruments of labour becomes inverted: the worker becomes the adjunct of the machine.[22] With further evolution towards a unified machinery system, workers are bound together by its preordained rhythm: the collective character of labour confronts the workers as a technical necessity. This vision of increasingly automated flow production reflects the early development of assembly-line technology, which reaches its apotheosis in the early twentieth century in Ford's Highland Park plant and in continuous flow production in the chemical and related industries; it becomes a primary subject for the analysis of modern capitalist production, whether from cheerleaders or critics, as well as a cultural reference point when contrasted with the supposed idyll of artisanal production, as in Fritz Lang's *Metropolis* or Chaplin's *Modern Times*.

In Marxist scholarship, this model of mass production is seen as dramatically accentuating the contradictions of capitalism. The need to valorize vast amounts of fixed capital accelerates the trend towards monopoly, the rise of trusts and cartels aimed at controlling markets; and at the same time, flow production systems make the collective nature of exploitation immediately apparent to the workers involved, encouraging thereby collective resistance on the shop floor and the rise of shop stewards and other forms of bottom-up self-organization. For example, Alfred Sohn-Rethel argued that the contradiction between the normal ebb and flow of price-competitive markets and the requirement of continuity of flow production amount to a 'dual economics of transition', which he identified historically in the support given by German heavy industry to the forms of state coordination and sector planning adopted by the Nazis.[23]

However, as is readily apparent to anyone examining more broadly the nature of capitalist labour processes, very few wage labourers in capitalism actually find themselves subordinated to a machine-based collective process in this way. Even within the engineering industries, heartland of the machine-paced assembly line, at the peak of manufacturing employment in the UK it was estimated that such systems covered only 30 per cent of workers.[24] The reality is that the disposition of labour in the modern workplace is for the most part not shaped by technology into an inflexible form that contradicts the fluidity that money capital seeks. As the pioneers of labour process studies showed in the 1970s, it is shaped by the choices of capitalist management and the resistance, whether individual or collective, of workers.[25] As we have seen only too clearly in recent decades, even the most apparently stable oligopolies, whether in manufacturing or services, are open to fundamental disruption through not only technological change, but also organizational innovations such as the relocation or outsourcing of production; the use of complex incentive schemes; the ever-closer monitoring of production activity through information systems; and above all, the constant and recently all too successful efforts of employers to remove hard-won legal rights from trade unions.

Already in 1986, Peter Meiksins suggested that the debates on class, and specifically the relation between the 'polar' model and the evident vertical and horizontal fracturing of the workforce in capitalism, required that 'the relationship between production relations and specific, historical patterns of class conflict needs to be reconsidered'.[26] Yet with the general decline in interest in class, these adjustments have not taken place, or at least not with the positive outcome that Meiksins hoped for. Indeed, the lack of progress is reflected in the similar call made nearly twenty years later by David Camfield, who draws attention not only to the continuing need to situate classes historically, but also to 'consciously incorporate social relations other than class, such as gender and race'.[27] In the remaining sections I will try to explain this and to suggest ways to begin to effect such changes in theory and in practice, and particularly to overcome the divisions that currently beset us in challenging the present social order.

CAPITALIST PRODUCTION AND SOCIAL REPRODUCTION

While the 1970s debates on the capitalist labour process certainly included consideration of this fragmentation of the working class, the turn to analyzing production and work also coincided with the rise of Marxist and feminist (including explicitly Marxist-feminist) work on the political economy of gender, where an important topic was the role of unwaged household work in capitalism, and more generally the reproduction of labour-power outside the direct production and sale of commodities.[28] One way of looking at reproduction was in terms of the vexed question of productive and unproductive labour, but looking back it is clear that the valiant attempts to sort this out by close study of Marxist texts never got very far. The role of non-wage labour in reproducing capitalism could not be denied, but as with work on the labour process, its critical analysis did not fundamentally transform Marxist theory and analysis as might have been expected.

In a recent essay, Nancy Fraser has sought to explore the reasons why 'we are living through a capitalist crisis of great severity without a critical theory that could adequately clarify it ... we lack conceptions of capitalism and capitalist crisis that are adequate to our time'.[29] She sees Marx's analysis as attributing four key features to capitalism: in order of precedence, they are private property, which presupposes the standard two-class division; the free labour market, through which non-capitalists must secure their subsistence and reproduction; the capitalists' compulsive pursuit of the accumulation of self-expanding value; and the distinctive role of markets, which allocate inputs to commodity production and determine how society's surplus is invested. This last element, she argues, should not be understood as an 'ever-increasing commodification of life as such', because the overall reproduction of capitalist society actually depends on a wide range of activities that do not take place within the production and exchange of commodities.[30] While Marx goes behind the appearance of capitalist markets as equal exchange by finding the secret of exploitation in the hidden abode of production, Fraser identifies social reproduction in abodes that are in turn hidden behind production. She argues that Marx only broaches such issues in his historical introduction to the rise of capitalism in Part VIII of *Capital I*, and we now need to explore these yet-more-hidden abodes. Social reproduction, she argues, is an 'indispensable background condition for the possibility of capitalist production ... moreover, the division between social reproduction and commodity production is central to capitalism – indeed, is an artefact of it'.[31] The remainder of her essay then explores these doubly hidden abodes, setting out a range of propositions on their relation to capitalist production and their role in capitalist crisis.

While I sympathize with Fraser's rejection of the 'dystopian fantasy' of ever-increasing commodification, her analysis of Marx ignores some very important elements in his critique of political economy – elements that, if restored to consideration, do much to soften the impact of her arguments, and point to a different way of placing social reproduction firmly at the heart of the analysis of class and of crisis. Fundamentally, this concerns Fraser's characterization of Marx's critique of capitalist production as 'economic' in content, and implicitly structural-functionalist rather than historical in method. The four features that she ascribes to Marx are set out in the opening two parts of *Capital*, which are highly abstract in content. However, if we read on into the later parts, we find not only the famous hidden abode of production, but also precisely Fraser's doubly hidden abodes of social reproduction. There we can find ample evidence that Marx's critique incorporated concretely not only aspects of the social order that would be understood, in the fragmented obscurity of bourgeois thought, as social, political, cultural or technological, but also the relation of humanity to nature. This is certainly not 'economics' as mainstream social science would define it; on the contrary, in discussing issues like the length of the working day, the forms that wages take in capitalist employment, or the effects of machinery on workplace relations, Marx draws extensively on the concrete experiences of workers, and on the social conditions that they endure at home, in their communities and in their relations with the state.

None of this is to claim that reading *Capital* is all we need to do, that somehow from Marx's brow there sprang forth a complete workshop manual for revolutionaries that would forever suffice us; or indeed that the task he bequeathed to us was simply to write the remaining books which he indicated (in a few casual passages which he himself never revised for publication) would round out the analysis. It is obvious, given the history of the twentieth century, not only that it is impossible to derive a completion from the fetishistic search for truth in Marx's own writings, but also that whole swathes of historical change have occurred which were not visible in Marx's lifetime – not least, the progress that has been made in addressing sources of oppression that lie outside capitalism as such. But that is precisely why the main benefits to be derived from studying Marx lie in his *method* of inquiry, which is developed in the opening chapters of *Capital* and exemplified not only in the historical account of the closing chapters, but also the chapters of concrete analysis of his own time that lie between.

So how does Marx go about his critique? There is a vast literature on Marx's method available for those who wish to mull over the many ways of answering this question, but I think it really boils down to a few basic principles. First, historical materialism entails locating social inquiry in historical context, using the principle of identifying those institutions, ideas and practices that together constitute distinct ways in which humanity structures its relationship to nature, that is, social reproduction. Social reproduction is indeed the primary purpose of social inquiry, and Fraser is right to privilege it over production insofar as she sees production as a narrowly economic process. Second, the historical thread running through Marx's analysis of the capitalist mode of production is not to be identified with specific visible features of capitalism (as in Fraser's list of property, free labour, accumulation and markets). Rather, it consists in the possibility of historical transcendence, of humanity developing a conscious and collective self-control, which Marx traces from its most abstract representation in the form of the commodity through to its most concrete historical manifestations in struggles over the organization of social reproduction.

Marx's *Capital* is not built around a historical account of capitalism, but around a critique of political economy, that is, the core ideology of the ascendant capitalist class. At the heart of this ideology, he reasons, lies the concept of the self-regulating market, freed from bondage to sovereign or state, and therefore his analysis begins with the commodity as the object of market exchange. He uncovers first the dual nature of commodities as useful objects (use-value) and as the carriers of exchange-value. He suggests that the exchange of two distinct use-values in definite quantities indicates that they have something in common, namely that they are products of labour. The value of a commodity is the amount of socially necessary labour embodied in it, abstracting from the specific or concrete labour that makes the product useful in meeting social needs. The labour undertaken by a worker in producing a commodity likewise has a dual character, as concrete useful labour, and as abstract value-producing labour, a distinction that is specifically absent in the apologetics of bourgeois political economy. The significance of this is brought out in the section on the fetishism of commodities, where he makes repeated presentations of the point from different perspectives.

This dual character of labour provides the starting point from which Marx elaborates his critique.[32] The elaboration follows a very specific sequence of concepts, first in the sphere of circulation from the commodity to labour to money to capital to surplus-value and exploitation. Then he goes into the sphere of production, where the labour process reproduces not only the commodities that go into it, but also capitalists, the workers and the social relations between them, through the extraction of surplus-value and the subsumption of labour to capital. Finally, he returns in Part V to circulation, where that surplus-value is realized, distributed and accumulated as capital. The way the analysis unfolds mirrors deliberately the circuit of capitalist production, because that is the reality that lies behind the veil of commodity fetishism, the 'magic of the market'. Along the way there emerges not only the capitalist, but also the worker; not only individuals pursuing their personal self-interest through free exchange, but capital and labour as social categories and as classes; not only the freedom of the market, but the coercion of the state; not only the apparent and common-sense logic of capital accumulation as organizing the production and sale of useful commodities, but the division of society into exploiters and exploited, the ravaging of communities and of nature, and all the hidden injuries of class.

However, there also appears at every stage of the argument the possibility of a different social order that humanity could establish, not on ideals plucked from the air, but on the basis of negating capitalist commodity production.[33] As a historical mode of production, capitalism contains within it not only the realm of value, the relentless logic that bourgeois political economy represents and tries to naturalize, but also the realm of use-value. In every facet of social production and reproduction, these two realms co-exist: the one driven by the imperative of capital accumulation, and the other by the application of labour time to nature to meet humanity's transhistorical need for subsistence.

Where does class, in the sense of the two-class model, fit in to this? Surely it is part of the realm of value; and just as surely, the potential for its negation – a classless society – lies in the realm of use-value, where concrete useful labour is expended to meet social needs. When Marx's two-class model is situated within the duality revealed by his critique of bourgeois thought, the historical character of its imposition upon society is revealed, and the possibility of its supercession also. Precisely because the capitalist form of class rule is co-constituted with the realm of value and capital, the starting point for its supercession must lie outside it, in aspects of society that must continue beyond capitalism, albeit in a different form. To envision socialism as a realm of freedom, and develop social practices that can begin to realize it, we have to start from use-values, concrete labour and social needs. This is what the critics of class politics have been arguing for; but it does not require the ditching of Marx's analysis of capital and class, only its re-interpretation as a critique of political economy rather than as Marxist economics.

FINDING BRIDGES TO SOCIALISM IN CAPITALISM TODAY

If the investigation of method in the previous section allows us to integrate the politics of production and of reproduction, then equally it can be argued that Marx's relational model of class, which is historically specific to capitalism, is generally compatible with sociological delineations of classes based like that of Savage and his collaborators upon the identification of clusters of economic, social and cultural characteristics within society. More than that, the integration of the two approaches to class into a single ontological and epistemological framework allows the weaknesses of each to be addressed. On the one hand, the real fragmentation of the 'relational' working class clearly bedevils attempts to develop an emancipatory politics of sufficiently wide appeal to mount a serious challenge to capitalism as it actually exists and as it is perceived. On the other hand, as noted at the outset, starting from the subjective attitudes and social practices of different segments of society makes it hard to see the wood for the trees – to grasp the commonalities that are concealed by a hegemonic common sense centred on individual aspirations in relation to property and consumption.

Nowhere has this been more visible recently than in the frustrating inability of 'the 99 per cent' identified by the Occupy movement to develop from a visceral hostility to the remaining 1 per cent into a serious political challenge to neoliberalism. The newer slogans of the social movements seem to have little more purchase than the older ones of the traditional labour movement, even when the two are able to coalesce at least in identifying the object of their wrath, as they did for a few years following the Battle of Seattle in 1999. What is more, as the current crisis has gone on, the common experience of shock and dislocation following the financial crash has been replaced by marked differences in how the resolution of the crisis affects different groups: not only between employed and unemployed, or skilled and unskilled, but between different countries and regions. In Britain, the coalition government and most of the media have scapegoated welfare recipients (whether unemployed, or receiving incomes so low that they must be topped up with state benefits) and above all immigrants, in a deliberate divide-and-rule strategy. Meanwhile, German workers protected from austerity policies have shown little or no solidarity either with their less-protected fellow Germans, or with workers in the Eurozone 'periphery' whose governments have been blamed for the crisis and forced to impose unprecedented cuts in living standards and state provision alike. The differential economic impact of crisis policies on women has also been widely noted.[34] Across the globe, employers and governments alike beat the drum of 'international competitiveness': work harder and longer, do as you're told, invest in skills (at your own expense) and then, just maybe, you can avoid losing your job to those industrious Chinese (Mexicans, Turks, etc.). Further, a crucial feature of capitalism in its modern neoliberal form is that the individualistic logic of competition is imposed far beyond the realm of capitalist production alone: such as within the higher education sector that employs many of you reading this, and even, it now seems, in the 'production' of protest.[35]

But this is the ideology of capital, the world seen from the standpoint of the law of value and the compulsion of profit. Meanwhile, within not only capitalist production, but also within the spheres of reproduction that lie outside the factory or office – those that Fraser identifies as doubly hidden – other forces are at work in contradiction to that ideology. In capitalist production, the relentless drive to deskill and control workers runs up, with equal necessity, against the capitalist's unavoidable dependence upon human beings. In his critique of the Ehrenreichs' thesis that the work of engineers essentially reproduces the pursuit of profit and thus the rule of capital, David

Noble insisted on the continuing ideology of professionalism that remains rooted in the exercise of scientific and practical knowledge, and the non-pecuniary satisfactions obtained from such work.[36] Much further down the workplace status hierarchy, Paul Durrenberger and Dimitra Doukas have argued that a 'gospel of work' continues to act as a counterweight to the 'gospel of wealth' among the US working class.[37]

More generally, the apparently abstract concept of the 'collective labourer' developed by Marx in his analysis of machinery and modern industry does not simply represent, as many people claim, the strategy of 'capital in command'; it also contains within it the necessity for elements of that collective labourer – in other words, individual workers – to combine their concrete activities creatively. Outside of the much-mythologized but rarely achieved 'fully automated' production process, most of us have to exercise our imagination and combine our talents with those of others in tasks from the most mundane to the most esoteric. If socialism is the 'free association of producers', then the capitalist workplace willy-nilly provides a foretaste of it. Nearly fifty years ago, in a relatively short chapter near the end of his study of Marx's *Capital*, Roman Rosdolsky examined what he called 'the historical limits of the law of value'.[38] He argued that contrary to the usual assertion that Marx was unwilling to make any predictions about a future socialist society, we 'constantly encounter discussions and remarks in *Capital*, and the works preparatory to it, which are concerned with the problems of a socialist society'. His suggestion that Marx's method both directs our attention to the historical past, and posits the 'historic presuppositions for a new state of society', supports the idea that bridges can indeed be found towards socialism within everyday capitalist production.

What about the work of social reproduction that takes place in households, in recuperative leisure activities, or in voluntary associations of all kinds that supplement or even replace the state-funded provision of goods or services? Surely it demonstrates also the unavoidable dependence of tasks, however mandated and by whom, upon concrete labour that entails forethought, initiative and creativity by individuals, typically exercised in cooperation with others. Insofar as such forms of labour shift to and fro across the boundary between capitalist and non-capitalist production, there is little change in the concrete labour performed; what changes is whether it generates pecuniary reward, and how far that reward is diminished by the interposing of private capital in the production process.

We should therefore look upon the world of work – by which I mean *all* kinds of work, not just that which takes place in the framework of capitalist wage-labour – not only as an external and alienating form of subordination to the other. It is equally, as Marx put it, 'the everlasting Nature-imposed condition of human existence, and therefore is independent of every social phase of that existence, or rather, is common to every such phase'.[39] But this very universality needs to be recognized, and to be seen as fundamental to the construction of a movement whose class purpose is, quite simply, the abolition of class society.

At this point we have to return to the vexed question of politics – no longer a politics 'of' class or a 'working-class politics', but a politics *against* class. This requires, in the first place, that we stop being coy about our eventual purpose, and start to spell out what exactly we envisage as the constitutive features of a post-capitalist society. By breaking this down into a picture of social needs and creative activities under socialism which people can compare directly with their day-to-day experiences under capitalism, we can challenge the relentless drumbeat of 'there is no alternative'. Capitalism is not a natural order, it is a social order; constructed by people in interaction with each other, it can equally be demolished and replaced. This is nothing more nor less than the original purpose of the Social Forum movement, to all appearances sidelined by the crisis of 2007-08 and its aftermath, but even at its most vigorous, bedevilled by the remnants of the failed party politics of the last century.

This leads to a second requirement: that we face up to the painful lessons of those failures. How can the grotesque inequalities of wealth and power in capitalism be challenged politically, if not by a robust insistence on the equal participation of all in any meaningful movement for change? This has to be rooted in the principles of citizenship and democracy that drove the pursuit of social justice in centuries past: there must be no more easy dismissal of 'bourgeois democracy', or insistence that enlightenment can only be brought to 'the masses' by a party élite. How many more attempts will be made to establish parties on the left in pursuit of the holy grail of a revolutionary politics that will brook no compromise with bourgeois politics? If we accept that bridges exist in day-to-day life that can help us to develop a popular and powerful movement for socialism, then there is nothing to be lost by working within existing organizations, whether parties, unions or social movements of all kinds. Given the compromises that we are forced to make every day of our lives, surely we can live with compromises in our political work; in many countries we have opportunities to do this in social democratic or green parties in which we will find people who share some vision of a better world. Above all, no amount of work to develop a more enlightening analysis of present-day capitalism is going to deliver a political awakening without a great deal of hard graft in the real world of compromised lives and confused aspirations. Perhaps it is time to read and write less, and instead plunge in to that world.

NOTES

This essay is part of a larger project on the critique of political economy and the prospects for socialism (see the citations in footnotes 7, 17 and 37). For advice and encouragement I am grateful to Logie Barrow, Anthony Barzey, Paul Blackledge, Dave Byrne, David Camfield, Daniele Tepe-Belfraege, Alfredo Saad-Filho, the editors of the *Socialist Register* and members of the CSE Transpennine Working Group.

1   Mike Savage et al., 'A New Model of Social Class? Findings from the Great British Class Survey Experiment', *Sociology*, 47(2), 2013, p. 220.

2   Richard Wilkinson and Kate Pickett, *The Spirit Level: Why More Equal Societies Almost Always Do Better*, London: Allen Lane, 2009; Daniel Dorling, *The No-Nonsense Guide to Inequality*, Oxford: New Internationalist, 2012; George Irvin, *Super Rich: The Rise in Inequality in Britain and the United States*, Cambridge: Polity Press, 2008.

3   See for example Owen Jones, *Chavs: The Demonization of the Working Class*, London: Verso, 2011; and Guy Standing, *The Precariat: The New Dangerous Class*, London: Bloomsbury, 2011.

4   Pierre Bourdieu, *Distinction*, London: Routledge, 1984.

5   Furthermore, the methodology of the LSE/BBC survey has been severely criticized by Colin Mills, 'The Great British Class Fiasco: A Comment on Savage et al.', *Sociology*, 48(3), 2014, pp. 437-44.

6   Thomas Piketty, *Capital in the Twenty-First Century*, Cambridge, MA: Harvard University Press, 2014.

7   Leo Panitch, Greg Albo and Vivek Chibber, 'Preface', *Socialist Register 2014: Registering Class*, London: Merlin Press, 2013, pp. ix-xi. This essay also draws on Hugo Radice, 'The Idea of Socialism: From 1968 to the Present-Day Crisis', *Antipode: A Radical Journal of Geography*, 41(S1), 2010, pp. 27-49; and 'The Prospects for Socialism: A Question of Capital and Class', in Henry Veltmeyer, ed., *21st-Century Socialism: Reinventing the Project*, Halifax, Nova Scotia: Fernwood Publishing, 2011.

8   See Sheila Rowbotham, Lynne Segal and Hilary Wainwright, *Beyond the Fragments: Feminism and the Making of Socialism*, 3rd edition, London: Merlin Press, 2013. On patriarchy in particular, see Heidi Hartmann, 'The Unhappy Marriage of Marxism and Feminism: Towards a More Progressive Union', *Capital & Class*, 8, 1979, pp. 1-33.

9   See David Camfield, 'Re-Orienting Class Analysis: Working Classes as Historical Formations', *Science & Society*, 68(4), 2005, esp. pp. 421-30.

10   For broadly Marxist accounts of the debates see Pat Walker, ed., *Between Labour and Capital*, Hassocks: Harvester Press, 1979; Nicholas Abercrombie and John Urry, *Capital, Labour and the Middle Classes*, London: Allen & Unwin, 1983; Bob Carter, *Capitalism, Class Conflict and the New Middle Class*, London:

Routledge & Kegan Paul, 1985; Erik Olin Wright, ed., *The Debate on Classes*, London: Verso, 1989; and Rosemary Crompton, *Class and Stratification: An Introduction to Current Debates*, Cambridge: Polity Press, 1993.

11   Thus Marx himself discusses the need in capitalist production, from its outset, for a 'special kind of wage-labourer' to supervise the work process: see Karl Marx, *Capital: A Critique of Political Economy, Volume I*, London: Lawrence & Wishart, 1970, p. 332.

12   See Thorstein Veblen, *The Theory of Business Enterprise*, New York: Charles Scribner's Sons, 1904; Adolf Berle and Gardner Means, *The Modern Corporation and Private Property*, New York: Macmillan, 1932; James Burnham, *The Managerial Revolution: Or, What is Happening in the World Now*, New York: John Day, 1941.

13   John Kenneth Galbraith, *The New Industrial State*, London: Deutsch, 1972; Paul Baran and Paul Sweezy, *Monopoly Capital: An Essay on the American Economic and Social Order*, New York: Monthly Review Press, 1966.

14   Barbara Ehrenreich and John Ehrenreich, 'The Professional-Managerial Class', *Radical America*, 11(2), 1977, pp. 7-31; and 'The New Left and the Professional-Managerial Class', *Radical America*, 11(3), 1977, pp. 7-22. Walker, *Between Labour and Capital*, includes critical assessments of their work by ten US left academics and activists. For other 'non-proletarianization' theses see Abercrombie and Urry, *Capital, Labour*, ch. 5.

15   A notable example is Alvin Gouldner, *The Future of Intellectuals and the Rise of the New Class*, New York: Seabury Press, 1979; see also the survey by Charles Kurzman and Lynne Owens, 'The Sociology of Intellectuals', *Annual Review of Sociology*, 28, 2002, pp. 63-90.

16   Hugo Radice, 'Marxism in Eastern Europe: From Socialist Dissidence to Capitalist Restoration', *Socialist History*, 42, 2012, pp. 43-59. For an integrated critical analysis of new class theories in capitalism and in Soviet socialism, see Lawrence King and Iván Szelényi, *Theories of the New Class: Intellectuals and Power*, Minneapolis: University of Minnesota Press, 2004.

17   For example Harry Braverman, *Labour and Monopoly Capital*, New York: Monthly Review Press, 1974; and Guglielmo Carchedi, *On the Economic Identification of Social Classes*, London: Routledge & Kegan Paul, 1977. See also Abercrombie and Urry, *Capital, Labour*, ch. 4.

18   The neoliberal demise of the PMC has been acknowledged by Barbara Ehrenreich and John Ehrenreich in 'Death of a Yuppie Dream: The Rise and Fall of the Professional-Managerial Class', New York: Rosa Luxemburg Stiftung, 2013, available at http://www.rosalux-nyc.org.

19   See notably Stanley Aronowitz and Peter Bratsis, eds, *Paradigm Lost: State Theory Reconsidered*, Minneapolis: University of Minnesota Press, 2002. Geoffrey Ingham has examined closely the forging of ruling class unity through the emerging hegemony of monetary wealth in *Capitalism*, Cambridge, UK: Polity Press, 2008.

20   The concept of false consciousness cannot be attributed to Marx. See J. McCarney, 'Ideology and False Consciousness', 2005, available at http://marxmyths.org.

21 See Marx, *Capital*, Part IV, and for the rest of this paragraph, see esp. ch. XV, sec. 3, 4 and 8.

22 Marx, *Capital*, ch. XV, sec. 1.

23 Alfred Sohn-Rethel, 'The Dual Economics of Transition', in Conference of Socialist Economists, *The Labour Process and Class Strategies*, London: Stage 1, 1976, pp. 26-45; and *Economy and Class Structure of German Fascism*, London: CSE Books, 1978.

24 See D. T. N. Williamson, 'The Anachronistic Factory', *Proceedings of the Royal Society of London*, A/331(1585), 1972, pp. 131-60.

25 See for example André Gorz, ed., *The Division of Labour: The Labour Process and Class Struggle in Modern Capitalism*, Brighton: Harvester, 1976; Richard Edwards, *Contested Terrain*, New York: Basic Books, 1979; Maxine Berg, ed., *Technology and Toil in Nineteenth Century Britain: Documents*, London: CSE Books, 1979.

26 Peter Meiksins, 'Beyond the Boundary Question', *New Left Review*, I/157, 1986, p. 110.

27 Camfield, 'Re-Orienting Class Analysis', p. 421. See also his more recent essay, 'Theoretical Foundations of an Anti-Racist Queer Feminist Historical Materialism', *Critical Sociology*, forthcoming.

28 For an excellent introduction to this question see Valerie Bryson, 'Production and Reproduction', in Georgina Blakely and Valerie Bryson, eds., *Marx and Other Four-Letter Words*, London: Pluto Press, 2005 (with thanks to Daniele Tepe-Belfraege for referring me to this source).

29 Nancy Fraser, 'Behind Marx's Hidden Abode: For an Expanded Conception of Capitalism', *New Left Review*, II/86, 2014, p. 56.

30 Fraser, 'Behind Marx's Hidden Abode', p. 59.

31 Fraser, 'Behind Marx's Hidden Abode', pp. 61-2.

32 This 'dialectics of labour' can also be understood as part of a historicist understanding of Marx, in which there is no sharp break found between his 'early' and 'mature' work. See Paul Walton and Andrew Gamble, *From Alienation to Surplus Value*, London: Sheed and Ward, 1972, esp. ch. 2, 'Alienation and the Dialectics of Labour', pp. 24-50.

33 This point is explored in Hugo Radice, 'Utopian Socialism and Marx's *Capital*: Envisioning Alternatives', in Lucia Pradella and Tom Marois, eds., *Polarizing Development: Alternatives to Neoliberalism and the Crisis*, Pluto Press, forthcoming.

34 See for example Jill Rubery and Anthony Rafferty, 'Women and Recession Revisited', *Work, Employment And Society*, 27(3), 2013, pp. 414-32.

35 On universities, see Andrew McGettigan, *The Great University Gamble: Money, Markets and the Future of Higher Education*, London: Pluto Press 2013; on campaigning, see Peter Dauvergne and Genevieve LeBaron, *Protest Inc: The Corporatization of Activism*, Cambridge: Polity Press, 2014.

36 David Noble, 'The PMC: a Critique', in Walker, *Between Labour and Capital*, pp. 121-42.

37 See E. Paul Durrenberger and Dimitra Doukas, 'Gospel of Wealth, Gospel of Work: Counterhegemony in the US Working Class', *American Anthropologist*, 110(2), 2008, pp. 214-25. For more on US working-class politics see

Paul Durrenberger, *American Fieldnotes: Collected Essays of an Existentialist Anthropologist*, West Branch, Iowa: Draco Hill Press, 2013; and Michael Yates, *In and Out of the Working Class*, Winnipeg: Arbeiter Ring Publishing, 2009; and on the UK, Selina Todd, *The People: The Rise and Fall of the Working Class, 1910-2010*, London: John Murray, 2014.

38   Roman Rosdolsky, *The Making of Marx's 'Capital'*, London: Pluto Press, 1977, ch. 28 (originally published in German in 1968). The quotations below are at p. 414 (the second quotation is from Marx, *Grundrisse: Foundations of the Critique of Political Economy*, Harmondsworth: Penguin Books, 1973, p. 461). See also the comprehensive account of Marx's concept of socialism in Peter Hudis, *Marx's Concept of the Alternative to Capitalism*, Chicago: Haymarket Books, 2013.

39   Marx, *Capital*, p. 184.

LABOUR AND THE LEFT IN THE USA
A Symposium

THE POLITICS OF US LABOUR: PARALYSIS AND POSSIBILITIES

KIM MOODY AND CHARLES POST

After nearly thirty years of political and economic retreat, the US labour movement is facing what is possibly its most serious crisis since the early 1930s. Historically, the US labour officialdom has practiced what we have called 'bureaucratic business unionism'.[1] Conceiving themselves as business people engaged in the sale of their members' labour-power, the leadership of the US unions have relied upon the National Labour Relations Board, and the resulting alliance with the pro-capitalist Democratic Party, to insure the regulation of labour-management relations since the late 1930s. The framework of industry-based pattern bargaining over wages, hours and working conditions (and the reliance on the bureaucratic grievance procedure to enforce written contracts) collapsed in the late 1970s. In the face of an aggressive capitalist offensive, the US labour bureaucracy has engaged in continuous *concessions bargaining*, reintroducing competition over wages and conditions among workers in the same industry, while seeking greater 'cooperation' with management and abandoning contract enforcement through routine grievance handling.

Since the onset of the global recession in 2008, the US labour movement has faced even greater challenges. Sectors of the US capitalist class and their Republican political representatives are going beyond the bipartisan calls for 'sacrifice' – more concessions in collective bargaining and the acceptance of neoliberal state policies. Today, the very *institutional basis* of the US trade union movement – state regulated union recognition and collective bargaining – are under attack across the United States.

Overall union density reached a post-Second World War height of 24.1 per cent in 1981. In 2013, only 11.2 per cent of US workers are members of a union.[2] The drop among *private sector* workers is even starker, from 24.2 per cent in 1973 to a mere 6.7 per cent in 2013. Only the public sector unions have gained density, rising from 23 per cent in 1973 to a height of 38.7 per cent in 1994, falling to 35.3 per cent in 2013, with even that under threat.

PRIVATE SECTOR UNION DECLINE:
'DEINDUSTRIALIZATION'?

The dramatic decline of private sector unionism since the 1970s is often attributed to deindustrialization or the flight of industry abroad. Yet the United States produces more goods today than ever. With the usual ups and downs, real industrial output has increased by over 200 per cent since the mid-1960s. As a percent of real GDP, measured by final product, goods production rose from 22 per cent during the 1960s and 1970s to 28 per cent in the 2000s and 31 per cent in 2010-12.[3] The loss of jobs in manufacturing has been great, but the loss of union members in manufacturing has been even greater. The number of production workers in manufacturing fell from 12,571,000 in 1994 to 8,444,000 in 2013, a drop of 33 per cent. The number of union members in manufacturing over the same period fell from 3,514,000 to 1,431,000, a decrease of 60 per cent.[4] Thus, while the employment loss explains about half of union decline, it cannot explain it all. Nor is this employment loss due mainly to lost production.

The major underlying causes of private sector union retreat lie in the geographic shift in manufacturing and related industries to the South that began after the Second World War, on the one hand; and, on the other, in the enormous productivity increases since the early 1980s due largely to the generalization of 'lean production'.[5] Value added by manufacturing in the South rose from 18 per cent of the US total in 1963 to 30.6 per cent in 1999, and 32.1 per cent in 2009.[6] In a somewhat belated recognition of the fact that the South is 'a major player in the new global economy and has become a haven for US manufacturing, foreign investments and finance capital', the AFL-CIO determined at its 2013 convention 'to develop a Southern organizing strategy'.[7] The defeat of the United Auto Workers at VW's Chattanooga, Tennessee plant in early 2014 is not a promising sign for such a project unless some lessons about the UAW's 'cooperative' approach toward management are learned.[8]

What has brought about the decline of the goods producing workforce is the productivity increases capital has extracted from labour since the long upturn that began in 1983. Since its appearance in the US in the 1980s, lean production has morphed into or been combined with various methods of extracting more work for less wages, such as Total Quality Management (TQM), modular and cellular production, or, under new brand names, CIM Logic's Manufacturing Execution System (MES) software. In the last decade and a half, practices once associated with auto plants have spread to all kinds of employment settings. In hospitals, to take one example, Six Sigma, a computerized Clinical Decision Support Systems (CDSS) and 'supply chain management' system, has been employed to guide the provision of healthcare as rapidly as possible. As with all applications of lean production, the standardization of healthcare has been one result, understaffing the other.[9]

Advocates of the 'high-wage, high-road' approach that often underlies labour-management cooperation programmes stress the combination of Human Resource Management 'best' practices with lean production organization creates a High Performance Work System (HPWS) which creates productivity gains and, therefore, higher wages. However, a 2004 study shows that such combinations seldom produce significant wage increases for non-management employees.[10] In a similar vein, a 2010 survey of Canadian manufacturing workers revealed, not surprisingly, that most preferred traditional work organization to 'Alternative Work Practices' and Human Resource Practices.[11]

Lean production methods along with just-in-time delivery systems, increased outsourcing or decentralizing of intermediate parts production (a major feature of lean production), and the rise of the 'Big Box' retailers have brought about another major change in both work and the workforce. Logistics, that combination of computer-driven intermodal transportation and vast warehouse centres that feed retailers like Wal-Mart on a just-in-time basis, have given rise to a growing 'blue collar' workforce. The number of production workers in transportation and warehousing rose from 2,545,100 in 1985 to 3,930,800 in 2013, an increase of 55 per cent.[12] To this must be added an unknown portion of the half a million who work in telecommunications and data processing. Some of these workers in transportation and telecommunications are already in unions, while many of those in warehousing are attempting to organize. Their efforts may be aided by the huge concentrations of warehouse workers in three 'hub' centres: 'the "Inland Empire" east of Los Angeles, a giant complex southwest of Chicago, and distribution centers along the New Jersey Turnpike'. Such intermodal systems are highly vulnerable to the actions of strategically placed groups of workers.[13]

For some time advances in logistics have increased intra-firm 'trade' in intermediate parts, some of it across borders within North America. That is, companies decentralize parts production, often to remote sites. As a study of logistics in Canadian affiliates of US corporations concluded, 'This reorganization generally involved adoption of JIT [just in time] logistics, global standardization of parts and processes, use of globally standardized common components across varieties of differentiated products, systems of global tracking of parts and components, and global sourcing. All these factors increased intra-firm trade in intermediates'.[14] This also applies to actual outsourcing to non-affiliated firms in the supply chain. In other words, the reorganization of intermodal transportation as logistics has facilitated the geographic dispersion of industry in North America. This means more outsourcing has occurred and more lean methods introduced with their impact on productivity, explaining some loss of manufacturing jobs as well as movement away from unionized firms and regions. It also explains the loss of railroad jobs, which are at the centre of logistics. So the three-person team that operated freight trains not so long ago has been reduced to two and now the employers want to cut it to one – the engineer.[15] Thus, the combination of lean production and advanced logistics also explains the loss of union jobs *within* unionized industries and firms as jobs are lost to lean methods or moved to non-union sites.

Overall, the generally high levels of productivity, in combination with the recession beginning in 2008, meant that the number of production workers in manufacturing fell from 12,550,000 in 1985 to 8,444,000 in 2013, with almost half of that drop occurring between 2006 and 2010, after which manufacturing employment rose again somewhat. But the shift from goods production to service providing continued to reshape the US working class. Altogether, the industrial core of the working class, including goods production, transportation and warehousing, utilities and information, has fallen from 32 per cent of the workforce in the 1980s to 21.4 per cent of all production workers in 2010-13.[16] The working class as a whole, however, has continued to grow. Many service-producing employees are exploited workers, many of them value producers. A good example of this are the 4.5 million hospital workers, whose industry has been reorganized along profit-making, increasingly capital intensive, capitalist lines in the last thirty years, who are joining unions at a faster rate than most workers.[17] Many more 'service' workers are among the most poorly paid. Thus, while the average hourly private sector wage in 2010 was $19.07, and that in manufacturing $18.61, the 11 million who work in accommodation and food services averaged $10.68 an hour.[18] Some value-producing workers are hidden in 'service' categories, such as the 2.7 million workers employed by employment agencies, many of whom actually work in manufacturing, transportation and warehousing or in hospitals. Indeed, as of 2005, 28 per cent of temp agency employees worked in manufacturing.[19]

Contrary to what many believe, about 90 per cent of all employed people in the US work in traditional employer-employee arrangements, with 83 per cent of those in full-time work. Bureau of Labor Statistics surveys done in 1995 and 2005 both showed that those working in 'alternative arrangements', such as independent contractors or temp agency workers, consistently compose about 10 per cent of the workforce.[20] There are no more recent figures for most of these non-traditional work arrangements. But while the number of those working through 'employment services' soared from 1,512,000 in 1990 to 3,849,000 in 2000, by 2010 their number had fallen to 2,717,000, a drop of 1,132,000.[21] Even if those in non-traditional jobs increase significantly as employers seek to expand production without taking on permanent hires, they are certain to remain a distinct minority. The vast majority of workers still have a workplace and a recognizable employer. Most of the 66 million employees in the private sector who are classified as production and nonsupervisory workers, along with many in the public sector as well, face 'the silent compulsion of economic relations', are exploited and subjected to the 'purely despotic' rule of capital, as Marx put it – with or without teams, circles or HPWSs.[22]

The biggest change in the ethnic/racial composition of the US working class has been the enormous growth of the Latino population in the last thirty years. Altogether, Latinos have gone from being a mere 6 per cent of the civilian labour force in 1980 to 23 per cent in 2010. By then, nearly 20 million Latino workers composed 14.3 per cent of those employed, compared to 10.8 per cent for African American workers, or 15 million.[23] By 2013, there were 1,952,000 Latino union members, not far behind the 2,081,000 black members. Whereas African American union members had seen their numbers decline from 2,513,000 in 1994, Latino members increased from 1,420,000 in that year. These largely immigrant workers have a strong incentive to join a union as they earn less than other groups: $578 a week compared to $802 for whites and $629 for blacks.[24] The potential power of Latino workers was demonstrated in the 2005 'Day Without Immigrants' demonstrations and strikes that affected workplaces across the country.[25] It is among these workers that the potential for significant growth in union membership is particularly strong.

THE ECONOMIC CONTEXT: CRISIS AND AUSTERITY

The bipartisan offensive against labour in the US was initiated amidst the crisis of profitability that characterized the 1970s.[26] A combination of an employers' offensive in the late 1970s that drove down wages and increased the rate of exploitation, the destruction of inefficient capitals with the loss of millions of manufacturing jobs, the creation of regional production chains and record low interest rates produced rising profits and spurred economic growth across the capitalist world from 1982 through 2007. The 'neoliberal' boom, with its falling rates of unemployment, *should* have been – like the post-Second World War boom – a period for major gains for the US labour movement. Instead, capital *intensified* its offensive against workers, demanding new concessions and generalizing 'lean production' methods. The US union leadership, wedded to bureaucratic business unionism, was incapable of mounting any sustained resistance.[27] Workdays lost from strike activity dropped precipitously, from a yearly average of 31,152,000 days during the strike wave of 1967-74, to a mere 9,061,000 at the depth of the recession in 1981, to an average of only 6,075,000 during the neoliberal boom of 1983-2007.[28]

The result of the continued employers' offensive was a sharp increase in labour productivity – the rate of exploitation. From 1983 to 2012, productivity in the nonfinancial corporate sector rose in an almost unbroken line by an average of 3 per cent a year – the equivalent of the postwar boom. From 1995 up to the Great Recession, manufacturing productivity increases averaged 3.6 per cent a year. They collapsed in 2008 as the recession hit, but made a remarkable recovery averaging almost 6 per cent in 2009 and 6.3 per cent in 2010. When the productivity index soared in 2009, *Business Week* wrote of 'The Dark Side of the Productivity Surge' as 'companies cut jobs and work hours' to squeeze out these gains. A consequence, it noted, was a fall of 3.6 per cent in unit labour costs over the year, 'the largest decrease since the series began in 1948'.[29] For 2011-13 the rate of productivity growth finally fell to an average of 1.5 per cent, as earlier rates of increase were unsustainable in more labour intensive, non-durable goods manufacturing industries over a long period. The productivity figures for durable manufacturing for 2011-13, however, were considerably higher than for manufacturing as a whole at 3 per cent.[30]

Massive overcapacity persists throughout the capitalist world economy, threatening long-term profitability and depressing investment. The results for working people in the US have been devastating.[31] Despite the growth in payrolls and a fall in the official unemployment rate since 2010, the number of 'discouraged' workers – those who have ceased looking for jobs – continues to grow. If they were to be included in the unemployment rate, unemployment would have remained over 10 per cent at the end of 2013. The long-term unemployed – those who have been jobless for six months or more – have also grown. The share of the unemployed out of work for more than six months peaked at around 45 per cent in 2010, but remains around 37 per cent – record levels for the postwar era. Hourly wages for workers in the bottom fifth of earners dropped 7 per cent, those in the middle of the wage distribution saw their wages drop 4.4 per cent and even those in the top fifth of wage earners saw wages erode by 2.6 per cent – despite renewed growth in productivity. As a result, workers are scrambling to sustain their buying power in the way they have for nearly three decades – working more, either through overtime or additional, part-time jobs. Union-busting, in particular an all-out assault on the last bastions of collective bargaining in the private and public sectors, is crucial to raising the rate of surplus-value as capital seeks to establish its *untrammelled* dictatorship in the workplace.

Although the unions had managed to gain 454,000 members in the public sector and 314,000 private sector members between 2006 and 2008 (the first such private sector gain in years), the 'Great Recession' wiped this gain out and brought new lows. Since public sector unions were the last bastion of capitalist state-sanctioned collective bargaining in the US, it was not surprising that they have borne the brunt of the post-2008 anti-labour offensive. Wisconsin's attack on public sector unions – with its abolition of an effective union-shop for public employees, restricting bargaining to wages, banning strikes and even binding arbitration in case of impasses in negotiations – has become the model for other states. According to a study by the union-backed Economic Policy Institute, twelve other Republican-dominated state governments have imposed similar restrictions on public employee union bargaining.[32] Emboldened by their victories, Republican governors in Indiana and Michigan introduced 'right to work' legislation for private sector workers. While the unions were able to defeat the Indiana measure, Michigan – the home of the United Automobile Workers – has become the first right-to-work state in the northern United States.

While the Republicans have spearheaded the attack on public employee unions in the US, the Democrats have not been far behind. Democratic governors and legislators, often elected with the support of unions, have joined the *bipartisan* neoliberal austerity drive against social services and public sector workers' wages and working conditions. Even the 'heroic' Democratic legislators in Wisconsin, whose boycott delayed the passage of Republican Governor Scott Walker's union-busting legislation, had agreed to massive cuts in social welfare and to the wages and pensions of public employees. In the wake of the defeat in Wisconsin, Democratic politicians, with New York's Governor Andrew Cuomo in the lead, have moved to gut public employee pensions in the so-called 'blue' states.[33] At the federal level, the Obama administration, elected and re-elected with labour's support, has reduced federal employment more than the Reagan administration,[34] imposed a wage freeze on federal workers,[35] and its 'educational reform' policies have unleashed a major attack teacher unions in the US.[36]

Although the Democrats generally have not attacked public sector union bargaining rights, relying on the unions for around 6 per cent of their funding and many of the 'get out the vote' troops needed to win elections, some Democratic state legislators have joined the fray.[37] In 2011, Democrats in Massachusetts supported legislation to strip public healthcare workers of bargaining rights, Connecticut Democrats attempted to reclassify college faculty as managers to make them ineligible for union representations, New Jersey Democrats joined Republicans in attempting to exclude healthcare from collective bargaining and Illinois Democrats succeeded in restricting teacher union rights.[38]

The assault on labour has not gone without a response in the past six years. Clearly, the highpoint of resistance was the Wisconsin Uprising of early 2011. However, the union leadership, whose material foundation in the ability to collect membership dues was under direct attack, was unable to successfully repel these attacks. Their exclusive political focus on elections – and their willingness to sacrifice promising mass mobilizations at the altar of the Democratic Party – has been labour's Achilles' heel.[39] Although the unions were central to Obama's re-election in 2012, they have continued to be unable to advance their political agenda through conventional means. The Clinton administration went beyond the traditional Democratic Party acceptance of the limits capital has imposed on reform in the US, and actively promoted neoliberal policies.[40] Many capitalists in the US have recognized the Democrats' service, contributing 41 per cent of their donations, $883 million, to Democrats in 2012 – 69 per cent of all contributions to the party.[41]

From 2008 through 2013, public sector union membership fell by a huge 622,000, no doubt a result of the attack on public worker rights of the last few years. Union membership in the private sector saw an even more precipitous drop between 2008 and 2012 of 1,228,000. Then in 2013, to everyone's surprise, private sector membership grew by 281,000. Over half of this increase was in construction, at 147,000, much of it likely the result of an increase of 171,000 production workers from January 2012 to December 2013 in that sector. In fact, over that period the number of production and nonsupervisory workers in the private sector grew by 3.5 million. Even manufacturing saw a gain of 121,000 workers. The tiny private sector gain of 134,000 union members in 2013 didn't even keep pace with employment growth. Membership figures reported by the AFL-CIO, for example, show a slight fall of 59,271 members between 2012 and 2013.[42]

Not surprisingly, wage compression and employer aggression have continued to be the norm, on average producing below inflation results in contract negotiations. Negotiated first-year wage increases have become more and more meagre, while the percentage of new contracts with no first-year increase has risen well above pre-recession levels, despite the recovery. Partly as a result of this poor showing and the declining ability of unions to affect non-union wages, at $294.93, average real weekly wages for production and nonsupervisory workers remain about 1 per cent below the 2010 level and 14 per cent below the 1972 highpoint of $341.73.[43] The story is no different for benefits, which fell slightly from a real value of $5.60 in 2007 to 5.57 in 2011, only 1.4 per cent above their 1989 value. The percentage of contracts in which 'measures to control health care costs' were included rose from 59 per cent in 2009 to 79 per cent in 2011.[44] No doubt the decline of the strike as labour's key weapon has played a major role in this long-term power shift in capital's favour.

Capital has done extremely well despite the setbacks of the recession, or perhaps even because of them. Labour costs were rising slightly just before the slump of 2008, but the recession brought these down for non-union workers, while union workers managed to raise their costs slightly by 2010, after which they remained more or less stable. On the other hand, domestic, nonfinancial corporate profits very nearly doubled after 2009, surpassing their pre-recession level. The impact of wage compression and labour cost containment, in combination with sizable productivity gains, can be seen in the shift of income from labour to capital. Between 2000 and 2010 'labour' income, as very broadly defined by the Economic Policy Institute, fell from 81.2 per cent to 73.8 per cent of national income, below even the 1959 level of 77.5 per cent.[45]

LABOUR'S CIVIL WAR

The continuing, even escalating retreat by organized labour comes after two decades of top-down 'reform' and organizing innovation, mostly associated with the leadership of AFL-CIO president John Sweeney. Yet, Sweeney's tenure oversaw little more than stagnation, as the number of private sector members held fairly steady from 9,400,000 in 1995 to 9,148,000 in 2000. But by 2004 membership dropped to 8,205,000, a loss of nearly a million members.[46] Not all unions had the same experience. Some, like UNITE-HERE's 'Hotel Workers Rising' and the National Nurses United, made significant gains. One union, however, whose leadership saw itself and its union as different and more effective was the Service Employees International Union (SEIU). While union membership overall stagnated between 1995 and 2000, SEIU reported a growth of 392,969 members. By 2004, while others were losing members, it had added another 328,339 members bringing it to 1.7 million.[47]

The SEIU first entered the national limelight in 1990 with its innovative and successful Justice for Janitors campaign in Los Angeles. But the SEIU of the 2000s was a different union. Under Andy Stern the union had centralized, 'staffed-up', and focused on growth through what became known as the 'organizing model'. This wasn't just a strategy for recruiting on a large scale; it involved the transformation of SEIU. Beginning in 2000 with the 'New Strength Unity' programme, locals were merged, many into multi-state mega-locals, often with no say in the process. The number of locals in the SEIU fell from 373 in 1995 to 140 in 2008, with 15 'mega-locals' encompassing 57 per cent of the membership – that is, just over one million members and agency fee payers in 15 local unions, or an average of about 73,000 per local spread out across several states. 'Servicing' and grievances were moved to call centres, known as Member Resource Centers, in some of the larger 'locals'.[48]

The crisis in the labour movement was registered when six unions left the AFL-CIO, joining the Carpenters who had already left the federation, to form Change to Win (CTW) in 2005.[49] The causes of war had been brewing for a while. While the SEIU conducted some important organizing drives among building service workers, notably in Houston and Miami, in the early 2000s, it simultaneously began to raid other unions in search of dues-payers. According to a report published by UNITE-HERE, the SEIU raided or intervened in the internal affairs of at least seven unions between 2002 and 2009.[50] By far the most spectacular and successful was the raid on UNITE-HERE itself. UNITE-HERE was the result of a merger in 2004, which apparently never really worked and the two top leaders soon fell out. Stern smelled blood and intervened, inviting both sides to join SEIU, but in fact, courted Bruce Raynor of the UNITE side of the rift while setting up a front group, Workers United, to absorb as many UNITE members as possible. A jump in SEIU members of about 60,000 in 2010 indicates about how many former UNITE members went to the SEIU.[51]

This outrageous raid brought verbal attacks from some 29 union leaders and saw both UNITE-HERE and the LIUNA eventually return to the AFL-CIO. The last major battle of the civil war was Stern's attempt to take away some 65,000 home care workers from the SEIU's giant United Healthcare West local, whose leader, Sol Roselli, had been a vocal critic of Stern's 'growth at any cost' policies. Facing trusteeship, another major Stern weapon, UHW members left the SEIU and formed the National Union of Healthcare Workers (NUHW). After two failed attempts to beat the combined opposition of the SEIU and Kaiser Permanente hospital management for its big bargaining unit, NUHW affiliated with the California Nurses Association. In 2010, Andy Stern retired as president of the SEIU and the civil war came to an end. So did the rapid growth of the SEIU, which saw its active membership fall slightly from 1,880,676 in 2010 to 1,831,998 in 2013. As UNITE-HERE left CTW in 2009 and the LIUNA following in 2010, CTW's membership dropped from 4,915,792 in 2009 to 4,253,617 in 2013.[52]

The 'organizing model' pioneered by the SEIU in the late 1980s and early 1990s appears to have become a routinized formula that no longer brings major gains, judging by the SEIU's stagnation since 2009. Employer neutrality card-check agreements, sometimes achieved by 'bargaining to organize' or 'concession organizing' (promising employers 'competitive' conditions if they remain neutral), have become harder to win or enforce as capital stiffens its resistance. It requires a great deal of time and resources to get the neutrality agreement. The result in the case of the SEIU, which used these agreements frequently, was that it took it '10 years to make a net gain of 600,000 members at a cost of $1 billion', as Janice Fine has noted; so that to 'reach the same goal in health care it would take upwards of thirty years at a cost of three billion'.[53] As Dorothy Benz warned, 'To evaluate the bargaining-to-organize strategy, we have to look at the process it takes to get *to* neutrality or card-check agreements as well as the results from such agreements'.[54] The major culprits may well be the employers and the broken system of union recognition under the National Labour Relations Board, but with the defeat of the Employee Fair Choice Act, it is highly unlikely that neutrality card-check agreements are a way around these barriers for very many.

Mergers, another panacea of the Sweeny era, were to make unions larger with more resources to organize or sustain strikes. It did not seem to matter whether the union merged with or absorbed another in the same industry or occupation. So, of the 42 union mergers in the 1990s 25 were multi-jurisdictional, while nine of the ten mergers from 2000 to 2005 had no jurisdictional or economic logic. Yet with the partial exception of the SEIU in membership growth, the five 'conglomerate unions' (SEIU, USWA, CWA, UFCW and IBT) that aggressively merged over these 15 years do not show any more growth or superior bargaining results in the private sector than those that merged less. All that can really be said for this 'strategy' is that it slowed the decline of those in industries losing jobs.[55]

The strike, which if used strategically might reverse some these trends, has continued to decline in frequency. As a mass phenomenon, strikes long ago fell into disuse. But the trend worsened in recent years as the incidence of strikes dropped from 394 a year in the second half of the 1990s, falling to 333 from 2000 through 2005, and then to 170 from 2006 through 2013.[56] The decline of the strike is not just a matter of caution by union leaders. Since the early 1980s employers have been increasingly willing to take advantage of the 1938 *Mackay Radio* case in which the Supreme Court found the use of *permanent* replacement workers during 'economic' strikes legal.[57] While the incidence of this is still relatively small, it has been on the increase. A survey conducted for the Federal Mediation and Conciliation Service (FMCS) found that while employers threatened to use replacements in 14 per cent of disputes in 1996, by 2003 they were doing this in 18 per cent of cases. The actual deployment of permanent replacements was much less, but still rising from 1 per cent of disputes to 3 per cent by 2003.[58]

Permanent replacements were used to defeat unions in high profile strikes in the 1990s, such as those at Caterpillar, Bridgestone/Firestone, A.E. Staley and the Detroit newspapers. This no doubt had an impact on how both leaders and members assess the wisdom of striking. But most strikers do not face permanent replacements. In some cases, notably the 20 or so local strikes at General Motors in the 1990s and the 1997 UPS strike, the use of any kind of scabs was not practical due to the size of the workforce and the mixture of skills required for production. In others, notably the 1989 United Mine Workers' strike against Pittston, constant mass mobilization, civil disobedience and a workplace occupation carried the day for labour. The cost of strikes has become negligible for capital. Any strategy for reviving the unions needs to increase this cost by going beyond the postwar conventional strike and the symbolic corporate campaign.[59]

IS THERE A FUTURE FOR ORGANIZED LABOUR IN THE US?

From this somewhat gloomy picture, it is all too easy to conclude that the days of the unions are numbered. For this to be the case, it requires more than bad news. It would require that class conflict either diminishes to the point of disappearance or that capital triumphs once and for all. We reject such a conclusion not only on the grounds of theory, but also of history. Class struggle is not a constant quantity, nor has its trajectory ever been one of incremental ascent. While we will not attempt to predict another upheaval any time soon, there are always signs of underlying class conflict.

First, there are the struggles which point to new tactics, even though they were not generally adopted across the labour movement nor even bringing lasting victories at the time. The occupation of the Republic Doors and Windows plant in Chicago in December 2008 is such an example. This struggle began four years before the occupation when the workers at Republic took matters into their own hands and threw out the corrupt Central State Joint Board, an independent teamster-type union, and brought in the independent but feisty United Electrical Workers in November 2004.

On 1 May 2005, many of Republic's 250 mostly Latino workers joined the massive 'Day Without Immigrants' demonstration-*cum*-strike, along with five million other immigrant workers. Then, when Republic management announced they were closing the plant without the required 60-day notice, the workers occupied the plant with the backing of the UE. This was illegal, but with support from many other unions and workers, and the local Latino community, the police did not even attempt to clear the plant.[60] The tactic did not spread as it had in 1937, but the process that led to it was not entirely unique: a rank-and-file rebellion that throws out a useless union, or more often union leadership, establishes a democratic organization, participates in the broad movement and is emboldened to try something new is a well-worn pattern.

Another tactic worthy of emulation was launched by the seasoned West Coast Longshore workers in the International Longshore and Warehouse Workers Union (ILWU). In July 2011, hundreds of ILWU Local 21 members blocked a train serving a new grain export facility on the Columbia River in Longview, Washington owned by EGT Development, which planned to run it non-union. For months the fight continued with invasions of EGT property – showing a healthy lack of respect for capitalist property – and mass demonstrations. Unfortunately, the ILWU international leadership physically disrupted meetings between West Coast Occupy activists and ILWU 21 and called off a final confrontation with a grain ship that might have involved the Coast Guard. While EGT was finally forced to recognize the ILWU, the contract did not include many of the features of ILWU master contract – a union-controlled hiring hall and Master Panel (arbitration board), and the right to hot-cargo goods and honour other union's picket lines.[61]

Perhaps the biggest example of new tactics used in the exercise of working-class power in recent years was the uprising of public sector workers in Wisconsin in response to Governor Walker's attempt to deprive them of collective bargaining rights. On 16 February 2011, 30,000 public sector workers and their supporters marched on the state capitol in Madison, some of them occupying the Capitol's rotunda. They had come to stop the passing of Walker's bill to end public sector collective bargaining. The protest did not end there. The occupation and weekend mass rallies numbering as many as 100,000 continued into the spring. There was even some talk of a general strike. Much of the turnout was from groups of union members who took the initiative on their own. In the end the mobilization was diverted into a dead-end electoral 'recall' campaign, and it was unable to stop the union-busting legislation. However, the mobilization of so many for so long presented one more picture of what labour can do.[62]

But most important as an indicator of union revival, going beyond the above singular incidents, was the 2010 victory of a genuine rank-and-file movement in the 30,000-member Chicago Teachers Union (CTU), the third largest local in the American Federation of Teachers (AFT). This movement, formed in 2008, calling itself the Caucus of Rank and File Educators (CORE) began preparing for what they knew would be a difficult fight to stop teacher layoffs, bigger classrooms and longer hours. Using one-on-one organizing they prepared the membership for what turned out to be a week-long strike in 2012 that took on Mayor Rahm Emanuel and won some important gains. Illinois law requires a 75 per cent vote of all members for a public sector union to strike; CORE produced a 90 per cent vote in favour.[63] This was a testament to what serious grassroots organizing *within* a union can produce.

Working-class resistances in even the worst of times are demonstrated by not only the victories at Republic Windows and Doors and the Chicago teachers' strike, but even the defeats of the Wisconsin uprising and the Longview struggle. However, whether these struggles end in victory or defeat is not random. The existence of a layer of experienced and sophisticated activists and leaders, who often learned important lessons confronting bureaucratic business unionists, was crucial to the ability of the Republic workers to carry out their successful sit-in and to the Chicago teachers' success in confronting the Obama-Emmanuel-Duncan neoliberal educational agenda. The absence of such a 'militant minority' allowed the labour officials to derail the mass mobilization and discussions of strike action in Wisconsin into the dead-end of Democratic electoral politics. Similarly, the absence of such a layer of organized activists in the ILWU permitted the leadership to physically disrupt the promising alliance between Occupy and the militant Longview local.

This victory in Chicago may be part of a trend in which incumbent, often entrenched, leaders who have failed to resist employer aggression or even to fight at all are being replaced by those more willing to fight and deploy mobilization tactics and direct action. This is a recurring phenomenon in US labour politics that sometimes comes in a wave of union reform and revitalization efforts from below. For example, in 2010, a rank-and-file slate of reformers beat incumbents in Teamster Local 804, the 7,000-member UPS-based local once led by Ron Carey. Aided by the Teamsters for a Democratic Union, these militants did not start with an election campaign, but with movement to defeat a contract offer that would have given up their hard-won 25 years-and-out pension.[64] In 2012, members of the 53,000-member Public Employees Federation in New York State voted out the incumbents, and the Proud Union caucus won following the rejection of a settlement backed by the old guard. After winning, the newly elected leaders set out to rebuild weak parts of the union and activate the members.[65] Other successful local-level rebellions in the last few years include reform victories in Teamster Local 743 in Chicago; Communications Workers of America Local 1101 in New York; the New York District Council of Carpenters; the 35,000-member New York State Nurses Association; the 20,000-member SEIU Local 1021 in Northern California; and the 5,200-member Teamster Local 251 in Rhode Island covering hospital, UPS and other workers.[66]

Not all rank-and-file organizations or networks run for union office. A caucus that began in Local 501 of the International Union of Operating Engineers (IUOE) in southern California has turned into a national network fighting for union democracy. It calls itself 'The Resistance', 'the men and women willing to fight'.[67] Another national rank-and-file organization spans the various unions that organize railroad workers. Railroad Workers United (RWU) and its publication *The Highball*, work for greater unity, democracy and militancy among rail workers in all crafts, unions and carriers. Major RWU campaigns include the fight against 'inward facing camera' surveillance and single-employee train crews.[68] As we will see, this organization could play a key role in the further unionization of the integrated logistics industry.

On an even larger scale, rebel movements have arisen in two national unions. In the face of mounting attacks on postal workers and services, in October 2013 the 'Members First' slate beat the incumbents of the 190,000-member American Postal Workers Union. The new leaders plan to activate the membership in a fight to stop the retreat on conditions and to build a movement to prevent the privatization of the Postal Service by Congress.[69] For the first time in half a century the International Association of Machinists is facing a similar revolt. The 'IAM Reform' slate appeared to be focused on reforming internal union practices (Lear jets, huge salaries, top heavy with officers). It began by successfully challenging an uncontested election in 2013, as a result of which the Labor Department ordered a new contested election. A concessionary contract at Boeing negotiated by the old leadership, however, has moved IAM Reform to deal with a broader range of issues. A caucus in District 751, covering Boeing workers, called 'Rosie's Machinists' has pushed matters in this direction.[70] Whether these reform movements are strong enough or politically farsighted enough to achieve real change remains to be seen. They nevertheless reveal the deep-seated anger of workers after three decades of attacks on living standards and working conditions, and offer one important channel for reviving not only the unions, but traditions of militancy and mobilization that can lead to renewed growth among working-class organizations.

The nation's private 'community' hospitals have become the site of growing, aggressive unionism. The underlying reason is the transformation of this one-time service into a profit-making industry and the adoption of lean production techniques. Union membership in hospitals grew from 689,416 in 2000 to a high of 951,000 in 2008, fell to 856,300 in 2012 and rose again to 894,994 in 2013.[71] Thus, while there were ups and downs, showing that healthcare is not recession-proof, the long-term trend is upward. A major problem is that there are about a dozen unions competing for different pieces of the workforce. By far the largest, however, are the SEIU which claims about 400,000 hospital workers, the National Nurses United (NNU) formed in 2009 with 154,339 dues-paying members in 2013, the American Federation of Teachers and the National Federation of Nurses, both claiming 70,000 members. In addition, there are state nurses' associations, some still affiliated with the American Nurses Association. Several other unions with smaller numbers of hospital workers, including the now CNA-affiliated National Union of Healthcare Workers (NUHW), also claim members in the hospitals.[72]

The militancy of hospital workers, especially nurses, was highlighted by the month-long strike by 1,000 nurses and 500 technicians who are members of the Pennsylvania Association of Staff Nurses and Allied Professionals (PASNAP) at the Temple University Hospital in Philadelphia in 2010. Indeed, in 2009 and 2010 there were 30 strike threats and 10 actual strikes involved in the nearly 100 labour contracts negotiated in those years with hospitals. Three were called by the SEIU, but seven of these were by nurses' unions, including PASNAP, but mostly by affiliates of the NNU. Frequently, the issues involved in these disputes are about patient care, issues such as nurse-patient ratios or limits on 'floating' (shifting nurses around).[73] At the same time, nurses are organizing. The ever-aggressive California Nurses Association grew from 65,665 dues-paying members in 2008 to 90,443 in 2013. The National Nurses United claims to have organized 14,000 nurses in 38 hospitals between its founding in 2009 and the end of 2012.[74] The SEIU and other unions also continue to organize and the growth of unionism in this growing industry seems irreversible.

Another major industry that bears watching is logistics. In transportation and warehousing, the heart of logistics, there were over 900,000 union members in 2013 out of a workforce of 3.9 million production and nonsupervisory workers, a higher than average density of 23 per cent. While this figure was down from a decade ago, it has risen since the end of the recession. Most of this is in transportation where many unions, 13 among railroad workers alone, have members. Various mergers have reduced this somewhat, with the railroad engineers and trainmen, for example, now in the Teamsters. The Railroad Workers United, along with the Teamsters for a Democratic Union, can play in important role in bringing these workers together.

The warehouse workers, who are among the lowest paid, on the other hand, are far less unionized. But in many ways the warehouse workers may prove to be the most dynamic element as they fight for organization. These warehouse workers represent not only key nodes in the logistics system, but a powerful link to the Big Box retailers, Wal-Mart in particular. Warehouse workers in three of the major warehouse centres that service Walmart have begun to organize along both informal and 'pre-union' lines in the three major concentrations described above. Inland from Los Angeles, Warehouse Workers United (WWU) has begun to organize among the 100,000 warehouse workers in that area. WWU is backed by Change To Win and linked to the United Food and Commercial Workers' OUR Walmart organization of Walmart retail workers. Outside of Chicago, where 150,000 warehouse workers are concentrated, the United Electrical Workers is backing a similar organization called Warehouse Workers for Justice (WWJ). In New Jersey a workers' centre calling itself New Labor has set up warehouse workers *consejos*, or workers' councils, in three cities. What is particularly significant in all three cases is that many of these workers work for temporary or workforce agencies rather than Walmart, but are part of Walmart's supply chain. Though the goal is unionization, they are avoiding the traditional route to organization for now in the hopes of mobilizing something like a movement that can impact Walmart as a whole. In Illinois and California, warehouse workers struck in 2012 even though they are not yet unionized, as did thousands of Wal-Mart workers in November 2013. Most of these workers are black and Latino, many are women and immigrants, all groups that are generally more union-prone.[75]

Finally, there is the South, in many ways the key to the future of unionism in the US. The AFL-CIO passed a resolution 'to develop a Southern organizing strategy' at its 2013 convention. Whether this becomes a reality or just another unfulfilled promise remains to be seen. The UAW's defeat at VW in Tennessee in early 2014 revealed how easily the 'neutrality' agreement was circumvented by the anti-union campaign conducted by Republican politicians and even by supervisors and salaried employees who simply ignored the agreement and openly opposed the union. It also showed the weaknesses in the UAW's 'cooperative', non-confrontational approach and the negative impact of its two-tier contracts with the Big

Three automakers.[76] If the South is to be organized a different approach will be needed.

In a positive development that shows some hope in this regard, union leaders and activists in North Carolina met in February 2014 to discuss just what southern workers are up against and how to build a movement that can confront these barriers and bring unionism to the South. It showed a unique spirit of unity including representatives from the AFL-CIO, the independent United Electrical Workers, the Farm Labor Organizing Committee, UFCW meatpackers from Smithfield Foods and pre-union fast food workers from 'NC Rising Up'. There was emphasis on building broad support for unionism and on direct action. The South today is a different place than in the 1940s when the CIO launched its 'Operation Dixie'. Due to Latino immigration as well as changing patterns of migration within the US, and especially African Americans moving south, the workforce in much of the region is more inclined to join unions if there is widespread support and the likelihood of victory.[77] Racism remains a barrier, but is now even more complicated with both immigrants and African Americans as targets. Hopefully, the AFL-CIO will follow through on their resolution and that its strategy will build on the experience of activists like those who attended the North Carolina meeting.

A major challenge for both leaders and activists across the labour movement in the US, however, is the crisis of the National Labour Relations Board framework. As Joe Burns has pointed out in his provocative *Reviving the Strike*, the labour movement's reliance on the NLRB framework for regulating collective bargaining required abandoning the type of massive, disruptive and often *illegal* tactics – sit-downs, secondary boycotts, solidarity strikes – that built industrial unionism and working-class power in the 1930s.[78] Since the mid-1950s, US labour law has stymied new organizing in the private sector, in particular in the South, the centre of US industry. There is a desperate need today for a strategic vision that transcends the NLRB framework, both in terms of new organizing and ongoing bargaining. While the goals of exclusive union recognition and the reestablishment (or establishment in some industries) of industry-wide bargaining remain central to any labour revival, they will not be established through the NLRB. Successful organizing will require going around the framework of NLRB supervised elections and return to the building of (initially non-majority) workplace union organizations that built the industrial unions in the 1930s. Winning recognition and making gains in bargaining will also have to violate the 'management rights' that the NLRB is pledged to maintain and a new willingness to break the law on the part of US labour.

The good news is that more and more union activists and those seeking union organization appear to be shaping up into a new layer of grassroots working-class leaders. They show up not only in the rank-and-file movements, but in the new organizing efforts as well. Such new leaders were certainly among the fast food workers who struck for a day in 100 cities across the country in early 2014 with some backing from the SEIU.[79] Some of these newer activists come to the local 'Troublemakers Schools' and the semi-annual conferences sponsored by *Labor Notes* – 'the media and organizing project that has been the voice of union activists who want to put the movement back in the labor movement since 1979'.[80] Its April 2014 conference was the largest yet, attended by 2000 labour activists. No doubt, this is as yet a small 'militant minority', but it is one that is willing to challenge the failed old ways of American business unionism, both in terms of demanding greater union democracy, increased workplace power and organization, and a willingness to use mobilizing, direct action tactics. Even though as yet small, such a layer has always been crucial to the building of working-class organizations and to periods of social upheaval.

NOTES

1   See Kim Moody, *An Injury to All: The Decline of American Unionism*, London: Verso, 1988.

2   All data on union density here is drawn from Barry T. Hirsch and David A. Macpherson's http://www.unionstats.com website.

3   Council of Economic Advisers, *Economic Report of the President 2013*, Washington, DC: US Government Printing Office, 2013, pp. 335, 384.

4   Bureau of Labor Statistics (BLS), 'Employment, Hours, and Earnings from the Current Employment Statistics Survey', Manufacturing, *Databases, Tables & Calculators by Subject*, 8 March 2014, available at http://data.bls.gov; BLS, 'Union Members in 1995', *News*, USDL-96-41, 9 February 1996, Table 3; BLS, 'Union Members – 2013', *News*, USDL-14-95, 24 January 2014, Table 3.

5   Mike Parker and Jane Slaughter, *Working Smart: A Union Guide to Participation Programs and Reengineering*, Detroit: A Labor Notes Book, 1994.

6   Kim Moody, *US Labor in Trouble and Transition*, London: Verso, 2007, p. 44; US Census Bureau, *Statistical Abstract of the United States, 2012*, Washington, DC: US Government Printing Office, p. 637.

7   The Institute for Southern Studies, 'AFL-CIO resolves to organize the South', 12 September 2013, available at www.southernstudies.org.

8   Mike Elk, 'Why Union Fell Short at VW', *Labor Notes*, 420(March), 2014, pp. 1, 3.

9   Alexandra Bradbury, 'Don't "Lean" on Me, Hospital Workers Say', *Labor Notes*, 412(July), 2013, pp. 8-10.

10   Michael J. Handel and Maury Gittleman, 'Is There a Wage Payoff to Innovative Work Practices?', *Industrial Relations*, 43(1), 2004, pp. 67-97.

11   John Godard, 'What Is Best for Workers? The Implications of Workplace and Human Resource Management Practices Revisited', *Industrial Relations*, 49(3), 2010, pp. 466-88.

12   BLS, 'Employment, Hours, and Earnings from the Current Employment Statistics Survey', *Databases, Tables & Calculators by Subject*, 8 March 2014.

13   Jane Slaughter, 'Supply Chain Workers Test Strength of Links', *Labor Notes*, 397(April), 2012, pp. 8-10.

14   Michael P. Keane and Susan E. Feinberg, 'Advances in Logistics and the Growth of Intra-firm Trade: The Case of Canadian Affiliates of U.S. Multinationals, 1984-1995', *The Journal of Industrial Economics*, 55(4), 2007, p. 626.

15   JP Wright and Ed Michael, 'Should a 15,000-ton Train be Operated Single-Handed?', *Labor Notes*, 405(December), 2012, pp. 16, 15.

16   BLS, 'Employment', 8 March 2014.

17   Kim Moody, 'Competition and conflict: Union growth in the US hospital industry', *Economic and Industrial Democracy*, 35(1), 2014, pp. 5-25.

18   US Census Bureau, *Statistical Abstract of the United States, 2012*, Washington, DC: US Government Printing Office, 2011, pp. 408-11.

19   BLS, 'Contingent and Alternative Employment Arrangements', *News*, USDL-05-1433, 27 July 2005, Table 8.

20   For the data on non-traditional employment, which includes independent contractors, on-call workers, temporary help agency workers and workers provided by contract, and data on percentage of traditional employees working full time, see BLS, 'New Data on Contingent and Alternative Employment Examined by BLS', *News*, USDL-95-318, 17 August 1995; and BLS, 'Contingent and Alternative Employment Arrangements', 27 July 2005.

21   US Census Bureau, *Statistical Abstract 2012*, p. 410.

22   Karl Marx, *Capital, Volume I*, London: Penguin Books, 1990, pp. 450, 899. For the argument concerning the exploitation of workers who do not produce surplus-value see Anwar M. Shaikh and E. Ahmet Tonak, *Measuring the Wealth of Nations: The Political Economy of National Accounts*, Cambridge: Cambridge University Press, 1994, pp. 30-1, 129-31.

23   US Census Bureau, *Statistical Abstract 2012*, pp. 377, 399.

24   BLS, 'Union Members in 1995', Table 1; BLS, 'Union Members – 2013', Table 1 and Table 2.

25   Moody, *US Labor in Trouble and Transition*, pp. 5-7.

26   Our discussion of the US and global economy over the past four decades is drawn from Anwar Shaikh, 'The First Great Depression of the 21st Century', *Socialist Register 2011*, Pontypool: Merlin Press, 2010, pp. 44-63; and David McNally, *Global Slump: The Economics and Politics of Crisis and Resistance*, Oakland, CA: PM Press, 2011.

27   Much of the following is drawn from Kim Moody, 'Contextualizing Organized Labour in Expansion and Crisis: The Case of the US', *Historical Materialism*, 20(1), 2012, pp. 3-30.

28 BLS, 'Work Stoppage Data: Number of Days of Idleness (in 000) from all Work Stoppages in Effect in Period, 1947-2014', Series ID: WSU001, available at http://www.bls.gov.

29 Peter Coy, 'The Dark Side of the Productivity Surge', *Business Week*, 5 November 2009, available at http://www.businessweek.com.

30 BLS, 'Industry analytical ratios for the Manufacturing sector, all employed persons', 6 March 2014; BLS, 'Productivity and Costs', *News*, USDL-14-0353, 6 March 2014, pp. 10-1.

31 Data on wages, hours and unemployment trends since 2008 drawn from Heidi Shierholz, 'Six Years From Its Beginnings, the Great Recession's Shadow Looms Over the Labor Market', *Economic Policy Institute Issue Brief*, No. 374, 9 January 2014, available at http://www.epi.org.

32 Gordon Lafer, 'The Legislative Attack on American Wages and Labour Standards, 2011-2012', *EPI Briefing Paper*, No. 364, 31 October 2013.

33 Mark Yzaguirre, 'The Other Big Winner in Wisconsin – Andrew Cuomo', *The Huffington Post*, 5 June 2012, available at http://www.huffingtonpost.com.

34 Floyd Norris, 'Under Obama, a Record Decline in Government Jobs', *New York Times*, 6 January 2012, available at http://economix.blogs.nytimes.com.

35 Dan Labotz, 'Obama's Federal Wage Freeze Will Become the Model', *Labor Notes*, 16 December 2010.

36 Claudio Sanchez, 'Relationship Chills Between Teacher Unions, Obama', *National Public Radio/All Things Considered*, 7 July 2010, available at http://www.npr.org; Paul Abowd, 'Race to the Top: Unions Asked to Play Ball for Education Dollars', *Labor Notes*, 28 January 2010.

37 Political contributions figure based on total contributions for the 2012 election cycle, see http://www.opensecrets.org.

38 Howard Ryan, 'Democrats Join the Raid on Union Bargaining Rights', *Labor Notes*, 23 May 2011.

39 Kim Moody, 'Wisconsin and Beyond', *Against the Current*, 152(May/June), 2011, available at http://www.solidarity-us.org.

40 Kenneth Baer, *Reinventing Democrats: The Politics of Liberalism from Reagan to Clinton*, Lawrence: University Press of Kansas, 2000.

41 See http://www.opensecrets.org.

42 BLS, 'Union Members', *News*, 2006-13; BLS, LM-2 Report for AFL-CIO. CTW figures for 2013 not available as of this writing, but these fell between 2009 and 2012. See http://kcerds.dol-esa.gov; BLS, 'Employment', 8 March 2014; BLS, LM-2 Reports for Change to Win.

43 BLS, 'Current and real earnings for production and nonsupervisory employees on private nonfarm payrolls', *Economic News Release*, Table A-2; Council of Economic Advisers, *Economic Report of the President 2013*, p. 380.

44 BNA, *Source Book on Collective Bargaining: Wages, Benefits, and Other Contract Issues*, Bloomberg BNA, 2010, p. 180. See also the 2012 edition, pp. 185-6.

45 Lawrence Mishel, Josh Bivens, Elsie Gould and Heidi Shierholz, *The State of Working America*, 12th Edition, Ithaca: Cornell University Press, 2012, pp. 102, 181.

46 BLS, 'Union Members', 1995 (USDL-96-41), 2000 (USDL-01-21), 2005 (USDL-06-99).

47   Department of Labor, LM-2 Reports, SEIU, 1996, 2001, 2005, available at http://kcerds.dol-esa.gov.

48   Adrienne Eaton, Janice Fine, Allison Porter and Saul Rubenstein, *Organizational Change at SEIU, 1996-2009*, commissioned by the SEIU, 2009, pp. 9, 25, 42-3.

49   The six were SEIU, UFCW, IBT, LIUNA, UNITE-HERE and the UFW. The Carpenters, who had already left the AFL-CIO, also signed on with CTW. This section is based primarily on Steve Early, *The Civil Wars in U.S. Labor: Birth of a New Workers' Movement or Death Throes of the Old?*, Chicago: Haymarket Books, 2011.

50   UNITE-HERE, *Growing Pains: SEIU Campaigns Against Other Unions*, unattributed, 2009.

51   See the US Department of Labor, SEIU LM-2 Reports from 2009 and 2010.

52   See the US Department of Labor, SEIU LM-2 Reports, 2009, 2010 and 2013; CTW LM-2 Report, 2009, 2010, 2011, 2012 and 2013.

53   Janice Fine, 'Why labour needs a plan b: Alternatives to conventional trade unionism', *New Labour Forum*, 16(2), 2007, p. 38.

54   Dorothy Benz, 'Organizing to survive, bargaining to organize', *Working USA*, 6(1), 2002, pp. 104-5.

55   Kim Moody, 'The Direction of Union Mergers in the United States: The Rise of Conglomerate Unionism', *British Journal of Industrial Relations*, 47(4), 2009, pp. 676-700.

56   Federal Mediation and Conciliation Service, *Annual Reports*, 2000-13, available at http://www.fmcs.gov.

57   Kim Moody, 'Striking Out in America: Is There an Alternative to the Strike?', in Gregor Gall, ed., *New Forms and Expressions of Conflict at Work*, Houndmills, UK: Palgrave Macmillan, 2013, pp. 233-52; Chris Rhomberg, *The Broken Table: The Detroit Newspaper Strike and the State of American Labor*, New York: Russell Sage Foundation, 2012, pp. 1-18, 178-80.

58   Thomas A. Kochan, Joel Cutcher-Gershenfeld and John-Paul Ferguson, *Report on the Federal Mediation and Conciliation Service Third National Survey*, Federal Mediation and Conciliation Service, July 2004.

59   For a good discussion of this see Joe Burns, *Reviving the Strike: How Working People Can Regain Power and Transform America*, Brooklyn, NY: IG Publishing, 2011.

60   Kari Lydersen, *Revolt on Goose Island: The Chicago Factory Takeover, and What it Says about the Economic Crisis*, Brooklyn, NY: Melville House, 2009.

61   Evan Rohar and Misha Gaus, 'Longshore Workers Block Train, Occupy Terminal', *Labor Notes*, 390(September), 2011, pp. 3, 15; Jack Gerson, 'Reply to Balderston: Longview Contract Was Not A Victory', *New Politics*, 8 August 2012, available at http://newpol.org.

62   Howard Ryan, 'Wisconsin Labor Jams Capitol To Resist Governor's Attacks', *Labor Notes*, 384(March), 2011, pp. 1, 6; Jane Slaughter, 'Wisconsin Changes Everything', *Labor Notes*, 385(April), 2011, pp. 1, 14; Jane Slaughter, 'The Mood in Wisconsin: Shaken, Angry, but Proud', *Labor Notes*, 386(May), 2011, pp. 1, 13.

63   Paul Abowd, 'Reformers to Lead Chicago Teachers', *Labor Notes*, 376(July), 2010, pp. 1, 13; Theresa Moran, 'Chicago Teachers Raise the Bar', *Labor Notes*, 403(October), 2012, pp. 1, 10.

64   Jane Slaughter, 'Look Out, Big Brown', *Labor Notes*, 370(January), 2010, p. 1-6.

65   Mark Brenner, 'NY Public Employees Hit Reset After Old Guard Pushes Contract Takeaways', *Labor Notes*, 402(September), 2012, p. 11.

66   Mark Brenner, 'Reform Rekindled', *Labor Notes*, 410(May), 2013, pp. 1-3; Jane Slaughter, 'Rank-and-File Reformers Oust "In Bed" Rhode Island Teamsters', *Labor Notes*, 417(December), 2013, pp. 10-1.

67   Association for Union Democracy, 'Letter: What is The Resistance?', 31 May 2013, available at http://aud2.uniondemocracy.org.

68   Railroad Workers United, *The Highball*, Winter 2014; Railroad Workers United, 'Rank and File Action', Special Supplement, *The Highball*, no date, available at http://www.railroadworkersunited.org.

69   David Yao, 'Activists Take The Helm of Postal Union', *Labor Notes*, 416(November), 2013, pp. 16, 15.

70   Jon Flanders, 'Reform Slate Boosted by Bum Boeing Deal', *Labor Notes*, 420(March), 2014, pp. 16, 15.

71   Barry Hirsch and David Macpherson, *Union Membership, Coverage, Density and Employment by Industry*, available at http://www.unionstats.gsu.edu.

72   Kim Moody, 'Competition and conflict: Union growth in the US hospital industry', *Economic and Industrial Democracy*, 35(1), 2014, pp. 5-25; Herman Benson, 'Unionization of the nurses in the US: Worker power, autonomy, and labour democracy', *Working USA*, 13(June), 2010, pp. 298-9. The recent development of nurses' unionism is complicated and beyond the scope of this article. For a more detailed look at this consult various issues of *Union Democracy Review* at the AUD website, http://aud2.unuiondemocracy.org.

73   Moody, 'Competition and conflict', pp. 16-8.

74   California Nurses Association LM-2 Reports, 2008-13, available at http://kcerds.dol-esa.gov; National Nurses United, 'Community Long Beach RNs Vote 76% to Join CNA/NNU', *News Releases*, 7 December 2102, available at http://www.nationalnursesunited.org.

75   Jane Slaughter, 'Supply Chain Workers Test Strength of Links', *Labor Notes*, 397(April), 2012, pp. 8-10; Adam Gabbatt, 'US fast-food workers strike over low wages in nationwide protests', *The Guardian*, 5 December 2013.

76   Elk, 'Why Union Fell Short at VW', pp. 1, 3.

77   Eric Fink, 'A Southern Workers' Movement Can Change the Nation', *Talking Union*, 24 February 2014, available at http://talkingunion.wordpress.com.

78   Burns, *Reviving the Strike*.

79   Victor Luckerson, 'The One-Day Strike: The New Labour Weapon of Last Resort', *Time*, 7 December 2013, available at http://nation.time.com; Gabbatt, 'US fast-food workers strike', *The Guardian*.

80   See http://www.labornotes.org.

FORGING NEW CLASS SOLIDARITIES: ORGANIZING HOSPITAL WORKERS

JANE MCALEVEY

In 1935, the US Congress, under pressure from an angry and increasingly activist labour force passed the Wagner Act, the legal framework that made it possible for workers who fought hard and smart to form strong unions. Twelve years and one world war later, Congress, under pressure from big business, passed the Taft-Hartley Act, which essentially gutted the Wagner Act. US workers have been slipping backward ever since. Over the past several decades, that slide became an avalanche, and today workers and the unemployed are all but buried. Amid the acrimonious debates about unions' future direction, too little attention is being paid to the central question of *power*. There is a fundamental lack of clarity about the relationship between power and strategy, and between what kinds of strategies lead to what kind of power. Far too little attention is paid to the following questions: Is this strategy actually expanding our base of organic worker leaders? Is this strategy deepening working-class solidarity? Is this strategy helping workers and the unemployed to overcome racism, sexism and the other 'isms' capitalists use as weapons to defeat the building of class? Is this strategy building measurable power?

Marx was right in his observation that large groups of (mostly) men, toiling side-by-side under an exploitive employer were likely to join together in sheer self-defence. But forging the kind of solidarity needed to actually win substantial concessions from capital requires high levels of unity and workplace organization, the building of worksite structures so tight that workers can routinely display their unity and strength to their employers. Between 1935 and 1947, workers were doing this in large numbers. It took Taft-Hartley, McCarthyism, self-serving business unionists, US postwar capitalist hegemony, jailings, expulsions and assassinations, to wrestle the US working class back into nearly complete submission; not to mention several decades of capital mobility that shifted jobs from highly organized states with better union laws to non-union and repressive political geographies in and outside the US.

Beverly Silver is probably right that oppressive factory conditions in other parts of the globe will reproduce the organizing impulse noted by Marx worldwide.[1] But what about in the US itself where there are many fewer industrial-era factories and many other kinds of worksites with different production processes? All of the fastest growing occupations in the US are in the female-dominated and people of color-heavy healthcare sector.[2] Hospitals, with five million non-management staff, have the largest concentrations of healthcare workers. Just barely 20 per cent of the current workforce is unionized, and the sector is growing, meaning the percentage of hospital workers in unions will drop unless strategic organizing expands. With four million unorganized workers presently, there's a cornucopia of possibilities.

This essay will focus on one example of mostly female healthcare workers who were engaged in bold organizing drives that substantially improved their material and nonmaterial condition at work and at home.[3] Their worksite organizations were every bit as strong as the industrial unions of the 1930s and 1940s. And they did it using many of the same methods. Central to their strategy, and to their subsequent ability to win substantial gains, was their decision to build their organizations wall-to-wall, putting not only registered nurses but all other hospital workers together in a single union. Nurses have more individual skill-based power than any other type of unionizable worker in a given healthcare system, but in a typical hospital they make up only 40 per cent of the total workforce.[4] There are several dozen typical job classifications in a common general medical and surgery hospital, including cooks, clericals, housekeepers, technologists and technicians, care aids and assistants, and many different strata among and between all of these categories as well as within the single largest workforce inside any hospital, the registered nurses. Typically, the physicians and managers are excluded from unionization efforts.

In 2006, hospital workers in Las Vegas made history when they walked off the job in the first-ever hospital strike in the Nevada city's history. The strikes came as part of a comprehensive city-and-suburbs-wide multiemployer hospital fight, also a first in the mostly non-union Southwest. Nine thousand hospital workers, nurses and non-nurses, from seven hospitals collectively struggled and succeeded in massively improving their quality of work life, and their home life, by winning region-wide wage scales and other standards that represented some of the largest single-contract gains in recent times in the entire southern US.[5] Significantly, other workers took part in the same struggle, including an additional 6,000 non-hospital municipal employees who were members of the organizing union, the Service Employees International Union (SEIU). These 15,000 workers not only won unprecedented workplace victories but also local elections; they thereby not only altered the power structure in the workplace, but also shifted the balance of power in the local government from politicians hostile to unions to those supportive of labour's cause.

Wall-to-wall hospital organizing of the type described in this essay has great potential implications. In terms of collective power against an employer, the sheer number of workers involved matters a lot. There can be little question that today, just as in the 1920s, 1930s and 1940s, uniting workers who are harder to replace with those who are easier to replace and building intense levels of solidarity among and between them on a large scale results in the strongest possible worker organization. But developing workplace solidarities that bridge intra-class differences, such as racism, sexism and more, has a ripple effect beyond the walls of the workplace, too. Forging a true labour alliance across skill, craft, experience, ethnicity, gender and more helps transform how workers understand their relationship to each other, to their neighbours, to their nation and even their world.

ORGANIZING HOSPITAL WORKERS TOGETHER

The mentality of a nurse is to care for those in need, at least it should be, and most of us are doing this because we want to care for those in need, meaning everyone, our entire team, our community, not just our patients. The few nurses who come with the elitist attitude, they should be doctors, not nurses. It's important to focus on why we went into nursing in the first place, to care for others. I didn't come into nursing to have initials behind my name. Some nurses do come into the field that way; until someone shits all over them and they realize they are just a nurse in a big system.[6] – Alfredo Serrano, Operating Room Nurse

Alfredo Serrano is Mexican-American, queer, a reformed alcoholic and a highly regarded nurse. He was one of ten children. He drives a pick-up truck so enormous it resembles one of those mountaintop removal machines found hulking in the Appalachian hills. His other wheels spin on a turbo-charged, Japanese-built motorcycle. He has three kids from an early marriage, before he came out, one of whom – his daughter, along with her husband and baby – recently moved back in with him: her husband lost his job just after the young couple gave birth to their first child. Serrano is without question the leader of all the workers in his hospital, starting with the nurses and right through the union-negotiated wage-scale classifications including the EVS (environmental services, a.k.a. housekeeping) and the dietary unit (cooks) and every type of worker in between, from techs to phlebotomists. He used to be the chief nursing steward, elected from among his nurse peers, but recently he decided he prefers the highest-level position in his union local, vice president, because it is elected by and responsible to all the workers in the hospital, not just the nurses. And as vice president, he gets to work on political and community issues, too, rather than simply handling worksite grievances. The vice president from each hospital also serves on the statewide union's executive board.

Serrano has been through three rounds of collective bargaining between 2003 and 2014. In 2003, and again in 2006, he experienced firsthand how hospital employers divide the nurses from the rest of the workers by offering them bigger raises and flattering them with praise for their suddenly appreciated profession while dismissing other health workers as nonessential and unimportant. Management had good reason to repeat an approach that had worked in 2000, when the workers negotiated the first contract for their newly formed union. In that year, the boss strategy succeeded: the union leadership was weak and incompetent and very few rank-and-file workers were involved, and management was able to divide and conquer by giving the nurses a bigger raise than the other members. That experience had demoralized and demobilized the rest of the workers. It would take new leadership and the involvement of many more workers in their own collective bargaining process – workers like Serrano – and several years before the nurses at the very same hospital would learn that they could get a *substantially* larger raise by standing united with all of the workers.

Serrano has been key among those new union leaders, helping to educate the nurses about the importance of solidarity between nurses and other hospital staff. This was a harder conversation for him, and other nurses like him, to carry during the 2003 negotiations because the nurses hadn't yet experienced winning significantly more by rejecting managements' divisive offers. Material self-interest aside, Serrano routinely challenges his fellow nurses to understand that all the hospital workers matter equally. 'I think it's funny', he told me. 'I ask the nurses, "Excuse me, does gasoline cost more for you and I than everyone else here? How about groceries? Why on earth would we be getting more when the cost of living is the same for everyone in our hospital and we already earn more money than everyone else based on our skill-based wage scale?"' He continued, 'I haven't ever said this, but I want the nerve to just say, "Is this your inferiority complex talking? Do you have an inferiority complex that management is playing on?"' Several years later, conversations about sticking together became significantly easier, because in 2003 the nurses won far better money and more rights by standing strong with their non-nurse coworkers.

Serrano works for the single largest hospital corporation in the US – in fact the largest in the world – the Healthcare Corporation of America or HCA, which owns more than 200 for-profit hospitals. Nearly all of them are in so-called right-to-work states; the employer takes advantage of the Taft-Hartley Act's provision that, even if a majority of workers vote to form a union which is certified as the bargaining agent, membership and dues are on a purely voluntarily basis. For hospital corporations like HCA, operating near exclusively in right-to-work states is a business model, a way to lower labour costs and squeeze even more profit out of the taxpayer-funded but privately managed, over-priced and substandard US healthcare system. Pay is kept lean and, worse, the conditions under which most employees work are frightful. HCA has an HR philosophy called 'staffing to the bone' – an interesting policy name for a healthcare corporation, which means saving costs by grossly understaffing their hospitals. And because this creates working conditions ripe for union organizing, they site their hospitals in union-busting states. The corporation's growth plan also depends on controlling federal healthcare regulations through its massive political power.[7]

Serrano and his colleagues work at Sunrise, a sprawling HCA hospital complex in the heart of the city that includes a children's hospital with specialized pediatric care, a level III trauma unit and outpatient clinics. HCA has two other Las Vegas area operations, Mountain View and Southern Hills, which they call their suburban hospitals (though to any urban dweller, all of Vegas looks like one continually expanding suburb). Sunrise was initially organized in 1998, in one of the first of the SEIU's top down, corporate campaigns in healthcare, resulting in a weak union inside the hospital. The corporate deal that resulted essentially condemned the workers to a bad first contract that also, as noted, drove a wedge between the nurses and other workers. But the foundation of a wall-to-wall union had been laid, and years later, after a change in union leadership, a real hospital workers' union was built on it.

Between the mid-1990s and the great recession in 2008, the population of Las Vegas exploded – showing the single highest growth rate in the nation – and the healthcare sector struggled to keep pace, opening one hospital after another, some right down the street from each other. Yet the hospital workers' union stagnated. The SEIU in Nevada was worse than weak and faced a very sophisticated employer in HCA, which was successfully pummelling its unionized Sunrise workers from the inside out, teaching them the lesson that forming a union was a futile endeavour. Nurses and Technical Workers (more than nurses, but less than the whole hospital) at two other private hospitals in the region, owned by Quest, had also organized in the 1990s, with help from the national, not local, union, but the employer there, too, was systematically reversing what little gains had been achieved in weak agreements. Several years later, Quest sold the hospitals to Universal Health Services (UHS). By 2002, under the new owners – viciously anti-union and, like HCA, grounded in a right-to-work-state business plan – the technical workers had voted to decertify the 'Techs' (technical unit) at one of the two UHS hospitals, and UHS began to campaign for decertification at the other.[8] The timing of this synced with healthcare division leadership changes in the national union; the new leaders had been analyzing a plan for an all-out organization of the US hospital industry. By 2003, the national union had come to see Vegas, with its hospital-sector growth and particular constellation of national chains with soaring profits, as a key launching pad for hospital union organizing nationwide.

LEMONS TO LEMONADE

Is there any nurses-only union that actually works well?[9]
– Joan Wells, Intensive Care Unit nurse

Joan Wells was born and raised in Canada. Her first full-time hospital job was in British Columbia. At that time, she was what US hospitals call a licensed practical nurse, or, LPN, not yet a registered nurse (RN). At Nanaimo Regional General Hospital there was a union, the Hospital Employees Union, HEU, but it didn't include the nurses, who were in a separate non-union association. Twenty years later, dissatisfied with her work, Joan returned to university to become a registered nurse. Recently divorced, with two daughters, a new degree in hand and needing a change, Joan left for the US, where she soon found herself working in right-to-work Texas, in Corpus Christi. On her first day, she asked a coworker what seemed like a normal question, 'Where do I sign up for the union?' She was immediately told you don't talk about unions in Texas.

This conversation would be repeated several years later, when she relocated to Vegas, lured by the whopping sign-on bonuses the hospitals were offering RNs. Except this time, the answer was a little different. There was a union, Joan's new colleagues told her – but then added the same hush-hush-we-don't-talk-union-here warning. Days later, because she had asked aloud for the union, a nurse approached her and handed her a card, but furtively, as if passing her the code to a secret society. Less than a year later, Joan Wells would become a leader in the resurgent effort to build a powerful hospital workers' union in Vegas. Her local union posted her picture high above the biggest freeway in Vegas on a massive billboard, declaring, 'We stand for patients before profits'. Within four years of coming to work in Vegas, Joan would be fired in the line of duty for taking on hospital management. She went on to work with the union as a full-time hospital organizer, entered a multiyear legal battle to win her job and her dignity back, and helped lead thousands of hospital workers to victory in the 2006 fight.

Before Joan was fired for union activity, she'd had 20 years of stellar reviews, including for her work as an ICU (intensive care unit) nurse in Vegas. Joan Wells is a nurse's nurse. Doctors requested her for their patients; other nurses turned to her for help. On the day they fired her, it wasn't just because there was a new billboard in town showing Joan in her scrubs, towering as big as the Vegas casinos. That day, when she arrived for her shift, the other nurses had told her, 'They are going to work us in the ICU at a 3:1 today'. In an intensive care unit, a 3:1 staffing level – three patients per nurse – is unacceptably high: a serious risk to patients' lives. Well-run ICUs operate on a 1:1 or at most 2:1 ratio. But in the hyper-greedy hospitals in right-to-work-states spreading across the US, ratios of 3:1 and even 4:1 are becoming more common. As Joan entered work, all of the dayshift nurses were waiting for her not because she had a union title – back then, she didn't – but because she was a top nurse whose first and foremost concern was caring for people, which meant her patients, as well as her team of coworkers.

The nurses asked her what they should do. If a patient is injured, it's the nurse, not the hospital, who loses the license. After a quick discussion, the nurses decided to refuse to 'take report', meaning that they wouldn't take over any patient-care duties from the nightshift nurses, and demanded that the hospital call in some backup nurses. When Joan was fired, she went from being a leader in her hospital to a heroine for all hospital workers in Vegas. By standing her ground for patient care, and, after surviving the humiliation of being fired when she had enormous pride in her work, she became an invaluable part of the effort to build power for workers in the region:

> In the US, the only time I've been in a union is in a right-to-work state, and that's Nevada. The climate politically is filled with corporate greed, the way the entire entrepreneurial system is set up in the US, you don't have much power unless you have big numbers and stand together with all your coworkers.

HOW THEY DID IT

From late 2003 to 2007, in spite of employer divide-and-conquer attempts, there was never disagreement between nurses and non-nurses about whether or not being in one union made sense. Nurses were winning more than they ever had, including on issues very specific to nurses, like staffing, and a related issue, floating (the process of the hospital management moving them around the hospital, generally against their will, to plug intentional short staffing). Every conversation in any hospital began and ended with a clear understanding that whatever issue the nurse or non-nurse wanted to resolve, a win would only be possible if every worker stood together and acted together. A new union-organizing team was hired and developed; it included more than a dozen nurses and a few other hospital workers brought onto full-time staff as organizers. Not all of them, like Joan, switched to full-time union work after being fired for their bold organizing. Most of them were nurses who had just experienced their first big contract wins and wanted to devote their energy full-time to expanding union ranks and growing union power. Because the union was making improvements in patient care, they understood the union as advancing their profession and their pay.

After the first decent Sunrise contract victory in 2003, when Serrano got involved, the hospital workers set new contract expiration dates for 2006, with the intention of aligning with the big public hospital expiration that was set for 2006. The Sunrise workers made a few real improvements in 2003, substantial enough to raise the expectation that they could win even more. The expanded union rights, which they immediately took advantage of, enabled two workers to do union work full-time for up to six months with the guarantee that afterward they could return to their positions and shifts in the hospital. Crucially, they won a 2006 contract expiration, the first of many steps in beginning to line up Vegas hospital contracts. Next, in 2004, the two UHS hospital contracts expired. Their contract terms had been so hideous that almost any improvement would have constituted a victory, but low expectations and weak settlements weren't the plan. The UHS workers, building on the 2003 Sunrise victory, led an incredible struggle, including taking their first strike votes, and secured a new contract that won average raises of 10 per cent a year for two years and the first fully employer-paid healthcare plans in Nevada's healthcare sector, along with improvements in on-call pay, shift differentials and more. Standards were escalating, and so were the hopes and dreams of the workers. The UHS workers demanded a 2006 expiration date, too. But by this time, it had dawned on the employers that hospital workers in Vegas were lining up their contract-expiration dates.

With total brinkmanship, the UHS workers made a 2006 expiration the final issue on the negotiating table for both UHS hospitals. Only because of intense and systematic worker-to-worker education about the importance of building worker power through lining up their contracts – discussions that began before the opening of negotiations and months before the eventual settlement – were the workers able to tell management across the table 'No' when the employer offered the richest financial package in Vegas history, but not the right expiration date. Under byzantine US labour laws, hospital workers legally must give their employer 10 days' notice before they strike. The 2006 expiration date was secured and the contract settled seven days into that countdown to what might have been the first hospital strikes in Vegas. The UHS workers prioritized union-leave language too, and immediately more nurses were brought out of their workplaces and into six-month rotating organizer positions. Six months is perfect, incidentally, to ask nurses to come out of their hospitals and do full-time union work, any more than that and they typically balk because there are constantly new procedures and techniques being introduced and they don't want to fall behind or get rusty. The UHS settlement was finalized in June 2004, with a two-year contract lining up their next period of negotiations with those of Sunrise and the big public hospital.

Within days of the UHS settlements, which received banner headlines, workers at two non-union hospitals, run by Catholic Healthcare West (CHW), called the union office and declared they wanted to do what it took to win the same contract. By mid-October 2004, 1,500 more hospital workers, nurses and non-nurses, had voted to form new wall-to-wall unions in their hospitals. And just six months later, workers at these two hospitals voted for contracts with standards that surpassed even the UHS workers' settlements. To top it off, the newly organized workers bargained for a 15-month agreement, far less than two years, so that they, too, would have their contract expiration set for 2006. And during the first contract negotiations for the CHW hospitals, the nurses and non-nurses also voted to form a union at a smaller, brand new hospital, HCA Southern Hills, bringing to three the number of wall-to-wall hospitals organized in five months.

When 2006 arrived, the payoff of all this solidarity of purpose and longsighted strategy surpassed all expectations. Hospital workers across southern Nevada ratified contracts with new standards unprecedented in the US South. The Catholic Healthcare West workers led off the 2006 negotiations because their employer was smart enough to realize a war was brewing and, being less ideologically bound, wanted to avoid it. The price tag for opting out of the fight was an even higher new contract standard, one that would establish the pattern for negotiations at the other hospitals. Their wages were already significantly above market, since their first union contract had been settled so recently, so the priority became other kinds of gains, including contractually negotiated mandatory staffing levels – the best ever negotiated in a US collective bargaining agreement at that time – and better work rules, pensions, retiree healthcare and more.[10]

The HCA Sunrise hospital workers, along with HCA Southern Hills (the hospital organized in early 2005), won a contract with average wage increases of 17 per cent over three years; 100 per cent employer-paid healthcare (employees had previously paid for their own healthcare through payroll deductions, if they could afford it; many lower-wage hospital workers simply did without); new differentials for evening and weekend work; a contractual right to strike over staffing mid-contract (breaking the US norm of signing no-strike clauses) and much more. Only UHS, with two hospitals, held out. The UHS workers sustained a brutal 12-month-long war with their employer and mounted the first-ever nurses' strike. For more than a year, two of the top private Pinkerton-style union-busting firms turned the two UHS hospitals into hell zones, revealing how little their employer cared about quality patient care or their employees. In the end, these workers also won the new area-wide wage and benefit standards, though there were many casualties along the way, such as the firing of Joan Wells.

On the heels of the 2006 Vegas wins, nurses in two more hospitals, in eastern and northern Nevada, also voted to form new unions, making Nevada the highest-density state in the US for registered nurses.[11] A crucial difference here from other states in the US was that all these Nevada nurses and hospital workers were in the *same* union, with commonality of purpose.

STRATEGIC CONSIDERATIONS

Theory and practice were merging in Nevada. Thousands of hours of discussion among and between the workers and with the organizers were required to move from conceptual discussions of power to the active construction of working-class identity formation and working-class solidarities. The following strategic considerations were key to the effort.

Struggling together

Hospitals have a fairly predictable stratification by ethnicity and gender. Among the nurses, the nurses with the most power, generally the Intensive Care Units (adults, neonatal, post-anaesthesia, etc), Surgical (operating room) and Emergency Department nurses, tend to be white. Among the Intermediate Care (IMC) and a catch-all category called General Medical-Surgical nurses (which includes telemetry, oncology, radiology, rehabilitation, etc), there can be larger numbers of Filipinas. But nursing units overall are more white than not, and the diversity generally stems from US schemes that import significant numbers of Filipinas. Most men in hospitals are found in the technical units, and are also typically more white than not. They crush and mix medicines in the pharmacy, administer EKG and X-rays and generally spend more time with machines than patients. Housekeeping staff trends Latino. Dietary trends Black.

Confronting racism and the many other 'isms' the boss throws in the way of a class-based movement is obviously done best when all of the hospital workers have to struggle together. By separating out the nurses, labour has destroyed the chance to help heal intra-class divisions. In Nevada, discussing the politics of race, gender and education/skill were central to building and holding hospital-wide solidarity. And because the union drove a community and political programme through the worksite structure and not outside of it, the workers were learning to overcome the bifurcation of work and home.[12] Undoing racism and sexism at work, through collective struggle that demanded total unity, was forging a better class politics inside and outside the workplace. The left was advanced on these issues in the 1930s early on, when simply pushing for the inclusion of blacks and women (whether they were wives or workers) was radical.[13] But the left's reaction to recent identity politics has been largely a failure, with far too many discussions about 'class versus race' or 'class versus gender'. It's how class, race, gender and more intersect, and in wall-to-wall organizing campaigns, workers' chances of winning are best when the discussions of intra-class divisions are explicit, not denied.

Developing a common vision

From early 2004 onward, a hospital by hospital, worker by worker conversation began about why Las Vegas healthcare workers in the state and region were so far behind their counterparts in places like New York, California, Pennsylvania and Washington. These conversations were rolled out as part of a plan to rebuild the union into a fighting force, and with a keen understanding that the best way to expand the union was for the existing workers to own and lead the plan. Expectations were being raised, and at all times the vision was anchored in the core principle of industrial unionism, commonly discussed as building wall-to-wall power, including registered nurses and everyone else. Winning would be contingent on mass participation and the word *power* was constantly discussed.

Vegas was in the boom years in its cyclical boom-bust tradition, and nurses from across the country, including quite a few from Canada and the Philippines, were arriving in droves, along with all other kinds of workers. This influx of hospital workers who had worked previously in strong union states or countries with union traditions helped make the conversations about what was possible more realistic. In every hospital there were workers like Tim Kearny, who helped build the hospital workers union in New York City two decades earlier at Columbia Presbyterian and had come to Vegas for cheap housing. And Shauna Hamel, another Canadian nurse who, like Joan Wells, had experienced a better healthcare system that had been heavily unionized. And Becky Estrella, a Filipina nurse who during tough negotiations would mutter under breath about going to get her machete when the employer was insulting the workers across the table. Becky had been a part of the revolutionary movements in the Philippines and all it took to get her involved was asking her. Becky brought an entire informal network of the Filipina nurse leaders along with her once she had confidence that the plan to win was real. Organizers deliberately plied these experiences at every turn so that workers were learning from workers that strong unions could extract big concessions and real changes.

Attending to semantics

Workers who don't know about unions (that's most in the USA today), or who are members of unions where participation is undervalued if not squashed regularly, base their initial ideas about the union on how union leaders, including organizers, talk about the union. Far from trivial, semantics are central. How leaders talk about the union is also how workers will talk about the union in conversations among themselves. In every one-on-one conversation, or speech, or interview, union leaders are giving an impression of what the union is to other workers. If the language conveys that the union is a fee for service, or only for professionals, or perhaps not for professionals at all, or a place where lawyers and negotiators work everything out, workers will be less likely to engage or see themselves as the union.

Talking about developing a wall-to-wall hospital union helped convey the power needed, but it would be another set of words that would reflect the mission-driven nature of most nurses and healthcare workers: a 'patient-centred hospital workers union'. By keeping the focus on patients, not professional status or lack thereof, semantics helped drive the discussion about what high quality patient care required. Was it sufficient to heal a patient if the cooks in the dietary unit accidentally delivered the wrong food to a diabetic patient? What if the anti-bacterial techniques were being compromised because of short staffing in housekeeping, or the technicians responsible for sterilizing equipment misses a millimeter of a piece when their boss called them away – would simply having a good nurse solve the problem? As Joan Wells put it:

Healing a patient is a team effort. If everyone is working well together, the patient heals faster. Being together in one union actually promoted team building in our hospitals by reducing animosity between workers, including the many layers of nurse-on-nurse power trips that can play out between ICU nurses and, say, less technically skilled nurses in the general medical surgical units.

This bottom-up approach was key to overcoming cynicism about genuine team building because just about every nurse and hospital worker has been forced by bad management into on-again-off-again 'Team Nursing' schemes, almost all of which are cost saving measures dressed up in colourful language.

The organizing teams in Nevada, comprised of a dozen nurses out on union leave at any one time and other organizers who were showing up in Vegas because the words 'real organizing' were spreading through the organizer grapevine, knew to expect 'semantics drills' almost every day. The organizing team was building a culture, along with the rest of the union, and the organizing culture demanded that every action, including every word, needed to help workers understand two ideas: power, 'all workers together up against management'; and purpose, 'patient-centred'. With their first or second cup of coffee in hand each morning, organizers at the mandatory 9 a.m. 'briefing meetings' would practice 'drills' and 'raps' regularly. Semantics, meaning how we talk, drives learning and discussions.

Leader identification

The process of correctly identifying what organizers call the 'organic leader' is what often separates winning from losing union campaigns. Unions have been losing a lot of campaigns in the US and it's not only due to external factors. Organic leader identification, or the building of a network of the 'most trusted workers in every shift and in every unit', isn't a new technique; nor, however, is it commonly done well, if at all, in many campaigns today. In every workplace, on every shift, among every type of worker, a power structure exists. Organizing is all about power, how to disrupt it, but also how to build it. Human social relationships and networks reflect power relations, whether it's overt, as in the military, or, subtle and informal, as it might be among a group of nurses, each with different years of experience and different types of training. When good organizers use the word *leader* it means only one thing: the person has *followers*. It has nothing to do with whether or not the person speaks well, dresses nicely, pleases people or even supports the union. The leader on a shift could be anti-union, which spells trouble if the identified leader doesn't come to change their position to pro-union. If the majority of real, informal organic leaders are pro-union, they can mobilize the majority of workers to stay the course, even during a tough fight.

In hospitals most workers are mission-driven, not just the nurses. People arrive at work with a calling to care for others. More often than not it's a nurse in any given unit and shift who actually leads most of the workers. For hospital workers to win, to build the strongest possible worksite organization, the organic leaders can't be in a separate union, expressing occasional solidarity. Solidarity is built in common struggle, with high stakes, where the accountability to take risk is between people.

Bargaining together

In Nevada, from 2003 to 2007, all hospital workers negotiated collective bargaining agreements together. Nurses of all types sat with every other worker in the union. Even though anti-worker labour laws cut up and divide various types of hospital workers into as many pieces as a surgeon's scalpel, workers can demand, and if strong enough win, the right to bargain together and negotiate a common collective bargaining agreement. By electing whole hospital bargaining teams, with representation from all types of workers across shifts and units, and preparing for and executing collective bargaining together, bottom-up team building flowers. As Serrano said: 'Nurses going to the bargaining table without the rest of the hospital workers is like going to a dollar store with 40 cents in your pocket. You can't really get anything.'

Of course, there are some issues, not many, that relate to specific groups of workers and that can be long, tedious and downright boring for other workers. A good example is what's called nurse floating rules. Floating is the term for when management wants to send, or *float*, a nurse from one unit, say, the ICU, into another unit, such as the general medical surgical unit or 'Med-Surg' unit, (the unit where patients go before being discharged, when they are on the mend, or at least not acute, where there can be anywhere from five to 12 patients). Nurses hate this practice; cheap or greedy hospitals love it. ICU nurses don't spend their day juggling multiple patients; their expertise is keeping one or two critical patients alive. Nurse floating discussions can be divisive among and between nurses, and can put everyone else to sleep as fast as any good anaesthesia. But it's incredibly easy to simply set up a side table in bargaining, where nurses and nurse managers can hammer out their floating policies. This simple solution is only possible when large numbers of workers are involved in their own collective bargaining process, because having several of each classification of worker from all different units in one room sets the stage for sub-teams to go off into their corners or adjacent rooms to work on specific issues.

Making commitments public

Just like a married couple can cheat, a public statement of commitment and a ring helps hold relationships together. It's true for other types of social relationships, too, including bargaining relationships among and between workers in the same hospital and across hospitals. In Nevada, to set the stage for the hospital-wide bargaining, all workers across all hospitals met as one giant bargaining team. Every other week hundreds of workers would arrive in the union hall by shift to discuss, strategize, update each other, eat a meal, break into hospital-specific breakouts, return to the big group and generally ratify plans of action for the weeks to come. Before the negotiations kicked off in the first hospitals, nurses and non-nurses had taken public votes together, including on what the minimum standards for bargaining would be, how they would support each other by attending, en masse, each others' bargaining tables and developing the camaraderie that allows for effectively implementing high-participation strategic planning.

CONCLUSION

Nurses are extraordinary natural leaders. To be good at their job, which the vast majority aspires to be, they either arrive with or have to develop a strong sense of confidence. Central to their job is making real decisions that impact patients' lives (decisions often made in the presence of distraught family members). Nurses possess persuasion skills, leading patients and their families through trying and scary moments where they must explain a plan of action for a successful recovery. They build instant and intimate relationships with patients and patients' families; the kind of intimacy that happens when they have to do what amounts to an invasion of their patients' most intimate personal space, their bodies. They are often the most trusted workers throughout the hospital. This means there's a large number of organic leaders, perhaps more than usual, but perhaps just more obvious. For nurses, learning how to quickly earn someone's trust is essential. Joan Wells explains it this way:

> Once we have the patient stable, our next most important job is making the family comfortable with our care. In order to do our job, our many tasks, with the patient, we have to be able to do it without a lot of interruptions. So if we don't establish a good rapport with the family right away, if they don't have confidence in you, your job becomes very difficult.

To waste this kind of compassion and this kind of leadership on a craft union, when nurses have and can lead thousands more workers around them, is a travesty. Some days it feels criminal. The qualities, skillsets and experiences of nurses are the same qualities and skillsets needed to build strong unions with all the workers. Nurses don't prioritize themselves; they are, in Serrano's words, about caring for people. The often repeated and accepted notion that nurses are 'professionals', and have a 'professional identity that requires a separate, professional union', is a myth constructed to rationalize the empire building objectives and turf wars of some union leaders. Nurses, as Serrano and Wells articulate, are mission-driven, caring people. It's a strategic choice to either play up their profession while playing down their care mission or play up their care mission and down their sense of professionalism.

Tragically, by early 2009, turf wars among rival unions would succeed where the employers had failed. The solidarity between nurses and non-nurses would be undone by a tightly-held secret national agreement between the California Nurses Association and the SEIU. The two national unions had been in a pitched turf war for several years, with CNA asserting it would be the 'only' national union for nurses. There was more to this battle, including ideological differences, outsized egos and political power ambitions between the heads of each national union. The nurses' organizing gains achieved in such a short timeframe in Nevada were unprecedented in the SEIU and a perceived threat to the CNA. Nevada workers got caught in the very ugly crosshairs of the escalating turf war between these national unions.[14] But Nevada's example of seven hospitals' worth of nurses choosing a wall-to-wall union model still provides plenty of evidence of what strategic choices are needed today for forging new working-class solidarities, even in the face of existing union organizations which do not value them.

NOTES

This article written with the support of a Boren Cherktov-Blue Mountain Center writing fellowship.

1   Beverly Silver, *Forces of Labor: Workers Movements and Globalization since 1870*, Cambridge: Cambridge University Press, 2003.

2   See http://www.bls.gov.

3   This account is based on my own personal involvement as Executive Director of the SEIU in Nevada, where I was hired by the Executive Board early in 2004 and stayed until 2008. This is also based on discussions and interviews I have undertaken with key rank-and-file activists in the spring of 2014. This essay goes beyond the account offered in my book *Raising Expectations and*

Raising Hell (London: Verso, 2012) by focusing on the strategic question of why nurses teamed up so readily with their non-nursing coworkers, and the broader implications of this for forging new class solidarities.

4   See http://www.bls.gov.

5   The hospitals included: the University Medical Center, UMC; Healthcare Corporation of America or HCA owned Sunrise and Southern Hills; Universal Health Services or UHS-owned Desert Springs and Valley; and Catholic Healthcare West or CHW-owned Rose Delima and Siena (CHW did a corporate branding name change to lose the word 'Catholic' and it now calls itself 'Dignity Health'). The municipal units included workers for the largest local government, Clark County, as well as three smaller city area housing authorities.

6   Author interview, April 2014.

7   Bill Frist, of the Frist family of Nashville, TN, world headquarters of HCA, was a two-term Republican senator who served as the Majority Leader in the George W. Bush years, from 2003 to 2007. The family founded HCA. See his page at http://en.wikipedia.org.

8   Part of 'management law' in the US, commonly called 'labour law', is that each different unit of workers has to vote to be certified or to decertify. There are up to eight different units, PROs or professionals, RNs, Techs (which of course isn't just techs, it's technical workers like EKG folks and all of many types, plus also, LPNs or Licensed Practical Nurses – what Joan Wells was prior to getting her Registered Nursing degree), the S & M or Service and Maintenance Units, the Operating Engineers units, and on and on.

9   Author interview, April 2014.

10   The uniqueness of the contractually negotiated nurse-to-patient staffing levels in the CHW Nevada contracts was that there was language stating that 'in the implementation of these new staffing ratios, the hospital agrees there will be no reduction in a single position in the non-nursing staff'. This language, according to the many nurses who had worked in California, where staffing ratios were set by a hard-fought state law, didn't have protections for the numbers of positions of the non-nurses and the result has been a profound undermining of the California law: the hospitals gutted thousands of positions in the non-nurse staff to pay for the increased nursing staff required by the law. So much so that nurses were asked to pick up new duties, duties that had been done by a more robust non-nursing staff. Though it wasn't the intent of the workers who campaigned to pass the California law, because it was only an RN focus, the RNs undermined themselves by creating a law that didn't actually solve the problem of RNs having workloads that are way too large to give the kind of patient care they desire.

11   By the end of 2007, nine out of 10 nurses were in the union. The Renown Hospital victory in Northern Nevada, in Reno, added 1,000 more RNs, and the Elko Regional hospital in eastern Nevada added first nurses and, in a second vote, the rest of the workers to the union.

12   Ira Katznelson, *City Trenches: Urban Politics and the Patterning of Class in the United States*, Chicago: University of Chicago Press, 1981.

13   William Z. Foster, *Organizing Steel*, New York: Workers Library Publishers, 1936.

14   The CNA spent much of 2008 attempting to 'raid' the nurses from the three CHW hospitals in Vegas. Despite the CNA setting up a ground operation in Vegas with forty nurses shipped in from California, churning out reams of literature about how the nurses didn't belong 'in a janitors union, but in a professional union', the CNA failed to win a majority of the nurses in two successive elections. But opportunity for rival union deal-making soon emerged when the SEIU was about to 'trustee' its big California healthcare local. Suddenly, it was in the SEIU's interest to give something to the CNA, something the CNA wanted. In a deal that succeeded in the SEIU preventing the CNA from joining forces with the new breakaway union that emerged out of the California local, one of the many poker chips the SEIU played was effectively handing over the nurses to the CNA. Notably, in his important essay 'Rethinking Unions, Registering Socialism' (*Socialist Register 2013*, Pontypool: Merlin Press, 2012), Sam Gindin speaks eloquently to the issue of rival unions competing for turf, and points to the urgent need for new left formations to succeed inside of unions so that solidarity and developing working-class power, not competing egos or business plans, dictate the mission of unions.

NEW WORKING-CLASS ORGANIZATION AND THE SOCIAL MOVEMENT LEFT

STEVE WILLIAMS AND RISHI AWATRAMANI

There is nothing more crucial, in this respect, than Gramsci's recognition that every crisis is also a moment of reconstruction; that there is no destruction which is not, also, reconstruction; that, historically nothing is dismantled without also attempting to put something new in its place; that every form of power not only excludes but produces something.[1]

Stuart Hall, 'Gramsci & Us'

New organizations are seeking to build power and organization from sectors of the working class previously relegated to the side stage of history. In these organizations, working-class African American, Latino, Asian, Pacific Islander and Indigenous communities are at the centre alongside working-class women, young people, queer and transgender people as well as organized white working-class communities. The constituencies of these organizations include service workers, bicycle messengers and fast food workers; informal workers including street vendors, day labourers and sex workers; unemployed workers and welfare recipients; people who have immigrated to the United States and people who are incarcerated; people fighting police brutality and home foreclosures and those fighting against the toxification of neighbourhoods in pursuit of clean and safe environments.

These organizations are developing leaders who will be positioned to forge the development of a broader anti-capitalist bloc inside the United States. From the San Francisco Bay Area to rural Mississippi, the efforts to organize working-class people in reaction to the immeasurable human and planetary suffering inflicted by the ruling class might appear as little more than mere resistance struggles, but closer examination reveals important potential. Each of these experiments is historically important in its own right, and together they represent a critical opening to expanding and sharpening class struggle guided by a vision of an alternative future, based on human development, ecological renewal and global solidarity. Of particular interest is the critical role that a small number of social movement leftists have played in sharpening the outlook, demands and practice of many of these organizations.[2] Socialists looking to build an anti-capitalist, anti-imperialist bloc should pay close attention to these efforts as the questions that they are grappling with 'and the practices they are innovating' will be critical in any effort to fight for an uncharted socialist future.

Franz Fanon famously counselled that 'Each generation must, out of relative obscurity, discover its mission, fulfill it, or betray it'.[3] In attempting to carry out that mission, revolutionaries of all eras must respond to certain foundational questions. None of those is more important than the question of the balance of social forces. What class has, or has the potential to develop, the consciousness, capacity and confidence to lead a larger social movement to transform society? Toppling the capitalist order and establishing the basis for a socialist future requires more than insurrectional fury and wishful thinking. Social transformation is a process of self-emancipation, and revolutionary movements must be animated by organizations comprised of the social forces with the interest in and social position to lead other forces in a struggle to transform society. No question is more important for socialists than identifying which sections of society are likely to take up direct and indirect struggle against bourgeois hegemony and play a leading role in that struggle. The answer to this question has tremendous implications on organizational strategy, objectives and practice. After identifying the leading class forces, revolutionaries must also identify the other social forces with whom the leading class can unite and lead in the transformative struggles. Once identified, revolutionaries must then work to cohere those forces so that they have the confidence and capacity to act collectively.

This question of which class forces have the best chance of leading a decisive movement to transform society and the economy is at the heart of all organizing efforts by leftists. Much of the organizing carried out by leftists in the United States, with some notable exceptions including the work of the Black Panther Party, the Young Lords and the National Welfare Rights Organization, operated from the assessment that the industrial working class would be the pivotal section of the working class in building a movement against capitalism and US imperialism. For some, this assessment was taken to an extreme such that the industrial working class was seen as the *only* section of the working class to have the potential to lead a revolutionary movement. According to such orthodoxy, all other sections of the working class came to be seen as peripheral at best, and sometimes as reactionary. Based on this assessment, trade unions and organizing at the point of production were seen as an exclusive arena of class struggle. Many left formations deployed cadre to organize in workplaces from the 1960s to the 1980s. Organizing efforts in other locations were paid little attention or viewed with suspicion. Whether or not that was an accurate assessment at that time, however, is not critical in advancing a new strategy in our current context. While the pronouncements of the death of industrial production in the United States have been premature, the position of working-class forces in the United States has experienced tectonic shifts in the last forty years.

This has been made even more acute since 2009, the only year of fiscal stimulus after the 2008 financial crisis. Neoliberal public austerity strategies, based on the ideological position that the crisis emerged because of over-spending and public debt, have established an approach to recovery that has cut the social safety net, formalized wage and public spending reductions already lowered during the crisis, and transformed employment relations into permanently unstable conditions. At work, workers find less and less stability in their hours and pay, and fewer protections from employer mistreatment and exploitation. Full-time jobs are transitioned to part-time, permanent jobs become temporary, stable work is subcontracted and immigrant workers are offered work arrangements linking their immigration status and family's future to a chain of contractors and employers that each deny responsibility for their workers' well-being.

The resulting new reality in the US is that class formation is no longer confined to the point of production, if it ever was; class formation now plays out in every aspect of life. With a state-subsidized private sector buttressed in most areas of the economy, workers and their families find increased insecurity in access to healthcare and education, and little ability to meet basic needs. Six years after the speculative bubble burst, what marginal recovery there has been for the ruling elite has come at the expense of working people and the climate. Living standards for working people and popular classes around the world continue to fall as sea levels and greenhouse gas emissions rise. With increased cutbacks and crackdowns, there have emerged significant pockets of stiffening resistance. The community, labour and environmental struggles happening today are cultivating popular power in ways that will shape the resolution of this crisis. Leftists have a responsibility to support, examine and help shape those struggles which are taking place. This essay is one attempt to shed light on a small but growing number of important organizing efforts which are attempting to heed Stuart Hall's insight and take up the challenge to transform the terrain on which struggles take place.

NEW WORKING-CLASS ORGANIZATION

Building from a desire to organize around the diversity of working-class life and experience, there are an increasing number of non-traditional working-class organizations that have set their sights on building membership in ways that complement the membership of traditional unions. Several campaigns have emerged over the past few years to bridge this chasm, including a national organizing drive of fast food workers, and a parallel effort of Walmart workers and many more. A new national initiative between the National Guestworker Alliance, Jobs With Justice and National People's Action is launching a long-term strategy to win new bargaining mechanisms for workers experiencing the most precarious and contingent circumstances. These organizations, which engage different sectors of the working class, have the potential to align an organizing programme that develops members and leaders through a political programme, and that sets its sights on transformations beyond unionization and towards the socialization of society's wealth. Committed and developed left leadership is necessary in order to realize this potential.

While all of these organizations are a part of mounting resistance to the ravages of neoliberal austerity, a small but critical minority of these organizations are moving to situate their efforts as part of larger efforts to build a socialist political presence in the US. The example of POWER (People Organized to Win Employment Rights) in the San Francisco Bay area demonstrates the importance of left leadership in supporting and sharpening the development of working-class organizations. POWER was founded in 1997 with the intention of uniting workfare workers and unionized public sector workers after the Clinton administration slashed the social safety net by passing its 'ending welfare as we know it' legislation the previous year. Amongst the organization's founding core and early staff were three social movement leftists who also happened to be members of STORM (Standing Together to Organize a Revolutionary Movement), a Marxist activist collective that operated in the Bay Area from 1995 to 2002. These activists integrated into, and built relationships and worked side-by-side with members of, San Francisco's working-class African American and Latino communities who had first joined specific campaigns initiated by POWER. After which a member of POWER's staff – often one of these social movement leftists – recruited them during outreach sessions at worksites, welfare offices, soup kitchens and public housing projects. Then, these members were encouraged to participate actively in all aspects of POWER's work, often taking leadership positions within an organization that especially cultivated a practice of identifying and fighting for what André

Gorz referred to as 'non-reformist reforms', or reforms that do not confine themselves to 'capitalist needs, criteria and rationalities'.[4]

POWER won important victories, including forcing the local welfare department to provide language interpretation and printed materials in multiple languages; securing the formation of a public body to resolve violations of health and housing codes in the City's public housing units; and leading a broad-based community and labour coalition which raised the local minimum wage in 2004 and increased the purchasing power of low-wage workers by more than $180 million per year.[5] No less significant are the advances that POWER made in deepening its members' leadership and intellectual capacities. The staff and members have created various mechanisms including a political training programme, reading and writing circles as well as an organizing internship for member-leaders. Although this required shifting organizational resources away from direct campaigning, the long-term benefit has been that members are more active and remain connected for longer periods of time than before these programmes were implemented. The result has been that scores of current and former staff and members now play key roles in various movement building efforts in San Francisco and across the country.

In 2011, POWER undertook a new campaign against the gentrification of San Francisco. The organization's leadership conducted a series of meetings to envision policies that would enable working-class families to stay and thrive in the city. They discussed the rising cost of living, never-ending cuts to public services as well as the mounting ecological crisis. They also noted how the market seemed to be encroaching into more and more aspects of their lives and how truly public space, once talked about as the commons, was disappearing. Central to the vision that emerged from the members' discussions was a commitment to the provision of free and quality public transportation for everyone – not just low-income people.[6] The members also mapped out all of the different social sectors that might have an interest in such a demand including the bicycle riders' coalition, advocates for smart growth and teachers, and they began building relationships with these forces. Realizing that the forces in favour of universal free public transit did not yet have the political power necessary to win such a demand. Yet, POWER made a tactical decision to limit the call for free transit initially to young people as a first step towards building the power and stoking the public imagination necessary to win the demand for free public transit for all. Among various contributing factors that led POWER to this decision, a key consideration was that over the previous five years, the cost of a monthly bus pass for young people had increased by more than 200 per cent, from

$10 to $22.[7] This was especially problematic since the City in 2013 had begun placing police officers on public buses to catch and issue citations to anyone without proof of having purchased a ticket. This combination of attacks on the community alarmed POWER members who saw this as yet another instance in a long string of city officials' criminalizing young African Americans and Latinos.

It would have been tempting for the members of POWER to issue a call for free transportation for students from low-income families. Instead, the organization developed a collective vision of quality public transportation which included comprehensive service, no-cost fares and quality wages and safe working conditions for all transit employees. The members then conducted an assessment of the City's transit system which included meetings with numerous transit policy analysts in the Bay Area. Finally, in April 2011, POWER members formed a coalition with other student and community organizations and supportive local officials, and they issued the demand for free public transit for *all* young people in San Francisco, regardless of their family's income. In their internal discussions, POWER members hoped that a victory would open the door to eventually winning a transit system that was fare-free for all riders. POWER's members saw this as especially important not only for countering the drive towards austerity but also for creating a new generation of transit riders, limiting greenhouse gas emissions and addressing the climate crisis. Emboldened by their commitment to the vision of a free transit system and acting as a leading force, POWER's membership of low-income students, domestic workers and public housing residents argued that *all* San Franciscans needed free transit – including the children of wealthy families.

Although the transit board ultimately rejected the demand for universal provision of free transportation, the members of POWER and the transit coalition were able to force the City to allocate more than $6 million to initiate a programme that allows all youth in families at or below the City's median income to ride public buses for free. Within the first months of this victory, more than 31,000 young people secured passes allowing them to ride the City's buses for free.[8] But just as important, POWER members no longer saw themselves as marginal. As Manuela Esteva, one of the campaign's leaders, said, 'I now know that our vision is key to making a better world for everyone. We're not just organizing to improve our lives. We're organizing to make the world a better place for everyone, and we're the ones who can do that'.[9]

While POWER's history and context are unique, it is hardly alone in its commitment to waging campaigns that strike at the logic of capital.

There are scores of organizations throughout the United States, and many more springing to life each year. For example, in a very different context, the National People's Action (NPA) is a national network of base-building organizations located in fourteen states with more than 200 organizers working on its campaigns. NPA traces its organizational lineage, very differently from POWER, to the anti-ideological organizing models developed by Saul Alinsky. Still, the terrain on which NPA is waging its campaigns has shifted very significantly, such that its organizers have become more open in their critique of 'the system', just as it has become more and more clear that the system is unable or unwilling to meet the needs of its members and its working-class constituency. The NPA recently completed an arduous process in which thousands of working-class members and leaders developed a forty-year long-term agenda ultimately directed at bringing about 'a new economy... that makes people – and not profits – the bottom line'.[10]

Unlike the neoliberal project's call for small government, the dominant call from these working-class organizing efforts has been for an active and accountable people's government. NPA's call for 'democratic control of government' and the work of groups like Community Voices Heard in New York are emblematic of this position. Extrapolating from this, twenty-first century socialism envisions a state apparatus to facilitate popular participation in ensuring that production meets specified criteria and goals (e.g. efficiency, stewardship of the earth, etc.) to protect society from the resurgence of pernicious forms of bourgeois society. Until a new socialism evolves into an organic, self-reproducing system of production and reproduction, much as contemporary capitalism is today, certain forms of state apparatuses will be necessary to act as a socialist regulator, defending against counter-revolution of the former capitalist class, enabling broad participation in decision-making and direct involvement in production, and setting some planning benchmarks. This form of the state will prioritize devolving its tasks and responsibilities to the regional, if not even more local, level. In other words, the old state must be committed to its own dissolution, even if it never gets all the way there. Though the state apparatus of a new socialism will have to find a way to deal with some critical old state functions, socialist state institutions will have a decidedly decentralized structure to allow for maximum participation and maximum protagonism, and will be tasked with being protectors of the socialist transition and the values of our new system. A new state system will be far more globally interconnected, with egalitarian global relations being a further expression of protagonism and human development.

This is an area in which numerous working-class organizations are experimenting. Over the last ten years, working-class organizations in Virginia, Florida, New York, Mississippi and California that had focused their efforts on organizing neighbourhoods or cities have begun to come together to engage their membership in the electoral arena with the intention of moving hundreds of thousands of people to take political action to shape their future, initially as voters and eventually as protagonists in transforming their communities and workplaces. Of these experiments, the one with the most explicit left programme is in Jackson, Mississippi. Anchored by the Malcolm X Grassroots Movement (MXGM), 'The Jackson Plan is an initiative to apply many of the best practices in the promotion of participatory democracy, solidarity economy, and sustainable development and combine them with progressive community organizing and electoral politics'.[11] The three components of the Jackson Plan include people's assemblies, solidarity economy and building a network of progressive political candidates. This fledging effort won an impressive victory when, as part of the MXGM goal of organizing the residents of that city to revitalize a city with failing infrastructure, they secured the election in July 2013 of the long-time activist from the Black Liberation Movement, Chokwe Lumumba, as the mayor of Jackson. These plans were rattled by Lumumba's untimely passing in February 2014, but MXGM is pushing forward their three-pronged efforts and these efforts demand the movement's attention and support. Efforts such as these develop the capacities of community leaders to engage in the governance of their own communities and experience the responsibility that comes from gaining the ability to make political decisions over an alien state.

Of course, without a vision for where participation in this political system may lead, it is quite possible for progressive elected officials to be absorbed into the bourgeois common sense of actually existing politics and, in fact, obstruct social movement interests and efforts. Vision and political programmes produced by social movement organizations create the opportunity for these experiments in electoral power to move us closer to full human development and protagonism, which leads to the critical role of social movement leftists.

DEVELOPING THE VISION

But what would it really mean to mount an economic, political and ideological challenge to up-end the capitalist system? While this question has deeply theoretical underpinnings, it is a question that has deeply practical implications for social movement activists, since demands, practice and strategy are all grounded in an organization's vision. Most successful movements throughout history have been guided by an overarching vision of what they were fighting for. Both past and contemporary movements, from South Africa to the Philippines, from China to Venezuela, have been and continue to be cohered by revolutionary imagination. The lack of a unifying vision in the United States splits the movement into issue-based silos; it causes organizers and activists to burn out more quickly; it means movements can't successfully challenge the capitalist vision of growth and development; and it limits their imagination to grow the movement to the scale needed to mount a serious challenge.

The need for a vision of twenty-first century socialism has not been universally embraced on the left. Some argue that the functions and process of a future socialism are impossible to predict. The nature of socialist society, they argue, will develop dialectically, reflecting the long struggle to transform the forces and relations of production. To develop a vision of socialism in advance of that struggle is anti-dialectical. However, to assume that socialism will emerge spontaneously out of an unfolding series of reform struggles in an undulating sea of capitalist hegemony ignores one half of the dialectic: the antithesis or counterpoint to the current mode of production. To ignore the need to develop a concrete alternative vision is, in fact, to rob the dialectic of its transformative potential. What follows are the outlines of a vision of a new type of socialism for the twenty-first century that builds on the work of movement intellectuals and on the practices, demands and approaches developed by social movements.

The central organizing principle of a systematic twenty-first century socialism is the goal of human development.[12] In contrast to capitalism's obsession with accumulating profit, twenty-first century socialism must centre on making the wealth of society available to develop the capacities of all human beings to live full, creative, healthy lives. This is a vision that is in line with the practice of many social movements, which connects the social goal of human development with Marx's concept of 'revolutionary practice' and Paolo Friere's 'pedagogy of the oppressed'.[13] This stresses that social transformation cannot be gifted from above, but must be created by the affected through their own efforts. This insight – that one is changed as one tries to make change in the world – is at the heart of the best contemporary working-class organizing efforts which have insisted that the members play key roles in the development and advancement of their organization's work.

Marx's concept of the alternative to capitalism as a 'free association of producers' is based on the premise that people themselves command production as the lead protagonists in shaping economic activity. The combination of this 'protagonism' with people's desire for good living and economic security motivates work and effort. The aspiration for society to be free of an 'alienated force' compelling people to work, alongside the drive to develop our full human creative potential, are at the heart of the project for twenty-first century socialism. In fact, the goal of human development must be the enduring measure of twenty-first century socialist aims advanced by social movements and the compass that determines strategic direction of the project for socialists fighting for a new society. In order for human development to occur, this new type of socialism revolves around three central features: 1) social ownership of the means of production; 2) reorienting production towards meeting social needs in balance with the reproductive capacity of earth; and 3) developing the capacities of workers and communities to guide and plan their own productive work.[14] Clarity of these three features can inform the demands advanced by social movements and the types of institutions developed by popular forces as they look to transcend capitalist relations. While the specific form and character of these demands and institutions will be shaped by the specific conditions in which they're advanced, there are certain characteristics that will flow from these three features.

A new socialism will have a different standard by which production is evaluated, based on a rigorous notion of 'socialist accountancy'. This is a concept which István Mészáros has described as involving a reorientation from exchange-value to use-value, so production is based on need rather than what is market-viable, while allowing for a significant increase in leisure time.[15] Such a reorientation would entail radically different understandings of economic planning. Efficiency, for example, in capitalist production means the production of as much surplus value as possible at the least cost, the growth of successful enterprises that are able to create the most surplus and the collapse of enterprises that are not, regardless of its human toll. But for socialist accountancy, efficiency in production would mean collecting data as quickly and accurately as possible on what use-values are needed, what production capacities are available, and then producing and distributing the most useful and necessary use-values in the least time.[16] Driven by the imperative of making protagonists out of workers, capable of shaping their own destinies, socialist accountancy is based on the understanding that feedback from workers and consumers in making ongoing production assessments can lead to greater efficiency.

Socialism must strive towards the fullest and highest possible development of all people in harmony with the natural world. This is one of the areas in which social movements are pushing most clearly around the need to challenge the logic of capitalism. With slogans like 'No war! No warming!

Build an economy for the people and the planet!', organizations and alliances like the Grassroots Global Justice, Climate Justice Alliance and the Indigenous Environmental Network have all confronted the inability of capital to operate in accordance with the limits of nature. Through dialogue with others social movements in gatherings such as the World Social Forum and the People's Assembly in Cochabamba in 2010, as well as online fora such as the Systemic Alternatives website, social movement leftists in the US are connecting to growing efforts to articulate a clear alternative to capitalist and socialist exploitation of the earth's capacity to reproduce.[17] While human development is the objective of this emerging vision of socialism, humankind must be understood as an element of the ecology, rather than separate from or dominant of ecology. Human development aims must be measured against consequences to the rest of the ecology. Considering the repair and survival of the planet's health in shaping the methods of production and consumption of natural resources is a means of achieving lasting and sustainable human development. In this framework, 'social ownership' of the means of production can be best re-articulated as non-ownership or collective stewardship of the means of production. Society would assume the responsibility for making production and consumption decisions that benefit the earth and humanity.

The question of global justice and international solidarity is also a critical and developing area of consideration for many of these new organizing efforts, as seen in the emphasis, for example, that Grassroots Global Justice and National Guestworker Alliance devote to building lasting relationships with social movement allies outside of the United States. Because the US state is still the dominant integrating force in world imperialism, care must be taken to avoid the potential chauvinism of US-centred socialism. A new socialism in the United States must be envisaged on the basis of social movements not only fighting for an end to capitalist imperialism, but ending once and for all the expropriation of resources from the Global South which inhibits the full expression of self-determination in the peripheries. Indeed, a socialist vision for the US must encompass how to facilitate and enforce redistribution of stolen resources and wealth, and reparations for centuries of colonialism and imperialism. This also requires envisioning such new international institutions as would be needed to create balanced and non-hierarchical global relations. Fostering the goal of ending imperialism and creating a system to promote global solidarity means we will need to revisit the political-territorial forms that can best meet people's needs, as most political territorial boundaries today have little to do with human development, socialist accountancy, freely associated labour or even self-determination.

COHERING THE SOCIAL MOVEMENT LEFT

In her ground-breaking work, Marta Harnecker has explored the differences and relationships that were pivotal in sparking the re-emergence of a vibrant and powerful left in Latin America.[18] As Harnecker points out, strong social movements typically build strong connections to critical social forces and often incorporate protagonist practices that support the development of new leaders, especially from popular sectors of women, people of color, indigenous people and youth. Alone, however, those same social movements are often unable to project a vision and demands beyond the scope of their immediate campaigns. This is where institutional or ideological left organizations can play a complementary role. Strong, organized left political vehicles are needed to allow social movements to turn their new approaches to organizing into victories against the totality of a multi-faceted system.

Social movements in the United States are experiencing positive breakthroughs in shaping and sharpening this post-capitalist vision. Nevertheless, these efforts are not without there own challenges. The fragmented nature of most of these struggles means that they remain resistance struggles, while rarely, if ever, rising to the level of an explicit challenge to the systems of capitalism, white supremacy and hetero-patriarchy. New organizing approaches that develop in isolated organizations, or in particular social movements, stand little chance of transforming capitalist relations that have developed an organic, embedded social character. In addition, with the exception of organizing in trade unions, much of this organizing is taking place through charitable non-profit organizations that operate within very specific constraints laid out by the capitalist state and the largely bourgeois-controlled philanthropic sector. As writers like Andrea Smith point out in *The Revolution Will Not Be Funded*, these funding sources create a social and political context which can stifle the transformative potential of well-intentioned organizing and activist projects. Social movement organizers yearning for a socialist transformation of political economy have bemoaned the fragmentation of social movements, the lack of vision and the absence of an organizational home to guide and steer our social movements to a vision like the one articulated above.[19] The pressing question facing US social movements is how can these social movement activists overcome these challenges and play their role in helping to connect the struggles and sectors with which they are engaged.

The fragmentation of social movements, however, is paralleled by the fragmentation amongst left and revolutionary parties in the US. Historically, this 'party left' has offered a rigorous practice of analysis of the conjuncture, as well as a disciplined approach to deploying resources to strategic locations.

Most critically, they provide a mechanism to develop cadre and engage different sections of the movement in a shared conversation. Most left party organizations possess a wealth of experience of fighting for anti-capitalist transformation. Several existing party organizations trace their origins and development through decades of US history, giving them a firmly rooted perspective on revolutionary strategy. The organizational left in the US, however, suffers from old and new divisions that serve to keep most of their organizations both small in number and culturally divisive. And, despite the social movement experience of many cadre in these organizations, the organizations themselves are disconnected from the very social sectors that have the greatest interest in building a transformative movement.

This is one of the areas where social movement leftists can make an invaluable contribution. Unorganized leftists are on the frontlines across many social movement spaces, and in addition to those social movement leftists in the organizations mentioned above who are attempting to tailor their organizing strategies to reflect an anti-capitalist programme, there are many more scattered throughout the country who are looking to develop the skills necessary to connect their day-to-day organizing work with the project of building a bloc of social forces prepared and capable of laying the foundations for twenty-first century socialism and confronting the capitalist class. The fact that many of these social movement leftists not only were radicalized after the dissolution of the Soviet Union, but never experienced any large-scale socialist party organizing, has contributed to a cultural dissonance with the party-oriented left on the one hand, and yet, on the other hand, a deep hunger to understand what left strategy across social movements may look like. An organization of the social movement left is needed that can produce a strata of organizers that are coordinated, ideologically trained, strategically literate and capable of implementing a strategy and articulating a grounded and compelling alternative. In order to address the complexity of conditions in a territory as large as the United States, to build cross-sectoral unity and to adjust to changing conditions, strategy needs an organizational instrument and a skilled base of cadre.

One emerging effort looking to filling this void is LeftRoots, whose goal as a national organization is to develop the individual and collective skills of social movement leftists across the United States to formulate, evaluate and carry out transformative, cross-sectoral strategy that is grounded in a concrete analysis of the current conjuncture. LeftRoots was launched in August 2013 with the initial development of a local branch in the San Francisco Bay Area that now includes fifty members, all of whom are actively involved in different social movement struggles as organizers, member-leaders or activists. In an effort to expand beyond those who normally see themselves as part of the left, the LeftRoots members reflect a deep involvement of people from oppressed and exploited communities with women, people of color and people under the age of 40 making up the great majority of the membership of the Bay Area branch.

Taking a non-sectarian approach to leadership development, LeftRoots plans to seed branches in other parts of the United States beginning in the spring of 2015. In order to safeguard the integrity of the project, LeftRoots members fund full-time staff and all of the organization's activities by paying monthly dues which are based on a percentage of each member's income. Building out from these locally-based branches, LeftRoots plans to spearhead a three-year long process which will lead up to a national congress in 2018, where members and social movement allies from the United States and abroad will come together to discuss long-term strategy to build twenty-first century socialism, based on concrete and evolving assessments of the present conjuncture. The aim of such an effort is to better position those organizers and activists already engaged with social movement struggles to strengthen and draw lessons from existing efforts, while also equipping those leaders to identify and act collectively during moments of strategic opening.

While there is reason to be hopeful about the work of LeftRoots, what is most significant is its recognition that throughout the country social movement leftists are beginning to confront fragmentation and cloudy vision as challenges to be overcome, not least by cultivating a new generation of committed, skilled and engaged cadre to lay the building blocks for mounting a concerted challenge to the existing capitalist order.

NOTES

1   Stuart Hall, 'Gramsci and Us', *Marxism Today*, June 1987, p. 19.
2   In using the term 'social movement leftists', we are drawing on the work of Marta Harnecker, who distinguishes this category from the party left, and considers both to constitute forces 'that oppose the capitalist system and its profit motive and which are fighting for an alternative humanist, solidarity-filled society, a socialist society, the building blocks of which are the interests of the working classes'. The social movement left are those leftists who specifically engage with social movements and whose primary political work is not inside a left party or organization. See Marta Harnecker, *Rebuilding the Left*, New York: Zed Books, 2007, p. 32-3.
3   Franz Fanon, *Wretched of the Earth*, New York: Grove Press, 1961, p. 206.
4   André Gorz, *Strategy for Labor: A Radical Proposal*, Boston: Beacon Press, 1967, p. 7.

5   POWER (People Organized to Win Employment Rights), 'What We Do', available at http://www.peopleorganized.org.

6   POWER, *Next Stop: Justice – Race and Environment at the Center of Transit Planning*, December 2012, pp. 2-3, available at http://www.peopleorganized. org.

7   To address budget cuts at the state government, school district officials announced plans in 2010 to stop transporting students to and from San Francisco's public schools. According to these plans, with very limited exceptions, all students would be responsible for finding their own way to and from school beginning in the 2012-13 school year. The impact was that most of the City's more than 15,000 young people would have to rely on San Francisco's public transit system.

8   John Coté and Marisa Lagos, 'Google says $6.8 million for youth Muni passes just a start', *San Francisco Chronicle*, 28 February 2014.

9   Personal interview by the authors, 19 May 2014.

10   National People's Action, 'Long-term Agenda to the New Economy', p. 2, available at http://npa-us.org.

11   'The Jackson Plan: A Struggle for Self-Determination, Participatory Democracy, and Economic Justice', available at http://mxgm.org.

12   Michael Lebowitz, *The Socialist Alternative*, New York: Monthly Review Press, 2010, p. 44.

13   Notably in his discussion of 'revolutionary practice', Lebowitz (p. 49) rightly highlights Freire, whose work and writings on liberatory pedagogy has been a major influence on many of the new organizations' approach toward leadership development.

14   See Lebowitz, *The Socialist Alternative*, pp. 86-7.

15   István Mészáros, *Beyond Capital*, New York: Monthly Review Press, 1995.

16   Michael Albert, *ParEcon: Life After Capitalism*, New York: Verso, 2003.

17   See the People's Agreement of Cochabamba, available at http://pwccc. wordpress.com; and the Systemic Alternatives Initiative, at http:// systemicalternatives.org.

18   Marta Harnecker, 'Forging a Union of the Party Left and the Social Left', *Studies in Political Economy*, 69, 2002.

19   NTanya Lee and Steve Williams, *More than We Imagined*, p. 17, available at http://eartothegroundproject.org,

THE CRISIS OF LABOUR AND THE LEFT IN THE UNITED STATES

MARK DUDZIC AND ADOLPH REED JR

The 2008 economic crisis and its aftermath were viewed by many as the 'Lazarus moment' for the US left. After all, here was a crisis brought about by the classic contradictions of capitalism playing out on a political landscape shaped by vast and growing disparities of wealth and power. In familiar left foundational mythologies, this was a moment that would give rise to revolution or, at the very least, a 'new New Deal'. And there was no shortage of commentary proclaiming no less than neoliberalism's death agonies.[1] Yet the left has been spectacularly unsuccessful in crafting a coherent response to this crisis, much less influence the terms of debate about its causes and solutions. The exaggerated proclamations of the beginning of the end of neoliberalism, unjustifiably inflated expectations of the Obama presidency, and the irrational exuberance stimulated by Occupy all point to the same reality: there is no left worth talking about in the United States and there has not been one for quite a while. That judgment may seem harsh, even sectarian, to some readers because many claimants to the labels radical, activist or left dot the political landscape.

By left we mean a reasonably coherent set of class-based and anti-capitalist ideas, programmes and policies that are embraced by a cohort of leaders and activists who are in a position to speak on behalf of and mobilize a broad constituency. Such a left would be, or would aspire to be, capable of setting the terms of debate in the ideological sphere and marshalling enough social power to intervene on behalf of the working class in the political economy. Some measures of that social power include: ability to affect both the enterprise wage and the social wage; power to affect urban planning and development regimes; strength to intervene in the judicial and regulatory apparatus to defend and promote working-class interests; power not only to defend the public sphere from encroachments by private capital but also to expand the domain of non-commoditized public goods; and generally to assert a force capable of influencing, even shaping, public policy in ways that advance the interests and security of the working-class majority. By any of these measures there is no longer a functioning left in the United States; nor has there been for a generation. Not only is there no organized left capable of contending for hegemony; in more mundane terms, the left is no longer even capable of affecting the wage structure in the auto industry or intervening in urban development decisions in Brooklyn. Whole swaths of the population, no doubt the vast majority, never come in contact with left institutions or ideas.

Historically, a left of the sort we describe has been anchored to a vibrant labour movement, which has provided the institutional resources, the living and breathing constituency, the core agenda and feet on the ground for any significant counterhegemonic intervention into the political economy. Indeed, it is difficult to imagine how a left capable of challenging corporate power and capitalist hegemony could be built, much less survive, without being linked to a dynamic labour movement. George Soros's Open Society Institute or other liberal foundations will not fund challenges to capitalist class power. Nor can a left capable of mounting such challenges be galvanized through appeals to an evanescent 'public' or the 'people'. For one thing, such appeals have to be projected through the corporate news and public information industry, which will never give serious left critiques or agendas fair hearing. Moreover, formation of a serious anti-capitalist force in American politics will not be sparked by dramatic actions or events, not least because the constituency for that sort of left does not yet exist; it must be created. That is a lesson that must be taken from the reality of our defeat: on the one hand, the relentlessness of the post-crash capitalist offensive understandably feeds a sense of urgency in fighting back; on the other hand, their relentlessness is possible only because we do not have the capacity to challenge them.

THE POSTWAR ROOTS OF TODAY'S DEFEATS

Of course, the left was always weak in the postwar US relative to other advanced capitalist nations. The simplest and most direct explanation of that difference is that, while European capitalist classes came out of the Second World War weakened politically and economically and discredited by their associations with fascism, the American bourgeoisie emerged from the war more powerful than ever and largely rehabilitated in public opinion. American capitalists were determined to curtail, if not roll back, the advance of the labour-left, and they had the social and political power to do so. The effects of the business mobilization were visible in the defeat of the

1945 Full Employment Bill, which would have established full employment as the cornerstone of national economic policy and mandated the federal government to take affirmative action, including public works jobs, to 'assure the existence at all times of sufficient employment opportunities for all Americans able to work and seeking work'. And this was matched by the defeat of the Wagner-Murray-Dingell bill that would have created national health insurance. Then came the Republican congressional victories in 1946, and in the following year the passage, over President Truman's veto, of the Taft-Hartley Act, which severely limited trade unions' occupational and geographical scope of operation and outlawed several important sources of their leverage against employers. The anti-communist offensive associated with the Cold War also isolated leftists and effectively proscribed anti-capitalist perspectives from public discourse – even within the labour movement.[2]

With respect to making sense of the state of the left today, however, that defeat of working-class politics in the late 1940s is less significant than the compromised terms on which it was possible to construct second-best victories within the framework of unchallenged capitalist power.[3] Even into the 1980s, the labour movement retained the capacity to negotiate basic wages and conditions for the first tier of the economy and, to some extent, trickle down conditions in the other tiers. On issues of broader working-class social power, the labour-left helped create and administer the regulatory state, set labour standards and minimum wages, establish and enforce equal pay provisions and win a series of incremental expansions of the social wage and the public sphere including food stamps, public housing, Medicaid, Medicare, publicly funded early childhood and higher education and more. The decline of trade union strength since the 1970s has obscured the extent to which other progressive movements, including what now are known as the 'social movements of the 1960s', depended on organic links to labour for their political capacity and popular successes.

As important as they have been, however, those successes were crafted within the context of the postwar 'grand bargain' of substantive class compromise that contained the seeds of its own undoing. The postwar system rested crucially on: cession of decisions concerning planning and production entirely to management; acceptance of a system of employer-provided social wage benefits negotiated through privatized collective bargaining rather than their universalization through the state; commoditization of housing security through federal subsidy of the private real estate market and suburbanization; and reliance on an economic policy of growth stimulation to sidestep a class politics of redistribution, which tied even left-liberals to support of military Keynesianism and thus Cold War interventionism.[4] Even though some labour-leftists continued to press for social-democratic policies into the 1960s, it is unlikely that more favourable arrangements for the working class could have been won in the context of the postwar reassertion of capitalist class power. Nevertheless, the grand bargain was struck on terms that assumed the inviolability of capitalist property rights and, to the extent that social wage provisions were tied to the privatized collective bargaining system, they were ultimately vulnerable to shifts in employers' prerogatives and a changing balance of class forces. Moreover, the two-tier framework of protections and benefits reinforced social hierarchies within the working class itself, in particular along racial lines. Racial and gender segmentation built into the semi-private social wage system created by New Deal social policy and the collective bargaining regime implanted a logic that reproduced a pattern of invidious inequalities over time.

For example, proliferation of the postwar 'American Dream' of privately owned, single-family housing, while providing many workers with a sense of wellbeing and relative economic security, also created space for articulation with a conservative 'home owner populism' based on commitments to property values and low taxes. That approach to housing policy materially reinforced racial and other starkly clear hierarchies because the privatized system of real estate valuation assigned a premium to white exclusivity in neighbourhoods, and federally subsidized mortgage financing adopted the industry's valuation framework. The real estate market was therefore structured on a racially discriminatory basis that all but denied minorities, especially but not only blacks, access to that important tier of the semiprivate welfare state. Worse, the threat that non-white 'encroachment' on a neighbourhood would ensue in reduction in residential market value gave material force to racial bigotry and exclusion, which occasionally erupted in violence against non-whites perceived as interlopers. In addition to direct disadvantage with respect to access to desirable housing, the pattern of discrimination and exclusion had intergenerational effects inasmuch as home equity was a primary source, along with defined-benefit pensions won through collective bargaining, of workers' asset accumulation and financial security.[5]

The postwar grand bargain in effect constituted a two-tier social compact. Its limited character created a secondary, more precarious labour market, disproportionately made up of non-whites and women, that was available to undercut concessions won by workers covered by collective bargaining and eligible for benefits accessible through the semiprivate welfare state. Despite the system's inherent fragility, the dominant trend within the labour movement, industrial relations experts, left-liberals, academics and pundits was to proclaim a new natural order, a distinctively American capitalism that had transcended class contradictions and antagonisms. The postwar regime was touted as a new era of post-ideological capitalism in which classes had been supplanted by interest groups united in a shared commitment to enhancing the general wellbeing through sharing in the proceeds of continuing growth. The mythology of the 'affluent society' had been so thoroughly consolidated as the normative truth of American society by the end of the 1950s that it spawned a genre of simultaneously celebratory and doleful ruminations on the supposed cultural malaise and crisis of values associated with having attained satiation of material needs and having transcended class conflict.[6] Trade unionists were more likely than others to recognize the system's limitations and mystifications, as they faced the realities of employer resistance and the exaggeration of working-class affluence. At the same time, labour leaders participated in propagating the ideology of American class harmony and economic growth internationally as a component of the Cold War programme.

Persisting and dramatic racial injustice presented a substantive challenge to exultation in the harmonious postwar order, but, when represented as a backward, pathological deviation from the American Way, it was just as easily incorporated as affirmation.[7] The racial liberalism that became orthodoxy in the postwar years detached racial inequality from its roots in political economy and addressed it as the product of benighted prejudice and intolerance, antecedent and therefore exogenous to the new arrangements. Characterization of 'racism' as an autonomous force in American life – the national 'disease' or its 'original sin' – gave the essentially psychologistic formulation an appearance of insurgent political criticism, but, notwithstanding a sometimes breathless rhetoric, attribution of the source of black inequality to racism was compatible with the premises of the grand bargain. In fact, by the early 1960s, conservative University of Chicago economist Gary Becker, who also had recently popularized the 'human capital' idea that similarly made class and political economy disappear, laid out an extended, albeit ahistorical, argument that racial discrimination was an irrational impediment to capitalist efficiency.[8]

That leftists were more likely than others to support struggles for racial equality fed an impression that support for equality of opportunity on racial lines was intrinsically a radical programme, particularly as southern segregationists and other opponents denounced racial egalitarianism as communist. But the struggle for racial justice was not at all necessarily tied to broader radical agendas, as was indicated in the popularity of the trope that racism was a betrayal of American ideals. The central thrust of postwar black political insurgency, understandably, was for inclusion into American political, economic and social institutions on more egalitarian terms and elimination of racial hierarchy. The victories on that front were and remain tremendously important, as anyone who can recall the racial *ancien regime* would attest, and have contributed greatly to democratizing American society writ large. However, those victories and the terms on which they were won, as well as the movements that produced them, were not directed at challenging the fundamental tenets of growth liberalism, and in fact generally took them as given. Even what appeared to be the radical turns in black activism, first to Black Power, thence to the various Marxist/nationalist hybrids of the 1970s, sidestepped systemic critique of the structural tensions at the core of the grand bargain and growth liberalism and focused on the postwar order's apparent racial disparities. Characterization of the black American situation as a form of domestic colonialism suggested a connection with Third World insurgencies that provided a radical-seeming patina to what was at bottom only a more militant version of hegemonic racial liberalism. As they became marginalized by the emerging political class of black officeholders and functionaries, radicals often slid into cultivation of fanciful, apocalyptic discourses of revolution which still abjured systemic critique of contemporary American capitalism.[9]

THE NEOLIBERAL ELIMINATION OF WORKING-CLASS OPPOSITION

When the project that would come to be known as neoliberalism began to take shape in the 1970s, most of the left was under the illusion that the postwar liberal consensus was an order set in stone.[10] The labour movement, as we have indicated, remained through much of the 1980s just barely capable enough of asserting itself against employers' demands for concessions so as to be able with some shred of credibility to override dissidents' arguments that a new class offensive was underway. Even though retrenchment actually had begun under Jimmy Carter's presidency, trade unionists and the broader left turned to Democrats for support and reinforcement against the accelerating onslaught then typically described as Reaganism. What ensued was a cycle of increasingly desperate defensive struggles aimed at preserving the last shards of the grand bargain. Ronald Reagan's peremptory firing in 1981 of more than 11,300 striking members of the Professional Air Traffic Controllers Organization (PATCO) symbolically punctuated an orgy of union-busting and deindustrialization that fundamentally altered the left in the United States and its capacity to intervene politically.[11]

The intensifying counterattack by capital and the political right also targeted broader social wage policy and Keynesianism in general. Culminating a decade of internal struggle within the Democratic Party, the Clinton presidency consolidated neoliberalism as the new baseline of the thinkable in American politics, consistent with Thatcher's infamous TINA. Clinton's original campaign for healthcare reform defined a single-payer insurance system on the Canadian model – the only option that enjoyed significant congressional or public support – as 'off the table' from the outset. His concern to placate the insurance and pharmaceutical industries accelerated the burgeoning crisis by setting in motion the debacle of corporate managed-care. Clinton ran on a pledge to 'end welfare as we know it'. The workfare component of Clinton's welfare reform effectively transferred public subsidies from poor people to employers of low-wage labour and terminated the federal government's sixty-year commitment to provide direct income support to the indigent. The Clinton administration also began the retreat from direct provision of affordable housing for the poor, with its HOPE-VI housing programme, which razed existing low-income public housing complexes and replaced them with combinations of market-rate owner-occupied and reduced numbers of subsidized rental housing units and offered rental vouchers for those displaced to use in the open housing market. The effect was to shift subsidies up the class ladder, from poor residents to real estate developers, landlords and middle-class homeowners. Clinton also pushed through the North American Free Trade Agreement (NAFTA) over intense opposition from much of his own party and its core constituencies, most of all labour. He advanced financial sector interests in other ways as well, most conspicuously in supporting and signing the Financial Services Modernization Act, which repealed the 1933 Glass-Steagall law that had established a firewall between commercial and investment banking (although it had been effectively breached long before its repeal with the support of the regulators and the Treasury during the 1990s). And his administration conducted nearly as many military interventions as Reagan and the elder Bush combined, and in four fewer years.[12] Clintonism completed the defanging of a labour-left that had subordinated itself to the Democrats less by suppression than by demanding accommodation to redefined limits of political possibility.

With few exceptions, even militant responses to the Clintonist consolidation in the 1990s and George W. Bush's further retrenchment failed to generate systemic critiques of capitalism. The NAFTA fight condensed frustrations among trade union activists and led to the changing of the guard in the leadership of the AFL-CIO. The 'New Voice' slate elected in 1995 reflected a shifting balance of power in the federation toward public sector unions, but it also was the institutional expression of a moment of labour insurgency, albeit a brief and in some ways self-limiting one.

THE LABOR PARTY EXPERIENCE AND AFTER

The most extensive and coherent expression of this insurgency was the effort in the 1990s to launch a Labor Party in the US.[13] Early in the decade, even before the NAFTA fight, several unions and labour leaders undertook systematic exploration into the possibility of establishing a labour-based political movement independent of the Democratic Party. The effort was led by veteran labour radical Tony Mazzocchi and fully supported by his union – the Oil, Chemical and Atomic Workers. It quickly caught fire and drew in thousands of union leaders and activists and hundreds of local, regional and national unions. Organizers focused on the need to build the party based on the felt concerns of the working-class constituency that would grow up around it. Mazzocchi was famous for stressing his 'union hall dictum': if you can't get something passed at your own union hall, don't bring it to the Labor Party. As organizers often had to point out to progressives whose initiatives focused either on electing candidates and/ or agitation for more incremental objectives that accepted the prevailing neoliberal policy constraints, the Labor Party's objective was not to organize the left, or become yet another platform for leftists to bear witness against injustice, but to be an institutional venue for articulation of a working-class politics.

The 1996 Founding Convention adopted a programme that had wide working-class support and gave a glimpse of what politics would look like if it were conducted on behalf of the vast majority of Americans who work for a living. The delegates also adopted an 'Organizing Model of Politics' centred around issue campaigns focused on identifying, educating and mobilizing supporters in unions and working-class communities. The first such campaign was for a constitutional amendment guaranteeing the right to a job and a living wage. Others subsequently adopted were for single-payer healthcare, reorientation of federal labour law around the 13th Amendment's protection against involuntary servitude and for free public higher education.[14] Subsequent Labor Party conventions adopted and re-fined an electoral strategy that grappled concretely with what it would take to disengage labour from a winner-take-all two-party system and run serious candidates that could challenge the neoliberal consensus and be held accountable to a living, breathing constituency. A principal focus was on preempting capricious protest candidacies or hopeless spoiler candidacies;

thus the electoral strategy required that prospective candidacies be supported by organized labour in a district and demonstrate access to adequate financial support and base of volunteers.

Although it won endorsement of a substantial section of the institutional labour movement, the Labor Party was never able to develop the 'exit strategy' that would make it feasible for unions to disengage from the two-party system. This flaw proved fatal in the early years of this century as labour experienced a series of strategic defeats and went into retreat. The last major effort of the Party was to establish a state party in South Carolina – one of the most conservative and least union-dense states in the US. Through one-on-one conversations with predominantly non-union working-class South Carolinians, organizers convinced more than 16,000 registered voters in the state to sign public petitions in support of the South Carolina Labor Party, proving that it was possible to build a party of labour in the heart of the right-to-work South. The South Carolina Labor Party was recognized by the state and awarded an official ballot in 2007. By that point, however, a diminished and defeated national labour movement was unable and unwilling to put in the necessary resources to capitalize on this advance. Many of the Labor Party chapters not connected with trade union organizations had devolved into little more than debating societies. To avoid becoming a Green-style party more concerned with a politics of personal testimony, Labor Party leaders decided it was best to put party-building efforts on hold until it could build a movement that could speak with an authentic working-class voice.

The Labor Party experience was in sharp contrast to two distinctive assessments of the state of the left and the task of movement-building. The electoral approach, exemplified by the Greens and its many offshoots, assumed that a constituency for a left politics already exists in a dormant state in the society and could simply be convoked around the properly appealing candidacy. The incrementalist approach abjured larger strategic vision and presumed that agitating for reforms imaginable within the context of Democratic neoliberalism could eventuate at some point in systemic change. The New Party and, after its meltdown, the Working Families Party in New York and elsewhere exemplified this latter approach. This tendency's fixation on fusion voting – endorsing a major party candidate and asking constituents to vote for her or him on a minor party line in hope to gain leverage for working-class issues – assured that it would never stray far from the Democrats' orbit.[15] At its worst, it has succumbed to a cynical collaboration with the anti-worker agenda of mainstream Democrats in order to achieve minor and temporary political gains.

Despite other heroic efforts to revive and reorient a political opposition, what we see today is a left devoid of agency and power. To some degree, this reflects the social experience of a working class that has been largely decollectivized. The catastrophic decline in union density means that in some sections of the US entire working-class communities have no organic relationship to labour organizations. But decimated unions are not the only nexus of decollectivized social experience. From flipping houses to accessing benefits under the Affordable Care Act, workers have been conditioned increasingly to believe that public goods and security are not the outcomes of collective struggle and are inferior to individual initiative and responsibility. This tendency has become more pronounced as bipartisan attacks have sharpened on the public sector, which is also among the last bastions of decent social-wage benefits like defined-benefit pensions.

The left has exhibited two dysfunctional responses to this new reality. One is to persist in the old forms of struggle with the hope that doing so will bear different fruit this time around. This mode assumes that there is still a terrain where assorted interest groups compete for power and resources within the framework of postwar pluralist liberalism. It hinges on an inside strategy of elite negotiation and an outside strategy of mobilizing popular forces to influence negotiations. This strategic approach assumes: 1) that all parties have a vested interest in maintaining the core relationships at the centre of the model; 2) therefore, that threats to walk away from the table carry significant weight; and 3) that elites purporting to speak on behalf of the popular forces actually have the capacity to foment social disruption if their concerns are not taken into account. Although clearly obsolescent since the beginning of the 1980s and the defeat of the PATCO strike, this model persists both as a cynical pageantry of protest as prelude to defeat and its mirror image in the magical thinking that produces the rank-and-file fetishism and 'activistist' fantasies that this or that spontaneous action will spark a mass movement.[16] This approach persists despite the failure of massive worldwide mobilizations to prevent the Bush administration's 2003 invasion of Iraq, and Occupy is its most flamboyant, if not its most desperate, expression to date.

The other mode openly accommodates neoliberalism. This is the version of a left that Clintonism, currently represented in the White House by Barack Obama, enables and cultivates within the Democratic Party; it is a left whose political horizon is limited to making the neoliberal order more equitable on its own terms. This is the left for which disparity and diversity have replaced inequality as the animating normative concern.[17] This accommodation ultimately preempts confronting capitalist class relations and power. If the core value of the labour-left was solidarity, the core value of this sort of left in the neoliberal era is diversity. Thus, for example, issues of structural unemployment become framed as problems of racial or gender justice, and low wages are problematic because they disproportionately affect women and people of colour. In naturalizing categories of ascriptive identity as the fundamental units of political life, this politics simultaneously naturalizes the social structures of capitalist reproduction by displacing contradictions rooted in those structural dynamics from political economy into the realm of culture – exactly as did postwar interest-group pluralism.

Attempts to combine identitarian and political-economic perspectives – e.g., via constructs like institutional or structural racism – demonstrate the primary commitment to the former. They effectively ontologize racism (or sexism or xenophobia) by vesting it with historical agency that rests on a 'takes on a life of its own' reification and acknowledges capitalist class dynamics only gesturally. Despite occasional, pro forma acknowledgments that it is important to oppose capitalism, this politics is strikingly dismissive of Marxism, when not viscerally anti-Marxist.[18] Defences of this view typically rest on appeals to realpolitik and claims that whites' racism and/or males' sexism have historically overwhelmed efforts to mobilize working-class unity. This perhaps explains the spasmodic recurrence of reparations talk in black American elite discourse since 2000; it reinforces assertion of the primacy of race and racial identity as the determinative force in American politics. Similarly, arguments that contemporary racial inequality is best understood via analogy to slavery or the southern segregationist regime that held sway in the first half of the twentieth century serve more to insist on the primacy of racism than to shed light on the reproduction of contemporary patterns of inequality. Michelle Alexander's popular book, *The New Jim Crow*, is a prime instance of this phenomenon. The analogy's appeal to Alexander is precisely that it asserts the ongoing and overriding causal power of racism by means of a rhetorical sleight-of-hand, yet even she finally acknowledges that it does not work because mass incarceration today is not significantly like the segregationist order.[19]

LABOUR AND THE IDENTITARIAN LEFT

The assertion of a fundamentally antagonistic history between labour and social movements, particularly those based on ascriptive identities like race, gender or sexual orientation, is a reflex in the discourse of the identitarian left fuelled by liberal stereotypes of the organized working class as definitively white, male and conservative. This political lore, despite having some basis in historical fact, has hardened into unexamined folk knowledge among many activists. The labour movement has hardly been immune –

either institutionally or as individual union members – from racist, sexist, homophobic or nativist currents in American political culture. The story of labour's inadequacies in that regard has been well told.[20] But labour hardly stands out from federal, state and local government, the academy, industry, organized religion or any other social institutions in generating and sustaining that framework of inequality or the hierarchies that constituted it. Moreover, the lore depends on denying or devaluing the significant connections between labour and other egalitarian social movements in the past as well as the present.

No matter what post-class self-images those who embrace identitarian politics may cherish, it is a politics rooted in neoliberal class dynamics. Its effacement of class as both an analytic and a strategic category dissolves working people's interests as working people – which have no place in neoliberalism – into populations defined by ascription or affinity rather than by location in the system of capitalist reproduction. The groupist discourse of diversity and opposition to disparity enables harmonizing the left's aspirational commitment to equality with neoliberalism's imperatives. From that perspective, the society would be just if one per cent of the population controlled ninety-five percent of the resources so long as significant identity groups were represented proportionately among the one per cent. This is, after all, the goal of liberal equality of opportunity in the market, as articulated historically by both elements of progressive social movements (e.g., a strain of the black civil rights movement and bourgeois feminism) and Becker's neoclassical brief against racial discrimination. It is also the only standard of social justice that neoliberalism recognizes.

Unsurprisingly, the impulse of this politics is not to organize and unify a single constituency defined by its broad relation to capitalism's class dynamics. Insofar as its notion of social justice centres on group parity and recognition, it is inclined toward courses of action that undermine the core unity necessary to build a movement strong enough to attack the roots of structural inequalities. Instead of unions, parties and civic organizations with living, breathing memberships whose financial support and votes bind leadership to some measure of accountability, much of the left's model in the neoliberal era is founded on the image of an NGO that is accountable only to its funders. In ventriloquizing population categories reified as groups or 'communities', the left is like NGOs that define their bases as helpless victims and/or abstract groups without real agency of their own. Other left-oriented tendencies that embrace broader social objectives continue to frame issues in those terms out of either pietistic habit or failure of political imagination. They substantively, and often enough explicitly, reject class politics.

Labour organizations often feel obliged to frame their issues using the language of disparity in pursuit of broader acceptance or do so in expression of the dominant normative reflex.[21] The national AFL-CIO conspicuously celebrates labour's diversity along lines of race, gender, age and sexual orientation. This is certainly defensible as union membership is, and has been, far more diverse along those lines than any other Democratic constituency. Celebrating labour's diversity is a useful affirmation directed toward both members and a general public steadily bombarded with anti-union propaganda, but that celebratory rhetoric also is embedded in and reinforces an implicitly penitent narrative of 'progress' from a benighted past of union bigotry. Popular catch phrases like 'this is not your father's labour movement' may cede too much to the discourse that disparages unions as backward-looking bastions of male, white and/or nativist privilege.[22] Defense of trade unionism through celebrating its diversity rather than through asserting its challenge to capital also marks the labour movement's acquiescence to neoliberal hegemony.

Within labour, concessions to neoliberalism go much deeper than disparity talk. Much of the movement has been hollowed out, and a dynamic relationship between a leadership that is accountable to a broad and active constituency has been displaced by a realpolitik that too often treats the felt concerns of the actual membership as an impediment to institutional survival. Thus unions, particularly at the national level, are now more a conduit from the Democratic National Committee to the labour movement than the reverse. They have become more like NGOs whose members are reduced to props in a shallow and anachronistic symbolism, all in the name of realism. The 'new unionism' commonly associated with the Service Employees International Union (SEIU) has exemplified this approach most clearly in combining what critics have described as a class collaborationist trade unionism with identitarian pageantry – choreographed representations, both rhetorical and visual, of non-white and female workers as embodiments of a new spirit of insurgency. This combination has been refined and advanced through a highly staff-driven organizational model that minimizes accountability to members and a technicistic discourse – propelled by neologisms like 'union density' – that repackages business unionism as a modernizing programme of rational worker-employer partnership. This aspect of the new unionism tends at least logically to reinvent the labour movement in the image of an industrial relations NGO.[23]

WHAT IS TO BE DONE?

Any serious discussion of the prospects for rebuilding a left must start from the understanding that the left in the US, as in the rest of the capitalist world, suffered a strategic defeat, and that capital has reorganized and emerged from the 2008 economic crisis even stronger.[24] While the extreme financialization of capital is likely to increase the frequency and intensity of episodic crises, this crisis once again confirms that there is no necessary correlation between crisis and revitalization of the left. In fact, notwithstanding glimmers of hope like SYRIZA in Greece and strong showings by anti-austerity parties in the spring 2014 European elections, the history of the post-2008 crisis politics in Europe would indicate that the more intense the crisis, the more deeply reactionary the response.

This does not mean that those who embrace a transformative vision must abandon all hope. Rather, the priorities, activities and resources of those who would rebuild a real left must be informed by this strategic sensibility. Building or rebuilding an effective left presence will be quite likely a decades-long process. This means that we are not well served by clambering after the Next Big Thing. We must start by excising the impulse – quite understandable for a political movement devoid of any real agency – toward utopian dreaming and wishful thinking. The spark will not ignite the prairie fire. Nor will the Ark float on its own account no matter how carefully we construct it.

Recognizing the left's political irrelevance can be emancipating, as it reduces the sense of urgency to try to mobilize around every one of neoliberalism's daily outrages. That should provide space for serious strategic discussion of how to begin to build a mass socialist movement based in the working class and the creation of new institutions capable of mobilizing cross-class solidarity, as Sam Gindin has articulated in a particularly clear and compelling way.[25] Certainly, the US left could benefit from a non-sectarian, organized force with a coherent strategic vision and programme. The absence of a disciplined, unified and sophisticated group of cadre is a major source of the left's incoherence, and helps explain why moments of spontaneous political upsurge have had, at best, an episodic impact and remain unconnected to similar moments in the past – even those in which the same activists have participated. Such organization, however, cannot be created in a vacuum. It can only emerge in tandem with a growing working-class movement.

We fear that in the specific context of US history and practice, the socialist project is too narrow a platform from which to launch a broad and far ranging left revitalization. Socialist practice in the US has become the domain of sectarian groups that drive away working-class support, and socialist consciousness has not embedded itself in any significant sections of the working class or a left capable of exercising social power. That failing reflects the cultural and ideological triumph of neoliberalism and the identitarian ideologies and programmes that serve as its left wing. In this environment, building socialism is exclusively a project of cadre development, albeit one that cannot hope to succeed apart from broader movement-building. Broad movement-building requires mobilizing around an agenda of substantively anti-capitalist reforms that directly and militantly assert the priority of social needs over market forces, bourgeois property rights and managerial prerogative in the workplace and production process. Struggles to preserve and expand public institutions and to decommoditize basic human needs like housing, transportation, healthcare and education could begin to address the immediate challenge, which is to create a new popular constituency for a revitalized movement, instead of reorganizing or re-mobilizing an already existing but totally marginalized left.[26]

Some question whether the current US labour movement is too narrow a platform on which to rebuild a left. In a widely circulated article, 'Fortress Unionism', Rich Yeselson correctly highlights the atrophy of the labour movement and shows how its decline began with the passage of the Taft-Hartley Act in 1947. He contends that labour's 'current institutional expression cannot, via a creative conceptual breakthrough ("tactics or broader strategy"), engender a vast growth in union strength comparable to its former peak. In short, "organized labor" can no longer create a space for workers to join their organizations by the millions'.[27] In grim statistical detail, Jake Rosenfeld's *What Unions No Longer Do* gives fuel to this thesis. He points out that despite decades of exemplary, heroic and pioneering organizing by Justice for Janitors in the immigrant community, 'Today only one in seven Hispanic janitors in the United States belongs to a union, down from one in five back in 1988, when Justice for Janitors began'.[28] Yeselson calls for a 'fortress unionism' that would 'defend the remaining high-density regions, sectors and companies' and then 'Wait for the workers to say they have had enough. When they demand in vast numbers collective solutions to their problems, seize upon that energy and institutionalize it.'[29]

This approach correctly identifies the urgent need to preserve the remnants of the current labour movement as an institutional base upon which to build a future revitalized movement. And it also correctly points out the haplessness of willy-nilly organizing schemes that do little to build power for working people while exposing their best leaders in unorganized workplaces to massive employer retaliation without any ability to defend them. But a strategy of waiting for workers to say they have had enough ultimately relies on magical thinking not unlike that of isolated Japanese soldiers scattered on island outposts at the end of the Second World War waiting for reinforcements from a defeated empire. Many of Yeselson's critics, however, are equally quixotic. Bruce Raynor and Andy Stern, two of the most cynical practitioners of a unionism that disempowers workers and is based on a model of global class collaboration, point out that the 'fortress' strategy will do little to reduce inequality. Instead, they place their hopes in 'strategic alliances with willing employers'; in unions developing value-added services to complement human resource departments; and in leveraging union and public-sector pension funds to rebuild union density.[30] This strategy would liquidate the very concept of an independent labour movement.

Given its decimation and marginalization, any revitalization movement would need to be built from a base that is far broader than the current institutional labour movement. A revitalized labour movement will have to embrace new organizational forms and some of the models emerging from new labour organizing show significant potential. Some are driven by necessity as the legal status of many immigrants and of workers in industries such as trucking, taxi driving and residential construction make organizing under current labour law virtually illegal. Much of this new organizing is being done by Worker Centers with heavy foundation funding and has the character of social work along the settlement house model of the early twentieth century. Much of it seems also, more or less openly, to fold class analysis into identitarian discourses that both substitute moralizing for political critique and fit comfortably within the NGO model. Such impulses, as well as the popularity of neologism, underlie arguments that current conditions have generated a new social formation, a 'precariat' that lies outside the traditional capitalist class structure.[31] But some associated with this category have begun to evolve into substantial, self-conscious worker-run organizations. The Taxi Workers Alliance grew from a small New York City advocacy group to become a national organization (whose members are classified as 'independent contractors' and thus ineligible for union representation under US labour law) and was recently admitted to the AFL-CIO.[32] In Vermont and elsewhere, strategic Workers Centers have built organic alliances with the labour movement and gone on to lead significant campaigns for healthcare for all, paid sick days and economic justice through the mobilization of a working-class constituency.[33]

Some argue that these campaigns and projects have the capacity to coalesce into geographically based class-conscious organizations and have called for the building of worker assemblies to give voice to this new movement.[34] Such an effort would require a level of ideological sophistication and institutional independence that does not currently exist. Attempts to establish these structures on the ground have been premature and could actually inhibit the kind of broad, class-based organizing that inspires this movement in much the same way that many Labor Party chapters became captured by an 'activistist' mentality that focused more on preaching to the converted than building a constituency, while driving away real working-class voices who represented something more than themselves.

New models are most successful when they can leverage existing organization and power to build outwards into new organization. Recent experiences organizing healthcare and homecare workers, hotel and casino workers and building services employees are fruitful examples of smart and strategic organizing that have leveraged existing union relationships and/or political opportunities to build power for working people. We also look to the logistics organizing campaigns – which focus on the chokepoints of global capitalism and build on existing union power on the docks and other shipping centres – as having the potential to develop a particularly powerful form of a strategic union presence in economic sectors at the very core of contemporary capitalism.[35]

THE CENTRAL TASK:
REBUILDING THE LABOUR MOVEMENT

Despite all of the excitement and pageantry of 'new labour', its efforts to rebuild a real workers' movement cannot progress without a class-conscious trade union movement providing the institutional structures, organizing capacity and working-class base to animate it. Transformation and revitalization of the institutional labour movement remains the central task. While much needs to change within labour if it is going to rebuild, our effort is not well served by those, like Robert Fitch, who see unions as a 'protection system' defined by 'poles of corruption and apathy'.[36] Such wrong-headed and irresponsible charges play to the peanut gallery and do nothing to engage with those who need to be in the room to start any conceivable revitalization project. They provide nothing of use for those who seek to embark on the long journey of reconstructing a left with the social power to be a transformative force.

There are indications that at least some sections of the institutional labour movement are reviving a social unionist orientation. Many unions are beginning to redefine their battles against voracious profiteers and privatizers not as defensive struggles to preserve rights, privileges, benefits and conditions already lost by most of the working class, but as far reaching campaigns for the public good, and they are sinking resources into building the kind of alliances necessary to win. The Amalgamated Transit Union has begun to call for free public transportation that is integrated into a planned urban ecosystem and to build bus riders' groups and other initiatives to advocate on behalf of the overwhelmingly working-class consumers of mass public transportation.[37] The Utility Workers Union, representing both public and private sector workers, has called for public ownership of all utilities and begun the difficult task of determining how the work done by their members can be disengaged from the carbon-based economy.[38] The California Nurses Association/National Nurses United has consistently linked organizing to the larger public struggle for quality healthcare, and the union is a stalwart voice on the AFL-CIO Executive Council urging support for single-payer healthcare. CNA/NNU has also been a driving force in the broader campaign for a financial transactions tax – the 'Robin Hood tax' – that resolutely asserts the interests of working people and their communities over Wall Street. And the new leadership of the American Postal Workers Union has characterized the current crisis in the postal service as a looting of an essential public resource by a gang of profiteers and has called for the revival of a postal banking system as a counterweight to the despicable payday loan, check cashing and other financial service industries that prey on the most vulnerable sections of the working class.[39]

Fights over public education are also central to a reconstructed and revitalized movement. The work of the Chicago Teachers Union in building a community and labour response to retrenchment and privatization of public education has been widely embraced by urban organizers and is sparking a wave of victories by union reformers in teachers' unions from Massachusetts to Los Angeles.[40] Higher education is also in crisis both from increasing debt burdens on students and a labour crisis of providers, and recently successful unionization efforts by faculty at the University of Oregon and the University of Illinois-Chicago have been linked to fights against corporatization and privatization of public universities. This situation is crying out for a unifying message such as free public higher education to pull the diverse organizations together around a common theme that will allow them to turn their defensive fights into a unified offensive against the power of capital in higher education.[41]

The recent election of big city mayors in New York, Boston, Minneapolis and elsewhere around economic populist agendas and critiques of inequality also deserves some attention, as does the rise of some local independent political victories in Seattle, Lorain County Ohio and elsewhere. Likewise, the emergence of viable campaigns for a real living wage (rather than a minimum wage) like the 'Fight for 15' campaign in Seattle and the recent calls to expand social security (rather than just defend the current inadequate system) also bode well. However, it is important not to be overly exuberant about these currents. In the absence of an organized left, the likely outcome is either outright marginalization and defeat or reabsorption into the neoliberal consensus, because most of them are forced to rely on structures embedded in a two-party system thoroughly under the control of capital.

In the ideological sphere, we need to take a page from the right-wing playbook and invest in a long-term project to seize the terms of debate. As Richard Seymour points out, 'The traditional ruling class is not merely good at exploiting opportunities; it thinks long-term in a way the left must learn to do'.[42] We must present a vision of a world outside of the constraints of neoliberalism. Neoliberalism is all about commodification and the inescapable dictatorship of the market over all of human activity. This movement must work to decommoditize the public and civic spheres by asserting the values of public goods and the public sphere in healthcare, education, housing, etc. It must work to revive the values of industrial and economic democracy and assert the right of people to participate in determining the conditions under which they work and distribute and consume the products of their labour. We need to begin to assert the possibility of a life beyond the constraints of capitalism.

The almost faddish embrace of Piketty's *Capital in the Twenty-First Century* is an indication of how eager many are for an analysis that identifies structural tendencies of capitalism itself as a driver of inequality. A critical understanding of the dynamics of capitalism and the mechanism of neoliberalism is no longer foreign at all levels of the labour movement, including some members of the executive council of the AFL-CIO. However, this understanding is often still coupled with a deep scepticism about the possibility that any radical organizational initiatives can succeed in building a substantial anti-capitalist movement. In practical terms, this analysis amounts to either an excuse for doing nothing or an embrace of magical thinking about some outside force that will arise to drive change. Its coupling with the pursuit of inconsequential and limited reforms will do little or nothing to undermine the system or build a movement. Piketty's own global wealth tax is an idea that scores the hat trick: it is utopian, devoid of any agency and therefore inconsequential.

The left must begin to build out from this ideological understanding by working to construct movements and campaigns around issues that facilitate an organic learning process and bring together a community of leaders and activists that is broad enough to actually coalesce as a social force. Organizations such as the Labor Campaign for Single-Payer Healthcare follow the Labor Party organizing model and challenge the underpinnings of neoliberal social policy around a demand that is central to the well being of the working class. Building a movement powerful enough to win such a demand under the conditions of neoliberalism would be a powerful learning experience and serve as a building block for a new, transformative political movement. Other initiatives, such as US Labor Against the War, serve a similar function. They pull together the best and the brightest in an expansive project that goes beyond narrow jurisdictional lines and seeks to affirm an agenda that exists beyond the next election cycle.

There are many other potential organizing initiatives that a revitalized left could work to organize and empower. The environmental movement is crying out for a class-based vision able to take on the entrenched corporate power at the heart of a system that is driving ecological degradation on a worldwide scale.[43] Movements to recapture some of the massive productivity increases of the global working class since the 1970s also have the potential to build out. These include fights for living wages, guaranteed income and a massive and systematic reduction in working hours and the working life.

None of these initiatives on their own will have the capacity to rebuild an effective left in the United States. The crisis is deep and profound. Merely rebuilding union density to numbers similar to the early 1980s is a task that is all but inconceivable under current conditions. But that does not mean that we cannot begin. We must start with the understanding that the grand coalitions of 1946 and 1968 have been defeated, and that these defeats, as we have suggested here, were rooted in their own limitations. In any case, conditions today are radically different. Capital and labour have become internationalized. There is no 'socialist model' in ideological and material contention with international capital; nor is there a hegemonic international socialist movement linked to such a model. Labour has become immensely more productive, but the labour process has become more fragmented and unintelligible. The political practice of decades obscures the centrality of class to any revived left movement. Therefore, we must marshal our forces around a structural critique of capitalism and its impact on those with the social power to change things. We need to focus on rebuilding a constituency. This requires a slow, steady, systematic organizing effort connected to the felt concerns and real daily struggles of working people. Such long-term organizing must be strategic and divorced as much as possible from the exigencies of the electoral cycle and the reactive circle-the-wagons politics that only feed the downward spiral.

Despite all the roadblocks and difficulties, the time to begin is now, when we still have the historic memory and some semblance of working-class institutions and resources. We must embrace a long-term view that focuses on waging ideological struggle, confronting both the millennial and utopian illusions of a disorganized and toothless left and the defeatist accommodation to neoliberalism that has consumed so much of the so-called 'progressive' movement. We can start by urging the institutional labour movement and other significant left organizations to shift a portion of their resources away from limited and self-defeating defensive struggles and electoral campaigns and towards expansive and transformative projects that will rebuild a fighting left with its own vision of a just future and a real plan to get there.

We believe the Labor Party experience is instructive because it was the most self-conscious and institutionally grounded attempt to mobilize around an explicitly working-class politics in the US within at least a generation. As we have argued, without links to a dynamic trade union movement an openly working-class politics cannot sink deep enough roots to grow organizationally or to broaden an actual working-class base. Only strategies aimed at challenging the bipartisan neoliberal austerity regime directly can challenge the juggernaut facing us, and the only plausible route to the working-class constituency that such strategies require runs through the organized labour movement.

While the conditions that gave rise to the Labor Party in the 1990s no longer exist, its approach to organizing must underpin any project to rebuild a left in the US. Its style of work – rooting itself in a dynamic network of working-class institutions and leaders; a slow, methodical approach to base-building that expands upon the life experiences of workers and gives voice to their common grievances, concerns and dreams while connecting them to a broader and systematic critique of neoliberal capitalism; and a rigorous rejection of both the utopian daydreaming and the self-defeating cynicism of a *realpolitik* that characterize much of the self-described 'left' in the US – remains in our view the only plausible method for generating an organic movement against capitalism.

NOTES

1   Merlin Chowkwanyun catalogues and responds to many of these proclamations in 'The Crisis in Thinking About the Crisis', *Renewal*, 17, 2009, pp. 57-66. As he points out, the fantasy that crises generate spontaneous revolutionary responses is a venerable one. See Russell Jacoby's 'Towards a Critique of Automatic Marxism: The Politics of Crisis Theory from Lukács to the Frankfurt School', *Telos*, Winter 1971, pp. 118-46 and 'The Politics of Crisis Theory: Toward

the Critique of Automatic Marxism II', *Telos*, Spring 1975, pp. 3-52. Ralph Miliband provided an important historical antidote to the premise that the left makes its greatest gains in crisis moments, and the tendency to prelapsarian yearnings for days of yore when the left was strong in 'Socialism and the Myth of the Golden Past', *Socialist Register 1964*, London: Merlin Press, 1964, pp. 92-103.

2   There is a substantial literature on that moment in American political history, but Nelson Lichtenstein, *State of the Union: A Century of American Labor*, Princeton and Oxford: Princeton University Press, 2002 and Kim Moody, *An Injury to All: The Decline of American Unionism*, London and New York: Verso, 1998 remain among the most astute accounts.

3   Sam Gindin, 'Unmaking Global Capitalism', *Jacobin*, 14, 2014, available at https://www.jacobinmag.com, lays out a perspective on the current state of the left and the sources of the current situation, and an argument about the necessary approach to rebuilding a credible left opposition that are almost identical with our own. That is not surprising, as we have been part of an ongoing conversation animated by shared perspectives and a common political project, although our view of the US labour movement in the 1950s and 1960s may be somewhat more sanguine than his. While agreeing with Gindin's larger point that the trade unions developed more as sectional and instrumental organizations, we would stress that even within that limited context the institutional labour movement and trade union culture provided space for articulation of a practice nearer class-struggle unionism and for cultivation of a more sharply politicized and broader class consciousness among rank-and-file workers.

4   Katherine van Wezel Stone, 'The Post-War Paradigm in American Labor Law', *The Yale Law Journal*, 90, June 1981, p. 1516. For a cogent overview of the postwar politics of growth at the national level, see Alan Wolfe, *America's Impasse: The Rise and Fall of the Politics of Growth*, Boston: South End Press, 1982; John Mollenkopf, *The Contested City*, Princeton, NJ: Princeton University Press, 1983; and Robert Collins, *More: The Politics of Economic Growth in Postwar America*, New York & London: Oxford University Press, 2002.

5   See Jeffrey M. Hornstein, *A Nation of Realtors: A Cultural History of the Twentieth Century American Middle Class*, Durham, NC: Duke University Press, 2005, esp. pp. 119-55; and Robert O. Self, *American Babylon: Race and the Struggle for Postwar Oakland*, Princeton and Oxford: Princeton University Press, 2005.

6   Ralph Miliband wonderfully debunked this mythology in his 'Professor Galbraith and American Capitalism', *Socialist Register 1968*, London: Merlin Press, 1968, pp. 215-29. The sleight-of-hand academics and pundits deployed to make class, and thus class conflict, disappear included shifting discussion of class as a meaningful social category from political economy to culture. This tendency is critiqued in Adolph Reed, Jr., 'Reinventing the Working Class: A Study in Elite Manipulation', *New Labor Forum*, 13, Fall 2004, pp. 18-26. Penny Lewis, *Hardhats, Hippies and Hawks: The Vietnam Antiwar Movement as Myth and Memory*, Ithaca and London: ILR Press, 2013, discusses the significance of this cultural construction of class in mystifying the sources of opposition to the Vietnam war and the notion of 'hardhat' patriotism.

7   Risa Goluboff, *The Lost Promise of Civil Rights*, Cambridge, MA and London: Harvard University Press, 2007, describes a shift away from an approach stressing the roots of racial inequality in political economy to one focused on individual equal protection and equality of opportunity in civil rights litigation in the late 1940s, a shift that was the result of a combination of incentives and disincentives, including successful challenges to *de jure* segregation, and the chilling effect of anticommunist hysteria on expression of views that could seem like economic radicalism.

8   Gary Becker, *The Economics of Discrimination*, Chicago: University of Chicago Press, 1962.

9   For critical discussion of those tendencies in late 1960s and 1970s black American radicalism, see Dean E. Robinson, *Black Nationalism in American Politics and Thought*, New York and Cambridge: Cambridge University Press, 2001, pp. 70-136 and 'Black Power Nationalism as Ethnic Pluralism', in Adolph Reed, Jr., Kenneth W. Warren et al., *Renewing Black Intellectual History: The Ideological and Material Foundations of African American Thought*, Denver, CO: Paradigm Publishers, 2010, pp. 186-214; and Cedric Johnson, *Revolutionaries to Race Leaders: Black Power and the Making of African American Politics*, Minneapolis and London: University of Minnesota Press, 2007.

10   Neoliberalism has become a catchword, of course, and taxonomizing it has become something of a cottage industry. Monica Prasad succinctly characterizes it as a practical programme consisting in 'taxation structures that favor capital accumulation over income redistribution, industrial policies that minimize the presence of the state in private industry, and retrenchment in welfare spending'. *The Politics of Free Markets: The Rise of Neoliberal Economic Policies in Britain, France, Germany, and the United States*, Chicago and London: University of Chicago Press, 2006, pp. 4-5. David Harvey cuts to the heart of the matter in describing neoliberalism as a programme for class power as well as a free-market utopia. *A Brief History of Neoliberalism*, Oxford: Oxford University Press, 2005, pp. 2-3. From our perspective, neoliberalism is best summarized as capitalism that has effectively eliminated working-class opposition.

11   Joseph A. McCartin, *Collision Course: Ronald Reagan, the Air Traffic Controllers, and the Strike that Changed America*, New York and Oxford: Oxford University Press, 2013.

12   Adolph Reed, Jr., 'Nothing Left: The Long, Slow Surrender of American Liberals', *Harper's*, March 2014, pp. 30-1.

13   In the spirit of full disclosure, both authors were intimately involved in that effort.

14   For discussion of the programme's specifics and more a thorough account of the Labor Party project and its history, see Mark Dudzic and Katherine Isaac, 'Labor Party Time? Not Yet', December 2012, available at http://www.thelaborparty.org; and Derek Seidman, 'Looking Back at the Labor Party: An Interview with Mark Dudzic', *New Labor Forum*, 23, Winter 2014, pp. 60-4 (and the response by Adolph Reed, Jr., pp. 65-7).

15   The New Party was formed to promote fusion voting as a model for national progressive political action. In 1997, the US Supreme Court ruled in *Timmins*

v. Twin Cities Area New Party that states could not be compelled to permit fusion voting, and the national party quickly faded away. Its offshoot, the Working Families Party (WFP), has thrived in New York, which has a long history of minor parties gaining limited influence through fusion voting. The WFP has been less successful in the seven other states that allow fusion voting, and recently the party expanded into some non-fusion states.

16   On 'activistism' see Liza Featherstone, Doug Henwood and Christian Parenti, '"Action Will Be Taken": Left Anti-Intellectualism and its Discontents', *Left Business Observer*, available at http://www.leftbusinessobserver.com. See also, Reed, 'Nothing Left'.

17   Adolph Reed, Jr. and Merlin Chowkwanyun, 'Race, Class, Crisis: The Discourse of Racial Disparity and its Analytical Discontents', *Socialist Register 2012*, Pontypool: Merlin Press, 2011, pp. 149-75; Walter Benn Michaels, *The Trouble with Diversity: How We Learned to Love Identity and Ignore Inequality*, New York and London: Metropolitan Books, 2006 and 'Against Diversity', *New Left Review*, 52(July/August), 2008, pp. 33-6; Adolph Reed, Jr., 'Marx, Race, and Neoliberalism', *New Labor Forum*, 22, Winter 2013, pp. 49-57.

18   Adolph Reed, Jr., 'The "Color Line" Then and Now: *The Souls of Black Folk* and the Changing Context of Black American Politics', in Reed, Warren et al, *Renewing Black Intellectual History,* pp. 271-3 and 'The Limits of Anti-racism', *Left Business Observer*, No. 121, September 2009, available at http://www. leftbusinessobserver.com.

19   Michelle Alexander, *The New Jim Crow: Mass Incarceration in the Age of Colorblindness*, New York: The New Press, 2010. For one powerful critique of Alexander's argument, see James Forman, Jr. 'Racial Critiques of Mass Incarceration: Beyond the New Jim Crow', *New York University Law Review*, 87, 2012, pp. 21-69.

20   Eric Arnesen provides a careful consideration of the history of scholarship on race and the labour movement in 'Passion and Politics: Race and the Writing of Working-Class History', *Journal of the Historical Society*, 6, September 2006, pp. 323-56.

21   Even the reliably working-class conscious *Labor Notes* sometimes lapses into this sort of formulation; see Steve Payne, 'Kellogg's Delivers Memphis a Slap in the Face', *Labor Notes*, 20 January 2014.

22   Jo Ann Mort, ed., *Not Your Father's Labor Movement*, New York: Verso, 1998.

23   See Herman Benson, 'Hybrid Unions: Dead End or Fertile Future?', *Dissent*, Winter 2009; Melvin Dubofsky, 'The Legacy of Andy Stern', *Dissent*, 12 May 2010, available at http://www.dissentmagazine.org; and Steve Early, *The Civil Wars in U.S. Labor: Birth of a New Workers' Movement or Death Throes of the Old?*, Chicago: Haymarket Books, 2011.

24   For discussion of this issue see Sam Gindin, 'Puzzle or Misreading? Stagnation, Austerity and Left Politics', *The Bullet*, No. 920, 31 December 2013, and 'Underestimating Capital, Overestimating Labour: A Response to Andrew Kliman', *The Bullet*, No. 953, 21 March 2014, available at http://www. socialistproject.ca.

25   Gindin, 'Unmaking Global Capitalism'.

26 Jane McAlevey, *Raising Expectations (and Raising Hell): My Decade Fighting for the Labor Movement*, New York and London: Verso, 2014, provides a pragmatically grounded and careful argument for developing a new social movement unionism in the US.

27 Rich Yeselson, 'Fortress Unionism', *Democracy*, Summer 2013, p. 76.

28 Jake Rosenfeld, *What Unions No Longer Do*, Cambridge and London: Harvard University Press, 2014, p. 158.

29 Yeselson, 'Fortress Unionism', p. 79.

30 Bruce Raynor and Andy Stern, 'Build Bridges. Not Fortresses', *Democracy*, Fall 2013, pp. 63-7.

31 Bryan D. Palmer criticizes these formulations persuasively in 'Reconsiderations of Class: Precariousness as Proletarianization', *Socialist Register 2014*, London: Merlin Press, 2014, pp. 40-62.

32 'Taxi! Taxi! Cabbies for Unlikely Union', available at http://www.aflcio.org.

33 See http://www.workerscenter.org.

34 Bill Fletcher and Fernando Gapasin, *Solidarity Divided: The Crisis in Organized Labor and a New Path toward Social Justice*, Berkeley and Los Angeles: University of California Press, 2009; and Sam Gindin, 'Working People's Assemblies: Can We Learn from American Activists?', *Canadian Dimension*, 40(September/October), 2006, available at http://canadiandimension.com.

35 G. Gonos and C. Martino, 'Temp Agency Workers in New Jersey's Logistics Hub: The Case for A Union Hiring Hall', *Working USA*, December 2011, pp. 499-525.

36 See Michael D. Yates, 'What's the Matter with US Labor? An Interview with Robert Fitch', *MRzine*, 30 March 2006, available at http://mrzine.monthlyreview.org.

37 'Transit Workers and Advocates to Mobilize 20 Million Riders to Unite for May Transit Action Month', available at http://www.atu.org.

38 'Utilities Are a Public Good and Should Be Owned by the Public', available at http://www.huffingtonpost.com.

39 APWU President Mark Dimondstein's remarkable speech at the 2014 Labor Notes Conference, 'APWU Pres. Mark Dimondstein Calls For Defense Of The People's Post Office', is available at https://www.youtube.com.

40 Micah Uetricht, *Strike for America: Chicago Teachers Against Austerity*, New York and London: Verso, 2014; and Labor Notes, *How To Jump Start Your Union: Lessons from the Chicago Teachers*, Detroit: LERP, 2014.

41 For a recent revival of this idea, see: 'Why can't college be free?', available at http://inthesetimes.com; and 'What's Out? Student Debt. What's In? Free College', *The Chronicle of Higher Education*, 11 June 2014.

42 Richard Seymour, 'How the Right Sold Austerity as the Only Economic Solution', *The Guardian*, 28 March 2014

43 Some of this work has begun at Cornell's Global Labor Institute and with organizations like the Labor Network for Sustainability, available at http://www.labor4sustainability.org.

Also available

Socialist Register 2014: Registering Class
Edited by Leo Panitch, Greg Albo & Vivek Chibber

The 50th volume of the Socialist Register is dedicated to the theme of 'registering class' in light of the spread and deepening of capitalist social relations around the globe. Today's economic crisis has been deployed to extend the class struggle from above while many resistances have been explicitly cast in terms of class struggles from below. This volume addresses how capitalist classes are reorganizing as well as the structure and composition of working classes in the 21st century. 352 pages.

Contents: Leo Panitch, Greg Albo & Vivek Chibber: Preface; Arun Gupta: The Walmart working class; Bryan Palmer: Reconsiderations of class: precariousness as proletarianization; Vivek Chibber: Capitalism, class and universalism: escaping the cul-de-sac of postcolonial theory; Ursula Huws: The underpinnings of class in the digital age: living, labour and value; Colin Leys: The British ruling class; Claude Serfati: The new configuration of the capitalist class; William Carroll: Whither the transnational capitalist class?; Bastiaan van Apeldoorn: The European capitalist class and the crisis of its hegemonic project; Virginia Fontes & Ana Garcia: Brazil's new imperial capitalism; Alfredo Saad-Filho & Lecio Morais: Mass protests: Brazilian spring or Brazilian malaise?; Ian MacDonald: Beyond the labour of Sisyphus: unions and the city; Andrew Murray: Left unity or class unity? Working-class politics in Britain; Madeleine Davis: Rethinking class: the lineage of the Socialist Register; Leo Panitch: Registering class and politics: fifty years of the Socialist Register.

Canada: Fernwood Publishing; USA: Monthly Review Press; UK and rest of world: The Merlin Press

Eugene V. Debs Reader: Socialism and the Class Struggle
Edited by William A. Pelz
With a new introduction by Mark A. Lause
and an original introduction by Howard Zinn

'This selection of Debs words will help introduce a new generation to an authentic American hero whose vision is as powerful today as in years past. ... Today, when capitalism, the free market, and private enterprise are being hailed as triumphant in the world, it is a good time to remember Debs and to rekindle the idea of socialism.' - Howard Zinn

Merlin Press paperback   248 pages   ISBN. 978-0-85036-613-6